Yosef Ofer
The Masora on Scripture and Its Methods

Fontes et Subsidia
ad Bibliam pertinentes
(FoSub)

Edited by
James K. Aitken, David S. du Toit, Jan Joosten,
and Loren T. Stuckenbruck

Volume 7

Yosef Ofer

The Masora on Scripture and Its Methods

—

DE GRUYTER

ISBN 978-3-11-059574-1
e-ISBN (PDF) 978-3-11-059456-0
e-ISBN (EPUB) 978-3-11-059348-8
ISSN 1861-602X

Library of Congress Control Number: 2018949262

Bibliographic information published by the Deutsche Nationalbibliothek
The Deutsche Nationalbibliothek lists this publication in the Deutsche Nationalbibliografie;
detailed bibliographic data are available on the Internet at http://dnb.dnb.de.

Typesetting: Integra Software Services Pvt. Ltd
Printing and binding: CPI books GmbH, Leck

www.degruyter.com

MIX
Papier aus verantwor-
tungsvollen Quellen
FSC® C083411

Contents

Part II: The Masoretic Text in Time and Space

Part III: The Masora in Interaction with Other Disciplines

Preface

The Bible was passed on from generation to generation over millennia in Jewish communities throughout the world. Thousands of copyists copied the books of the Scriptures, and millions of Jews read them and pronounced their words following traditions that were transmitted from a father to his children and a sage to his pupils. Naturally many disagreements arose regarding every aspect of the text: orthography, the spacing of sections and the writing of poetic passages, pronunciation, cantillation, pauses, how to divide the passages for public reading etc. Experts in every generation occupied themselves with making decisions about disputed issues, trying to achieve a uniform and single text that would reflect the word of God. For this purpose the Masora was created, including various compositions, thousands of rules and tens of thousands of short and long notes. All of these together comprise a sophisticated and integrated defense mechanism for the preservation of the text.

The Masora was the work of hundreds of sages, most of them anonymous, who devoted their lives to preserving the text of the Bible and standardizing it with precision. Each and every letter in the Bible, every vowel, every cantillation mark – were given attention; and all of this in order to pass on precisely the word of God in the twenty-four books of Scripture.

Due to the development of means of copying and preserving texts – mainly printing and the computer – only a few experts still deal with the accuracy of the Biblical text. In earlier times every copy of the Bible was written specifically by a scribe with expertise in the Masora, and each one needed to devote great time and effort to producing one single copy of the Bible or a part of it. However, today editions of the Bible are printed and reprinted over and over and distributed in computer programs and computerized editions. Most of these editions were prepared by experts, but these are few, and only a small number of experts still have the ability to use Masoretic notes and compositions.

The purpose of this book is to tell the story of the Masora, and to enable the wide community of people who study the Bible to enter its gates.

Among the few introductory books on the Masora I should mention in particular that of my late teacher, Israel Prize laureate, Prof. Israel Yeivin, *Hamasora Lamiqra* (The Biblical Masorah). This book originated in a modest textbook published in 1972. It was translated to English by E.J. Revell in 1980. An updated Hebrew edition, which I edited, appeared in 2003.

This book differs in character from that one. It does not give encyclopedic descriptions of the manuscripts, types of Masoretic notes and Masoretic compositions; nor does it sum up all the studies of the Masora in the last generations. Its purpose is to present the basic questions that have been discussed in research on the Masora and the problems raised by its study, particularly in recent years. I have not refrained from giving my opinion on central research questions which have been dealt with by researchers of the Masora, and in some cases I have based my writing on my own sci-

https://doi.org/10.1515/9783110594560-201

entific articles, which were published in a number of venues. The discussion includes many examples and photographs of manuscripts, which demonstrate and enrich the theoretical discussion.

The chapters of the book are divided into three sections:

The first section describes the areas with which the Masora deals – orthography, vocalization signs and cantillation marks, spacing of passages and poetic sections, distinctions between the written text and its traditional reading – and the way in which the Masora works: important manuscripts, the techniques used by the Masora in different types of notes, the efficiency of Masora mechanisms and the degree to which it has succeeded in preserving the text.

The second section describes the text of the Bible according to the Masora: the role of the Masoretic text in the history of the biblical text, differences between the Babylonian Masora and that of Tiberias, the special status of the Aleppo Codex and the effort to find or reconstruct its missing parts, the difference between the system of marking *ge'ayot* (secondary stress marks) in manuscripts and printed editions, various printed editions of the Bible and their degree of proximity to the Masoretic texts and that of the Aleppo Codex.

The third and final section of the book deals with the relation between the Masora and other related areas that interact with it: Hebrew grammar, biblical exegesis and Halakha.

The chapters of the book are a product of courses on the Masora that I taught at Bar-Ilan University and Herzog College.

I want to thank Mr. Michael Glatzer, who translated my book to English, and made many remarks and suggestions. Beit Shalom Foundation (Kyoto, Japan) supported some of the translation costs. Thanks to all the libraries, institutions and individuals, the owners of the photographs presented, for their permission to include them in the book. Thanks to De Gruyter Academic Publishing House, to its editorial director Dr. Albrecht Döhnert and the entire publishing team for their help and devoted work.

My hope is that these chapters will provide students and other interested individuals entrance into the world of the Masora, enable them to familiarize themselves with its riches, and appreciate its secrets.

Yosef Ofer

Part I: **The Biblical Masora and its Methods**

1 What is the Masora?

The Masora, strictly defined, is the system of rules created in order to transmit the text of Scripture from one generation to the next. Masoretic notes were usually written in the books of the Bible, in the margins of the pages on which the text itself was written. Some Masoretic rules were written independently on separate pages in the biblical codex or in separate books devoted exclusively to the Masora.

A broader definition of the Masora includes everything that was done in order to transmit the text of Scripture, including signs for vocalization and cantillation as well as decisions regarding textual accuracy.

Vocalization and Cantillation Signs

Before vocalization and cantillation signs were determined, the Torah would be read from a scroll that contained letters only, just as one reads the Torah in the Jewish synagogue today. According to Halakha vocalization and cantillation signs may not be written in a Torah scroll, and regarding this the writer of Mahzor Vitri[1] (ed. Horowitz, p. 462) stipulates:

> The cantillation was given to Moses... but the cantillation signs were made up by scribes... and since cantillation tends to be forgotten they made up signs, relying on what is written: "It is time to act for the Lord, for they have violated your teaching" (Ps. 119:126).[2] And therefore a Torah scroll cannot be vocalized. Although the [division into] verses, and the cantillation melody were given on Sinai in a tradition, as it is written "and giving the sense" (Neh. 8:8) – it was transmitted orally, and not in vocalization signs in the book.[3]

The biblical scrolls from the Judean Desert, written at the end of the Second Temple period, are in principle like contemporary Torah scrolls: the scroll is made of sheets of parchment, sewn together and written on one side only. Before reading, the scroll needs to be <u>rolled</u> (*liglol*) to the desired point in the text, and for that reason it is called a <u>scroll</u> (*megilla*).

---

1 Mahzor Vitri is a halakhic-liturgical composition by Simḥah b. Samuel of Vitry, France, pupil of Rashi, who lived in the eleventh and twelfth centuries

2 The Talmud (Temura 14b) deduces from this verse homiletically that sometimes the sages need to violate teachings of the Torah in order to make a change required by circumstances. The Midrash reads the verse in this way: "It is time to act for the Lord, and therefore the sages ought to violate your teaching".

3 שטעמי לנגינות הם שנאמרו למשה... אבל סימני הנגינות סופרים הוא שתקנום... ומפני שהטעמים והנגינות משתכחין הוא שתקנום, וסמכו על מה שאמר הכתוב "עת לעשות ליי הפרו תורתך" (תה' קיט, קכו). ולפיכך לא ניתן ספר תורה לינקד. שאע"פ שניתנו פסוקי הטעמים ונגינות הקרייה מסיני במסורת, דכתיב "ושום שכל" (נחמ' ח, ח) - על פה נאמרו, ולא בסימני נקידה בספר.

https://doi.org/10.1515/9783110594560-001

The scrolls contain letters only (which for the most part signify only the consonants in every word), and therefore anyone who wants to read from them in public needs to be familiar with the reading, i.e. he needs to know what vowels he will pronounce when reading the consonants, and with what melody he will chant the verse. This knowledge had to be imparted to him by another person, his father or teacher, who was himself expert in reading, and thus the manner of reading passed from one generation to the next orally.

The Masoretes changed this when they created the signs for vocalization and cantillation. They developed written signs – vocalization – which indicate the vowels in every word, and other phonetic matters, such as doubled consonants (indicated by a *dagesh forte* – a dot inside the letter), distinguishing between the two sounds produced by the letter *shin*, the two ways of pronouncing the letters ב,ג,ד,כ,פ,ת (*dagesh lene [qal]*), and the difference between the letter ה at the end of the word that indicates the consonant hand when it is only serving as a vowel (*mappiq*).

The Masoretes also developed signs for cantillation (*te'amim*), that indicate how to chant the scriptural text (and indirectly how to divide the words in the verse, which influences its meaning). By doing so they resemble someone who knows songs and melodies, and in order to pass them on to someone else, he *creates* for the first time musical notation to record the melodies he knows.

The vocalization and cantillation signs are not mentioned in the Talmud, from which we may conclude that they were not created before its completion (circa 500 CE). Creation of the complex and ramified system of vocalization and cantillation was not completed at one time. We find it in its final sophisticated form in the tenth century and maybe in the ninth, thus it is generally presumed that they originated in the seventh and eighth centuries.

In summary: The Masoretes transformed an oral tradition that was passed from one generation to the next into a written tradition. This effort was in a way parallel to that of the Sages, who allowed the Oral Law to be written in books. The Babylonian Talmud (Temura 14b) says that "oral things – you may not write them down" yet nevertheless they allowed the Oral Law to be written because 'It is time to act for the Lord, for they have violated your teaching'" since "it is better for one teaching to be violated, than for the teachings of Israel to be forgotten." The writer of Mahzor Vitri (quoted above) cites the same Talmudic passage, when he explains why the vocalization and cantillation signs were created.

In addition to the vocalization and cantillation signs mention should also be made of *ge'ayot* (or *metagim*), which were also created by the Masoretes and appear in the ancient Bible Manuscripts. These are vertical lines beneath a word, which indicate a slowing of the reading, a secondary stress in the word. In chapter eleven below, we will discuss this issue in depth.

Decisions regarding Textual Accuracy

The primary purpose of the Masoretes was to determine a single, uniform text that would be regarded as the accurate and precise text of Scripture. In order to achieve that goal they needed to decide in many instances regarding which there were differences of opinion. From the oldest witnesses of the biblical text, among them the Dead Sea Scrolls and ancient translations, we learn that at the end of the Second Temple period textual differences in copies of the Torah, the Prophets and the Writings were widespread. The Masoretes decided which text was more accurate and recorded their choices in books written for that purpose.

An ancient *baraitha* [Tannaitic saying][4] testifies to how early Masoretes made their choices. It tells about three Torah scrolls found in the '*Azara*, i.e. in the Temple in Jerusalem, which contained textual differences. It relates that three cases of disputation were found in these scrolls, and in each case the text in one (other) scroll differed from that of the other two. The sages ruled according to the majority and "maintained two, negating the third", creating a uniform and consensual text. This schematic story evidently reveals the working of the Masoretes whenever they encountered conflicting versions: they sought out manuscripts that were regarded as ancient and authoritative, compared the texts, and decided on the basis of a majority of authoritative manuscripts. In this way they were able "to overcome" the great number of scriptural texts, and created a single, uniform text.

This text, which the Masoretes determined, they sought to preserve for future generations and to prevent its corruption or deviation from it. For this purpose they created the system of Masoretic notes that will be presented below.

From Scroll to Codex

Vocalization and cantillation signs were not written in scrolls but in codices (*mitshafim*), i.e. books made of parchment in which every leaf was written on both sides, much like modern books. The term *mitshaf*, taken from Geez and Arabic, was adopted into Hebrew by the Geonim as the equivalent of the Latin term codex. This writing technique was invented in Rome in the second century CE, and implemented in the writing of Hebrew literature centuries later.

This technique of writing allows turning the pages of the book easily and moving quickly from one section to another. The book is made of quires, each one consisting of parchment sheets folded in the middle. In ancient Bible manuscripts quires of five sheets folded in the middle are common. Each quire would thus contain ten

---

4 Sifre Devarim, par. 356; Yerushalmi, Ta'aniyot 68a; Sofrim 6:4.

leaves, which comprised twenty pages. The text of Scripture was written in two or three narrow columns on every page.

In order to appreciate the efficiency of writing codices, it is useful to point out an historical analogy from the improvement of technology in recent decades. From the 1960s until the 1990s audio and video cassettes were widely used. In the recent digital revolution these were replaced by CDs and DVDs. Cassettes are like scrolls. In order to move from the beginning to the end they had to be rolled, which took time. However a disk allows immediate access to each section, just as in the pages of a codex (see Figure 1.1).

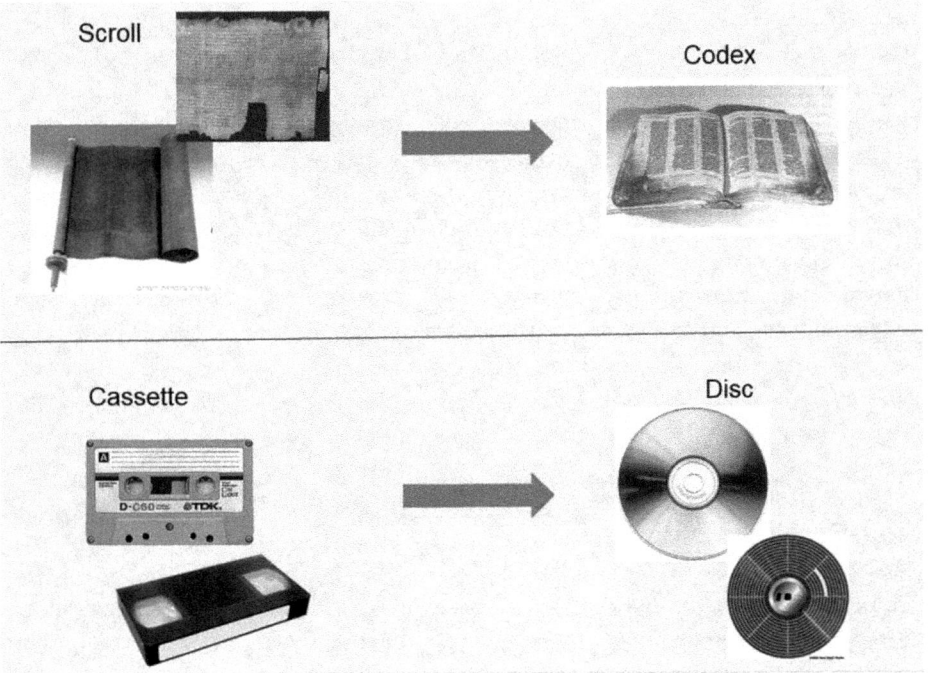

Figure 1.1: Scroll and codex, cassette and disk.

In fact, both types – the scroll and the codex – are found in Jewish synagogues today. The Torah is read from a scroll, without vocalization and cantillation signs, which preserves the ancient methods of writing and reading. But the congregation follows the reading in *ḥumashim* (printed books containing the Five Books of Moses), much like ancient codices, including vocalization and cantillation signs. A reader who did not prepare sufficiently may err in his reading, and the congregation wastes no time in correcting him – and he then repeats the passage correctly.

Ancient Manuscripts of the Masoretes

The most famous Masoretic codex is the Aleppo Codex (*Keter Aram Zova*). This is a complete Tanakh (Hebrew Bible; Torah, Prophets and Writings), which contained 490 leaves. The Masorete who added the vocalization and cantillation signs as well as the Masoretic notes was Aharon Ben Asher. This codex was evidently written in Tiberias circa 930. Scholars of the Masora cite the various manuscripts by letter, and the Aleppo Codex is cited as **A**. Another complete manuscript of the Hebrew Bible is Ms. Leningrad, which is generally cited as **L**. This manuscript was written in Egypt in 1009 by Shmuel ben Ya'akov, as we learn from the colophon of the manuscript, i.e. information recorded by the scribe himself at the end of the manuscript. He wrote as follows:

> Shmuel ben Ya'akov wrote and pointed and added Masoretic notes to this cycle of Scripture on the basis of books corrected by the teacher Aharon ben Moshe ben Asher, may he rest in Paradise.[5]

Thus we see that Shmuel ben Ya'akov prided himself on his reliance upon books of Aharon ben Moshe ben Asher, a renowned and authoritative Masorete.

The Aleppo Codex had no colophon, from which we could learn the precise date of its writing. However at the beginning of the manuscript there was a dedicatory inscription, written in the eleventh century, when the manuscript was dedicated to the Karaite synagogue in Jerusalem. It reads as follows:

> This complete codex of twenty four books which was written by our master and Rabbi Shlomo, known as ben Buya'a the swift scribe, may the spirit of the Lord give him rest. And the great learned and wise scholar father of sages and first of scholars, swift in his deeds and understanding in his action, unique in his time, Rabbi Aharon ben Rabbi Asher, may his soul be bound in the bonds of life, vocalized and added Masoretic notes to it... It was dedicated by the great leader... Israel of the city of Basra ... to Jerusalem the holy city...[6]

The names of the two individuals who created the manuscript are given with the blessing for the deceased, i.e. neither of them was still alive when the manuscript was dedicated. The former, Shlomo ben Buya'a, wrote the codex, that is the letters, and he was entitled the "swift scribe", while the latter, Aharon ben Asher, who added the vocalization and wrote the Masoretic notes, receives a long list of superlatives. From this text we may learn the division of labor between the two: The scribe, who was

---

5 שמואל בן יעקב כתב ונקד ומסר את המחזור הזה שלמק'[רא] מן הספרים המוגהים המבוא'[ר]'[ים] אשר עשה המלמד אהרן בן משה בן אשר נוחו בגן עדן

6 זה המצחף השלם של עשרים וארבעה ספרים שכתב אותו מרי ורבנא שלמה הנודע בבן בויאעא הסופר המהיר רוח יוי תניחנו ונקד ומסר אותו באר הטיב המלמד הגדול החכם הנבון אדון הסופרים ואבי החכמים וראש המלמדים המהיר במעשיו המבין במפעליו היחיד בדורותיו מר רב אהרן בן מר רב אשר תהי נפשו צרורה בצרור החיים... הקדיש אותו השר הגדול... ישראל ממדינת בצרה... לירושלים עיר הקדש...

an expert in calligraphy, like scribes today, who are well practiced in writing Torah scrolls, phylacteries and *mezuzot*. But the Masorete was responsible for the text, a more specialized task. He added the tradition of Bible reading that he received from his ancestors and teachers, and he was responsible for checking the letters written by the scribe.

Here we shall list a few of the ancient manuscripts from the tenth and eleventh centuries:

- Ms. **S1** is a codex of the entire Tanakh, which belonged to the collector Suleiman Sassoon, Ms. 1053 in his collection. It is noteworthy that writing the entire Tanakh was not a common practice in ancient times, and generally a codex was of only the Torah, Prophets or Writings. This manuscript is one of a few complete codices of the Tanakh that were written in the tenth and eleventh centuries and survived till today. Other than the Aleppo Codex and the Leningrad Codex, only one or two additional manuscripts belong to this category. The Masorete of this manuscript used the Aleppo Codex; in one of the Masoretic notes he quoted a note from it, stating "and we found them in the work of the great teacher Aharon ben Asher in his cycle (=the entire Tanakh) known as *al-Taj* (*taj* in Arabic means crown = *keter*)." From the lack of a blessing for the deceased we may conclude that the note was written in the lifetime of Aharon ben Asher.

- A manuscript of the Prophets kept in the Karaite synagogue in Cairo, cited as **C**. This manuscript is unique in two respects: first of all, this is the earliest dated Hebrew Bible manuscript, and according to its detailed colophon it was written in 895. Secondly, according to the same colophon, the scribe and Masorete was Moshe ben Asher, the father of Aharon ben Asher, the Masorete of the Aleppo Codex. The colophon at the end of the manuscript reads as follows:

  > I, Moshe ben Asher, wrote this cycle of the Bible on the basis of... as G-d's good hand for me, well annotated, in Medinat Ma'azia Tiberias, the noble city [...] and it was written 827 years after the destruction of the Second Temple.

  However some scholars have cast doubts regarding the authenticity of this colophon. One claim relates to the colophon itself: The writer mentions "this cycle of the Bible", i.e. the entire Tanakh. But the inscription appears at the end of the manuscript, which contains only the books of Prophets. Consequently scholars have presumed that the words were originally written by Moshe ben Asher, but that in Ms. **C** the colophon is a copy and not the original.[7]

- Ms. **B**, in the British Library (Or. 4445). This manuscript contains the Torah, but the beginning and end have been missing from it for centuries, and consequently it has no colophon, telling us when or where it was written or the name of the

---

7 Cf. M. Glatzer, "The Aleppo Codex: Codicological and Paleographical Aspects", *Sefunot* 19 (1989), pp. 250–259 (Heb.).

scribe. Recently the name of the Masorete of this manuscript was discovered –
Nisi ben Daniel Ha-Cohen (for details of the discovery see below in Chapter Four).
In the Masora of this manuscript "the great teacher Ben Asher" is mentioned twice
(Gen. 49:20; Lev. 20:17; and also "of the great teacher" in Ex. 35 without citing his
name). From the lack of the blessing for the deceased it was concluded that these
notes were written during Ben Asher's lifetime and therefore the manuscript is a
contemporary of the Aleppo Codex.

- Ms. **S** (also from the Sassoon Collection), was acquired by the National Library
of Israel (Ms. Heb. 24°5702). This is also a manuscript of the Torah and lacks a
colophon. It is presumed to date from the tenth century. Ben Asher is mentioned
in its Masora as "the teacher" (*HaMelammed*). Figure 1.2 below gives the *Masora
Parva* on Num. 23:23, which presents the dispute over the stressed syllable in the
word פָּעַל (*pa'al*, 'acted') in that verse: "according to the teacher פָּעַל penultimate
stress, according to Ben Naftali פָּעַל ultimate stress." The manuscript shows indications of corrections that were inserted: First the cantillation mark was beneath
the letter ע following the system of Ben Naftali and afterwards it was erased and
re-written beneath the letter פ following Ben Asher's system. This correction, and
the reference to Ben Asher as "the teacher" without citing his name, reflects the
respect given to the Masorete.

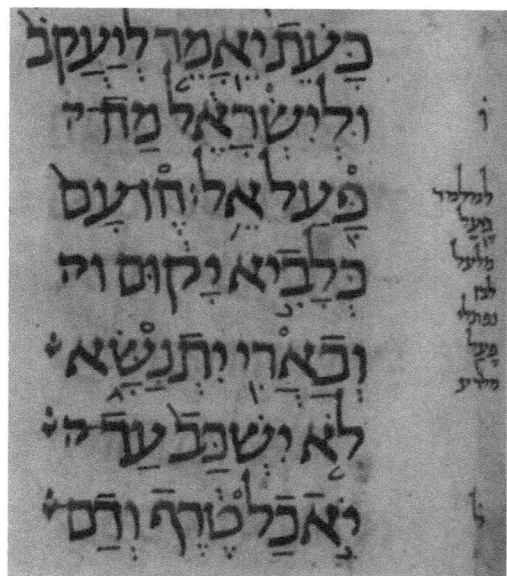

Figure 1.2: Ms. **S** – the Masoretic note on
the word פָּעַל.

The manuscripts we have mentioned are related to the Ben Asher family and in particular to Aharon ben Moshe ben Asher, who is referred to by Masoretes as "the great
teacher." The study of these manuscripts began already in the nineteenth century,

and researchers into the Masora described them and examined their texts. There are dozens of additional early codices of Scripture, most of which have not been studied sufficiently. Some of them contain large sections of the Torah, the Prophets or the Writings and some of them have barely survived and contain only a few leaves. They are found in many libraries throughout the world, but the largest and most important collection is that in the National Library of Russia in St. Petersburg (formerly Leningrad). These manuscripts were brought from the Middle East to Russia in the nineteenth century by the learned Karaite traveler Avraham Firkowich. (Only in the early 1990s did Israeli scholars obtain free access to these manuscripts and were photographs of it made available in Jerusalem).[8]

In the sixteenth century the age of printing reached the Masora. The early and most important printing was that of Venice 1524–1525, under the supervision of Ya'akov ben Haim Adoniyahu, which later came to be known as "*Miqraot Gedolot.*" Adoniyahu included in the printed edition all of the elements found in the manuscripts: vocalization, cantillation signs, secondary stress marks (*ge'ayot*), notes of *Masora Magna* and *Masora Parva*. Adoniyahu edited the Masoretic notes according to the manuscripts that were available to him. His edition was widely disseminated and has been republished many times.

How does a typical page of the Tiberian Masora codex look?

As an example of the product of the Tiberian Masora we shall examine one page from the Aleppo Codex (Figure 1.3).

As mentioned above, this is one page from a codex, in which every leaf is written on both sides. This page has three columns, which was the customary way in which ancient codices of the Masora were written. The words are vocalized and include cantillation signs. Many Masoretic notes are written between the columns in small script. These are the notes called *Masora Parva* (the Small Masora). At the top of the page and the bottom longer Masoretic notes also appear. These are the notes of the *Masora Magna* (the Large Masora).[9]

Returning to the letters of the Biblical text, spaces at the end of lines or in the middle of lines are noticeable. These are the spaces that indicate sections: In two places on the page the next section appears after a blank line, and these are called

8 Cf. Israel Yeivin, *The Biblical Masorah*, Jerusalem 2003, pp. 6–28 (Heb.). (compare: Israel Yeivin, *Introduction to the Tiberian Masorah*; translated and edited by E.J. Revell, Missoula, Montana 1980, pp. 15–29).
9 These are the terms used in the study of the Masora, but are not documented in the ancient Masoretic literature itself. Below, in Chapter Four, we shall see that the term Masora Magna (in Hebrew: *Masora Gedola*) was used to refer to a special compilation of Masoretic notes, today known as *Okhla we-Okhla*.

Figure 1.3: A page from the Aleppo Codex – Deut. 32:50–33:29. All photos from the Aleppo Codex are published courtesy of the Ben Zvi Institute and the Committee of Trustees of the Aleppo Codex.

parashot petuhot = open sections (in the right column: זאת הברכה [l. 9], וללוי [last line]). An open section can also be designed without an empty line, if the former section ends at the beginning of the line, and the new section begins from the right side of the next line. In other cases the section comes after a small indentation at the beginning of the line (left column [1.1]: ולזבולן) or after a space in the middle of a line (left column [l. 6]: ולגד). These are called *parashot setumot* (closed sections). Scribes writing Torah scrolls are expected to implement these open and closed sections, with the same care with which they copy the letters of the text themselves. A *baraitha* in

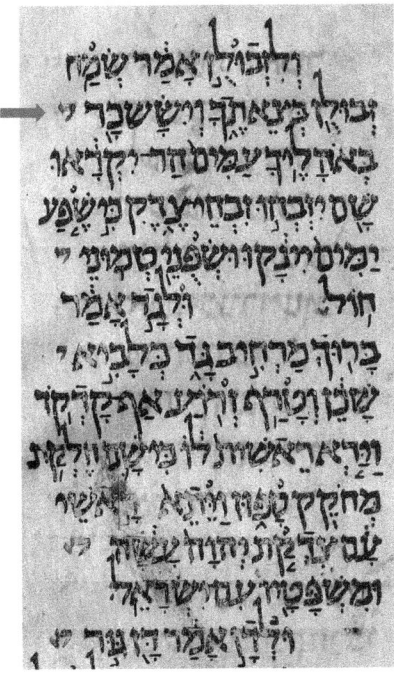

Figure 1.4: Detail from the Aleppo Codex.

Tractate Shabbat (103b – cited as a binding regulation in Maimonides, Laws of the Torah Scroll 7:11) states: "An open section may not be made closed, a closed may not be made open."[10]

At the end of lines partial letters may be observed. The enlarged photograph above (Figure 1.4) shows part of the left column of the page. The letter *yod* is visible after the word וישׁשׂכר (l. 2; see the arrow) and other marks in different shapes after the words טמוני, כלביא, עשׂה, גור (lines 5, 7, 11, 13). These are **line fillers**. Their purpose is to fill in the ends of the line so that no one thinks by mistake that the space left at the end of the line is meant to be an open section. As is well known, word processors today create straight margins automatically. Professional scribes of Torah scrolls expand certain letters (אהלת"ם) when they need to fill out the line because the next word is too long and needs to be written on the following line. The Masoretes did not follow this practice. They did not expand letters artificially, and if there was space left at the end of the line they used line fillers. The shape of the line fillers was not standardized, and each scribe chose the shape that he preferred: Parts of the letters י, א, שׁ, ם or dots and angles. In some cases these line fillers may help to identify the work of a certain scribe or to determine that two codices were written by the same scribe.

---

10 The design and place of various sections will be discussed below in Chapter Five, pp. 68–70.

Before clarifying some Masoretic notes on this page, we should point out three important kinds of notes that appear in the upper right column (Figure 1.5). This is the beginning of the section called *weZot HaBerakha*, the last of the weekly portions in the yearly cycle that is customary today throughout the Jewish world.[11] On the right side of the column is a decoration in which the letters פרש are written, i.e. *parasha* (= portion). In the blank line before the new portion the letters נ"ב were written. That gives the number of verses in the preceding Torah portion (*Ha'azinu*), 52 verses. On the right there also appears the letter ס', which pertains to a different custom of reading, by which the Torah was divided into about 150 *sedarim* (= orders), and the cycle lasted about three years. The Talmud relates that the triennial cycle was customary in Eretz Israel, and the one-year cycle in Babylonia (Megilla 29b). Over time the yearly cycle gained popularity and came to replace the triennial cycle.

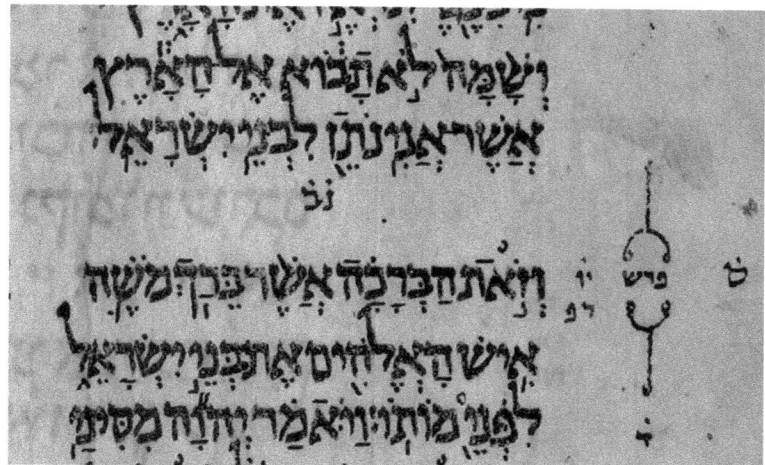

Figure 1.5: Detail from the Aleppo Codex.

Masora Magna and Masora Parva

Now we shall return to the Masoretic notes, which served to preserve the text of Scripture in every detail. The notes of the Masora Parva are brief, in some cases terse, some of them consisting of a single letter. The notes are connected to the text by tiny circles

---

11 Note the distinction between *"parasha petuha"* and *"parasha setuma"* on the one hand – referring to how Scripture is to be written, and *"parshat hashavua"* on the other, which refers to a section for public reading. Quite often the word *"parasha"* is used to refer to the weekly portion, and then it should be distinguished from the other terms by the context.

above the relevant word. The Masoretic note relates to a word in the line to the right or on the left of the note. The most common note is 'ל, an abbreviation of the Aramaic expression לית דכוותיה (*leth dikhwatheh*), i.e. there is no other occurrence of the word under discussion in this form – it is unique in the entire scripture. For example the word ולנפתלי (*ulNaftali*; Figure 1.3, left column, l. 14) is unique, although the name *Naftali* appears many times in Scripture.

Other Masoretic notes tell how many times a certain word appears in scripture. For example on the word ראם (*re'em*, 'oryx', middle column, l. 4 f.b.) the note is 'ג, i.e. the word appears three times in Scripture (in this verse; in Num. 23:22, and 24:8).

Information regarding the distinction between the written text (*Kethiv*) and the way it is to be read (*Qere*) are included in the Masoretic notes. An example may be seen in the middle column: above the word בָּנָו (*banaw*, 'his sons', l. 5) there is a circle, and in the right margin the note בניו ק', indicating how it to be read. An additional note of this kind appears on the word אשדת (*eshdat*, right column, l. 14). The note of the Masora Parva on the right says "כת' מלה חדה וקרי תרת מלין", i.e. the word is written as one word but read as two: אֵשׁ דָּת ('a fiery law').

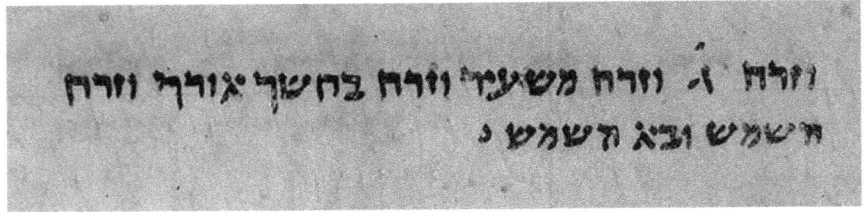

Figure 1.6: A note from Masora Magna in the Aleppo Codex.

The notes of the Masora Parva usually give a number, without citing references to the verse, but the notes of the Masora Magna are longer and more detailed. For example, the first note of the Masora Magna on this page (Figure 1.6) reads: "זרח ג': זרח משעיר. וזרח בחשך אורך. זרח השמש ובא השמש", i.e. the word וְזָרַח (*weZarah*, 'and rose') appears three times: in this passage (the second verse of *weZot HaBerakh*a), in Is. 58:10 and in Eccl. 1:5. The notes of the Masora Magna are not connected to the relevant words by a circle, and the reader needs to look for it on the page. They always relate to a word on the same page, and exceptions to this rule are very rare.

What is the difference between notes of the Masora Magna and the Masora Parva, and why did the Masoretes create a double apparatus? Scholars have suggested various hypotheses for the development of two kinds of Masora and which came first. However, the question is not very important. From the perspective of the creators of the codices there was a double apparatus, and the Masorete of every manuscript inserted notes of both kinds. The notes of the Masora Parva are brief, and usually give a number, but not details (such as 'ג, 'ד, 'ה = 3, 4, 5, and sometimes even larger numbers such as 91 or 134). Notes of the Masora Magna are longer and include both a number and references to the relevant verses. The two apparatuses complement each other: the number is repeated several times in the Masora Parva, and the reader who encounters it seeks out the note in the Masora Magna that gives the details.

It should be emphasized that the notes of the Tiberian Masora do not come in a permanent order, a standardized text or a permanent place. On the contrary, in no two codices are the Masoretic notes identical over a number of pages. Every Masorete wrote the notes in his manuscript in a process of selection and revision. He rephrased the notes that he received, expanded them or abridged them at will and in accordance with the designated space for Masoretic notes in the manuscript.[12] The Masora Magna is usually assigned a given number of lines on the page. In the Aleppo Codex, for example, it is given two lines at the top of the page and two lines on the bottom, and only in a few cases did the Masorete depart from that scheme and give it a third line.

From this description the student and scholar may draw an important conclusion: if he wants to find a certain Masoretic note, it is not sufficient to choose one manuscript and open it to the point in the text that interests him. He should look in many manuscripts, lest a certain note that is lacking in one appears in another; and in every manuscript he should look in sev   given in any place where the word appears in Scrip   iple and it pays to use indices and various research

Secondary Stress Marks

Leaving aside the Masoretic notes for now, let us take a look at the secondary stress marks (*ge'ayot*). In the middle column on l. 5 (see Figure 1.7), the word שָׁמְרוּ appears. To the left of the letter ו is a *pashta*, in the form of a diagonal line rising towards the left from the top of the letter. Beneath the letter שׁ, to the left of the *qamaṣ*, there is a vertical line, called a *ga'aya*. The same sign is used to indicate the end of a verse (as in the word יִנְצֹרוּ [*yinṣoru*, 'they keep'] on l. 6). The cantillation sign *merkha* is marked similarly, slightly pointing to the left, but the slant is not always noticeable (cf. for example in the word וּפֹעַל [*ufo'al*, 'and the work'] on l. 10). The *ga'aya* is distinguished from other uses of the vertical line by the fact that it occurs beneath a word <u>in addition to another cantillation sign</u>. The word שָׁמְרוּ (*shameru*, 'guarded') is marked with a *pashta*, and consequently the vertical line is a *ga'aya*. The *ga'aya* informs the reader to lengthen the qamaṣ under the letter שׁ slightly, while the major stress remains on the final syllable רוּ. Additional occurrences on this page may

---

12 About one exception of this rule, see: Kim Phillips, "The Masora Magna of two Biblical Fragments", *Tyndale Bulletin* 67,2 (2016), pp. 287–307.

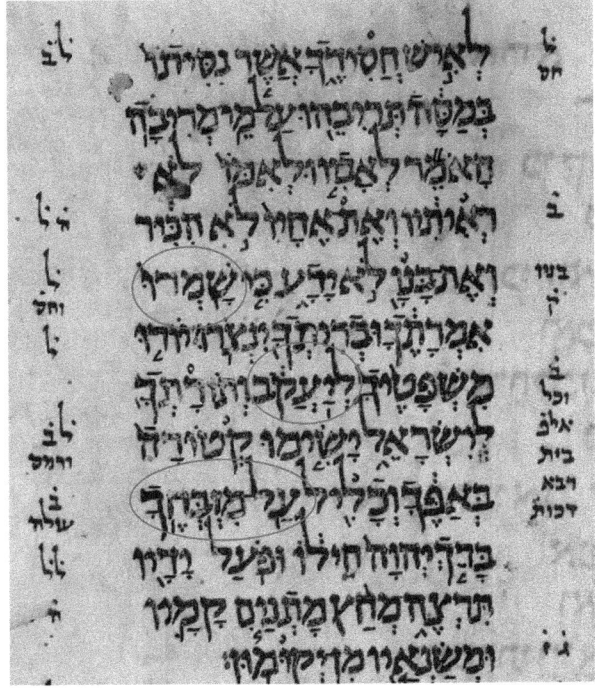

Figure 1.7: Aleppo Codex – three words marked with *ge'ayot*.

be observed in the word לְיַעֲקֹב (*leYa'akov*, 'to Jacob', l. 7) and the combined words עַל־מִזְבְּחֶךָ ('*al-mizbehekha*, 'upon your altar', l. 9): the two words are joined by a hyphen (*maqaf*), and the cantillation mark for the word is the *sof pasuq* (end of the verse) that appears beneath the letter ח. The additional vertical line beneath the letter ע is thus a *ga'aya*. The reader may examine the page (Figure 1.3 above) and find two more occurrences of *ga'aya* (there are only two more on this page!). You will notice that the distinction between the *ga'aya* and similar marks is not easy. Making use of a printed edition of the Tanakh, you may observe that it contains more such signs that do not appear in the manuscript. This will be explained in Chapter Eleven, which deals with *ge'ayot* extensively.

More on Masoretic notes

The Masora Parva enables the Masorete to include a very large number notes on one page. For example, the page we are describing contains no less than 65 notes of the Masora Parva! Sometimes they occur tightly spaced: In the space between the second and third columns (l. 9 f.b.) we find the sign ל'ל', which is the abbreviated note לית (*leth* [*dikhwatheh*], 'there is no [other occurrence]'), three times. The reader needs to discern to which circle each note refers. In order to do so he must remember several rules: (1) the note always begins on the same line as the word to which it applies; (2) a Masoretic note may appear in the space to the right or the left of the word; (3) the notes always appear in the same order as the words to which they apply.

To illustrate this point, the reader should examine the circles and Masoretic notes in the three columns of l. 16 (see also Figure 1.8). In the right column there is one circle, in the middle – one and in the left column – two; between the right and middle columns there is one note, and between the middle and left – three notes. To what word does the note ב between the middle column and the left one refer? (Cf. Gen. 41:50).

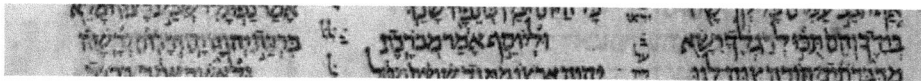

Figure 1.8: Aleppo Codex – example of notes in the Masora Parva.

Notice that the most common note in the Masora Parva is ל׳. These notes do not require expansion in the Masora Magna, since the only occurrence of the word in this form is here. However, in some cases the Masora Magna accumulates many notes of this kind which have a common feature. Such notes are called "Accumulative Masora" and will be discussed at length in Chapter Four.

The note ב׳ (= 'this word occurs twice in the Bible') is an intermediate kind of note. It can be used in the normal way: citing the number alone in the Masora Parva and providing the references in the Masora Magna. But since there is only one additional occurrence of the word in that form, sometimes the Masora abridges the process giving the reference in the Masora Parva. For example, in the right column (l. 13) next to the word מֵרִבְבֹת (*meRivvot*, 'from ten thousands') the note reads: ב׳ לא אירא. The words לא אירא (*lo 'ira*, 'I am not afraid') refer to the second occurrence of the word in Scripture (Ps. 3:7). The reader should find five more such notes on this page, and identify the verses to which they refer [A Concordance or a computer software of the biblical text may be used, of course].

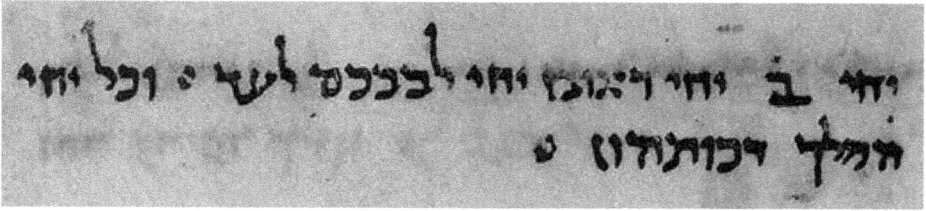

Figure 1.9: Aleppo Codex: a note from the Masora Magna.

We conclude this chapter with remarks on the second note of the Masora Magna on the page (Figure 1.9): יחי ב׳ יחי ראובן יחי לבבכם לעד. וכל יחי המלך דכותהון. The note details the occurrences of the word יְחִי (yeḥi, 'let [he] live'), evidently distinguishing them from other verses in which the form יִחְיֶה (yiḥye, 'will live') occurs. The two occurrences are in Deut. 33:6 (in the page we are discussing) and Ps. 22:27. However, in fact, there are many more occurrences of the word. The Masora adds a group of verses in which the expression יְחִי הַמֶּלֶךְ (yeḥi haMelekh, 'let the king live') appears using the same form. For this purpose the Masora uses an Aramaic Masoretic term: דכותהון (dikhwathon) – which means "like them". In short, it says that every verse in which this combination appears is like the two examples given. This style of Masoretic note is very common, and we will discuss it at length in Chapter Two.

2 Methods of Description and Classification

Principles of writing Masoretic notes in scientific editions

We shall begin this chapter with a technical, but essential issue: how we write references to notes from the Masora Magna in scholarly literature. In the manuscripts the notes are written in one way, but the accepted practice is to record them another way, in order to make clear to the contemporary reader matters that are not explicit in the manuscript.

Let us examine a typical note from the Masora Magna in the Aleppo Codex (Figure 2.1; detail from Figure 1.3). In the second line we read:

ירחים ד' ותצפנהו וממגד במספר תספר

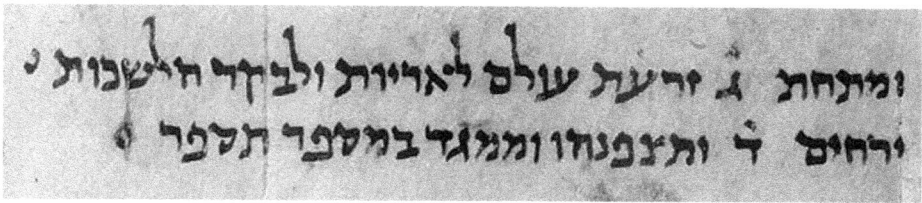

Figure 2.1: Two Masora Magna notes from the Aleppo Codex.

The meaning of this note is that the word יְרָחִים ('months') appears four times in the Tanakh (Hebrew Bible), without reference to orthography, i.e. whether the word is written with or without the second *yod* (יְרָחִם or יְרָחִים).

The next four words in the note refer to four verses in which the word under discussion appears. For example, the first word, ותצפנהו ('and she hid him') refers to the expression "ותצפנהו שלשה ירחים" ('and she hid him three months') in Ex. 2:2. In conformity with the customary practice in the Masora Magna, one of the references is to a verse on the page where the note appears, in this case וממגד תבואת שמש ('with the bounteous yield of the sun', Deut. 33:14).

How can we write this note clearly? We transcribe it in a number of lines. In the first line the title of the note: ירחים ד'. Below we copy the four words in the note that refer to the verses, each in a separate line:

ירחים ד'

ותצפנהו

וממגד

במספר

תספר

https://doi.org/10.1515/9783110594560-002

Thus far we have not added a single letter to the original note, but the note is clearer because of the separation into lines. This is particularly helpful when the note gives more than one word for each reference, and the differentiation between the words is not entirely clear. For example in the following note (Figure 2.2; Detail from Figure 1.3):

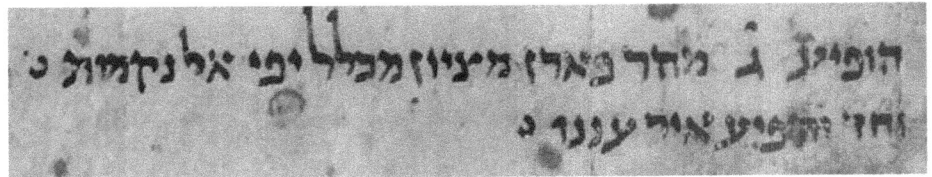

הופיע ג' מהר פארן מציון מכלל יפי אל נקמות

Figure 2.2: A Masora Magna note from the Aleppo Codex (Deut. 33:2).

In order to differentiate the verses to which this note refers, one has to recognize them or find them using a concordance or computer program:

('appeared' – 3 [times])	הופיע ג'
(from Mount Paran)	מהר פארן
(from Zion the totality of beauty)	מציון מכלל יפי
(God of vengeance)	אל נקמות

Look again at the previous note on the word ירחים. First of all, let us add the vocalization: יְרָחִים. This clarifies the accurate reading of the word the Masora is dealing with. The editor of the Masoretic note and the reader agree, as it were, that the vocalization of the title was added by the editor and not found in the text of the masora itself.[1]

The second addition is references to the verses in the note. These are cited in a separate column following the reference words themselves:

	יְרָחִים ד'
Ex. 2:2	ותצפנהו
Deut. 33:14	וממגד
Job 3:6	במספר
Job 39:2	תספר

How do we locate these verses? The easiest way to do so is by use of a computer program that contains the entire text of the Tanakh. An additional, classical way is to

---

1 In most cases the vocalization is certain, because it can be found in the biblical text. If the vocalization is found in the text of the masora, it should be indicated in a footnote.

track the verse using a concordance. Our note is simple and finding the verses may be done with ease.

In this way Masoretic notes are transcribed in various editions, such as the huge collection of the Masora by C.D. Ginsburg, which is based on many manuscripts and arranged alphabetically (*The Masorah Compiled from Manuscripts, Alphabetically and Lexically Arranged*, London 1885) and in the following editions based on individual manuscripts and arranging their Masora notes in the order of the appearance in the manuscript: Beit Zipporah: the Masora Magna according to Ms. Leningrad B19a (ed. G. Weil, Rome 1971); Masora Magna of the Aleppo Codex (ed. D.S. Loewinger, Jerusalem 1977); The Masorah Magna to the Pentateuch by Shemuel ben Ya'aqov: Ms. L^M (ed. M. Breuer, New York 1992); The **Masora Thesaurus** Module in *Accordance* software [based on the Masora of Ms. Leningrad B19a], by Aron Dotan and Nurit Reich, 2013 on.[2]

Methods of classification in Masoretic notes

Let us see how Masoretic notes describe the biblical text. The examples below are taken from the Aleppo Codex, but the principles are not exclusive to the Masora in that codex.

Below is the note of the Masora Magna in the Aleppo Codex on Jos. 4:14:

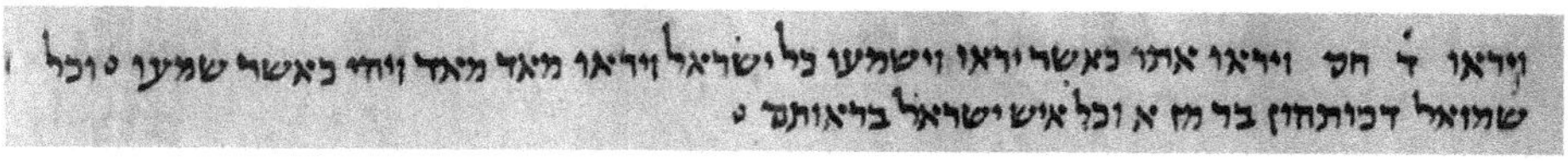

ויראו ד׳ חס ויראו אתו כאשר יראו וישמעו כל ישראל ויראו מאד מאד ויהי כאשר שמעו ׃ וכל שמואל דכותהון בד מח א וכל איש ישראל בראותם ׃

Figure 2.3: A Masora Magna note from the Aleppo Codex (Jos. 4:14).

וַיִּרְאוּ ד׳ חסר
(*wa-yir'u* [and they feared]: 4 defective occurrences)

Jos. 4:14	ויראו אתו כאשר יראו
	(and they revered him as they revered)
I Kings 3:28	וישמעו כל ישראל
	(When all Israel heard)
II Kings 10:4	ויראו מאד מאד
	(But they were overcome by fear)
Neh. 6:16	ויהי כאשר שמעו
	(When all heard it)

---

2 Some of the principles of this transcription are found in ancient manuscripts, such as *Okhla weOkhla*, in which each reference appears on a separate line. Apparently Ginsburg developed the system in its entirety: vocalization of the word under discussion and writing the references in a separate column.

וכל שמואל דכותהון בר מן א'

(And all the book of Samuel is like these [i.e. defective], except one occurrence
[which is plene])

I Sam. 17:24   וכל איש ישראל בראותם

(When the men of Israel saw the man)

The Masora reports that the word וַיִּרְאוּ appears four times in the Tanakh in defective spelling, and details the verses. The references are to the word וַיִּרְאוּ from the root יר"א, meaning 'to fear'. This note does not relate to the similar form from the root רא"י, meaning 'to see'.[3]

The choice of reference words (key words) to the verses in Masoretic notes does not reflect a uniform system: sometimes one word from the verse is given (as in the note on the word ירחים above) and sometimes several words as in the last example above. Sometimes they are the first words of the verse, but other times words from the continuation of the verse. Sometimes the word being discussed is included in the reference, but other times not. Sometimes identical notes appear in two manuscripts, but the choice of key words is different. At any rate, the key words refer to the four verses in which the word וַיִּרְאוּ is written in defective spelling.

Reading the note, one might get the impression from the title that in the entire Tanakh there are only four verses in which the word appears in defective spelling, but in the continuation of the note one learns that there are more than four. The four cases are from the rest of the Tanakh, besides the Book of Samuel, but in that book there are more defective occurrences; as the matter of fact, **all** occurrences of וַיִּרְאוּ throughout the Book of Samuel are defective except for one!

Why did the Masora use such an indirect method instead of listing all the *plene* occurrences or all the defective ones? It did so for brevity and to reduce to a minimum the exceptional verses to which it needed to refer. For that purpose it divided the entire Scripture into two "areas of reference", referring to each one separately. In one area most of the occurrences are *plene*, so only the exceptions are recorded; in the other most of them are defective, and only the occurrences of *plene* are recorded.[4]

---

3 וַיִּרְאוּ meaning 'to see' is always written in defective spelling, and it may be distinguished from the word וַיִּרְאוּ that is the subject of this Masoretic note, because the shewa beneath the letter 'ר is quiescent, and there is never a *ga'aya* (secondary stress mark) beneath the letter 'י.

4 *Sifre* on Deuteronomy (Par. 100 and Par. 103) points out a similar principle with regard to the language of the Torah itself: "Scripture always details the minority." Using this principle the Midrash explains (and following it Rashi on Deut. 14:13) why the Torah details the list of clean animals and unclean fowl. Shmuel b. Ya'akov, a masorete who lived in the eleventh century, phrased the principle of the Masora as follows: "the minority is always recorded in the Masora" (Cf. Y. Ofer, "Masoretic Comments on Grammar in MS לׄ (A Manuscript from St. Petersburg Containing the *Tafsir* of Saadia Gaon)" (Heb.), in: A. Maman (ed.), *Language Studies* VIII: David Tene Memorial Volume, Jerusalem 2001, p. 59).

We can present the data provided in this Masoretic note in the form of a table:

	וַיְּרְאוּ	וַיִּירְאוּ
Throughout the Tanakh except in the Book of Samuel	4	All other occurrences
In the Book of Samuel	All other occurrences	1

On top of the table we write the *two different forms* that the Masora wants to differentiate. On the left we record the two *areas of reference* as defined in the Masoretic note. In the table itself we fill in the numbers and data culled from the note, without listing the verses themselves.

From the note it is impossible to know exactly how many times the defective spelling occurs in the Book of Samuel or how many times the *plene* spelling occurs in the rest of the Scriptures. One can only presume that in the Book of Samuel there is more than one occurrence of defective spelling, and in the rest of the books more than four occurrences of *plene* spelling, and consequently the Masora cited the minority in each area.

With the help of this Masoretic note we can know regarding every verse in the Tanakh in which this word appears, if it is in *plene* or defective form. For example, if we examine a verse from Genesis (such as וייראו/?ויראו? האנשים כי הובאו בית יוסף, Gen. 43:18), we should look at the first line of the table. Since the verse is not listed among the four instances of defective spelling, we may conclude that its spelling is *plene*.

To complete the picture, we use a concordance (or computer software) and add in brackets the numerical data that the Masora did not provide. Here are the results regarding this note:

	וַיְּרְאוּ	וַיִּירְאוּ
Throughout the Tanakh except in the Book of Samuel	4	All other occurrences [11]
In the Book of Samuel	All other occurrences [5]	1

Thus we see that the Masora could have detailed 9 instances of defective spelling of the word throughout Scripture or 12 instances of *plene* spelling. Instead of doing so it makes use of the system of reference areas and cites only five exceptions (4 + 1). Note the economy and reduction achieved: A note of one and half lines in the Aleppo Codex provides the spelling of the word in 21 verses!

The Masora is phrased in *alternating phrases*, like a chain. First it lists the defective occurrences, then it establishes that all the occurrences in the Book of Samuel are also defective like them (using the Aramaic term דכוותהון, 'like them'), except for one verse.

In determining the areas of reference in the table, it should be noted that the first area is not defined explicitly, but by a process of negation. Only when we have seen the definition of the second area ("all the Book of Samuel"), do we realize that the first area is not the entire Tanakh, but all the books except that of Samuel.

We may ask whether there is any significance to the fact that the Book of Samuel differs from the rest of Scripture on this issue. That is to say, *why* is the defective spelling וַיִּרְאוּ routine in the Book of Samuel, while in the rest of Scripture the *plene* form וַיִּירְאוּ is the norm? However, before answering this question, we must stress that it does not pertain to the Masora as such. The Masorete did not divide his discussion into two areas of reference because he regarded the Book of Samuel as a special case, but because he found ad hoc that this division would serve his purpose of transmitting a short and accurate description of the spelling of the word וַיִּירְאוּ in all of Scripture. In order to ask this question, one would have to change from Masorete to grammarian or exegete. The newly phrased question would be: Is there any linguistic or exegetical meaning to the fact *discovered by chance* in the writing of the Masorete, that the defective spelling of the word וַיִּירְאוּ is more common in the Book of Samuel than in the rest of the Scriptures?

It is difficult to answer this question unequivocally. The grammarian would respond most likely that the picture given here is too partial, and these data are insufficient to determine whether we have here a genuine linguistic phenomenon or only something incidental. He would ask concerning the status of similar words, such as יִינְקוּ, יִישְׁנוּ, יִישְׁנוּ, וְיִירְאוּ, יִירְאוּ, and concerning the situation with regards to *plene* and defective spelling in every book of Scripture. Only on the basis of broader and persuasive evidence, could the grammarian draw a clear conclusion that the Masoretic text of the Book of Samuel was inclined toward defective spelling, and if so, ask what does that tells us about the book, its redaction and transmission.

Let us turn to an additional example, the note of the Masora Magna in the Aleppo Codex on I Sam. 19:1. This is how it appears in the manuscript:

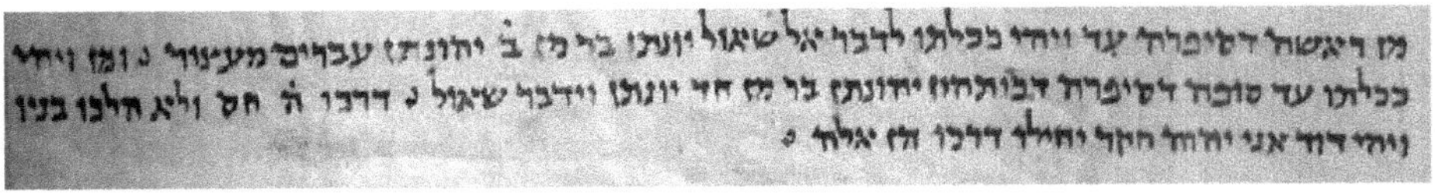

Figure 2.4: A Masora Magna note from the Aleppo Codex (I Sam. 19:1).

"מן ראשה דסיפרה עד ויהי ככלתו לדבר אל שאול יונתן בר מן ב' יהונתן עברים מעצור. ומן ויהי
ככלתו עד סופה דסיפרה דכותהון יהונתן בר מן חד יונתן וידבר שאול".

"From the beginning of the book till אל לדבר ככלתו ויהי [the form used is] יונתן, except for 2 יהונתן [whose catchwords are:] עברים, מעצור. And [all occurrences] from ויהי ככלתו till the end of the book are like them, יהונתן, except for one יונתן [which is:] שאול וידבר."

From this terse form we could transcribe the note into the scientific format, as we have seen above (vocalization of the words under discussion, presenting each verse in a separate line, adding references). We shall not do so in this case, but only present the main idea of the note in table form:

	יונתן	יהונתן
From the beginning of the Book of Samuel until I Sam. 18:1	The rest [28]	2
From I Sam. 18:1 to the end of the Book of Samuel	1	The rest [67]

A note of one line and a half in the manuscript is able to describe the distribution of the name Jonathan spelled with or without the letter ה after the י throughout the Book of Samuel, in which it appears 98 times! The Masora does so by dividing the book into two parts: in the first part of the book the form יונתן is the norm, and in the second part the form יהונתן.[5]

If we leave the sphere of Masora and address this issue from the perspective of exegesis or Biblical scholarship, we must remark that it discloses a significant fact that should not be ignored: The name of the son of Saul changes in the middle of the Book of Samuel. This may be explained from a literary point of view: Scripture wants to say something about Jonathan by changing the orthography of his name, as we have seen explicitly in other cases in Scripture with regards to other figures, such as Abraham, Sarah and Joshua (the first two had the letter ה added to their name and the last the letter י: "But Moses changed the name of Hosea son of Nun to Joshua", Num. 13:16). Another way of looking at it would be that the fact reflects different dialects of Hebrew that are used in the Book of Samuel or its redaction by different writers (cf. I Chr. 29:29). Either way, it is important to emphasize that this does not interest the Masorete. His job is to describe the accurate version of the Book of Samuel with regards to the spelling of the name Jonathan, and he found a brilliant way to do so briefly, pointing out only three exceptional cases: עברים ("Hebrews" – I Sam. 14:8) and מעצור ("prevention" – 14:6) in the first part and וידבר שאול ("and Saul spoke" – I Sam. 19:1) in the second part.

At this stage it is important to emphasize the approach towards exceptions from the perspective of linguistic research as opposed to that of the Masorete. A philologist may sometimes ignore exceptions, claiming that the rule expressed in the majority of verses is the main thing that should be considered, and exceptions are less important. Sometimes he may look for an explanation for exceptions, but if he does not find one he will make due with the general rule and add "Every rule has its exceptions". The Masorete sees this differently. For him to say "In the first part of the book the form יונתן

---

5 The book is divided at I Sam. 18:1, and this verse belongs to the second area of reference in the note. This division is made "ad hoc" for the purpose of this note alone. In general the Masora treats the Book of Samuel as one book and does not divide it into two books (the same applies to Kings, Chronicles and Ezra-Nehemiah).

generally appears and in the second part יהונתן" has no importance! His intention is to determine the precise version of Scripture in every single verse, and the general rules that have exceptions, do not help him!

Here is an additional example of the Masora that indirectly provides a linguistic fact, the note of the Masora Magna in the Aleppo Codex on I Sam. 9:21:

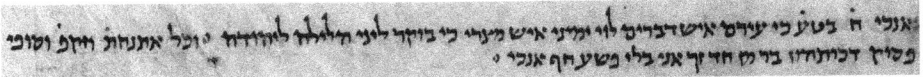

Figure 2.5: A Masora Magna note from the Aleppo Codex (I Sam 9:21).

אנכי ח' בטע' כי עירם איש דברים לוי ימיני איש מצרי[6] כי בוקר ליני הלילה ליהודה. וכל אתנחת'
וזקף' וסופי פסוק דכותהון בר מן חד זך אני בלי פשע חף אנכי

"אנכי appears 8 times in this stress (i.e. penultimate stress): Gen. 3:10; Ex. 4:10; Jud. 17:9; I Sam. 9:21; I Sam. 30:13; Amos 7:14; Ruth 3:13; II Sam. 3:8; and all [the words accented with] *etnaḥta*, *zaqef* or *sof pasuq* are like these (i.e. their stress is penultimate), except for one: Job 33:9"

We shall leave to the reader the challenge of identifying the catchwords of the Masora in the verses referred to, and present only the table of differences in stress of the word אנכי (I):

	אָנֹכִי (*aNOkhi* = I) (penultimate stress)	אָנֹכִֽי (*anoKHI* = I) (stress on last syllable)
The word is marked with another cantillation accent	8	All other occurrences
The word is marked with an *etnah* or *zaqef* or *sof pasuq*	All other occurrences	1

The division into reference areas is made here on the basis of cantillation marks. With three of the accents the stress is generally penultimate (with only one exception) and with all other accents the stress is generally on the final syllable with eight exceptions. Notice that in this note, as in many other notes, the first area of reference is not defined explicitly, but must be deduced from the definition of its opposite (i.e. in all occurrences in Scripture other than those with the three accents mentioned).

The grammarian will immediately notice the reason for this phenomenon: the three accents that are mentioned are the strongest indicators of a pause,[7] and

---

6 It should read נער מצרי (I Sam. 30:13), but the Masorete of the Aleppo Codex erred here under the influence of the adjacent verse (I Sam. 30:11).

7 The cantillation accent *segol* is also indicative of a strong pause, but the word אנכי never appears with that accent, so there is no need for the Masora to mention it.

consequently the form of the word that is appropriate to a pause occurs with those accents: אָנֹכִי with penultimate stress. But in the case of other signs, the pause is of a lower degree, and therefore the form of the word will conform to the context: אָנֹכִי with the stress on the final syllable. The grammarian may choose to ignore the exceptions and regard them as irrelevant, or try to explain the deviations.

For example: one of the exceptions is כִּי בוקר אָנֹכִי in Amos 7:14. In this case the word has a penultimate stress despite being marked with a *tipḥa*. Examining the entire verse reveals the reason for the deviation:

וַיַּעַן עָמוֹס וַיֹּאמֶר אֶל אֲמַצְיָה: לֹא נָבִיא אָנֹכִי / וְלֹא בֶן נָבִיא אָנֹכִי / כִּי בוֹקֵר אָנֹכִי / וּבוֹלֵס שִׁקְמִים.

"Amos answered Amaziah; **I am** not a prophet / and **I am** not a prophet's disciple. / **I am** a cattle breeder / and tender of sycamore figs".

Note the rhythm of the verse. The word אנכי (I) appears three times. The first two have strong pauses (the first a *zaqef* and the second an *etnah*), and evidently they influenced the third, which appears in a clause that is in contrast to the first two.

Another exception that can be explained easily is in the opposite direction: the word אנכי is marked with an *etnah* and nevertheless not given the form it should have in a position of pause! Here too an examination of the entire verse (Job 33:9) reveals the reason for the deviation from the rule:

זַךְ אֲנִי בְּלִי פָשַׁע // חַף אָנֹכִי וְלֹא עָוֹן לִי

"I am guiltless, free from transgression; I am innocent, without iniquity".

The main division of the verse occurs on the word פָשַׁע (transgression), and that word appears in its pausal form. The word אנכי is indeed accented with an *etnah*, but in this verse it does not indicate the main pause in the verse. This verse is from the Book of Job, and in the three books called תהלים, משלי, איוב) ספרי אמ"ת = Job, Proverbs and Psalms) there is sometimes a stronger pause than the *etnah*, called *oleh we-yored*. This is the strongest mark in the verse and it appears on the word פָשַׁע. Here the *etnah* indicates a secondary pause that is not strong enough to require the pausal form.

Once more it is important to emphasize that these explanations interest the grammarian, but not the Masorete. The latter only sought to transmit the details of the accurate text, as briefly as possible. Here too he did so with astonishing success: In this short note that refers to nine exceptional verses, he was able to describe the stress of over 350 occurrences of the word אנכי in Scripture!

Aron Dotan, one of the leading experts on the Masora today wrote:

The grammarian sees the entire forest; the Masorete looks for individual trees. Grammar books present a system of rules that describe linguistic phenomena; deviations are treated like unimportant details, a kind of nuisance that interferes with the uniformity of the rule, and causes the grammarian unease. The Masora, on the other hand celebrates the minority, it is a festivity for exceptional forms, giving them center stage, and giving them greater importance for the very reason that they differ from the systematic majority. (A. Dotan, "From the Masora to Grammar" (Heb.), *Leshonenu* 54, 1990, p. 158)

I would like to define the relationship between the Masorete and the grammarian slightly differently, using a contemporary analogy. We are familiar with the desire and need to compress data, photos, films or recordings. There are two ways to do so: One is called "Lossless data compression" by which a large file is reduced into a zip file, far smaller. The recipient can open the "package" and restore the original file. Another form is called "Lossy data compression". For example: a photograph of excellent quality that is stored in a "heavy" file that may delay the work of the computer or be too large to be sent over the internet – for practical purposes a photograph in lower resolution may be produced from it, weighing much less, but the indiscriminating eye would not notice the difference.

Thus I would say that the grammarian performs "Lossy data compression". He says that *anoKHI* is the contextual form and *aNOkhi* is the form for a pause. And there are some deviations. The Masorete, on the other hand, performs "Lossless data compression". He says that with certain cantillation signs the word has penultimate stress except for a few exceptions, *which he details*. By doing so he has asserted accurately the stress on the word in every occurrence in Scripture, but is spared of listing every verse. Reverting to Dotan's remarks – the Masorete does not prefer the exceptions to those that conform to the rule. He must detail the exceptions in order to preserve the accurate text in every detail.

The next Masoretic note is taken from the Masora Magna on Judges 16:23. This time we will present the note in scientific format:

	Jud. 16:23	וסרני פלשתים
The lords of the Philistines		
	Jud. 16:24	ושלאחריו
And in the following verse		
		אויבנו כתב
The word אויבנו is thus spelled		

וכל עזרא אויבינו כתב בר מן חד כתב כתב איבינו

And throughout the Book of Ezra the word appears thus: אויבינו except once when it is written איבינו

	Neh. 6:1	ולגשם הערבי וליתר איבינו
And to Geshem the Arab and the rest of our enemies		

וכל שאר קרייה דכותה איבינו כתב

And in all the rest of Scripture it is written איבינו

This note is more complicated than the previous ones because it deals with a word that contains two issues of *plene* and defective spelling. In the word אויבינו (our enemies) both the first letter *vav* and the second letter *yod* could be written or omitted, without affecting the pronunciation of the word. Thus there are theoretically four possible spellings of the word: איבנו (this orthography is sometimes called defective of defective); אויבינו (*plene* of *plene*); אויבנו (*plene* of defective); איבינו (defective of *plene*). The first form does not appear anywhere in Scripture; thus three forms remain.

The data from the Masoretic note appear in the following table[8]:

	אויבנו	איבינו	אויבינו
In the remainder of Scripture	2	All the rest	0
In the Book of Ezra (including Nehemiah)	0	1	All the rest

At this point we should notice a fact that seems astonishing at first sight: The Masoretic note lumps together two different grammatical forms: The form אויבנו meaning "our enemy" and the form אויבינו meaning "our enemies." The Masora does not refer at all to the difference in meaning between the two forms, presenting them as exclusively orthographic differences!

A basic principle of the Masora lies behind this fact. The starting point for the discussion of the Masora is the pronounced word, and from the perspective of pronunciation there is no difference between the singular and plural forms of this word. Therefore the Masora treats all the occurrences of this word as one item, and sorts them by orthography alone. In some verses it may be difficult to decide by the context whether the meaning is enemy or enemies, and the Masora, which is concerned with the accurate text and not its interpretation, can sidestep the problem and address only the spelling of the word disregarding its meaning.

In this context it is interesting to see how S. Mandelkern dealt with this question in his Concordance to Scripture. The system of the concordance differs from that of the Masora, analyzing the grammatical forms and sorting them according to their roots, conjugation (of verbs), person etc. Thus in making a concordance, one has to decide whether the form is singular or plural. Here is how Mandelkern presented his results (for the root א"יב, pp. 41–42):

---

8 Note that the Masoretic note does not regard the Book of Judges as a separate area of reference, but the two verses from Judges are the exceptions in the area of reference of all of Scripture except the Book of Ezra (which, as we pointed out above, includes Nehemiah).

אֹיְבִים *pl.*		1S 19,17	ותשלחי את־איבי וימלט		(8) אֹיֵב, אוֹיֵב *pl.*
Ps 127,5	כי ידברו את־א' בשער	1R 21,20	המצאתני איבי	Ex 15,6	ימינך ' תרעץ אויב
		Ps 13,3	עד־אנה ' ירום איבי עלי	Ex 15,9	אמר אויב ארדוף אשיג
אויבינו		Ps 13,5	פן יאמר איבי יכלתיו	Lev 26,25	ונתתם ביד־אויב
		Ps 41,12	כי לא־יריע איבי עלי	Nu 35,23	והוא לא־אויב לו
אויבינו		Job 27,7	יהי כרשע איבי	Dt 32,27	לולי כעם אויב אגור
1S 4,3	וישיענו מכף איבינו	Thr 2,22	אשר־טפחתי ורביתי אי' כלם	Dt 32,42	...מראש פרעות אויב
1S 12,10	ועתה הצילנו מיד איבינו			Dt 33,27	ויגרש מפניך אויב
Thr 3,46	פצו עלינו פיהם כל־איבינו	**מאיבי**		1S 18,29	ויהי שאול איב את־דוד
Neh 4,9	ויהי כאשר שמעו אויבינו	2S 22,18	יצילני מאיבי עז	1R 8,33	בהנגף...לפני אויב
Neh 5,9	מחרפת הגוים אויבינו	Ps 18,18	יצילני מאיבי עז	1R 8,46	ונתתם לפני אויב
Neh 6,1	לסנבלט...וליתר איבינו			Jer 18,17	...אפיצם לפני אויב
Neh 6,16	ויהי כאשר שמעו כל־א'	**איבנו**		Jer 30,14	מכת אויב הכיתיך
		Jud 16,23	נתן...את שמשון איובנו	Jer 31,16(15)	ושבו מארץ אויב
ואיבינו		Jud 16,24	נ'־אלהינו בידינו את־אויבנו	Hos 8,3	...אויב ירדפו
Dt 32,31	ואיבינו פלילים	2S 19,10	המלך הצילנו ׀ מכף איבנו		
Ps 80,7	ואיבינו ילעגו־למו				

Figure 2.6: Parts of the entry "אויב" in Mandelkern's Concordance.

As opposed to the Masoretic note that cites two verses with the spelling אויבנו (without a *yod* after the *bet*), here there are three. The additional verse, II Sam. 19:10 reads: המלך הצילנו מכף איבנו ("The king saved us from the hands of our **enemy**"). Thus the Biblical text on which Mandelkern based this entry differed from the Masora, bringing him to an erroneous grammatical conclusion. If Mandelkern had taken the context into consideration, he might have arrived at the conclusion that the plural form is more appropriate, and he would have explained the spelling before him as defective spelling of the plural: וַיְהִי כָל הָעָם נָדוֹן בְּכָל שִׁבְטֵי יִשְׂרָאֵל לֵאמֹר: הַמֶּלֶךְ הִצִּילָנוּ מִכַּף אֹיְבֵנוּ וְהוּא מִלְּטָנוּ מִכַּף פְּלִשְׁתִּים, וְעַתָּה בָּרַח מִן הָאָרֶץ מֵעַל אַבְשָׁלוֹם (= "All the people throughout the tribes of Israel were arguing. [Some said:] 'The king saved us from the hands of our **enemies**, and he delivered us from the hands of the Philistines; and just now he had to flee the country because of Absalom'".) However Mandelkern followed the (erroneous) orthography before him, and drew the wrong grammatical conclusion.

The next Masoretic note appears easy to describe, but contains a problem[9]: Masora Magna in Ms. **S1** on Num. 26:53:

כל אורית' שמת חס' בר מן ט' מל' וסימנה' [...] וכל נביאים וכתוב' דכות' מל'

In all of the Torah the word שֵׁמֹת ('names') is spelled defectively except 9 occurrences and they are signified by [...]. And all the Prophets and Writings are *plene*, like the latter."

---

9 The note and its discussion follow M. Breuer, *The Aleppo Codex and the Accepted Text of the Bible*, Jerusalem 1977 (Heb.), p. 205.

	שֵׁמֹות *Shemot* = names (plene spelling)	שֵׁמֹת Shemot = names (defective spelling)
Torah	9	All the rest
Prophets and Writings	All occurrences	0

The problem here is what is the extent of the usage of the word to which the Masora refers here? Does it deal with the word *shemot* alone, or with its occurrence with prefixes as well? The table below describes the occurrences of the word throughout scripture:

	Defective	Plene
Torah	9 שֵׁמֹת, 2 בְּשֵׁמֹת, 1 וּבְשֵׁמֹת, 1 כַּשֵּׁמֹת	9 שֵׁמֹות
Prophets and Writings	0	5 שֵׁמֹות, 9 בְּשֵׁמֹות

On the basis of these data we can explain that the Masoretic note refers to all occurrences of the word. Stating that it appears in the Torah in *plene* form 9 times means that the other 13 occurrences in all forms are defective.

However in one of the examples there is a serious ancient controversy – the last word in the verse וַיִּקַּח מֹשֶׁה וְאַהֲרֹן אֵת הָאֲנָשִׁים הָאֵלֶּה אֲשֶׁר נִקְּבוּ בְּשֵׁמֹ[ו]ת ("So Moses and Aaron took those men, who were designated by name" – Num. 1:17). The ancient manuscripts differ regarding this verse. In Mss. **L** and **S** and in the printed *Miqraot Gedolot* the word appears in *plene* form, but in Mss. **B** and **S1** it is defective; Rabbi Meir Halevy Abulafia (Spain, 12–13 cent.) expressed doubt about the correct reading in his book *Masoret Seyag laTorah*; Jewish communities the world over have written this word differently: The Torah scrolls of Sefardim and Ashkenazim use the *plene* form and those of the Jews of Yemen the defective form.

Accepting the opinion that the spelling should be *plene*, the table should be revised as follows:

	Defective	Plene
Torah	9 שֵׁמֹת, 1 בְּשֵׁמֹת, 1 וּבְשֵׁמֹת, 1 כַּשֵּׁמֹת	9 שֵׁמֹות, 1 בְּשֵׁמֹות
Prophets and Writings	0	5 שֵׁמֹות, 9 בְּשֵׁמֹות

The Masoretic note that says there are 9 occurrences in the *plene* form in the Torah may be explained in that the note discusses the word שמות alone without prefixes.

What we see here is that sometimes the extent of reference of a Masoretic note is unclear. In this example the lack of clarity caused the controversy.

However, it is more likely that the extent referred to in the note is broad, and we may conclude that the spelling of the word in Num. 1:17 was defective (בְּשֵׁמֹת).

Two matters support this conclusion: First of all, if the Masora wanted to describe the spelling of the word *shemot* alone, it could have listed the 9 occurrences of defective spelling in Scripture (all of them in the Torah) alone. That would have been simpler since it did not require distinguishing between Torah on the one hand and Prophets and Writings on the other. As we have seen the method of the Masora is to use the most concise description and detail the minority of occurrences. Secondly, the fact that in all the manuscripts that Breuer checked not one Masoretic note was found that deals explicitly with the *plene* or defective spelling of the word *beshemot* (with the prefix ב) in Scripture is most astonishing. It simply means that the Masora meant to deal with all the occurrences of the word in every form in one note.

And indeed today we can give two strong arguments for determining the spelling of the word in Num. 1:17. Testimony regarding the text of the Aleppo Codex indicates that the spelling in that manuscript was defective, and the Babylonian Masora on the verse states explicitly "*beshemot* defective".[10]

We shall conclude this discussion with an additional Masoretic note that illustrates the difference between the approach of the Masora and that of the grammarian or concordance writer. The Masora cites three occurrences in Scripture in which the word וְהֶבֶל (*wehevel*) is read. This note appears in many places in the Masoretic literature. In some of them (such as the Masora Magna in Ms. L on Prov. 31:30) the note is written without any reference to the difference in meaning between the usage in Proverbs – שקר החן והבל היפי ("Charm is deceptive and beauty *vain* [*wehevel*]" and the usage in Genesis – והבל הביא גם הוא ("and *Abel* [*wehevel*] also brought" [Gen. 4:4]). In other places (such as the Masora Magna of Ms. L on Gen. 4:4) the Masora does mention at the end of the list of common occurrences the fact that it includes homonyms with different meaning. The Masora says there: קדמיה שם אנש (= "the first is a name of a man"), meaning that in the first verse in the list, the verse from Genesis, the word is a man's name. However, listing such words together would be inappropriate in a grammatical treatise, and for that reason Mandelkern harshly criticizes one of his predecessors in writing concordances, who was influenced by the masoretes (preface to the concordance, p. xvi):

> In Buxtorf's concordance along with תהו וְהֶבֶל נסכיהם (should be: לתהו והבל – Is. 49:4) and שקר החן וְהֶבֶל היפי he cites also וְהֶבֶל הביא גם הוא (Gen. 4:4), and regarding this one of the comedians wrote in the margins: והבל הביא גם הוא (= [the concordance writer] also wrote in vain!).

---

10 Cf. Y. Ofer, "M.D. Cassuto's Notes on the Aleppo Codex", *Sefunot – Studies and Sources on the History of the Jewish Communities in the East*, NS 4 (19), Jerusalem 1989, pp. 309, 335 (Heb.); Y. Ofer, *The Babylonian Masora of the Pentateuch, its Principles and Methods*, The Academy of the Hebrew Language and the Hebrew University Magnes Press, Jerusalem 2001 (Heb.), p. 496.

For further reading

Y. Ofer, "The Relation of Different Masora Types to Grammar", in: M. Bar-Asher (ed.), *Hebrew Through the Ages – In Memory of Shoshanna Bahat*, Studies in Language II, Jerusalem 1997, pp. 51–69 (Heb.).

For further study

Examine the Masoretic notes below, quoted from the Aleppo Codex. Transcribe each note scientifically according to the principles expounded in this chapter. In order to identify the verses make use of a concordance or a computer program.

The Masoretic note may be viewed in the digital photograph of the Aleppo Codex in the following website: http://www.aleppocodex.org/homepage.html

You can compare what you have written to the edition of *Miqraot Gedolot Haketer*, edited by M. Cohen and published by Bar-Ilan University (in print or on-line: www.mgketer.org.il), in which references to the verses are given in the section called עין המסורה.

List the data found in the Masora in a table as in the examples in the chapter. Always define clearly the distinguishing forms in the vertical column heads and the areas of reference at the beginning of the horizontal lines.

1. Masora Magna on I Sam. 23:16

ויחזק ה' וסימנהון חרשה חרש את המצודות את המלוֹא עזר. וכל דסמיך לאדכרה דכות'

2. Masora Magna on Jos. 6:14

אחת ו' זקפ' פת' וסימנהון צנצנת ויסבו סגר ויחלק גזרו ככר. וכל חקה מדה שנה תורה דכות' בר מן חד
נקי יהיה לביתו שנה אחת. וכל אתנח' וסוף' פסו' דכות'

3. Masora Magna on Jud. 17:1

מיכיהו ד' ויהי איש וישב את הכסף וישמע ויגד להם. וכל מלכים ומן אלה המשרתים עד סופה דסיפ'
דכותהון מיכיהו בר מן ב' מיכה ויבא אל המלך ואת עבדון בן מיכה

3 Determining Orthography on the Basis of Masoretic Notes

Do the ancient Tiberian biblical manuscripts reflect a uniform text of Scripture?

The question posed in the title of this sub-topic is a question of principle in the study of the Masora. It may be asked more directly in the form "Does *the* Masoretic text of the Bible really exist?"

This question needs to be clarified in two respects. First of all we are concerned here only with manuscripts of the Masora and not with other witnesses of the scriptural text, like the Dead Sea Scrolls or the Septuagint. The text reflected in those sources is significantly different from that of the Masora: Addition (or omission) of words, verses or even passages of Scripture, in some cases changes of order of lengthy passages in Scripture. In other places in this book (above, p. 5, and below, chapter 10, pp. 170–177) we pointed out that the Masoretes sought to determine a uniform text and succeeded to avoid the introduction of such changes in the manuscripts of the Masoretic text. Our question here concerns other, more minor differences.

The second clarification relates to the relativity of distance. It is impossible to give a definitive answer to questions like "Is Jerusalem close to Tel Aviv?" or "Is New York close to Boston?" The answer depends on the context, since those distances are far greater than the distance between atomic particles, but far smaller than the distance between the earth and the sun. In a similar way it is difficult to answer definitively whether the texts of Masoretic manuscripts are close to one another. Compared to the distance between the Septuagint and Hebrew manuscripts of Scripture, the distance between one manuscript and another in this group appears minute. However, if we examine carefully the group of manuscripts, we find that some are closer to the Aleppo Codex and some farther away from it.

The group of manuscripts of the Masoretic text is not uniform. Here we refer to manuscripts of all or parts of Scripture that were vocalized using the Tiberian system and have notes of Masora Magna and Masora Parva in the margins. Manuscripts may be distinguished by the time of their writing, and also by the geographical provenance. Some manuscripts have survived completely or nearly completely, others only in the form of a few leaves or even a single leaf or fragment of a leaf. The earlier manuscripts are from the tenth and eleventh centuries. Most of them were written in the East: Eretz Israel, Egypt or other lands. These manuscripts are close in time and provenance to the creation of the Tiberian Masora, and are consequently highly important for research.

There are also later manuscripts, from the twelfth to the fifteenth centuries. These are generally categorized by their provenance: Spain, Germany (Ashkenaz), Italy, Yemen and the Orient. Each region is characterized by a different tradition of writing, revealed by the shape of the letters. Only a few of them include a colophon providing

https://doi.org/10.1515/9783110594560-003

information on the names of the scribe, vocalizer and Masorete, the precise date of writing and the venue. Nevertheless experts can determine on the basis of the script and technique of writing the manuscript where and in what century it was written.

In the sixteenth century printed editions of the Tanakh (Hebrew Bible) started to appear, and they quickly took the place of manuscripts. Naturally, the text of the different printed editions is also an interesting subject for research.

The manuscripts can be compared from a number of perspectives. We can compare matters of writing the text, such as *plene* (מלא) and defective (חסר) orthography, the spacing of sections, and the manner of writing poetic passages in Scripture. We can also compare elements that belong to the tradition of reading, such as vocalization, cantillation marks and *ge'ayot*. The results of the comparison in one area may differ from the results in another area.

In this chapter we shall discuss questions of *plene* vs. defective spelling, such as the spelling of the word שֵׁמוֹת vs. שֵׁמֹת (*shemot*, 'names'), דָּוִיד vs. דָּוִד (David). The discussion centers on whether the vowel should be written or not. Of the four letters used as vowels (*aleph, he, waw* and *yod*), two are generally written: *aleph* and *he*. The question of whether to write the letters *waw* and *yod* mainly arises in the middle of a word, since at the end of a word ending in a vowel, the appropriate vowel is usually written. Thus we may reduce the question to the writing of *waw* or *yod* in the middle of a word.

We shall examine the two most famous manuscripts from the Masoretic period: the Aleppo Codex (**A**) and the Leningrad manuscript (**L**). We have already seen that both of these are manuscripts of the entire Tanakh and both stem either directly or indirectly from Ben Asher. A careful comparison of the two manuscripts, **A** and **L**, shows that they have nearly no differences between them with regards to letters that effect the reading or meaning (such as adding or deleting the *waw* that means "and" at the beginning of a word), but they do have differences of orthography. These two manuscripts have differences in the orthography of approximately 280 words in the books of Prophets. In order to appreciate this statistic, we should point out that in *Biblia Hebraica Stuttgartensia* Bible edition (1967), the books of Prophets take up 733 pages. That is to say that on every two or three pages in this edition there is a difference of spelling of one word on the average between these two manuscripts. This "distance" is infinitesimal compared to the distance between them and the Dead Sea Scrolls, which if compared to the Masoretic text show many differences in every verse. But in relation to the goal of the Masoretes, to achieve uniformity in every case, the distance is still great. The question must be asked how we can decide between these differences of opinion regarding orthography, and whether our decision will conform to that of the Masoretes.

It is important to emphasize that these disagreements over spelling cannot be decided on the basis of grammatical rules. Biblical orthography does not follow standardized rules. The same word may be spelled in defective form in some places and *plene* form in others.

Apparently, the simple way would be to examine additional manuscripts and decide on the basis of the majority, which is how Halakha works. This method would lead us to a practical decision. But would it necessarily reveal the choice of the ancient Masoretes? Maybe they themselves could not decide in certain places, and thus left us many manuscripts that reflect methods and sub-methods regarding which no clear decision was made!

Can the Masoretic notes help us to solve this problem? Many Masoretic notes deal with the question of *plene* vs. defective spelling. Can these Masoretic notes help reach a decision regarding orthography?

Here we reach a central point: Masoretic notes appear in the margins of the manuscript, and every manuscript brings a different choice of notes, phrased in its own way and in its own order. What then is the connection between the Masoretic notes in every manuscript and the Scriptural text that appears in the same manuscript?

Theoretically there are two main possibilities, and they are presented in the sketches below. Let us presume that we have two manuscripts **A** and **L**, which differ regarding the spelling of a particular word, and that in both of them we found Masoretic notes pertaining to the spelling of that word. Do not forget that this Masoretic note does not have to appear on the same page in which the word under discussion is found in the text. It may appear in a different place in scripture on which the same word appears.

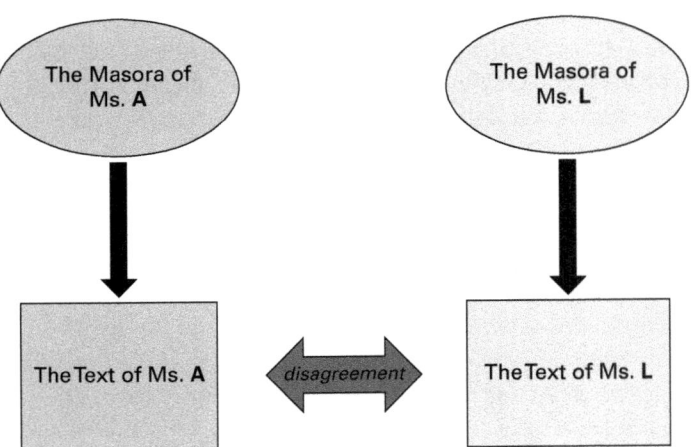

Figure 3.1: Situation no. 1 - The Masora does not contribute towards a decision.

Figure 3.1 presents theoretical situation no. 1: The Masora of each manuscript supports the spelling presented in the text of the manuscript. Every manuscript has a system of its own, reflected in the body of the text and also in the Masoretic notes. In this situation we cannot determine that the text of one manuscript is "correct" or better suits the Masora. At most we can decide which reading should be preferred, on the basis of the more authoritative manuscript or the reading that corresponds to a majority of manuscripts.

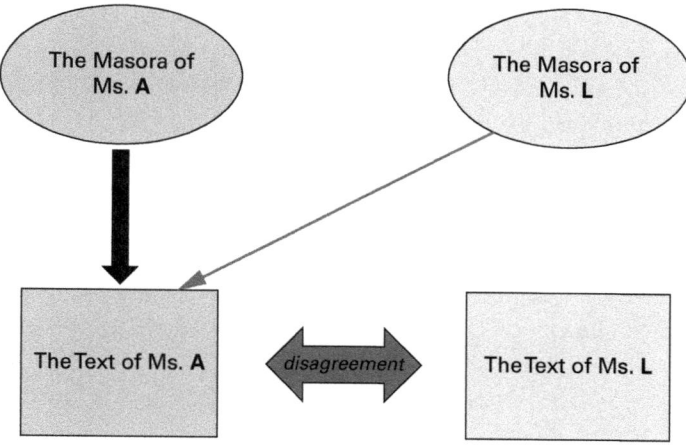

Figure 3.2: Situation no. 2 - The Masora contributes towards a decision.

The situation is different in situation no. 2 (Figure 3.2): The Masora of Ms. **A** supports the text in that manuscript, and the Masora in Ms. **L** also supports the text in Ms. **A**, and not that of Ms. **L** itself. In such a case the position of Ms. **L** is inferior, and we cannot claim that it was created by an expert Masorete, who held a different view. If he did, he would not have written a Masoretic note that contradicted what he wrote in the text on a different page.

We have described here a theoretical examination of one place. In order to arrive at a comprehensive picture we need to examine many hundreds of instances, and the conclusions may be drawn from a compilation of the results of those examinations: Is the more characteristic situation that of situation no. 1 or situation no. 2?

Rabbi Mordechai Breuer made such an examination when he wanted to determine the text of Scripture according to the Masora,[1] and he chose the technique of examining some ancient manuscripts from the Masoretic period and the Masoretic notes in their margins. This was a novel technique among traditional Jewish scholars for determining the text, since other Jewish Bible editions (such as that of Koren), followed the decisions made by Masoretes of later generations, such as the author of *Minḥat Shai* (R. Yedidya Norzi, 1560–1626) and R. Wolf Heidenheim (רו"ה, 1757–1832). Breuer decided according to the "early authorities" and not the "later authorities". Early manuscripts from the Masoretic period became known to modern scholars at

---

1 Breuer's text of Scripture appeared in different editions, among them *Da'at Miqra* and the Jerusalem Crown edition. The process of deciding is described in detail in his book M. Breuer, *The Aleppo Codex and the Accepted Text of the Bible*, Jerusalem 1976 (Heb.; Henceforth: Breuer, Aleppo Codex) and this chapter is based mostly on that book.

the end of the nineteenth and the beginning of the twentieth centuries, and Breuer based his work on them.

Breuer's edition also has a novelty in relation to the Western world. *Biblia Hebraica* Editions, first published in the early twentieth century, were based on the Venice Edition (second rabbinical Bible, 1524–1525). The third edition of *Biblia Hebraica* (completed in 1937) and subsequent editions (BHS and BHQ) follow the text of Leningrad manuscript B19a. Breuer, however, based his Bible editions on a group of ancient manuscripts, including the Aleppo Codex.

Here are two characteristic examples from Breuer's examination. The first is the spelling of the name גיחזי (Gehazi).

וַיֹּאמֶר אֶל גֵּיחֲזִי נַעֲרוֹ קְרָא לַשּׁוּנַמִּית הַזֹּאת וַיִּקְרָא לָהּ וַתַּעֲמֹד לְפָנָיו

He said to his servant Gehazi, "Call that Shunammite woman." He called her and she stood before him. (II Kings 4:12)

The two manuscripts differ regarding the spelling of Gehazi in this verse. The Aleppo Codex gives the name in *plene* form (גיחזי) and Ms. **L** in defective form (גחזי). In both manuscripts, the note of the Masora Magna regarding this word appears in a different place: II Kings 8. Let us compare the Masoretic notes in detail (Figures 3.3 and 3.4):

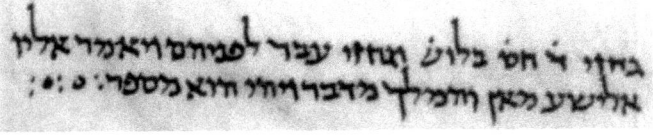

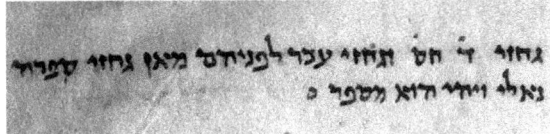

Figures 3.3 and 3.4: Masoretic Notes on "Gehazi" in Ms. **L** (above) and the Aleppo Codex (below) on II Kings 8:4–5.

Masora Magna – Ms. A		Masora Magna – Ms. L	
	גֵּחֲזִי ד' חס'		גֵּחֲזִי ד' חס' בליש'
II Kings 4:31	וגחזי עבר לפניהם	II Kings 4:31	וגחזי עבר לפניהם
II Kings 5:25	מאן גחזי	II Kings 5:25	ויאמר אליו אלישע מאן
II Kings 8:4	ספרה נא לי	II Kings 8:4	והמלך מדבר
II Kings 8:5	ויהי הוא מספר	II Kings 8:5	ויהי הוא מספר

Masora Magna – Aleppo Codex

Geḥazi – 4 times defective:

And Geḥazi had gone
on before them (II Kings 4:31)
Where, Geḥazi (II Kings 5:25)
Tell me (II Kings 8:4)
While he was telling (II Kings 8:5)

Masora Magna – Ms. L

Geḥazi – 4 times defective
(also with prefixes):
And Geḥazi had gone on
before them
And Elisha said to him where
The king was talking
While he was telling

Ms. **L** adds one word to the title of the note: בלישנא (literally: in this tongue; i.e. including all similar forms). This word clarifies that the note deals not only with the form גיחזי, but also with the word with prefixes i.e. וגיחזי, לגיחזי. Ms. **A** does not say that explicitly, but has the same intention, as may be seen in the first verse quoted which contains the form וגחזי. In fact, in every Masoretic note that deals with a particular word, it is possible that the intention is only to the word as it is, but it could also be that the note relates to forms of the word with prefixes as well, and when studying a note, one must check which definition applies.

Although the references to the four occurrences of the defective form are not identical in the two notes, the intention is the same. For example, in II Kings 8:4 the Masorete of Ms. **L** chose the first words of the verse: "The king was talking", while the Masorete of Ms. **A** preferred to cite specific words from the same verse that stand out and make it easy to identify and remember, such as "Tell me". Both references are to the same verse and to the subject of the same word in the verse (גחזי).

From this Masoretic note – in its two versions – the conclusion is that in the verse under discussion (II Kings 4:12) the spelling of Geḥazi should be *plene* (גיחזי). The Masora says that the defective spelling occurs only four times, and the verse under discussion is not one of them. So we see that not only the Masora of Ms. **A** supports the use of *plene*, but also the Masoretic note of Ms. **L**, contradicting the spelling that appears in the text itself. This is the case described as "situation no. 2" above.

The question arises how could this strange situation happen? How can we explain this failure in the work of the Masorete of Ms. **L**? The problem is exacerbated by the fact that the Masorete and the scribe of Ms. **L** were one and the same: Shmuel ben Yaakov was the scribe, vocalizer and Masorete of the manuscript. How did he not notice the contradiction between what he wrote in the text and in the note?

We can find the answer if we consider how the Masorete worked. The Masoretic note we are discussing takes up two short lines in Ms. **L**. If the Masorete found the note in some Masoretic composition and copied it, it took him a very short time: one or maybe two minutes. But it is much more difficult to check that the instructions in the note conform to every occurrence in Scripture. A Masorete who wanted to check that would need to check the four verses mentioned in the note and make sure that the name Geḥazi is written defectively in all of them. But that would not suffice. He would have to check that all the other occurrences of the name Geḥazi throughout the Tanakh to make sure that they are written in *plene* form. An examination in a concordance shows that the name Geḥazi appears only in Kings, and if the Masorete knows that with certainty, his work would be easier. However with regard to more common words, all of Scripture would have to be examined systematically. That is a more difficult task that would require a few hours of work. Here is the test of the Masorete: Is he only a copyist, whose task is to complete the job as quickly as possible and receive his compensation, or is he an expert Masorete, who is willing to invest the many hours of checking and rechecking in order to arrive at the most accurate text possible that will be devoid of internal contradictions.

The next example is from II Sam. 18:15.

וַיָּסֹבּוּ עֲשָׂרָה נְעָרִים נֹשְׂאֵי כְּלֵי יוֹאָב וַיַּכּוּ אֶת אַבְשָׁלוֹם וַיְמִתֻהוּ

Then ten young men who were Joab's armour-bearers closed in on Absalom, struck at him and killed him.

The word וַיְמִתֻהוּ (and killed him) presents two spelling issues: The vowel *yod* could come after the letter *mem* and the vowel *waw* could come after the letter *taw*. Regarding this verse there is agreement that the second case is defective (no *waw* after the letter *taw*); but regarding the first issue there is a disagreement: In the Aleppo Codex, the spelling is defective (וַיְמִתֻהוּ) and according to Ms. L *plene* (וַיְמִיתֻהוּ). Presuming that we have discovered this disagreement between manuscripts, how could we find a Masoretic note dealing with the question that might help resolve the difference of opinion? It is not an easy task. Such a note could appear anywhere in

המקרא	לק	א**ש**ׁ**ד**	הערות מסורה המסייעות לא**ש**ׁ**ד**
שופ׳ ב, ב	בקלי	בקולי	מ״ג~**ש**ׁ שמ׳ ד, ח: וכל בקלי דאור׳ חס׳ ב] [חד׳ מל (וכו׳) וכל נביא׳ וכת׳ מל י
״ יב, יב	אלון	אילון	מ״ג~**ש** (מ״ק~לד), מ״ג~ל: ראה ק שופ׳ יב,יא
ש״א ה, יא	למקמו	למקומו	מ״ג~ד (מ״ק~אלק**ש**ׁ): למקומו ג׳ חסרי׳...×
״ ל,ז 2,1	האפד	האפוד	מ״ג~**ש**ׁ**ד**: אפד האפוד ט׳ מלי בתורה (וכו׳) וכל נביאיא וכתיביא דכותהון.
ש״ב יח, טו	וימיתהו	וימתהו	מ״ג~**ש**ׁ**ולד** (מ״ק~א): וימיתהו ו׳ (וכו׳) נביאים וימתהו חס דחס׳ כתיביא וימיתהו.

למקומו. ד מ״ס קמ 26; אלק**ש**ׁ ש״ב יט, מ. האפוד. ש שמ׳ כח, כז; ד שם ד. **וימתהו.**
ש**ולד**א מ״ב יד, יט. וחצות. ש במ׳ כב, לט; ל יר׳ ה, א; דש**ג** במ׳ שם; א מש׳ ח, כו; ש**ג**ק מ״א כ, לד.

Figure 3.5: From Breuer, *Keter* (Mosad Harav Kook ed.), p. 114; followed by English translation of framed passages.

which the word וַיְמִתֻהוּ occurs and in every manuscript being examined.[2] Breuer carried out such a study, and recorded his findings in his book as follows:

The verse	MSS L and C	MSS A, S1 and D (=second rabbinic Bible)	Masora Comments that support MSS A, S1 and D
II Sam. 18:15	וימיתהו (plene)	וימתהו (defective)	MM of S1,L,D and MP of A: וימיתהו: 6 times…; [all occurrences in] Prophets are וימתהו (twice defective); [Those of] Writings [are] וימיתהו
וימתהו – Masora Comments of S1,L,D,A appear on II Kings 14:19			

From these data we can see that in two manuscripts the spelling is in *plene* form, Ms. **L** (ל) and Ms. **C** (ק). In two other manuscripts, **A** (א) and **S1** (1ש) – defective, and also in the printed edition of *Miqraot Gedolot*, Venice 1525 (known as 'second rabbinic Bible'; indicated as **D** (ד) – *defus*=print). A Masoretic note on this matter may be found in four of these sources on the page in II Kings 14:19. From the language of the Masora Magna note of Ms. **S1**, quoted in Figure 3.5, it appears that in all the books of the Prophets the spelling is חסר דחסר (literally: defective of defective), i.e. in both cases the spelling is defective. Thus this Masoretic note supports the text of **A, S1** and **D**. Such a note does appear in these three sources, as we would have expected. But it also appears in an additional source: Ms. **L**! Here is the Masoretic note in that manuscript (Figure 3.6):

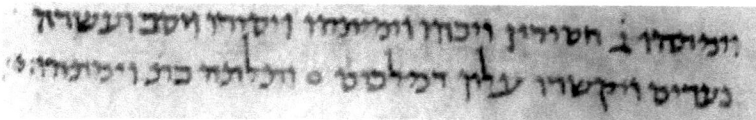

Figure 3.6: A Masoretic note from Ms. **L** on II Kings 14:19.

	וַיְמִתֻהוּ - 3 times defective	וַיְמִתֻהוּ ג' חסירין
II Sam. 4:7	They struck him dead and cut off [his head]	ויכהו וימיתהו ויסירו
II Sam. 18:15	Ten young men closed in	ויסבו עשרה נערים
II Kings 14:19	And they conspired against him (in Kings)[3]	ויקשרו עליו דמלכים
	And three [other cases] are spelled וימיתהו	ותלתה כת' וימתהו[4]

---

2 Masoretic notes on a certain matter appear in different places in Scripture in different manuscripts. For example, in the bottom of Figure 3.5 there are references to Masoretic notes dealing with the orthography of the word חוצות in Scripture. They appear in Ms. **S** and **S1** in Numbers, in Ms. **L** in Jeremiah, in Ms. **A** in Proverbs and in Ms. **C** in Kings.

3 The reference דמלכים (=of Kings) does not appear in order to help the reader identify the verse, but to distinguish this verse from a parallel one, II Chr. 25:27. In the latter verse the word under discussion is written in *plene* form: וימיתהו, so the Masora emphasizes that וימתהו in the verse in Kings is included in the list of defective occurrences.

4 Should be: וימיתהו.

The way of demonstrating the facts in this Masoretic note is entirely different from that in Ms. **S1**. While the note in **S1** stated that throughout the books of Prophets the word is written in defective form, this note cites each and every verse in which the word appears in defective form. However, the conclusion is the same: There are six occurrences of this word in the Tanakh: three of them are in the books of Prophets – and all of them defective; the other three are in the books of Writings – and they are all in *plene* form. The note of the Masora Parva in the Aleppo Codex (חסר 'ג = 3 defective) also reiterates the note of the Masora Magna in Ms. **L**.

Once again, the Masoretic note of Ms. **L** supports the text written in **A** in the relevant verse (II Sam. 18:15), and not the text as written in Ms. **L** in that verse. Once again we have here an example of situation no. 2, demonstrating the superiority of the Masorete of the Aleppo Codex.

In order to determine the correct spelling of the entire Tanakh thousands of examinations of manuscripts and Masoretic notes need to be carried out, and Breuer did so when he wanted to prepare an edition of Scripture on the basis of the Masora. His findings led him to an unequivocal conclusion: Of the two situations stated above, no. 2 was much more characteristic than no. 1. In most cases, all of the Masoretic notes conform to one version of the text, and that is usually the version of Ms. **A**, the Aleppo Codex.

Breuer described his work as follows (quoted freely with omissions):

When we started to prepare the text, we still did not have the Aleppo Codex available to us.[5] Therefore we selected the five oldest manuscripts closest to the Masoretic period as the basis for the edition. The following was the technique for determining the text on the basis of these sources: We presumed that in every case where there is no disagreement between the manuscripts the text they gave was the original Masoretic text. When there was a discrepancy, we decided it on the basis of the majority or on the basis of the Masora. However, the greatest caution needed to be taken in making these decisions: We should not rely on the majority unless the minority opinion was negligible (a single version alone). Moreover Masoretic notes should not be relied on without careful examination: Only if the Masoretic note is found to be the opinion of many sources without disagreement, can it be relied upon to decide between alternate versions.

The resulting version was a new one that was not to be found in any existing manuscript of Scripture. It always conformed to some of the ancient manuscripts – but never in its entirety to any one of them. It was impossible not to question this technique: What right did we have to propose a new version of Scripture, contradicted by all the ancient manuscripts and differing from the "accepted" text? And who would believe the claim that all of these were wrong – and only the new text is the genuine ancient Masoretic text?

Only after the work was completed was this technique proved to be correct. After completing the preparation of the text of most of the Writings and Prophets, we received a photograph of the

---

5 The Aleppo Codex reached Israel in 1958; but only in 1976 a photocopy of the manuscript was published, and the Codex became available to all scholars.

Aleppo Codex. We compared the text of this manuscript to that which we prepared followed the technique described above. And we found that the two texts were nearly identical!

We can illustrate this numerically: In the text of Prophets in Ms. Leningrad there are more than 250 words the spelling of which does not conform to the Masora. In the Cairo Prophets manuscript there are about 130 such words, and in Ms. **S1** there are about 500 such words in Prophets, but in the Aleppo Codex there are no more than five words in the entire Tanakh in which the scribe erred in their spelling.

Thus the text was determined in two ways that are generally considered contradictory. It is a text that was collated from different texts on the basis of the majority of them and the testimony of the Masora, using a system that was accepted for generations by the sages of Israel, but nevertheless, the text conformed in most of Scripture to one tradition, as the system used in modern times by editors and scholars. It is both an eclectic and a diplomatic version!

(M. Breuer, *Tanakh*, ed. Mosad Harav Kook, pp. 394–395)

Breuer points out that he did the work and clarified the text before he received a photograph of the Aleppo Codex, and the results he arrived at with the help of other manuscripts and their Masoretic notes was close to the version of the Aleppo Codex. In his book on the Aleppo Codex the results are given differently, and the data from that manuscript are included in his description of the process, as may be observed in Figure 3.2 above (א = Aleppo Codex). However it is important to stress that the Aleppo Codex did not receive a priori preference! For the purpose of the examination five or six manuscripts were selected and examined together, and at this stage the authority of every one was equivalent. Only after completing the examination, after the text was decided according to the majority of the manuscripts and the Masoretic notes – did the time to evaluate the quality of each one of the manuscripts used in determining the accurate text. The "text decided upon" in the first stage was then compared to each manuscript individually, and thus they were evaluated.

And these are the results that Breuer presented (English translation of Breuer, *Keter*, p. 139):

I will present here the number of places in which the spelling of MSS. A,L,B,C,S,S1 differ from the spelling of the Masora – in the Torah and in the Prophets:

Manuscript	No. of places in the Torah	No. of places in the Prophets
A	[about 3]	about 7
C	–	about 150
L	about 120	about 280
S1	about 20	about 500
B	about 65	–
S	about 25	–

This table shows the degree of conformity of the text to the Masora in six manuscripts that were compared. Two of the manuscripts (ב=**B** and ש=**S**) are of the Torah alone, and one (ק=**C**) is of the Prophets alone. The Aleppo Codex (א=A) originally included the entire Tanakh, but the Torah part was almost entirely lost, and consequently the data on the spelling used in it cannot be examined directly (The number in brackets does not appear in Breuer's book and was revealed by Cassuto's lists. See below, p. 147).

A comparison of the numbers in Prophets shows a dramatic gap between the manuscripts, the number of "errors" or "discrepancies" in them ranges between 150 and 500. However, in the Aleppo Codex only seven errors were found. Such a difference is not only quantitative; it is qualitative and reflects the enormous effort of the Masorete of the Aleppo Codex to ensure that the text he was preparing conformed to the Masoretic text.

Of course the seven places in which the Aleppo Codex "failed" are each of special interest, and it is appropriate to examine each one scrupulously. Now that the accuracy and "authority" of the Aleppo Codex have been established, there is reason to presume that it relied in those cases on another authoritative source. Indeed, since the publication of Breuer's book those seven cases have been investigated thoroughly, both by him and by others, and the number has been reduced to one! In other words, the edition of the Tanakh called *"Keter Yerushalayim"*, which appeared in 2000 following Breuer's system and in conjunction with him, has **only one place** in the Prophets where its spelling differs from that of the Aleppo Codex: the word אשיב (*ashiv* = "I will restore") in Jer. 33:26. According to the Masoretic note in the Aleppo Codex the spelling should be אשוב (*ashuv* = "I will return"), but the scribe who wrote the manuscript wrote אשיב, which was the *qere*, the word as it should be pronounced as opposed to the *ketiv*, the word as it should be written, and the Masorete did not notice and correct the spelling.

Here I would like to present an example of a decision in favor of the text of the Aleppo Codex that was made in the second stage, even though the first examination had decided against it. The word וְנוֹדַד ("and fly away" Nah. 3:17) is unique in all of Scripture. It appears in *plene* form in mss. **L,C**, and **S1** and in the printed *Miqraot Gedolot* (**D**), and a note in the Masora Parva of Ms **C** supports that spelling stating ל' ומל' ("no other occurrence, and *plene*"). As opposed to all of this evidence, the Aleppo Codex reads וְנֹדַד in defective form, and no Masoretic note supports this spelling. Following Breuer's system the decision should be against the Aleppo Codex. However, considering the accuracy and the excellent work of the Masorete of the Aleppo Codex, there is room to suspect that this may reflect a weakness in the technique of examination. In fact not all of the ancient manuscripts from the Masoretic period were checked, but only some of the most famous and most complete ones. In this case the examination should be expanded to see if it reveals a different picture. And indeed it did change! In an additional examination ten manuscripts were found that agree with the Aleppo Codex, some of them early and accurate manuscripts, and likewise a Masoretic note supporting the text of the Aleppo Codex (defective spelling). On the other hand two more manuscripts were found that disagreed with the Aleppo

Codex (*plene* spelling). The conclusion of this expanded study is that most of the manuscripts checked support the text of the Aleppo Codex, but both forms have support in a Masoretic note, so the decision for the edition *"Keter Yerushalayim"* was like the text of the Aleppo Codex.[6]

To conclude this discussion of Prophets we shall return and explain what Breuer wrote: The system he outlined is "eclectic", i.e. based on combining different sources. This system conforms to the way decisions are made in Halakha according to majority opinion and to the *Baraitha* that tells about three books found in the Temple court.[7] However, scientific scholars usually prefer a "diplomatic version", i.e. a version based systematically on one authoritative manuscript, and not on a mixture of versions from which the editor decides in each case which reading he prefers. In this case it turns out that for determining spelling in the Prophets, the eclectic version based on a majority of manuscripts and their Masoretic notes, and the diplomatic version found in the Aleppo Codex – are one and the same!

Criticism of Breuer's Method

Masora scholars Prof. Menahem Cohen and Prof. Jordan S. Penkower agreed that the text of Scripture that Breuer established is the best reflection of the Tiberian Masoretic text, but they criticize the method he used. Cohen wrote:

> Rabbi Breuer's success in achieving such good results by means of his method of majority is derived from the fact that most of the manuscripts he chose were indeed close to the top range of accuracy, and only the selection of the Printed edition by Ben-Haim (Venice 1525) [as one of his sources] partially spoiled the work. How much his results depended on accident may be seen from the fact that if he had taken into consideration even one more manuscript with the [low] degree of accuracy of Ben-Haim's edition, the results would have been substantially different.[8]

---

6 See: Y. Ofer, "The Preparation of the Jerusalem Crown Edition of the Bible Text", *Hebrew Studies* XLIV (2003), p. 95.

7 "Three books were found in the Azara (=the Temple court): one of מעונים, and one of היא הוא, and one called זעטוטים. In one was written מען אלהי קדם and in two מעונה אלהי קדם (= 'The ancient God is a refuge', Deut. 33:27) – the sages dismissed the one and maintained the two. In one היא (= 'she') was written nine times and in two eleven times – the sages dismissed the one and maintained the two. In one was written, וישלח את נערי בני ישראל, וישלח את זעטוטי בני ישראל and in two ואל זעטוטי בני ישראל ('He designated some young men among the Israelites', Ex. 24:5), ואל אצילי בני ישראל ('against the leaders of the Israelites', Ex. 24:11) – the sages dismissed the one and maintained the two" (*Sifrei* Deut. 356).

8 M. Cohen, *Mikra'ot Gedolot HaKeter: Based on the Aleppo codex and Early Medieval MSS, Joshua & Jodges with a general Introduction*, Ramat-Gan 1992, Introduction, pp. 54*-55* (Heb.). J.S. Penkower wrote similarly in his Ph.D. dissertation, *Jacob Ben Hayyim and the Rise of the Biblia Rabinica*, Jerusalem 1982, pp. 437–438 [item 28 – refers to note 449a].

The orthography of the Torah

Let us examine the results regarding spelling in the Torah (cf. the Table on p. 43). The first finding that strikes the eye is the small number of discrepancies in Ms. **S1**: only 20 compared to nearly 500 in the Prophets. In fact the Prophets are about 80% lengthier than the Torah, but that does not suffice to explain why there are 25 times more discrepancies in the Prophets than in the Torah! The explanation is that evidently the Masorete of the manuscript was more exacting to be accurate in the orthography of the Torah, using accurate books and following Masoretic notes, and less so in Prophets and Writings – or perhaps did not complete his checking of those books.

As we mentioned before, we do not have direct data regarding the version of the Aleppo Codex of most of the Torah. However, we do have indirect data. From that data, regarding which we will expand in Chapter 8, we learn that in three places in the Torah the spelling in the Aleppo Codex differed from the Masora. In that case the accuracy of the Aleppo Codex in the Torah as well was greater than that of all the other manuscripts.

It is appropriate at this point to examine the accepted version of the Torah scrolls in use in Jewish communities. Over generations a version came to be accepted for use by scribes writing Torah scrolls. The version used among Sephardi and Ashkenazi communities[9] differs from that in use among Yemeni Jews in nine places, regarding plene and defective spelling. Of course, the two versions are not directly dependent on manuscripts that Breuer examined. The version used by Sephardi and Ashkenazi communities was determined mainly by R. Meir Halevy Abulafia (Haramah) in Spain in the early thirteenth century in his book *Masoret Seyag laTorah* ("Tradition is a Fence for the Torah"), but we do not know with certainty how the Yemeni version was determined.

For the moment we may ignore these nine differences, and address the version that is held in common among all Jewish communities regarding all the rest of the words in the Torah. This version agrees completely with the Masoretic version that Breuer established on the basis of manuscripts and Masoretic notes. This finding is surprising: The accepted version in Jewish communities, which was determined over

---

9 The accepted version today in Sefardi and Ashkenazi communities is based on the work of R. Menahem di Lonzano (Turkey and Eretz Israel, seventeenth century) and R. Yedidya Shelomo Norzi (Italy, seventeenth century), who revised and corrected the printed edition of Venice 1547. Both of them relied on the work of R. Meir Halevy Abulafia (Spain, thirteenth century), who clarified the text of the Torah on the basis of accurate manuscripts and detailed it in his work *Masoret Seyag la-Torah*. The version of the Torah in Spain, Italy and Ashkenaz in the Middle Ages, before the work of Lonzano and Norzi, differed much for from the Masoretic text. Testimony on that is found in an examination of many Biblical manuscripts that have come down from different areas: Cf. Y. Peretz, Open and Closed Passages and the Forms of Songs, Ph.D. dissertation, Ramat Gan 2008 (Heb.); O. Kolodny, The Torah in Italian Codices and Handbooks for Scribes from the Middle Ages, Ph.D. dissertation, Ramat Gan 2008 (Heb.).

generations on the basis of unknown and relatively late manuscripts, conforms to the Masoretic text more than manuscripts from the Masoretic period, such as Ms. Sassoon (**S1**) and Ms. Leningrad (**L**), which have between twenty and 120 discrepancies from the Masoretic text.

As for the nine differences between the Sephardi and Ashkenazi version and that of Yemen: In six cases the manuscripts support the Yemeni version unequivocally; in two cases the manuscripts themselves disagree, but the Aleppo Codex supports the Yemeni version; in only one place the opinion of the manuscripts is evenly split, and the evidence from the Aleppo Codex is conflicted (Num. 22:5 בעור or בער – The name Beor, spelled with or without the letter *waw*).[10]

It is unlikely to assume that the research evidence about the Masoretic text and about the ancient manuscripts will bring Jewish communities to change the text of their Torah scrolls and adopt the tradition of the Yemeni community that corresponds to the Masora. After all, they rely upon a stable halachic tradition practiced for several centuries, and it is possible that their versions are also ancient and wide spread, even though the Masora sages preferred a different version.

Rabbi Breuer made the following hypothetical suggestion a few years ago: "A new settlement that does not have a regular custom – and consists of people from different communities – perhaps it should prefer a Torah scroll written according to the Yemeni custom" (Breuer, *Keter*, p. 9). However, it is doubtful whether anyone adopted that practice.

Orthography of the Prophets and Writings in practice

The situation differs regarding the books of the Prophets and Writings. No clear tradition with an authoritative imprimatur of Halakha was established regarding the orthography of these books. In fact in most communities it was not customary to write the books of prophets or writings on parchment following the regulations for the writing of Torah scrolls. The *haftarot* (passages from Prophets) and most of the "Scrolls" (from Writings: Song of Songs, Ruth, Lamentations and Ecclesiastes with the exception of the Scroll of Esther) were read in the synagogue from printed texts. The version of the texts was not uniform, and even though some of the later authorities have tried to introduce greater accuracy, the issue was never concluded authoritatively. Recently, since the publication of Breuer's studies and his Bible editions, many scribes have started to write the Prophets and the Scrolls following his version that conforms to the Masora, either from his editions or on the basis of special guides for scribes (*Tiqunei Soferim*) that were influenced by him.

---

10 See: Breuer, *Aleppo Codex*, p. 87; Y. Ofer, "M.D. Cassuto's Notes on the Aleppo Codex", **Sefunot** NS vol. 4 (19), Jerusalem 1989 (Heb.), pp. 309, 335.

In addition it should be noted that some of the books of Writings do not exist in the Aleppo Codex as it is today. Breuer recorded about twenty words from Ecclesiastes, Daniel and Ezra regarding which the manuscripts differ and no decisive Masoretic note has been found that could resolve the disagreement. Breuer's decisions as to the spelling of these words are not beyond doubt.[11]

Conclusion

The major conclusion presented in this chapter is that the system of Masoretic notes – found in dozens of manuscripts in various versions – was able to preserve a uniform text regarding the spelling of every word in Scripture. The total number of disagreements reflected in the Masoretic notes is not great, so that in nearly every place in which there is a disagreement between the ancient manuscripts, it is possible to find a clear decision in the Masora. This version of the orthography found a nearly perfect expression in the Aleppo Codex. For the Torah this version was accepted in all Jewish communities, except for nine words that remained disputed between different communities. For the books of Prophets no such accepted and accurate spelling tradition was formulated in Jewish communities until the last generation. But since the discovery of the Aleppo Codex and the manuscripts that are close to it, it is possible to know how the Masora ruled regarding nearly every word in the Prophets and Writings.

---

11 M. Breuer, 'Insoluble Problems', *Leshonenu* 58 (1994–1995), pp. 294–295 (Heb.).

4 The Accumulative Masora

In this chapter we shall consider one kind of Masoretic notes, those called accumulative Masora. We shall explain what they are, when they are used and why they are structured in a certain way.

Figure 4.1: A full page from Ms. B (Or. 4445), fol. 44v, reduced (Courtesy of the British library, London).

First we shall examine a page from Ms. B (Figure 4.1). This is an ancient manuscript of the Torah from the tenth century, contemporary to the Aleppo Codex, preserved today in the British Library (Ms BL Or. 4445). The beginning and end of the manuscript were damaged in an ancient period, and most of the books of Genesis and

https://doi.org/10.1515/9783110594560-004

Deuteronomy are missing; the missing sections were recopied in Yemeni script in the sixteenth century, several centuries after the writing of the original manuscript. For that reason we cannot know if it had at the beginning or end a colophon giving details of its writing. Nor do we know the name of the Masorete who wrote it.

At the top of page we find a Masoretic note, and what stands out is the letter *lamed* that occurs repeatedly on the line and above the line. From afar it looks like a forest of *lamed*s with their flags waving high. This is an accumulative Masoretic note: It presents together words that appear only once in Scripture.[1]

The standard type of note in the Masora Magna is a "detailing note". It usually discusses a word that appears several times in Scripture: twice, three times, five or more. The Masora Parva gives the number of occurrences by letter, *bet, gimmel, he* etc; and the Masora Magna gives verbal references to the verses. When a word is unique, coming only once in the entire Tanakh (Hebrew Bible), the Masora Parva points that out by use of the letter *lamed*, an abbreviation of לית דכוותיה (*let dikhwateh*; "no more like it"). In that case there is no place for the detailed Masora since the only occurrence is the one before us, and there is no need to detail other places.

However, here an accumulative Masoretic note may be given: If this is a unique word, many other unique words that are similar to it may be listed together with it. In order to examine this example, we shall copy here the first line of the note (see also Figure 4.2):

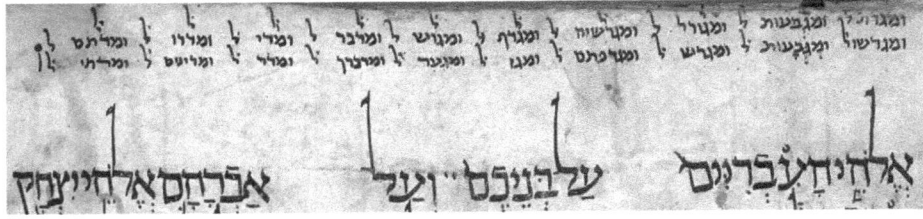

Figure 4.2: The Masoretic note at the top of the page.

"ומגרת ל' ומגבעות ל' ומגורל ל' ומגרשיה ל' ומגדף ל' ומגיש ל' ומדבר ל' ומדי ל' ומדדו ל'
ומדתם ל'"

Here we have ten words (and ten more in the second line), that are all unique occurrences. What else do they have in common? They all begin with the letters *waw mem*. The first six begin with the letters *waw mem gimmel* and the next four with the letters *waw mem dalet*.

---

1 The "uniqueness" of words included in Masoretic notes means that no additional word occurs with precisely the same pronunciation. This term must be distinguished from the linguistic term *hapax legomenon*. For example, the second word mentioned in the Masoretic note in Figure 4.2 is וּמִגְּבָעֹות (= "and from the heights"). This form is unique, because it appears in all of Scripture only in Num. 23:9. However the word גִּבְעָה (= "height, hill") in its many forms appears dozens of times throughout Scripture and thus וּמִגְּבָעֹות is not a *hapax legomenon*.

Why were these words cited? We have to find the connection between them and the text on the page. By chance, or perhaps not by chance, it is the first word וּמְגֶּרֶת ("and the lodger" Ex. 3:22). Together with this word additional unique words are cited that begin with the same first three letters, and when there are no more such words, the Masorete cites words that begin with the same combination, but the third letter is the next letter in the alphabet (*dalet* instead of *gimmel*). He continued using this system until he completed the line intended for the Masoretic note, and then stopped.

This model of Masoretic notes is very flexible; it can be extensive or brief, depending on space available. It does not have to bring all the letters of the alphabet, and in this case made do with the letters *gimmel* and *dalet*. Moreover the Masorete did not cite every word he could have in which the third letter is *gimmel*. An examination shows that besides the 12 words he cited (six in each line), there are nine more unique words, that he could have cited, but refrained from doing so, such as וּמִגָּרְנְךָ ("and from your threshing floor" Deut. 15:14) and וּמָגִנֵּנוּ ("and our shield" Ps. 33:20). This is not an error of the Masorete, since he never claimed that he intended to cite every word that could be cited. In other words: many accumulative Masoretic notes do not exhaust their subject.

Incidentally the notes of the detailing Masora mentioned above are not flexible like the notes of the accumulative Masora. If a Masoretic note details five occurrences of a particular word in Scripture, the Masorete cannot cite only four of them because he does not have enough space on the page, and, naturally, he cannot cite six. He does have some room for flexibility in choosing how to cite the references. He can refer to the entire Tanakh or only the Torah or the Prophets. However, the Masorete preparing accumulative notes is entirely free to add additional examples or to omit them as he wishes. Because after all this is not a single note, but a combination of many notes: A certain word is unique, and another word is unique, and another and another. Every note of this kind could stand on its own (as it indeed does in the Masora Parva). But the accumulative Masora presents it together with other similar Masoretic notes.

How did the Masorete find all of these unique words? He may have had a list of unique words that begin with the letters *waw mem*. This list was arranged alphabetically according to the third letter of the word. It contained words that began *waw mem aleph, waw mem bet, waw mem gimmel* etc. This is not only a supposition. Such a list exists in the work called *Okhla weOkhla*, a compilation of numerous Masoretic notes, written as a separate treatise and not in the margins of a Bible manuscript. List no. 18 in this compilation (Figure 4.3) contains over 200 such words, and it is reasonable to assume that the Masorete of Ms. B used such a list. However, the list he used was evidently richer than the one in *Okhla weOkhla*, which cites only two words under *gimmel* and three under *dalet*.

An additional list of accumulative Masora is written vertically on the same page of Ms. B, in the right margin (see Figure 4.4). Here too are words that begin with the letters *waw mem*, but one word is cited with each letter: וּמֵאֲצִילֶיהָ ("and from its far corners" Is. 41:9) וּמִבָּנוֹת ("and of daughters" Is. 56:5) וּמְגֶּרֶת ("and the lodger" Ex. 3:22) וּמִדְבָּרֵךְ ("and your mouth" Cant. 4:3) etc., and this fact is expressed explicitly at the end of the list under the entry *alphabet*. Here too the word *umigarat* is the key word, i.e. the detail

18.

א"ב מן חד חד ומ' ברי' תיבות' ולי' דכותהון וסי'

Ein alphabetisches Verzeichniss von einmal vorkom-
menden Wörtern, die mit 'וּמ anfangen.

ומאז באתי אל פרעה	וּמֵאָז	Ex. 5, 23.
כה אמר ה' אל דרך	וּמֵאֹתוֹת	Jer. 10, 2.
כל רעיך תרעה רוח	וּמְאַהֲבַיִךְ	Jer. 22, 22.
אשר תאכלנו במשקול	וּמַאֲכָלְךָ	Ez. 4, 10.
	[- - -]	
ועתה הואלת לברך · ד"ה	וּמִבֹּרַךְ	1 Chr. 17, 27.
ויהי לאסא חיל	וּמִבִּנְיָמִן[1]	2 Chr. 14, 7.
והיו לאחד מבני	וּמִגֹּרַל	Num. 36, 3.
אם לא ברכוני חלצו	וּמִגֵּז	Job 31, 20.
ואתה בן אדם· קדמ' דפ'	וּמִדָּבְרֵיהֶם	Ez. 2, 6.
והיה מדי חדש בחדשו	וּמִדֵּי	Jes. 66, 22.
שרים רדפוני חנם	וּמִדְּבָרֶיךָ	Ps. 119, 161.
כי איש איש מבית	וּמֵהַגֵּר	Ez. 14, 7.
והוכן בחסד כסא	וּמַהֵר	Jes. 16, 5.

Figure 4.3: Passages from list 18 in Okhla weOkhla (Ms. Paris, Frensdorff Edition).

Figure 4.4: Enlargement of the list in the right margin of the same page in Ms. B.

from the list that links it to the page of Scripture on which it is written. In this case the word does not appear at the top of the list, but in its place in alphabetical order.

Accumulative Masora lists are convenient for filling pages and decorating them. Figure 4.5 is an example of an accumulative Masoretic note from Ms. Cairo (of Prophets) that also cites words that begin with the letters *waw mem aleph*. Besides the letters themselves there are also word references to verses, written in micrographic script, in various geometric shapes: triangles, a hexagon, a circle with a

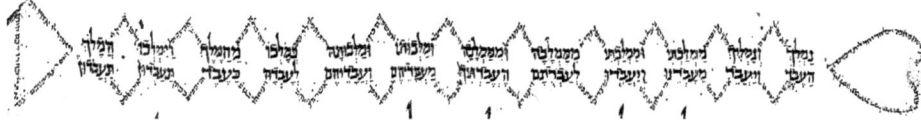

Figure 4.5: Ms. Cairo, an accumulative Masoretic note on II Sam. 22:4; fol. 150r.

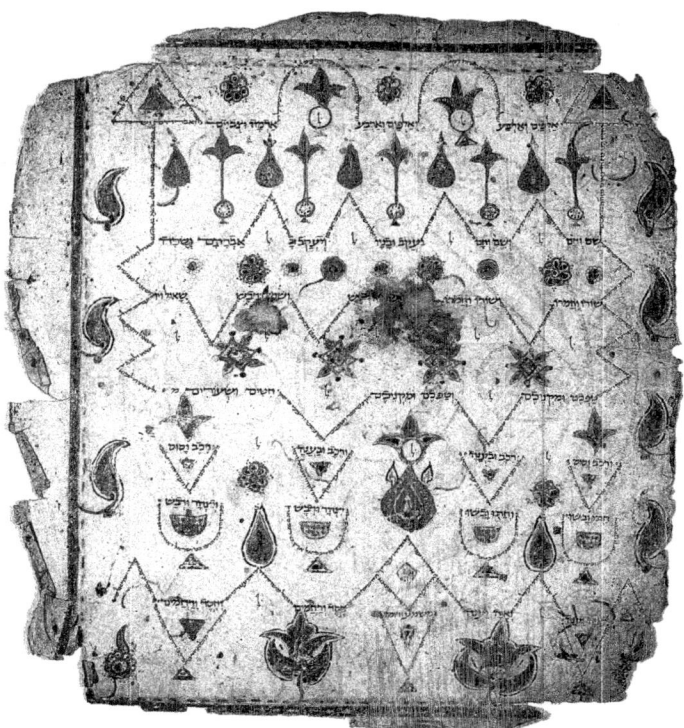

Figure 4.6: An illustrated 'Carpet Page' from Ms. Cairo, fol. 5r .

stem and the like. We shall read one word as an example: the third word on the second line is וּמַאֲכָל ("and food"), and the triangle to the left of the word is comprised of the words ומשתה ושמן לצידנם, ("drink and oil to the Sidonians"), referring to Ezra 3:7.

The next illustration (Figure 4.6) is even more impressive aesthetically, with its bright colors of gold and silver in the origin! This page, and pages like it, come at the beginning of Ms. Cairo in order to decorate it. The text on the page contains a single, accumulative Masoretic note. The items in the note are written in large, vocalized letters, and the words that refer to verses are written in various geometrical forms that link the items themselves. Every detail is dual, for example (from the top of the page): the combination אַלְפַּיִם וְאַרְבַּע ("two thousand and four") is unique in Scripture (Num. 7:85) and likewise the combination

וְאַלְפַּיִם וְאַרְבַּע ("and two thousand and four" Ex. 38:29). The other entries are given in a similar style, such as the combination in the second row: שֵׁם וְחָם ("Shem and Ham" Gen. 9:18) opposite the combination וְשֵׁם וְחָם ("and Shem and Ham" Gen. 7:13) with the prefix *waw* (and) before the first name.

Incidentally, even with the sophisticated means available today it is difficult to find such details as those presented in this kind of accumulative Masora. Try to find a combination that appears only once in Scripture containing "X and Y" and one time "and X and Y". In these cases neither a concordance nor a regular computer program would suffice. A special program designed by a computer programmer would be needed to answer such a request for data. Of course, in the time of the Masoretes both comprehensive knowledge of Scripture and exhaustive work were required in order to create such a note, and I can imagine that there were masoretes who were able to create a rich collection of such examples and took great pride in what they had done.

The principles of combination in the accumulative Masora are many and varied. Words can be put together on the basis of the letters with which they begin (as in the Figures 4.2–4.4 above). They may be combined on the basis of the last syllable, or by the "root" of the word (as in Figure 4.5). And there are additional techniques, such as that in Figure 4.6 ("X and Y" vs. "and X and Y"). The main question to be asked is: What was the purpose of this Masora? Why create lists of unique words in many different ways?

Is the accumulative Masora a useful tool for the main purpose of the Masora, i.e. preserving the Biblical text? When a problem arises regarding a particular word, it is difficult to check in what list of the accumulative Masora the word appears. The accumulative Masora might be useful if we doubt whether some word is unique in Scripture and find it in an accumulative masora list. But the different techniques for combining words would make it difficult to track down the word.

The same applies to entire tracts devoted to accumulative Masora, such *Okhla weOkhla*. But this is particularly true regarding accumulative Masora in the margins of Scripture. As we have seen, the notes are partial and fragmentary. They look as if they only serve to fill the space on the page that is set aside for Masoretic notes, decorating it with a forest of ornate *lamed*s and different geometric patterns.

It seems that Masoretes who included accumulative Masora in their Masora Magna comments had a different purpose in mind. It is combination for its own sake. The Masoretes enjoyed making notes that reflected cleverness and sophistication. Complex and intricate construction like this, which involves enormous effort to make, was regarded by them as appropriate for ornamenting Scripture. It is a kind of amusement, expressing love for the Holy Scriptures, its words and letters. This love was given a double expression: both in the contents of the sophisticated Masoretic note and in the geometric designs in micrographic script that ornamented the page.

It is interesting to point out in this context that in some of the major manuscripts, the Masoretes refrained entirely, or almost entirely, from the use of accumulative notes. There are no notes of this kind in the Aleppo Codex, and they are very rare in the famous Ms. L (which also contains the entire Tanakh). One cannot presume that this was accidental. We may presume that the Masoretes noticed the inefficacy of the accumulative Masora in the margins of a Bible manuscript, and preferred to include the detailing Masoretic notes, which have direct and immediate bearing on the accurate text of Scripture.[2]

In conclusion here is an unusual accumulative Masoretic note, also from Ms. B, from which we began this discussion of the accumulative notes (Figure 4.7):

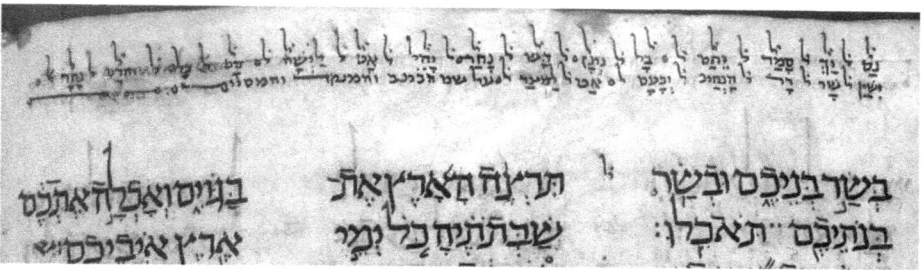

Figure 4.7: Ms. B, fol. 113v: the Masorete's acrostic on Leviticus 26 (Courtesy of the British library, London).

It is easy to discern here an accumulative Masoretic note, just from the multitude of *lamed*s. However it is difficult to find the guiding principle for collecting the words: נַס ל' יָד ל' סָמַר ל' יֵחַם ל' etc. A look at the end of the note will clarify the matter beyond any doubt: עַל שם הכתב והמנקד והמסיים (=after the name of the scribe, the vocalizer and the completer [=Masorete]). In other words the list is an acrostic, and the initials of the words in it give the name of the scribe, who was also the vocalizer and the Masorete. His name was ניסי בן דניאל הכהן (Nisi ben Daniel HaCohen). This Masorete is unknown to us from any other source, but he found a rare and special way to perpetuate his name, within the Masoretic notes he made. Three such notes have survived in this manuscript, and thanks to them his name was discovered (by scholars of the Masora, D. Lyons and A. Dotan), although the beginning and end of the manuscript are not extant, where it was customary to inscribe the names of the scribe and Masorete in a colophon. Only accumulative Masoretic notes can be structured in the form of an acrostic since only these notes give the Masorete the freedom to choose the verses to which he wishes to refer, and he can thus select them in order to create an acrostic. Only a few Masoretes made use of this option. Till today, five additional Masoretic notes designed in acrostic form and referring to the name of the Masorete were revealed. One gives the name שעיד בר כדרוי (Said son of Kadroi), and two other – the name חנניה הלוי בן שלומה (Hananya Halevy son of Shelomo).

---

2 Another opinion about the efficiency of the accumulative Masora, contrary to that expressed here, is presented in an appendix at the end of this chapter.

The Masoretic Collection *Okhla weOkhla*

The Masoretic collection *Okhla weOkhla* is an early Masoretic work, presumed to stem from the ninth century. The name by which it is called is related to the opening list of accumulative Masora, which includes pairs of words, each one of them unique: The second is identical to the first, but with addition of the letter *waw* (=and). The list is long and includes items that begin with all the letters of the alphabet. The first pair in the letter *aleph* is אָכְלָה אחרי חנה ותקם ("and Hannah rose after eating" I Sam. 1:9; beneath the letter *aleph* is a *qamaṣ qatan*) and קום נא שבה וְאָכְלָה מצידי ("Pray sit up and eat of my game" Gen. 27:19). These two words, *Okhla* and *weOkhla*, gave the collection its name, and this name has been known since the days of R. David Kimhi (Radak). However Rashi and Rabbenu Tam called it *"Masoret Hagedola"* (note: the names *Masora Gedola* [Masora Magna] and *Masora Qetana* [Masora Parva] referring to the notes in upper and lower margins of the page and the notes between the columns – are not ancient names).

The compilation *Okhla weOkhla* has come down in two ancient and complete manuscripts. Ms. Paris was published in the mid-nineteenth century (ed. S. Frensdorff) and is better known and more frequently cited. Ms. Halle was published in Spain in 1975 by F. Diaz Esteban. Fragments of pages from additional manuscripts have also been discovered. The Frensdorff edition contains 374 lists of accumulative Masoretic notes.

It is noteworthy that among the lists are some that deal with Ketiv and Qere (words that should be pronounced not as they are written). The lists are categorized systematically, such as list 113 (ed. Frensdorff), which cites 14 words ending in the letter *he*, but pronounced as if they ended in the letter *waw*, that is they are pronounced with the sound u at the end of the word (e.g. יִקְרָחֶה, שָׁפְכָה, נִשְׁבְּרָה). For example the word נשברה (I Kings 22:49) written with the letter *he* at the end, reflecting the form נִשְׁבְּרָה (*nishbera*, 'broken' fem. singular), but pronounced נִשְׁבְּרוּ (*nishberu*, plural).

Two of the Masoretic lists in the compilation *Okhla weOkhla* are especially important. List no 5 (ed. Frensdorff; Figure 4.8) includes the terms מלעיל (*mil'el*) and מלרע (*milra'*):

א"ב מן חד וחד, חד מלעיל וחד מלרע דלוג ולית דכותי'

(=Alphabet, i.e., an alphabetical list, containing pairs of words, one *mil'el* and the other *milra'*, the alphabetical list is not complete, and there are none like them, i.e. unique words.)

As in the first comment of *Okhla weOkhla*, here too pairs of unique words appear. In every pair one word is defined *mil'el* and the other *milra'*. However there is no connection between these terms and the same terms as used in contemporary grammatical usage, indicating which syllable should be stressed. The terms are used here to illustrate the differentiation of vowels in the words discussed. For example, in the

5.

א״ב מן חד וחד חד מלעיל וחד מלרע דלוג ולית
דכותי׳ וסי׳

Ein unvollständig alphabetisches Verzeichniss von Wörtern, die nur zwei Mal vorkommen, und zwar ein Mal mit
einem langen und ein Mal mit einem kürzern (langen) oder
kurzen Vocal.

כה אמר ה׳ אלהים יען	אָמֹר	Ez. 25, 8.
כי טוב אמר לך עלה	אָמָר	Prov. 25, 7.
משא בערב ביער	אֹרְחוֹת	Jes. 21, 13.
וישבו לאכול לחם	אֹרְחַת	Gen. 37, 25.
ואלה העולים מתל מלח	אֻרן	Neh. 7, 61.
וחברו ואלה העולים	אַדָן	Esr. 2, 59.
והשתיה כדת	אֹנֶם	Est. 1, 8.
בלטשאצר רב	אָנֶם	Dan. 4, 6.
עלי מרעים	בִּקְרֹב	Ps. 27, 2.
והיה בקרב אי״ש	בִּקְרַב	2 S. 15, 5.

Figure 4.8: The beginning of list no. 5 in the compilation *Oklha weOkhla*.

first pair אָמֹר-אָמָר, the differentiation is between the *holam* and *qamaṣ qatan*; in the second pair אֹרְחוֹת-אֹרְחַת, between *holam* (*orḥot*) and *patah* (*orḥat*) etc.

We shall discuss the grammatical significance of this list below, in chapter fourteen.

Another list of special importance is no. 59 (Figure 4.9):

א״ב מן ב׳ ב׳ ותרויהון תרין לישנין

(An alphabetical list of pairs of words, both of them with different meanings = hom-onyms)

The list comprises pairs of words, which appear twice in Scripture, but each time with a different meaning. This note is important because it carries an exeget-ical element. Such a thing is exceptional in the Masora, which mainly concerns pronunciation and not meaning. However in this list of homonyms, by referring to two different meanings of the word, the Masora is taking an exegetical stand. In some of the pairs, any reader would easily discern the distinction in meaning. For example, the word אָמִיר (*amir*): In the verse כבודם בקלון אָמִיר ("**I will change** their dignity to dishonor" Hos. 4:7) the word is a verb in the future tense. But in the verse שנים שלשה גרגרים בראש אָמִיר ("Two berries or three on the topmost branch" Is. 17:6) it is a noun meaning "the topmost branch". However in other items in this list it cannot be taken for granted that the words have different meanings, such as הָאָבְנָיִם (*haovnayim*), which refers to two surfaces: one used for childbirth ("the birthstool" Ex. 1:16) and the other for the work of the potter ("the wheel" Jer. 18:3). The beginning of the list also appears in a decorated page of Ms. Cairo (see below, Figure 4.10).

We shall discuss the exegetical ramifications of this list below, in chapter fifteen.

59.

א"ב מן ב' ב' ותרוייהון תרין לישנין וסימ'

Ein alphabetisches Verzeichniss von Wörtern, die zwei Mal
vorkommen in gleicher Form aber in verschiedener
Bedeutung.

ואני שלשת החצים	אוֹרֶה	1 S. 20, 20.
אתכם ביד אל	אוֹרֶה	Job 27, 11.
ויצא אחד אל השדה	אֹרֹת	2 Reg. 4, 39.
יחיו מתיך נבלתי	אוֹרֹת	Jes. 26, 19.
לולי כעס אויב	אָגוּר	Deut. 32, 27.
דברי אגור בן יקה	אָגוּר	Prov. 30, 1.
ונשאר בו עללות	אָמִיר	Jes. 17, 6.
כרבם כן חטאו לי	אָמִיר	Hos. 4, 7.
ואני בבאי מפדן	אֶפְרָת	Gen. 48, 7.
ותמת עזובה ויקח	אֶפְרָת	1 Chr. 2, 19.
וישאל שאול בה'	בָּאוּרִים	1 S. 28, 6.
על כן באים כבדו ה'	בָּאָרִים	Jes. 24, 15.
מי כמכה באלם ה'	בָּאֵלִם	Ex. 15, 11.
הנחמים באלים	בָּאֵלִים	Jes. 57, 5.
ותתפשהו בבגדו	בְּבִגְדוֹ	Gen. 39, 12.
אם רעה בעיני אדניה	בְּבִגְדוֹ	Ex. 21, 8.
או בשתי או בערב	בְּעֵרֶב	Lev. 13, 48.
בנשף בערב יום באישׁן	בְּעֶרֶב	Prov. 7, 9.

Figure 4.9: The beginning of list 59 of
Oklha weOkhla: pairs of homonyms.

For further study

Regarding the accumulative Masora and its techniques see: D. Lyons, *The Cumulative
Masora: Text, Form, and Transmission*, Beer Sheva 1999 (Heb.). The author collected
all of the accumulative Masoretic notes in the Cairo Prophets Codex and presented
them in facsimile and transcription, categorized them and discussed phenomena
related to the accumulative Masora.

Regarding acrostics in accumulative Masoretic lists see: D. Lyons "Acrostic signa-
ture in lists of the Masora", *Qiryat Sefer* 61 (1987), pp. 141–145 (Heb.). A. Dotan, 'Reflec-
tions Towards a critical Edition of Pentateuch Codex Or. 4445', *Estudios Masoreticos*
(X Congreso de la IOMS), Madrid 1993, pp. 39–51; Y. Ofer, "An acrostic signature in a
Masoretic note", *The Babylonian Masora of the Pentateuch, its Principles and Methods*,
Jerusalem 2001, pp. 253–259 (Heb.); Y. Ofer, "Acrostic Signatures in Masoretic Notes",
Vetus Testamentum 65 (2015), pp. 230–246; Y. Ofer, "Acrostic Signatures in Masoretic
Notes and their Development", *Leshonenu* 78 (2016), pp. 60–77 (Heb.).

Figure 4.10: Ms. Cairo, p. 6r: an ornamental page of accumulative Masora.

As a challenge for readers, the photograph below contains two more accumulative Masoretic notes from Ms. Cairo. The first is on Hosea, Ch. 14 (Figure 4.11) and the second on II Kings, Ch. 16 (Figure 4.12).

Figure 4.11: Ms. Cairo, p. 279v: Accumulative Masora.

Figure 4.12: Ms. Cairo, p. 143r: Accumulative Masora.

By examining the Masoretic note, you can copy the title (in the second note, the title is hidden in the micro-graphic letters), find the references by using a search program, identify the word that links each note to this particular page of the Prophets, and verify the accuracy of the words in the list. A particularly challenging task is to see if the notes exhaust the possibilities they could: Are there additional occurrences of the same sort that could have been added to the list?

Appendix: Effective Accumulative Masora

Contrary to what we have said above about the ineffectiveness of the accumulative Masora comments that are written in the margins of the biblical manuscripts (as Masora Magna), certain lists in the *Okhla weOkhla* collection are effective comments that help to preserve the text of the Bible. These comments deal with large-scale issues, such as the existence of conjunctive *waw* and the distribution of the prepositions אֶל and עַל.

Thus, for example, the word אֶל has 3542 occurrences in the Hebrew Bible and the word עַל comes 3547 times. The task of determining which one is used in each verse is not an easy task, given that there is no clear linguistic distinction between the two. Many accumulative Masora comments in Ms H of the treatise *Okhla weOkhla* deal with these prepositions, joining together and creating a comprehensive and effective mechanism for dealing with this issue.

5 Open and Closed Passages and the Writing of Songs

Introduction

The purpose of the spaces between passages is to indicate to the reader where one subject ends and another begins. According to the sages the division of the Torah into passages is as old as the Torah itself, and when the Torah was given to Moses, he was also informed of the spaces between them: "to give a space to Moses to separate one passage from another and one subject from another" (*Sifra Lev.* 1:1, ed. Finkelstein, p. 6). Spaces indicating open and closed passages are found in the earliest biblical fragments – the Dead Sea Scrolls.

Generally speaking an open passage (פרשה פתוחה) expresses a stronger break than a closed passage (פרשה סתומה). One could generalize and say that an open passage comes at the beginning of an entirely new subject, and a closed passage indicates a change from one sub-topic to another. For example: Figure 5.1, from the Aleppo Codex, contains the description of the inheritance of the tribe of Judah (Joshua 15). The description begins with an open passage, marked with an empty line in the second column. The other spaces are closed passages, each indicating a new set of cities within the list.

For further illustration look at Chapters 16–18 of Leviticus: An open passage comes at the beginning of a new subject, such as the first verse in Chapters 16, 17 and 18; closed passages come between each element in the passage of incest (ch. 18). Nevertheless, there is not a clear and unequivocal criterion for the use of an open passage or a closed one, and it ultimately depends on tradition.

The Tanaitic sources stressed the importance of keeping the tradition of open and closed passages, as for example a Halakhic Midrash (*Sifre Deut.*, par. 36, ed. Finkelstein, pp. 65–66):

> And you will write them – a complete writing. From this they said: [...] if he wrote a closed passage in place of an open one, or an open one in place of a closed one, wrote without ink or wrote a song as if it was a prose text [...] – these should be set aside.[1]

The Babylonian Talmud uses similar language (Shabbat 103b), making it clear that the homily is based on the word וּכְתַבְתָּם ("and you will write them", Deut. 6:9) treating the word as two words כְּתָב תָּם ("writing completely") – "and you will write them – the writing should be complete."[2]

---

1 וכתבתם – כתב שלם. מיכן אמרו: [...] כתב לפרשה סתומה פתוחה, לפתוחה סתומה, כתב שלא בדיו או שכתב שירה כיוצא בה [...] - הרי אלו יגנזו.

2 And the text continues there: if he wrote a closed passage in place of an open one, or an open one in place of a closed one; wrote a prose text as a song or a song like a prose text [...] – these should be set aside.

https://doi.org/10.1515/9783110594560-005

Figure 5.1: A page from the Aleppo Codex, Joshua 15.

The lack of treatment by the Tiberian Masora of the issue of passages

One of the puzzles of the Masora is the fact that the Tiberian Masora ignores the subject problem of open and closed passages. Whereas matters of orthography (*plene* vs. defective spelling) occupy a central place in notes of both the Masora Magna and Masora Parva, the Masora ignores entirely the way the passages are written, and does not address itself to them in the notes in the margins of the page. Nor are there lists of open and closed passage in the Masoretic appendices to ancient Tiberian manuscripts. You might think the Masoretes relied on the scribes to copy the manuscripts accurately with regard to passages; however that is not so simple – an examination of ancient manuscripts reveals a lack of uniformity in this matter. While in matters of *plene* and defective spelling the Masoretes did not rely on the scribes to copy Scripture directly from manuscripts, but developed a complex system of Masoretic notes, they did no such thing with regards to passages. Occasionally we find that a late Masorete corrects the tradition of passages of a scribe in a specific place in Scripture, and writes a Masoretic note in the margins of the manuscript. However a systematic discussion of passages is not to be found in the notes of the Tiberian Masora.

Menahem Cohen addressed this problem and made the following proposal:

> a. The intention of the mentioned warning [in Sifre and in the Talmud] was only to prevent the carelessness of scribes in copying open and closed passages as they were transmitted in local tradition. [...] b. The Masoretes of Tiberias did not want to grant their authority to any of the systems of passages that were current in the local traditions of scribes and consequently did not make lists or Masoretic notes on this subject.
>
> (Introduction to *Miqraot Gedolot HaKeter*: Joshua, Judges and Introduction, Ramat Gan, 1992, pp. 50*-51*)

In my opinion, it is difficult to accept Cohen's interpretation of the sources of Halakhah (section a). As for the position of the Tiberian Masoretes (section b), things look reasonable, but the question remains **why** did the Masoretes refrain from granting their authority in this matter the way they did regarding orthography. The key to the answer may be found in Maimonides' ruling, that points out the difficulty of correcting spaces for passages in a Torah scroll:

> A [Torah] scroll that is not well-checked regarding *plene* and defective [spelling] can be corrected as we have explained above. However, if he erred regarding the space of passages and wrote an open passage closed or a closed passage open, or left a space where there is no [new] passage or continued writing as he was and did not leave a space where there is a passage, or changed the form of songs – this is invalid and cannot be repaired, except by removing the entire page in which he erred (Laws of the Torah Scroll, 8:3).[3]

Unlike matters of *plene* or defective spelling, which may be easily corrected by erasing or adding a single letter, filling in a superfluous blank or creating a space

---

3 Some of the early authorities questioned Maimonides regarding this, asking why it was not permissible to erase a few lines and fix the passage that was written erroneously. Cf. *Kesef Mishne* (Rabbi Yosef Karo's commentary on Maimonides' *Mishne Torah*, ad. loc.; Responsa of Rabbi Izhak bar Sheshet no. 7 (ed. Vilna 1839, 2a-b); R. Menahem Ha-Meiri, *Qiryat Sefer*, Second article, Part 2, (Jerusalem 1956), p. 47.

where none was left to begin with require erasing many lines and writing very condensed or expanded letters. Thus, maybe, the accepted approach of the Tiberian Masoretes was to regard every scroll that was written according to an existing tradition as valid without a need to correct or change it. It is important to keep in mind that most vocalized codices of Scripture were written by a scribe and passed on to an expert Masorete. He added the vocalization and cantillation marks and the Masoretic notes, and also checked the spelling and corrected it according to the Masoretic notes. Correcting the passages was difficult and the results of such a correction unaesthetic.

Passages in the Babylonian Masora

The Jews of Babylon developed their own methods of punctuation signs, cantillation signs and Masoretic comments, different from the methods developed in Tiberias and used in the land of Israel. Unlike their Tiberian counterparts, the Babylonian Masoretes did deal in detail with open and closed passages. This discussion had two paths: the first was composing the Babylonian Masora that followed the order of Scripture and the second was the composition of special lists on the subject of passages.

The Babylonian Masora follows the order of Scripture and details its Masoretic notes verse after verse. The beginning of every verse is indicated in a special note, citing it as ר"פ, an abbreviation of ראש פסוק, "beginning of a verse", and followed by the other notes that pertain to that verse. The beginning of the verse is pointed out even when there are no Masoretic notes on that verse. If there is an open or closed passage it is indicated together with the beginning of the verse. The Babylonian Masora refers to a passage by the term פיסקא (*pisqa*). Here is a section from the Babylonian Masora that refers to Deuteronomy, Ch. 6:

ואמרת. (=the beginning of vs. 20, which is a closed passage) כי ישאלך ר"פ ופיס' סת'
ר"פ (=the beginning of vs. 21); ויציאנו כת' (=a Masoretic note on the spelling of one word in the verse); ויתן ר"פ (=the beginning of vs. 22).

The second path is the passages lists. Babylonian lists of passages have been found in the Cairo Geniza,[4] and they are edited in different ways. A long list detailing only the closed passages, and we should presume that its continuation (which is not

---

4 The Cairo Geniza was discovered in 1896 in Fustat, Old Cairo. It contains remainders of about 300,000 fragments and books in Hebrew, Arabic and Aramaic. It contains Biblical and later Rabbinic works, liturgical materials as well as letters and documents that reflect the economic and cultural life of the Eastern Mediterranean regions from the tenth century on. The Geniza materials enlarge our knowledge about the tradition of reading the Bible in Babylonia and about the special tradition of the Hebrew language among Babylonian Jews.

extant) detailed the open passages.[5] Other lists do detail both open and closed passages. Here is a typical passage from one such list (Ms. St. Petersburg, National Library of Russia, Evr. II C 156):

ויהי רעב ("And there was a famine", Gen. 12:10)

ויהי בימי אמרפל ("And it came to pass in the days of Amraphel", Gen. 14:1)

פת' (=open)

אחר הדברים ("After these events", Gen. 15:1)

ושרי ("And Sarai", Gen. 16:1)

ויהי אברם ("And Abram was", Gen. 17:1)

שרי אשתך ("Sarai your wife", Gen. 17:15)

סת' (=closed)

וירא אליו ("And he appeared to him", Gen. 18:1)

פת' (=open)

ויסע משם ("And he traveled from there", Gen. 20:1)

וייי פקד ("The Lord took note", Gen. 21:1)

סת' (=closed)

Such lists were found in the Cairo Geniza and elsewhere, and it is usually evident that they came from Babylonia since they mention disagreements between different Babylonian schools of Masora, such as the list entitled: "These are the passages regarding which the scribes of Nehardea (in Babylonia, nowadays Iraq) disagreed", and like the following description of disagreements:

ויעש את הקרשים [שמות לו, כ] - סת'

ופליגתא דנהרדעי ודסוראי הלין אמרי פת' והלין אמרי סת'

ולא פשיטה לי עד דאתי עזרא לעלמא דאתי ויאמר.

"They made the planks" (Ex. 36:20) – Closed passage
And there was a disagreement between [the school of] Nehardea and [the school of] Sura – these said an open passage and those said a closed passage.
And it will not be resolved for me until Ezra comes in the next world and says.

The maker of this list presents here a case of disagreement between the schools of Nehardea and Sura regarding which kind of passage begins in this particular verse, adding that he does not know how to resolve the disagreement, and we must wait until Ezra the Scribe comes in the next world, in order to decide. From this example, and also by comparison of different Babylonian passage lists, we must conclude that the Masoretes of Babylonia

---

5 Published by C.D. Ginsburg on the basis of Ms. New York, JTS L715. Cf. C.D. Ginsburg, *Introduction to the Massoretico-Critical Edition of the Hebrew Bible*, with Prolegomenon by Harry M. Orlinsky[2], New York 1966, pp. 977–982.

were unable to arrive at a total consensus and agreement by use of these lists. The various lists did not agree with each other, and the Masoretes who wrote them were unable to arrive at an agreement. Perhaps that is why the Tiberian Masoretes refrained from dealing with the issue: The experience of the Babylonian Masoretes taught them that it is difficult to reach agreement between the disputing traditions regarding the passages.

For further study

Yosef Ofer, "A Babylonian List of Open and Closed Parashiyot in the Pentateuch", in: M. Bar-Asher and C. E. Cohen (eds.), *Mas'at Aharon: Linguistic Studies Presented to Aron Dotan*, Jerusalem 2009, pp. 392–434 (Heb.).

Maimonides' ruling

About 200 years after the creation of the Aleppo Codex and the biblical manuscripts close to it, Maimonides described the poor state of affairs with regard to determining passages and the writing of songs:

> And as I saw great confusion in all the books that I have seen in these matters, and the Masoretes, who copy and write in order to inform [us] about open and closed passages disagree in this like the codices they rely upon, I saw the need to write here the closed and open passages of the Torah and the form for writing songs in order to write the [Torah] scrolls according to them and check and correct from them. etc.
>
> (Laws of Tefillin and Mezuza and Torah Scroll, 8:4)

Maimonides found many disagreements between the books – Torah scrolls and codices of the Torah. He was familiar with lists of passages like the Babylonian lists described above, and he knew that they did not agree with each other and did not succeed to resolve the disagreement. Consequently Maimonides himself created a list, hoping that his list would be accepted by Jewish communities and would become the authoritative list. Surprisingly, historically speaking, that is in fact what really happened: Maimonides' list was accepted in all communities, and all the Jewish communities followed his ruling. However, this did not happen at one time: Maimonides' list was accepted relatively quickly in the communities of Yemen and Spain, and more slowly in Italy and Ashkenaz, where the final decision in favor of Maimonides' tradition fell only in the seventeenth century.[6] In only a few places there was some doubt

---

6 Cf.: Jordan S. Penkower, "A Sheet of Parchment from a tenth or eleventh Century Torah Scroll: Determining its Type among Four Traditions (Oriental, Sefardi, Ashkenazi, Yemenite)", *Textus* 21 (2002), pp. 235–264; see also the Ph. D. dissertations of Yosef Perez, Bar Ilan University, 2008 and Orlit Kolodny, Bar Ilan University, 2008.

regarding Maimonides' intention and in one place (Lev. ch.7) there was a disagreement between the communities as to the meaning of Maimonides' formulation, which we shall discuss below (p. 72 and pp. 116–120).

And how did Maimonides determine his list of passages? He decided to select one reliable and accurate manuscript and accept its tradition of passages. This was a novel decision since he could have proposed a different way to arrive at a decision, such as checking a variety of manuscripts and lists of passages, locating the various disagreements and deciding in every case according to the majority. Maimonides did not take that path, saying (Ibid.):

> And the book that we relied upon in these matters is the well-known book in Egypt, which contains twenty-four books, that was in Jerusalem some years ago, to revise the books from it, and everyone relied on it, since it was revised by Ben Asher, and he worked meticulously on it for many years and revised it many times, according to tradition.[7] And I have relied on it in the Torah Scroll that I wrote according to the Halakha.

To what book is Maimonides referring here? Many traditions have identified it as the Aleppo Codex, which is indeed a complete Tanakh revised by Ben Asher that was in Jerusalem for some time. Much evidence supports this hypothesis, and the question will be discussed at length below in Chapter 8 (pp. 144–146).

For the purpose of this discussion, we shall accept the identification, but a difficult question arises: Aharon Ben Asher did not write the Aleppo Codex! The dedicatory inscription of the codex reports that the scribe who wrote the letters was Shlomo Ben Buya'a, and Aharon Ben Asher's part was adding the vocalization, cantillation marks and Masoretic notes. The question that arises is how could Maimonides rely on Ben Asher regarding passages, which he did not write himself?

We can propose two different solutions to this quandary. The first possibility stems from the study by Mordechai Glatzer, who examined the writing of the Aleppo Codex and arrived at the following conclusion:

> It appears that the codex was written for Aharon Ben Asher himself, at his own initiative. There were no other owners besides him at that time. Otherwise it would be impossible to explain how Ben Asher was able to work on it perpetually for many years. If the codex had been in the hands of another private person after its completion, Ben Asher could not have been able to revise it again and again. [...] **One may presume that he also instructed the scribe before its writing.** Therefore it is not surprising that this copy [...] became the classic copy for copyists of Scripture regarding, which "everyone relied on."[8]

---

7 As to the meaning (and the English translation) of the last words see: Mordechai Glatzer, "The Aleppo Codex: Codicological and Paleographical Aspects", *Sefunot* 19 [1988], p. 226 and n. 6 (in Hebrew). According to another explanation, Maimonides intends to say that traditions have reached him with respect to Ben Asher's expertise. According to this explanation the expression כמו שהעתיקו should be to translated: "as people have transmited".

8 Glatzer, pp. 249–250.

Nevertheless a problem remains: Maybe the Aleppo Codex was written under the guidance of Aharon Ben Asher. But is it reasonable to presume that Maimonides knew that? The codex was written in Tiberias in the early tenth century, and Maimonides made use of it in Egypt in the second half of the twelfth century. How did Maimonides know just how the codex was written about 250 years before his time?

Therefore we can propose a different answer to the problem: Maimonides did not claim that the passages in the codex were written according to Ben Asher's Masora. Maimonides only wanted to justify his choice of one manuscript of the Torah and his preference for it over all other traditions. For that reason he cited its lineage and the qualities it had over generations: (1) the codex is an ancient manuscript ("some years ago") that was in Jerusalem, a central and influential place; (2) everyone relied on it; (3) Ben Asher himself revised the codex over many years, giving it its aura; (4) Maimonides himself relied on the codex when he wrote a Torah scroll according to it.

In the light of all these qualities of the codex, Maimonides claimed, it is better to prefer the tradition of this manuscript over all other traditions.

For further study

S.Z. Havlin "Decision by majority or by authority" in E. Fleischer et al. (eds.), *Meah She`arim – Isadore Twersky Memorial Volume*, Jerusalem 2001, pp. 241–265 (in Hebrew).

The form of open and closed passages

The early rabbinic authorities had different opinions regarding the form of open and closed passages. They all agreed that if the scribe finished a passage at the beginning of a line and left a space, starting the next passage on the same line – this next section is a closed passage. They also agreed that if the scribe finished the passage close to the beginning of the line, left the rest of the line blank and started the next passage at the beginning of the next line – that next section is an open passage.

In other cases, for example if the scribe finished a passage near the end of a line or at the very end of the line, they had different opinions. Maimonides was of the opinion that in that case the next passage should begin in the middle of the following line for a closed passage, and in the case of an open passage he should leave the next line blank and start the new passage on the third line (Laws of the Torah Scroll 8:1–2). Rabbenu Asher (*HaRosh*) had the opposite opinion: If a passage begins in the middle of the second line, it is an open passage, and if an entire line is left blank and the passage starts on the third line, it is a closed passage (*Halakhot Qetanot la-Rosh*, Laws of the Torah Scroll, no. 13).

Most of the Torah scrolls to be found today try to satisfy both opinions. The scribes make an effort to end every passage near the beginning of the line, and not close to the end of the line, thus eliminating the need to decide between Maimonides' opinion and that of Rabbenu Asher. That is the recommendation of Rabbi Yosef Karo, the author of the *Shulhan Arukh*, (*Yore De`a*, par. 275:2). Contemporary scribes have no problem to do so, since most of them copy the scrolls from a *Tiqqun Soferim* ("Guide for Scribes") that indicates how to divide the words into lines.

What was the opinion of the Masoretes and scribes who wrote the ancient manuscripts (such as the Aleppo Codex) regarding the form of open and closed passages? There is no explicit definition of the form the passages should take, but it can be argued that they were of the same opinion as Maimonides. When there is a series of open or closed passages, and one of them ends close to the end of a line – for example: in the list of David's heroes in II Sam. Ch. 23 – closed passages separate each name from the next. In the Aleppo Codex (Figure 5.2), in most cases there is a space in the middle of the line, but before the name Aviezer (אביעזר) the previous line was long and the scribe started the next name in the middle of the next line. Similarly at the beginning of the book of Amos (Figure 5.3): The text gives a series of prophecies regarding different nations, and each one begins with the words "Thus said the Lord: For three transgression... and for four"; each prophecy begins with an open passage, and in three of them the Aleppo Codex separates them with a blank line.

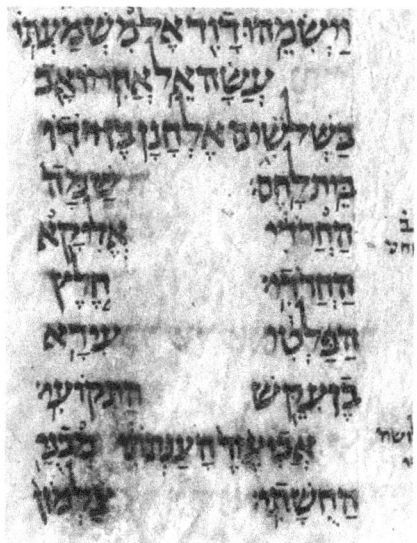

Figure 5.2: Aleppo Codex, II Sam. Chapter 23, right-hand column.

The opinion of the scribes may be demonstrated in additional ways: (1) by comparing the passages in two manuscripts such as the Aleppo Codex and the Leningrad Manuscript, presuming that their traditions regarding the passages were close (although not identical). (2) Comparing the passages in Psalms to the list prescribed in the Babylonian Masora (published by I. Yeivin in *Textus* 7 [1969], pp. 76–102). The tradition of

Figure 5.3: Aleppo Codex, Amos Chapter 1.

passages in the Aleppo Codex is very much like that list, presuming that a blank line was meant to indicate an open passage.

For further study

Y. Ofer, "On Masora matters – indicating passages", *Megadim* 2 (1986), pp. 91–104 (in Hebrew); E. B. Halivni, "Open and closed forms: the disagreement between Maimonides and Rabbenu Asher in the light of the Aleppo Codex and Ms. Leningrad", *Netu'im* 8 (2002), pp. 73–82 (in Hebrew); D. Yitzhaki, "The system of Ben Asher in the form of open and closed passages", *Sefer Ashreinu: the Masora of the Torah Codex of Ben Asher*, Bnei Beraq 1995 (in Hebrew), pp. 106–107.

Is it really possible to satisfy all opinions?

The attempt to satisfy all opinions – that of Maimonides and that of Rabbenu Asher – created some problems. One question concerns the form of the two songs in the Torah: the Song at the Sea (Ex. 15) and the Song of Haazinu (Deut. 32). It is customary to leave a blank line before and after each song. Maimonides, faithful to his own system, stated that both songs begin with open passages (and likewise the verses that follow them: "And Miriam... took" [Ex. 15:20]; "And Moses came" [Deut. 32:44]). However, following the system of Rabbenu Asher the space of a line indicates a closed passage!

In the wake of this problem in some manuscripts the lines before the songs were constructed in such a way that the line preceding the song would contain only one word (giving a clear indication of an open passage). However, this solution did not apply to the end of the songs. Some later authorities opposed this suggestion, and asserted that Halakha demanded a blank line before and after the songs. Maimonides, as befitted his system, called the line an open passage, and Rabbenu Asher agreed that a blank line should be left, but he asserted that it was nevertheless either a closed passage, or a part of the writing of the song, not to be regarded as an open or closed passage (Responsum of R. Shalom Shachna Yellin, *Qol Arye*, no. 1).

But there is an even greater and broader problem here: The list of passages on which we base the writing of Torah scrolls is derived from the list that Maimonides drew up on the basis of "the well-known book in Egypt". Maimonides examined this manuscript and defined every space as an open or closed passage. However, according to Rabbenu Asher's system the passages should be defined differently. For example: if in the codex that Maimonides relied upon there was a blank line, he defined it as an open passage, but according to Rabbenu Asher it was a closed passage. Since we cannot know what was the exact form of each section in the codex on which Maimonides relied, we cannot satisfy Rabbenu Asher's opinion!

Some of the later authorities asked this question.[9] Some suggested that perhaps there were no passages in the codex that Maimonides relied upon regarding which a disagreement might arise. However, that would not be likely, and now that the Aleppo Codex can be examined, we can observe that in the part of the Torah that has survived some of the passages do appear in such a way that Maimonides and Rabbenu Asher would have disagreed about their definition. The only remaining possibility to reconcile the quandary is to assert that the list Maimonides prepared was accepted *en bloc*,

---

9 Among them were R. Yom Tov Lippman Milhausen (*Hilkhot Sefer Torah*, published at *Sinai* 60, 1967, p. 253); R. Nathan Adler, the teacher of the Hatam Sofer (see the *Responsa of the Hatam Sofer, Yore De'a*, no. 261); R. Arye Lev b. R. Shalom Shachna Yellin (*Qol Aryeh*, Vilna 1872, Responsum 1, fol. 54b); and R. Shelomo Ganzfried (*Lishkat Hasofer*, Investigation 16, in: *Qeset HaSofer*, Brooklyn 1984, p. 211).

without consideration of the manuscript on which it was based, and this list should be implemented in Torah scrolls in accordance with both opinions.

The disagreement between Jewish communities regarding Leviticus, Chapter 7

The Torah scrolls in use today disagree in one place regarding where a passage begins. In Ashkenazi and Sephardi scrolls there is no new passage – either open or closed – beginning with Lev. 7:22 "And the Lord spoke to Moses, saying: Speak to the Israelite people thus: You shall eat no fat of ox or sheep or goat". In the Torah scrolls of the Yemeni community, this verse begins an open passage, but there is no space before vs. 28, which begins "And the Lord spoke to Moses, saying: Speak to the Israelite people thus: He that offers etc."

The source of the disagreement is interpretation of Maimonides' list of passages, which was accepted by all the communities as the basis for writing Torah scrolls. Maimonides lists six consecutive open passages in this part of Leviticus (6:12-8:1), the fifth of them beginning with the words "And the Lord spoke to Moses, saying: Speak to the Israelite people". That is what is found in the most accurate manuscripts of Maimonides, but it may be understood as referring to vs. 22 (as in the Yemeni Torah scrolls) or vs. 28 (as in the Ashkenazi and Sephardi scrolls).

How does this passage appear in the Aleppo Codex? As mentioned above, most of the Torah from it has been lost (except for the last pages of Deuteronomy), so that we have to rely on the testimony of scholars who examined the codex when it was still complete. According to the testimony of R. Yehuda Attiya, one of the rabbis of Aleppo, who examined the Aleppo Codex at the request of Prof. U. Cassuto, there was an open passage in the codex at both vs. 22 and vs. 28. This testimony is also confirmed by an earlier list copied in the Responsa of *Be'er Mayim Hayim*, written by R. Shmuel Vital of the seventeenth century, which stated: "[...] no fat of ox – open". A third testimony regarding the version of the Aleppo Codex is found in a printed Torah proofread in the sixteenth-century by Yishai Hacohen Amadi, who wrote: "In the Keter written by Ezra – an open passage." A comparison with other testimonies demonstrates, in my opinion, that "Keter written by Ezra" is none other than the Aleppo Codex.

Why did Maimonides deviate here from the tradition of the passages of the Aleppo Codex? An answer to this question will be given below in chapter 7 (p. 119).

For further study

J. S. Penkower, "Maimonides and the Aleppo Codex", *Textus* 9 (1981), pp. 88–99; Y. Ofer, "M.D. Cassuto's Notes on the Aleppo Codex", *Sefunot* N.S. 4 (19), 1988 (in Hebrew), pp. 325–330, 334–341; J.S. Penkower, *New Evidence for the Pentateuch Text in the Aleppo Codex*, Ramat Gan 1992 (in Hebrew), pp. 50–51, 76–78, 88.

Open and closed passages in scrolls of the Prophets and the "Five Scrolls"

Up to now we have discussed passages in the Torah. But what about passages in books of the Prophets and Writings? Manuscripts produced by the Masoretes do not provide a uniform tradition regarding the passages, either for the Torah or for the Prophets and Writings. As we have seen Maimonides was able to establish a uniform tradition regarding passages in the Torah, which he did on the basis of the Aleppo Codex. However, Maimonides dealt only with the Torah, and not with the books of the Prophets or Writings.

In most Jewish communities the books of the Prophets and Writings are not read from parchment scrolls. The *haftarot* (readings from the Prophets) read on Sabbaths and holidays, and four of the five scrolls read on festivals or the Fast of the Ninth of Av – are read in most congregations from printed *ḥumashim* (Pentateuchs) or a printed edition of the Tanakh, and not from parchment scrolls. The only exception is the book of Esther, which is read on Purim from a parchment scroll, as stipulated by Halakha.

In the opinion of the Vilna Gaon (R. Eliyahu Hasid, 1720–1797) the *haftarot* should be read from complete scrolls of the Prophets books written on parchment and according to the requirements for a Torah scroll (cf. his book, *Ma'ase Rav*, no. 136), and since that time this is the accepted in practice in congregations of the *"Perushim"*, who follow the customs of the Vilna Gaon. Consequently establishing open and closed passages became a practical question that needed to be decided, and in circles that subscribe to the practices of the Gaon a tradition developed for writing scrolls of the Prophets.

When the Aleppo Codex arrived in Israel in the mid-twentieth century, and its details became known, it became possible to write scrolls of the Prophets according to it, since the books of the Prophets in the Aleppo Codex remained nearly complete. If Maimonides regarded the book revised by Ben Asher as authoritative for establishing the passages in the Torah, why should we not follow the same principle regarding books of the Prophets (and Writings)?

Moreover: In the 1860s an emissary was dispatched from Jerusalem to Aleppo in order to copy the list of passages in Prophets and Writings from the Codex. This was done at the initiative of R. Shalom Shachna Yellin with the encouragement of the leading rabbis of Jerusalem, led by the Ashkenazi rabbi of Jerusalem, R. Shmuel Salant. The passages in the Aleppo Codex were marked in the margins of a printed Tanakh, by the emissary, Moshe Yehoshua Kimhi. This Tanakh, which for many years was thought to have been lost, was discovered in Jerusalem in 1987 (see Figure 5.4).

Discovery of this Tanakh led to an additional discovery: Many scrolls of the Prophets were written in Jerusalem in accordance with the list of passages from the Aleppo Codex that were indicated in the margins of this Tanakh. These scrolls exist today in some synagogues in Jerusalem – for example, in the Sha'arei Hesed

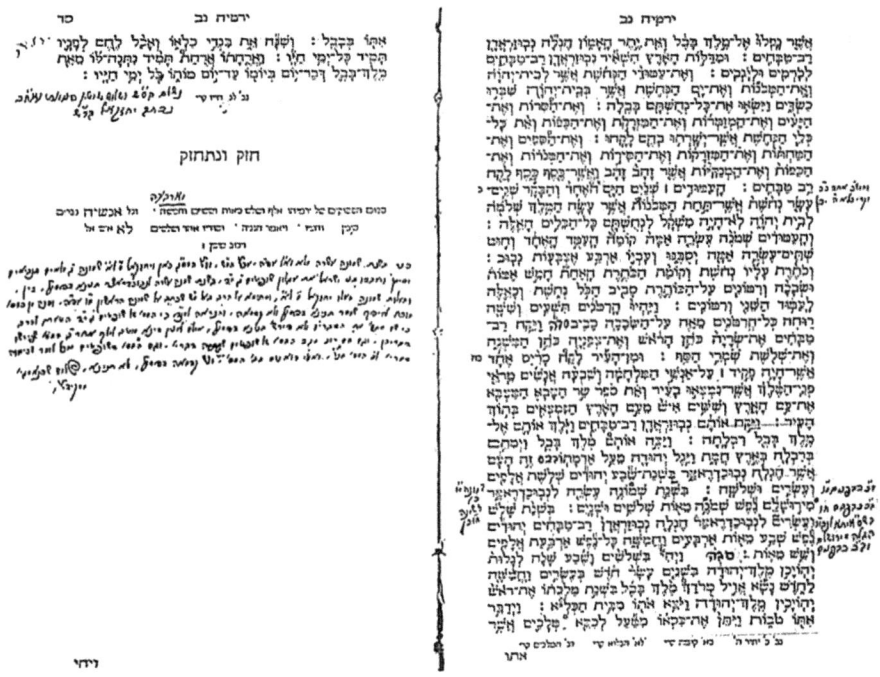

Figure 5.4: A page from the Kimhi Tanakh with Yellin's notes and signature, and Kimhi's testimony on the orthography and passages in the Aleppo Codex.

neighborhood, the 'Ets Haim Yeshiva and the Katamon neighborhood – to which they were evidently brought during the Israel War of Independence from the Old City and from the Yemin Moshe neighborhood.

These discoveries were doubly important: both practically and from the point of view of halakha. Practically, they allowed the reconstruction of the passages from the Keter in the lost sections from Prophets and Writings, since when the list of passages was prepared in the nineteenth century, the Keter was still complete. From the point of view of halakha, a precedent from the nineteenth century carries weight since the scrolls were written with the approval of the great rabbis of Jerusalem.

In 1995 a stormy dispute broke out in the ultra-Orthodox world over the writing of passages in the Prophets and Writings. On one side were scribes and rabbis who had started to write scrolls according to the passages in the Aleppo Codex. The opposing group claimed that there was "a tradition from generation to generation" of how to write the Prophets, and there was no justification for changing the accepted practice and following that of a "new" manuscript recently made known. Each side acquired letters of agreement and support from rabbis, and both sides published pamphlets by which they proved their positions and debunked the claims of their opponents. The title pages of two polemic pamphlets are presented in Figure 5.5.

Figure 5.5: Title pages of two polemic pamphlets about the Aleppo Codex. On the left: supporting the adoption of the system of the Aleppo Codex; on the right: against it.

Today, more than twenty years later, it seems the dispute has died down. It is hard to say who won, but it seems that a great part of the new-written scrolls of the Prophets and Writings follow the Aleppo Codex.

For further study

Y. Ofer, "The Aleppo Codex and the Bible of R. Shalom Shachna Yelin", in: M. Bar-Asher (ed.),
Rabbi Mordechai Breuer Festschrift – *Collected Papers in Jewish Studies*, Jerusalem 1992, pp.
295–353 (Heb.).
D. Itzhaki, *Sefer Ashrenu: The Tradition of Ben Asher's Keter Torah*, Bnei Beraq 1995 (Heb.).

Passages in the Scroll of Esther

The Scroll of Esther differs in two ways from the other books of Prophets and from the other four "Megillot" (scrolls): First of all, writing a scroll (*megilla*) is stipulated by the Halakha, since on Purim the book of Esther is read from a kosher scroll. Secondly, the passages in the Scroll of Esther were established in a ruling by R. Moshes Isserles in the *Shulhan Arukh* (Laws of the *Megilla, Oraḥ Ḥayim*, par. 691, b): "And all the passages are made closed, and if he made them open – it is invalid".

The Book of Esther is missing from the Aleppo Codex today. However, the evidence regarding its passages was recorded in the Tanakh by Kimhi (as mentioned above). From the evidence it appears that there were open passages in the Book of Esther, such as "And Memucan said" (1:16). A tradition of open passages in the Scroll of Esther is also recorded in the book *Or Zaru'a* (written in Vienna in the 13th cent.; Laws of the *Megilla*, no. 373), as well as in many ancient and later manuscripts throughout the world, as J. Penkower showed in a comprehensive study. However since the halakha was established in the *Shulhan Arukh* that all sections of the book of Esther should be made closed and Jewish communities accepted the ruling and followed it, the writing of the Scroll of Esther has not been altered. This is similar to the places in which the orthography of the Torah or its passages do not conform to the Masora or to Aleppo Codex, since accepted writing practices are not to be changed.

For further study

Jordan S. Penkower, "An Esther Scroll from the 15th century: determining its type among five traditions (Oriental, Sefardi, Ashkenazi, Italian, Yemenite)", *Textus* 26 (2016), pp. 209–270

The biblical Songs – three ways to write them

The songs in the Tanakh appear in different ways.[10] The Jerusalem Talmud (Megilla 3:8, 74b) describes two ways and stipulates as follows:

> R. Za'ura, R. Yirmiya in the name of Rav: The Song at the Sea [Ex. 15] and the Song of Deborah [Jud. 5] are written blank over print and print over blank. The ten sons of Haman [Esther 9:7-9] and the kings of Canaan [Jos. 12: 9-24] are written blank over blank and print over print.

A third technique is described in the tractate Soferim[11]:

---

10 The three ways of writing songs were described by M. Breuer, *The Aleppo Codex and the Accepted Text of the Bible*, Jerusalem 1976, pp. 149–189. I published an ancient fragment of Masora that displays different forms of writing songs in my article, Y. Ofer, "A Babylonian List of Open and Closed *Parashiyot* in the Pentateuch", in: M. Bar-Asher and C. E. Cohen (eds.), **Mas'at Aharon: Linguistic Studies Presented to Aron Dotan**, Jerusalem 2009 (in Hebrew), pp. 407–408, 434.

11 Soferim, 12:12 (ed. Higger, pp. 236–237; in the printed Talmud, 13:1): אבל בשירות דוד שבשמואל ובתילים לא נתנו חכמים שיעור, אבל לבלר מובהק מרצפן בפתיחות באתנחייתא וסופי פסוקים. וכן תילים כולו ואיוב ומשלי.

But in the Song of David in Samuel and in Psalms, the sages did not prescribe an exact way of writing, but the skilled scribe writes them by putting spaces in the middle of the verses and at their end. And similarly all of Psalms and Job and Proverbs.

The manner in which the Song at the Sea and the Song of Deborah are written ("blank over print") is unique, used for those two songs alone, and will be discussed below.

However, the way in which the sons of Haman and the kings of Canaan are written ("print over print") is a very common way of writing Biblical manuscripts: From the point of view of contents these are not songs, but lists of names. These lists were written in the common form of closed passages so that each element of the list is separated from the next one. However these spaces are arranged attractively each one below the previous, creating two straight columns. This technique was used in the list of the sons of Haman (see Figure 5.6) as also in many other lists: the spoils of David (I Sam. 30:26-31; see Figure 5.7), David's warriors (II Sam. 23), the poem of times in Ecclesiastes (Ch. 3) the priestly watches (I Chr. 24) etc. In many cases the long list is festive, celebrating victory over enemies or listing the priestly watches in the Temple, for example. But sometimes these spaces of closed passage repeat themselves in lists that have no festive element, such as the list of incestuous relations (Lev. 18) or those who are cursed (Deut. 27). The aesthetic arrangement of the spaces between the repetitive elements depends on the skill of the scribe and his taste, and also on technical factors such as the length of the elements and the width of the column. However, in

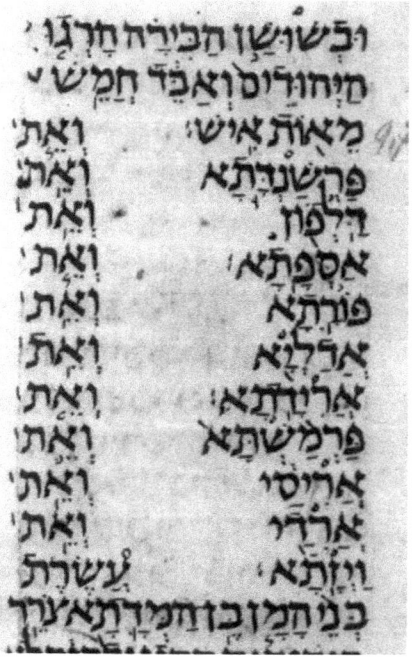

Figure 5.6: The ten sons of Haman in Ms. Leningrad.

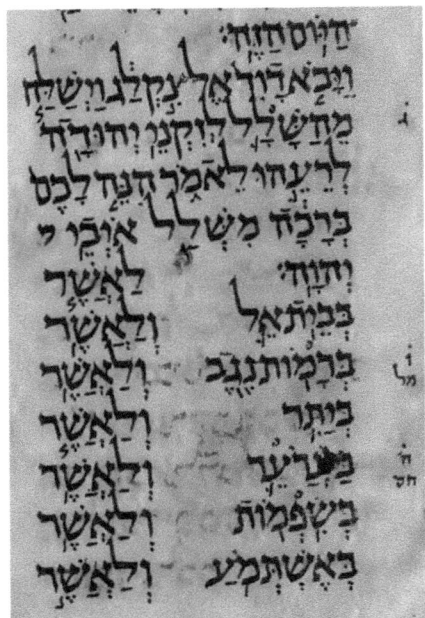

Figure 5.7: David's spoils (I Sam. 30) in the Aleppo Codex.

some cases, like that of the sons of Haman or the kings of Canaan, the form was stipulated by the Halakha.

The third way is used in three books of Writings (Job, Proverbs and Psalms, which are known by the Hebrew acronym ת"אמ ספרי = תהלים, מִשְׁלֵי, אִיּוֹב, a word play for *emet*, which thus means "books of truth") and also the Song of David (II Sam. 22). Here no definite points in the text were set for leaving space, but it is a function of the writing of the entire leaf: In every line the scribe leaves a space, usually not too large, and the result is a wide column within which a kind of snake path of spaces appears (see Figure 5.8). The scribe usually tries to split the line logically, where there is an *etnaḥta* (a cantillation mark that indicates the syntactic middle of the verse; sometimes equivalent to a semicolon) or a *sof pasuq* (end of verse), but sometimes that is not feasible or he does not make the effort and the line is split after a word that should go together with the next word.

In many cases a verse will be written on one entire line, and the space will come after the *etnaḥta* that divides the verse into two parts. There are manuscripts in which the scribes make a point of writing this way, and in order to facilitate this technique they use a wide column in the books of Psalms, Proverbs and Job. This is especially the case in manuscripts with Babylonian vocalization (see Figure 5.9). The result is that both the ends of the lines and the space in the middle of the lines indicate a pause, in contradistinction to the other kind of lists (as the sons of Haman and David's spoils), in which only the spaces indicate pauses and not the end of the lines.

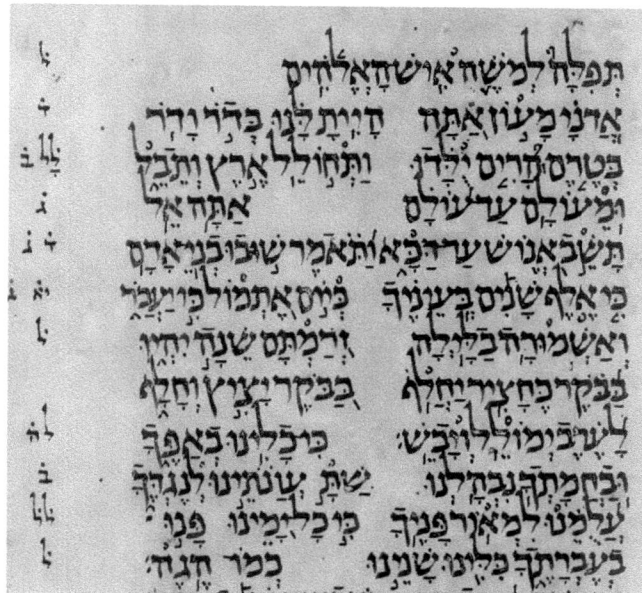

Figure 5.8: The Aleppo Codex, Psalm 90. In five out of the six bottom lines in the photograph, the end of the verse comes in the middle of the line.

From various sources it appears that the Song of *Haazinu* (Deut. 32) also belongs to the third way of writing songs. That is evidently why it was not mentioned in the passage from the Jerusalem Talmud on how to write songs. It is stated explicitly in a *baraitha* that corresponds to Tractate Soferim, quoted in the Laws of the Torah Scroll ascribed to R. Yehuda Barceloni:[12]

> Continuous made intermittently, intermittently made continuous – it should not be read from. And what is continuous? That which is written as it should be. Intermittently – like *Haazinu* and the book of Psalms, [and the books of] Job and Proverbs.

According to this view, there is no importance to the number of lines in the Song of *Haazinu*, which depends on the width of the column devoted to its writing. The scribe has only to make sure to write the entire song in two hemistiches, like the books Job, Proverbs and Psalms. A fine proof of this point of view is found in an ancient manuscript in the Firkowich Collection in St. Petersburg (Evr II B 159; Figure 5.10). The scribe started writing the song on a leaf on which one of the three usual columns was already written. The width of the song was made to fit the width of the remaining two columns, and the hemistiches are divided in the usual way. However, when the

---

12 Elhanan Adler (ed.), *Ginzei Misraim: Hilkhot Sefer Torah le-R. Yehuda Hanasi Elbargiloni*, Oxford 1897, p. 35: רצוף שעשה מסורג, מסורג שעשאו רצוף – לא יקרא בו. ואי זה רצוף? זה שכתוב כהילכתו. מסורג – כגן האזינו וספר תילין איוב וממשלות.

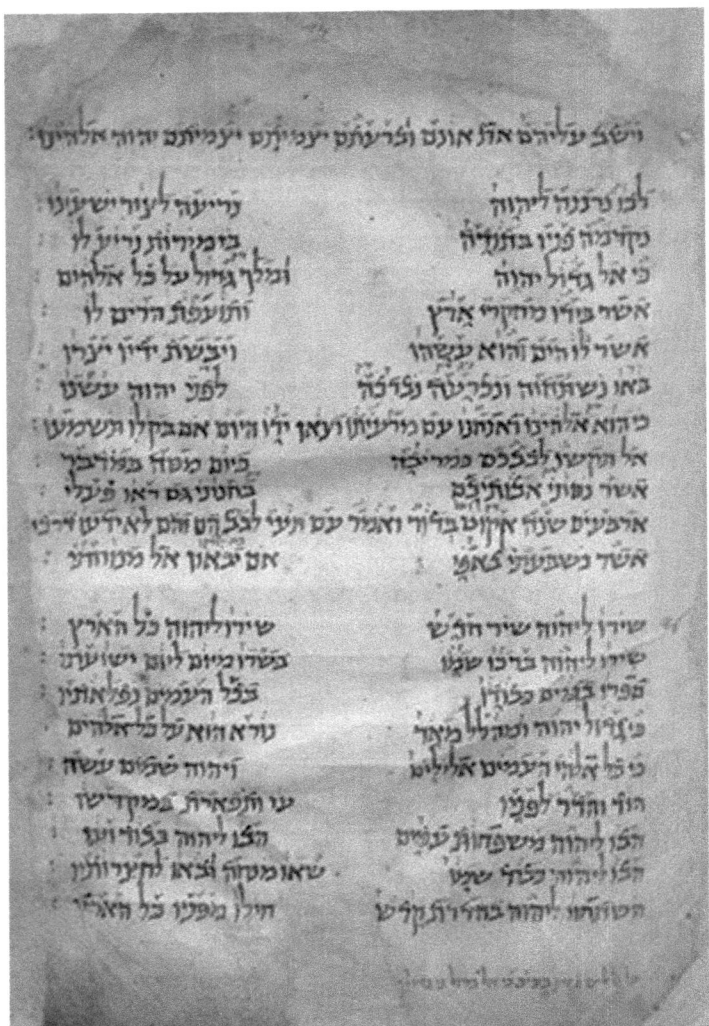

Figure 5.9: A manuscript with Babylonian vocalization in which the scribe wrote each verse on a separate line. Staatsbibliothek zu Berlin - Preussischer Kulturbesitz, Orientabteilung, Ms. or. quart. 680, fol. 14r: Psalms 94–96.

scribe moved on to the next page, he used the full width (of three columns) looking in every line for the most suitable place to put a space, not with accordance with the usual technique.[13]

---

[13] The manuscript was described by Israel Yeivin in his article "Ms. Leningrad L2", *Textus* 10, 1982, pp. 51–65.

Figure 5.10: The Song of *Haazinu* in Ms. St. Petersburg NL Evr II B 159.

However, at a later stage, the importance of *Haazinu* meant that its form needed to be determined more precisely by the Halakha. Both Tractate Soferim and Maimonides stipulated the first word in every line and the first word in the second hemistich of every line. Moreover, even the lines before the song and after it were stipulated precisely.

Below (in Chapter 8, pp. 145–146) we shall see that Maimonides followed the example of the Aleppo Codex, stipulating that *Haazinu* should be written in 67 lines, but in most communities the practice was to write it in 70 lines, as documented in Tractate Soferim, and even Maimonides' text was altered to conform to that opinion.

Let us return to the first way that songs are written, i.e. that of the Song at the Sea and the Song of Deborah. Here too we can observe that the spaces between the hemistiches are the starting point: Here we are not speaking of repetitive elements with a word in common, but the fact that this is a song dictated the required pause after each hemistich, and this pause was treated as a closed passage (like in "songs" of the second type). The arrangement of all the spaces in the format "blank over print and print over blank" is simply an aesthetic way of arranging the spaces.

The last line in the Song at the Sea provides the criterion for defining the way it should be written. For the sake of symmetry the graphic form of the song requires a space before the last word in the song, because in every second line in the song there is a space after the first word and before the last word. Accordingly, the last line in the Song at the Sea should be written as follows:

הים	ובני ישראל הלכו ביבשה בתוך	הים
the sea	And the children of Israel walked on dry land within	the sea

A close examination of this format provides a pleasant surprise: At both ends of the line we find "the sea" and between its two parts "the children of Israel walked on dry land". However, contrary to these considerations is the view that regards each space as a kind of closed passage dividing the hemistiches. Such a space cannot come between the combination בתוך (within) and הים (the sea). And indeed ancient manuscripts – such as the Aleppo Codex (as testified by Yishai Amadi) and Ms. Leningrad – did not leave a space between these two words. On the other hand, according to the tradition practiced in Torah scrolls of Ashkenazi and Sephardi Jews the last line is written as presented above, and the consideration of symmetry overcame the view that the spaces provide the appropriate pauses for reciting the song.

The titles in Psalms

In his book *Bar Kokhba*, Yiga'el Yadin relates the discovery of a fragment from a scroll of Psalms in the "Cave of Letters" in Naḥal Ḥever. An enlarged color photograph of the fragment appears there on p. 122 (see Figure 5.11). The fragment is of Psalm 15, and even though it is torn on both sides, the manner in which the entire psalm was written can be reconstructed. It is clear that every verse was written on a separate line, divided into two parts with a space between them conforming to the syntax of the verse. Thus this style of writing, which is also found in several

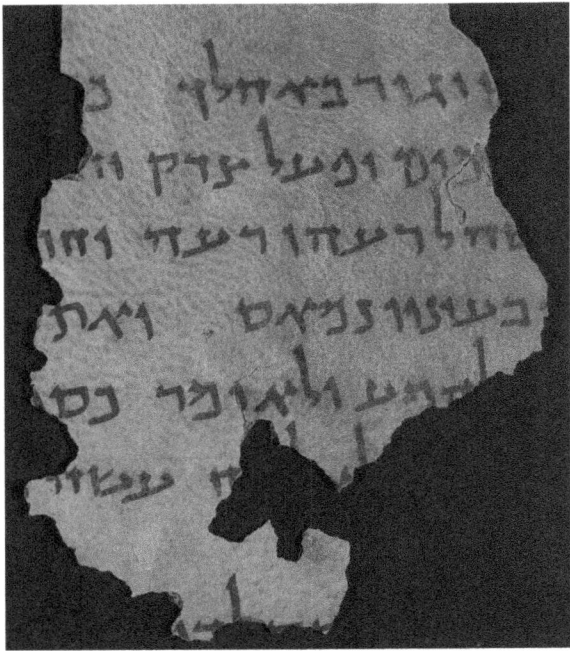

Figure 5.11: Fragment of a Psalm from Naḥal Ḥever.

manuscripts from the Masoretic period is the ancient way of writing Job, Proverbs and Psalms.

At the bottom of the fragment we can discern remnants of letters, which come from the title of the next psalm (16) מכתם לדוד ("a *mikhtam* of David"). A blank line separates the two psalms.

Writing the title in the middle of the column is aesthetic, and suits the symmetry of the psalm, which is written in two columns. However, examining the Book of Psalms in the Aleppo Codex, we can discern that the titles of the psalms were written in a different way. They always begin on the right of the column and not in the middle. In some cases the entire line is devoted to the title: If it is lengthy it may fill the entire line, if it is brief, comprising only one or two words, the space on the left remains blank (see Figure 5.8 above). In other cases the title takes up the right side of the column, and the text of the psalm itself begins on the left side.

How can we explain this phenomenon? Why do the titles not appear in the middle of the column?

The quandary is even more severe when we examine the Book of Job in the Aleppo Codex: The titles of the responses to Job do appear in the middle of the line, after a space, just as in the psalm fragment from Naḥal Ḥever. Also in Proverbs there is one title, משלי שלמה ("the proverbs of Solomon") at the beginning of Chapter 10, which appears in the same way.

Moreover, there are not a few manuscripts that do insert the titles in the middle of the line in Psalms, among them ancient manuscripts that stem from the same system as the Aleppo Codex, such as three manuscripts from the Second Firkowich Collection in St. Petersburg (Evr II B): Ms. 115 (from the year 994), Ms. 34 (from the tenth century) and Ms. 1475.

The answer to this question may be found in an ancient list of passages of Babylonian origin discovered in the Geniza, and published by I. Yeivin.[14] From this list it is apparent that the titles of psalms were regarded as open or closed passages. This view applied as well to the space between the previous psalm and the title of the next one, and also to the space between the title and the psalm itself, but not to the space in the middle of the lines of the psalm. They are not considered spaces that constitute a passage, but only an aesthetic way of writing the psalm.

According to the approach reflected in this list, a title that appears on the right side of the column after a blank line is regarded as an open passage. If the title came in the middle of the column, it would be regarded as a closed passage. A title like that would create a paradox: Only a closed passage separates the psalm from the preceding psalm, but an open passage would be separating the title from the text that belongs to it, since the psalm itself begins on a new line after a space. That is why there are no titles in the middle of the line in Psalms in some codices.

---

14 I. Yeivin, "The Division into sections in the Book of Psalms", *Textus* 7 (1969), pp. 76–102.

The Aleppo Codex conforms to this list of passages in almost every detail, thus it appears that the scribe of the codex (or the Masorete, if he supervised the scribe's work) used this list and the concept underlying it and applied it. For some reason the list does not deal with Proverbs and Job, and that may be why they do have centered titles: either because they did not think that these titles should be considered open and closed, or because the Masorete accepted the guidelines of the list, but followed an ancient tradition regarding titles in books with which the list does not deal.

6 *Ketiv* and *Qere*

Introduction

Anyone reading the Hebrew Scriptures is familiar with the phenomenon of *ketiv* (כתיב) and *qere* (קרי). In hundreds of places in Scripture a word is written in a certain way (*ketiv*), but in the margins of the page there is a note citing how the word should be read (*qere*). Sometimes the difference between the two forms is not great, such as: תחתו (*ketiv*) - תַּחְתָּיו ק' (only the addition of the letter *yod* – to be pronounced *taḥtav*, "beneath him", II Sam. 2:23), or והמבי (*ketiv*) - וְהַמֵּבִיא ק' (the addition of an *aleph* at the end of the word – to be pronounced *vehamevi*, "and bringing", II Sam. 5:2). Other times the difference is great, such as in these two places: העיר (*ketiv*) - חָצֵר ק' (written: *ha'ir*, "the city"; read *hazer*, "court", II Kings 20:4), בָּנָיו קרי ולא כתב (read: *banav*, "his sons", but not written at all, II Kings 19:37). Figure 6.1 shows the first place in the Aleppo Codex. Figure 6.2 shows both places in *Biblia Hebraica* Bible Edition.

The *ketiv* and *qere* phenomenon looks strange and hard to understand, and many explanations have been given for it. The way it is explained here is based on the interpretation of Rabbi Mordechai Breuer, which is surprising in its simplicity.[1]

Scripture was transmitted from one generation to the next in a double way – in writing and orally. To illustrate this we shall give two testimonies from Scripture. The first deals with the entire Torah and the second with the prophecies of Jeremiah.

The Book of Deuteronomy tells about the completion of the Torah and its transmission to the people by Moses:

> When Moses had **put down in writing** the words of this teaching (Torah) to the very end, Moses charged the Levites who carried the Ark of the Covenant of the Lord, saying: Take this book of Teaching and place it beside the Ark of the Covenant of the Lord your God, and let it remain there as a witness against you (Deut. 31: 24-26).

And at the beginning of the same chapter it says:

> And Moses **wrote** this law, and delivered it unto the priests the sons of Levi... And Moses instructed them as follows: Every seventh year... you shall **read** this Teaching aloud in the presence of all Israel. Gather (*haqhel*) the people – men, women, children and strangers in your communities – that they may hear and so learn to revere the Lord your God and to observe faithfully every word of this Teaching (Deut. 31:9-13).

---

1 M. Breuer, "Faith and Science in the Biblical Text", *De'ot* 47 (1978), pp. 102–114 (Heb.); M. Breuer, "*Ketiv* and *Qere*", in M. Bar-Asher (ed.), *Hebrew Through the Ages: In Memory of Shoshanna Bahat*, Jerusalem 1997, pp. 7–13 (Heb.). On the phenomenon of *ketiv* and *qere* and references to it in ancient writings, cf. Y. Ofer, "Ketiv and Qere: The Phenomenon, Its Notation, and Its Reflection in Early Rabbinic Literature", *Leshonenu* 70 (2008), pp. 55–73; 71 (2009), pp. 255–279 (Heb.).

https://doi.org/10.1515/9783110594560-006

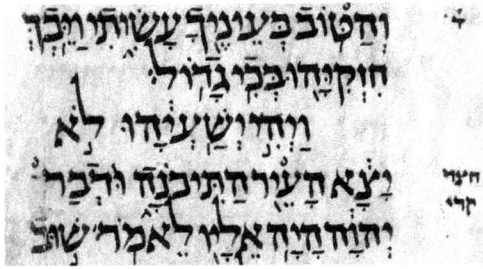

Figure 6.1: A *qere* comment in the Masora parva of the Aleppo Codex : II Kings 20:4. Note the tiny circle above the *ketiv* word, referring to the *qere* note in the margin.

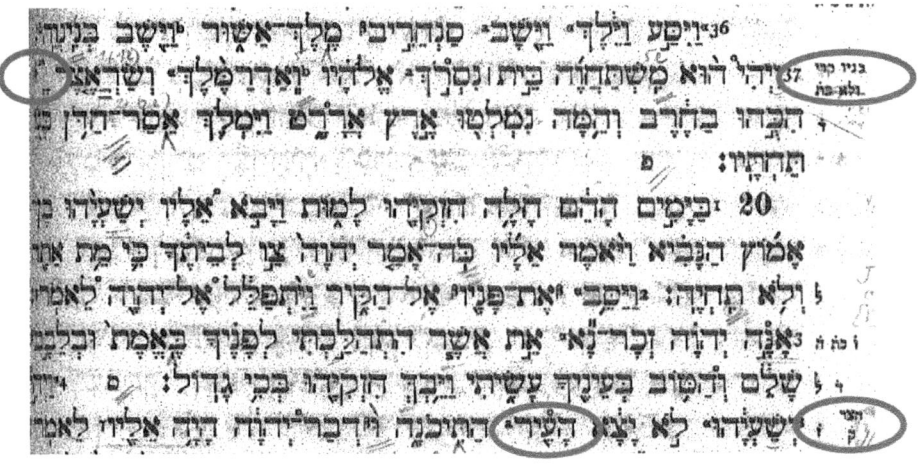

Figure 6.2: Two *qere* comments in *Biblia Hebraica* Bible Edition (BH3): II Kings 19:36-20:4.

Thus we see that the Torah was given to the people of Israel in two ways: First of all, Moses wrote the Torah as a scroll, and the scroll was given to Israel to be kept in a sacred place next to the Ark of the Covenant. Secondly, Moses commanded future generations to read the Torah aloud in a gathering (*haqhel*) in order to teach it to the people. This gathering resembled the scene at Mt. Sinai: just as there the people heard the words of the Torah from the God himself, so in the gathering of *Haqhel* the people heard the words of the Torah read aloud.

And how was Jeremiah's prophecy transmitted to the people: Jeremiah 36 reports as follows:

> And Baruch wrote down in the scroll, at Jeremiah's dictation, all the words which the Lord had spoken to him. ... Then all the officials sent... to say to Baruch, "Take that scroll from which you read to the people and come along!" They said, "Sit down and read it to us." And Baruch read it to them [...] And they questioned Baruch further: "Tell us how you wrote down all these words that he spoke." And Baruch answered them: "He himself recited all those words to me, and I would write them down in the scroll in ink" (4; 14-15; 17-18).

Note the process: Jeremiah dictated the words of prophecy to Baruch, and Baruch wrote them on a scroll, and afterwards Baruch read the prophecy before the people, and repeated it before the officials. Thus the prophecy was transmitted in two ways: in writing and orally. Baruch is the faithful person who could read the words as they were spoken to him.

Transmission of Scripture in two parallel channels

This is how the Tanakh (Hebrew Bible) has been transmitted from generation to generation. This transmission was by necessity a double one, in two parallel channels: in one channel it was copied by scribes from one scroll to another, and in the second transmitted orally, from father to son or rabbi to disciple. Neither channel could function independently of the other: in the book only letters are written, and there is no information of how it should be read. The letters עבד could be read *eved* (slave, context form) or *aved* (slave, pausal form), the letters אחת – *ahat* (one, context form) or *ehat* (one, pausal form), מדבר – *medaber* (speaks [*piel*]) or *middabber* (speaking [by itself; *hithpael*] – Num 7:89), יראה – *yireh* (will see [*qal*]) or *yeraeh* (will appear [*niphal*]), נראה – *nir'eh* (is seen) or *nir'ah* (was seen). Likewise there is no information in the scroll regarding the cantillation or what syllable should be stressed. All of these matters depended only on oral traditions of reading.

If that is the case, why was it necessary to write the Torah at all? Could it not have been transmitted orally from generation to generations exactly as heard from God or from his prophets? Indeed, in some cultures, sacred texts were successfully transmitted orally for centuries – without a written language at all. Nevertheless, only by writing, can wide-scope texts be disseminated among large communities of readers and scholars. The writing stabilizes the book or the text, and determines precise limits to it. Only by writing, can the sacred text be preserved uniformly for many generations in many distant communities.

Moreover, the written tradition establishes factors that are not found at all in the oral tradition. The writing is transmitted with absolute precision regarding every letter and every space. *Plene* and defective spelling, the way that songs should be written and the space between passages – all of these are transmitted only in the written tradition. Thus Scripture could be passed on from one generation to the next only by a combination of both these transmissions.

When Scripture was transmitted over generations in two parallel channels – and essentially by two groups: the scribes and the readers – some discrepancies could develop between them. In fact, the readers are not reading orally but from a scroll, however nothing prevents them from being aided by the scroll and still maintaining correct reading as they were taught: the reader learns and internalizes that when he sees in the scroll the word ירושלם (Jerusalem) he should read יְרוּשָׁלַיִם, adding the omitted letter *yod*, and pronouncing the word *yerushalayim* instead of *yerushalem*, as written.

When the word יששכר (Issachar) is written he will know to pronounce it יִשָּׂכָר, *Yissak-har*, ignoring the second שׂ. When he sees the Tetragrammaton he will know that it should be read *adonay* (and sometimes *elohim*). He will also know that the word הוא (*hu* = he) is sometimes to be read as *hi* (= she); the word אחת (= one) is sometimes read as *ahat* and at other times *ehat* – depending on the oral tradition. The reader would also learn that in a certain verse in Genesis (8:17) the word הוצא (*hotze* = bring out) should be read as *haytze* (in the same meaning but another and unusual pronunciation).

This discussion centers on the question of transmission of Scripture, and refrains from dealing with the question of how the discrepancies between *ketiv* and *qere* came about. This question will be considered later on. But in order to understand the issue of *ketiv* and *qere* it is important to clarify first how and why they were maintained, and how they were understood. So the discussion will concentrate first on the transmission of Scripture, in which the root of the phenomenon is found.

Why did they not just "solve the problem" by correcting the written text or the reading? Breuer explains it this way: There is no problem here that needs correction. What could they correct? Could they change the Torah and write היא instead of הוא? Could the text of the Torah be changed? Could they change the reading tradition and pronounce ירושלם *yerushalem* because that pronunciation conforms to the letters in the text? The Torah was given to Moses both in writing and orally, and each tradition stands on its own and the Jewish People is totally committed to maintaining them without alteration.

A different type of discrepancy could occur: a disagreement between scrolls regarding the text of the Torah. That would be an important halakhic question and the Halakha determines how it should be resolved: according to the majority of reliable books, as in the case of three scrolls found in the Temple court, as told in *Sifre Deuteronomy* and in additional parallel sources. Here is the version in *Sifre*, par. 356:

> Three scrolls were found in the Temple court, one of *me'onim*, one of *hi-hi*, and one called the book of *za'atutim*.
>
> In one was written מעון אלהי קדם (Deut. 33:27 – "The ancient God is a refuge") and in two מעונה אלהי קדם (the difference is the additional letter *he* at the end of the word *ma'on*). The sages rejected the one and maintained the two.
>
> In one was written the word היא nine times (in the Torah with *yod*, and not הֻוא as usual) and in the others eleven times. The sages rejected the one and maintained the two.
>
> In one was written וישלח את נערי and in the others וישלח את זעטוטי בני ישראל and ואל זעטוטי בני ישראל (Ex. 24:5 – "He designated some young men among the Israelites") and ואל אצילי בני ישראל בני ישראל (Ex. 24:11 – "against the leaders of the Israelites"). The sages rejected the one and maintained the two. (In this case in the minority scroll the word זעטוטי ["youngsters"] came instead נערי in the first instance and instead of אצילי ["leaders"] in the second.)

A disagreement could also arise between the readers regarding the correct way to read the Torah, and this is also a disagreement in which a decision should be made according to the tradition of expert readers.

Such disagreements within each group would be decided in the accepted way among the Jewish people – according to the majority of expert sages. But a disagreement between the scribes and the readers need not be 'resolved': the former should continue to write as they were accustomed and the latter to read following their own custom.

Ketiv and *qere* before the invention of vocalization marks

The difference between the written tradition and the reading tradition can also come into play from another perspective. Everyone that studies the Torah needs to ask himself what can be learned from this difference. For example, the following passage from the Babylonian Talmud treats one instance of *ketiv* and *qere*:

> "The meal offering with it shall be two-tenths of a measure...and the libation with it a quarter of a *hin*" (Lev. 23:13) – Rabbi Elazar said: it is written with the letter *he*, תנסכה ("and *her* libation"), but read with the letter *waw*, ונסכו (*wenisko*, "and *his* libation"). The libation of the meal offering (fem.) is like the libation of wine (mas.): just as the wine is a quarter measure, so the oil is a quarter measure.
>
> (*Bab. Tal., Menahot* 89b)

Rabbi Elazar points out the special spelling of the word for libation – *wenisko* in this verse that concerns the offering of the *Omer* (first sheaf). He could have explained the spelling as an unusual form like that of the words כֹּה (*ko* – thus) or פֹּה (*po* – here) or like the names שִׁילֹה (Shilo) and פַּרְעֹה (Pharaoh). However Rabbi Elazar saw this spelling as a reflection of the reading וְנִסְכָּה (*weniskah*), concluding that the spelling came to teach a halakhic matter regarding the measure of oil in the meal offering brought together with the lamb of the Omer. Thus we see that sages of the Talmud recognized the difference between the two traditions (written and oral), and in some cases they explained the meaning that difference held.

In this context – of the description of the situation that existed before vocalization and cantillation signs were invented – it is appropriate to refer to an unusual sign that appears on the page of some manuscripts regarding *qere* and *ketiv*. The sign looks like a final *nun* or the letter *zayin*, and its meaning is not clear. It seems to be a sign that was used by readers before vocalization and cantillation. They would write in the margins a reminder, a kind of warning sign that instructed them to take care in these places to read according to the oral tradition, and not to err by reading the word as written. The sign has come down in manuscripts that do have vocalization, or at least partial vocalization. It is reasonable to presume that this sign goes back farther and was used before the development of vocalization signs. It is hard to know if this sign was also used (in that meaning) in Torah scrolls that were used for public reading. Below are examples of the sign in a few manuscripts. Evidence that this sign preceded the installation of the vocalization signs is that

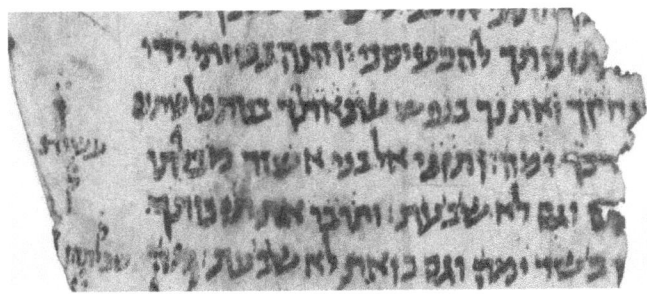

Figure 6.3: A final *nun* in the margin of a manuscript with Palestinian vocalization, Ms. Cambridge University Library, T-S 20.59, 1r. With permission of the Syndics of CUL.

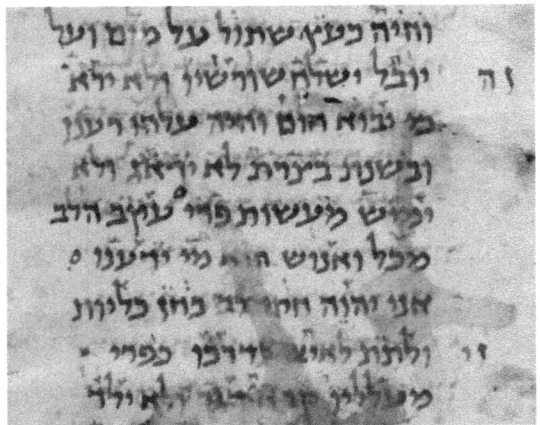

Figure 6.4: Final *nun* in the margin of a manuscript with Babylonian vocalization: Ms. Cambridge University Library A39.9, 2v. With permission of the Syndics of CUL.

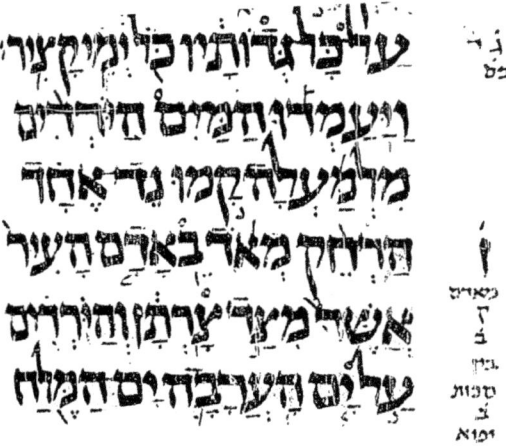

Figure 6.5: Final *nun* in the margins of a manuscript with Tiberian vocalization: Ms. Cairo, Jos. 3:16.

it can be found in manuscripts with each of the three main vocalization systems known to us: the Palestinian vocalization (Figure 6.3), the Babylonian vocalization (Figure 6.4) and the Tiberian vocalization (Figure 6.5).

The phenomenon of *ketiv* and *qere* and the addition of vocalization signs

And then something happened that changed everything completely.

In the seventh or eighth century sages came and established signs for vocalization and cantillation, following the precept "It is time to act for the Lord, for they have violated your teaching" (Ps. 119:126), i.e. there was a suspicion that the oral tradition would be forgotten.[2] However, a Torah Scroll that contains vocalization and cantillation signs is invalid for public reading! Consequently they made special books, which were called *ḥumashim* (Pentateuchs) or *mizḥafim* (codices) in which they wrote the signs for vocalization and cantillation. These books were not written in scroll form, but in the form of books like we use today, in which the pages could be conveniently turned from the beginning to the end.

This stage is a qualitative change in the transmission of Scripture. From this point copies of Scripture were created in which both traditions were written – the reading tradition and the written tradition – together, on the same page. This was made possible thanks to graphic signs for vocalization and cantillation, according to the following principle: The letters that had been written in scrolls heretofore were written exactly the same way in the codices. However, in addition to them – above, below and within the letters – two new systems of signs were added, one for vocalization and the other for cantillation, signifying the vowels and the melody for reading.

The discrepancies between the two traditions – which up to now had been hidden from view and apparent only under close study – became a practical problem: It was impossible to write the word עפלים (*afolim;* the ketiv form of 'hemorrhoids'), and add its vocalization in such a way that the reading tradition could be related: טחורים (*teḥorim* = hemorrhoids)! (Cf. Deut. 28:27 and more). The word may be vocalized with the appropriate vowels עֳפָלִים, but that does not suffice to present the correct reading. If the traditional reading is to be preserved not only orally, a note needs to be added on the page specifying how the word should be read: "טחרים קרי". Therefore, recording the notes of *qere* on the page became an integral part of the *niqud* (vocalization) system! (Note that the vowels for the correct pronunciation of the *qere* are given on the word in the *ketiv*.)

---

2 See *Mahzor Vitri*, Horovitz edition, Berlin 1893, p, 462.

In some cases such notes were not written, relying on oral transmission of the tradition. For example the Tetragrammaton is vocalized with a *shwa* and *qamaṣ*, (the vowels that belong to the letters *aleph* and *nun* in "*Adonai*") without an accompanying note, and only by oral tradition does the reader know how to interpret the signs. The same applies to the writing of יְרוּשָׁלַם without the second letter *yod*, יִשָּׂשכָר with the silent letter שׁ and the writing of the word הוא (to be pronounced *hi*) without accompanying notes. However, these are individual words that appear frequently, and this practice is called 'permanent *qere*'. In all other cases a note appears in the margin, and it constitutes a necessary supplement to the vocalization system.

The idea that permanent *qere* applies to very few words requires clarification: it is true that this practice applies to a very small number of words, but from the perspective of occurrences, they are an absolute majority of the cases of *qere* and *ketiv*, since the Tetragrammaton alone occurs more than six thousand times throughout Scripture, many times more than all of the other occurrences of *qere* and *ketiv*.

To conclude: The appending of vocalization signs brought the gap between *ketiv* and *qere* to the fore, and required writing explicit notes on the page that referred to the phenomenon.

The number of *qere* and *ketiv* notes in Scripture

How many notes of *qere* and *ketiv* are there in the Tanakh? Introductory books on Scripture point out that there is a great gap between manuscripts regarding these notes. The estimates range between 800 such notes at least and 1300–1500 at most.[3] This gap may appear to reflect many disagreements over the text of Scripture between the manuscripts. However, that would be a false impression as we shall explain below.

Here are a few disagreements on *qere* and *ketiv* between Ms. Leningrad (L) and the Aleppo Codex (A):

	The verse	Masora Parva Ms. L	Masora Parva Ms. A
Jer. 3:4	הֲלוֹא מֵעַתָּה קָרָאתי לִי אָבִי	קראת קרי	יתיר י'
Jos. 9:7	וְאֵיךְ אֶכְרָות־לְךָ בְרִית	אכרת ק'	ב' מל'
II Sam. 16:8	בֵּית שָׁאוּל אֲשֶׁר מָלַכְתָּ תַּחְתָּו	תחתיו ק'	ד' חס'
II Sam. 11:24	וַיֹּראו הַמּוֹראִים אֶל עֲבָדֶיךָ	ויורו ק'	ל' כת' א'

In all four cases the Masorete of Ms. **L** wrote a *qere* note, while the Masorete of Ms. A gave a different kind of note: יתיר (=a superfluous letter); מלא (=*plene*); חסר (=*defective*);

---

3 Cf. Israel Yeivin, *Introduction to the Tiberian Masorah*; translated and edited by E. J. Revell, Missoula, Mont 1980, p. 55; I. Yeivin, *The Biblical Masorah*, Jerusalem 2003, p. 53 (Heb.).

א כתיב' (=written with a [superfluous] letter aleph). According to both Masoretes the words should be written as follows: קראתי, אכרות, תחתו, וייראו; and according to both of them they should be read in this way: קָרָאת (*qarat*, "you called"), אֶכְרָת- (*ekhrot*, "I shall make [a covenant]", תַּחְתָּיו (*taḥtaw*, "in whose stead"), וַיֹּרוּ (*wa-yoru*, "and they shot"). They both agreed that a note should be added concerning the spelling (which was exceptional or unexpected). However the Masorete of Ms. **L** chose to give a clear note of *qere*, while the Masorete of Ms. **A** preferred to describe the spelling in a "moderate" or "routine" kind of note: In the first case he used the term יתיר (superfluous), which is much like a *qere* note, and in the other cases he preferred to use the usual technique of the Masora regarding *plene* and defective reading, and even cited the number of times that similar forms appear in the entire Tanakh.

Similar disagreements may be found in contemporary editions of the Tanakh.[4] For example: In the last two cases above, *Miqraot Gedolot* of Venice, Ginsburg and *Biblia Hebraica* editions add notes on the reading (or the note "the aleph is superfluous"). However, the Koren edition and the Breuer edition give no notes at all; their editors think that the vocalization of the words וייראו, תַּחְתָּוו suffices to instruct the reader on the accurate pronunciation of the words, and there is no need for a marginal note on *qere*.

Returning to the previous point, before vocalization there were many places in Scripture where there was a potential contradiction between the written tradition and the oral tradition. Since the vocalization was added to the letters, these contradictions came to light. Sometimes the contrast was clear, and there is no way to indicate the correct reading of the word without a note regarding *qere* (except for the routine cases that everyone was familiar with, and the readers' knowledge could be relied upon These cases became 'permanent *qere*'). In other cases the contradiction was less extreme and adding vocalization to the word could provide enough information. In fact the spelling may look awkward or exceptional, but the reader could pronounce the word without error. Regarding these cases the Masoretes and the editors of printed editions of Scripture were not in agreement: Some add *qere* notes here as well, in order to clarify the matter for the reader, and others keep their reading notes to a minimum, and give such notes only when absolutely necessary.

Ways of indicating *qere*

It is taken for granted that the vocalization of words that have both *qere* and *ketiv* applies to the *qere* form. After all, the system of vocalization was created only in order to facilitate the accurate reading of Scripture.[5] Consequently some editors of Scripture,

---

4 For a description of contemporary editions of the Tanakh, see below Chapter Twelve.
5 Abravanel's remarks and those of Elias Levita are strange and reflect a wrong perception of the phenomenon: "And why did Ezra [...] add vocalization that always conformed to the *qere* and not to

such as Ginsburg, Koren and Dotan, vocalized the *qere* and left the *ketiv* without vocalization. For example in Judges 13:17 – כִּי יָבֹא דבריך ("when your words come true") the
ketiv word in the text appears without vocalization and the *qere* reading in the margin
is vocalized: דְבָרְךָ. [The difference in meaning between the *ketiv* and *qere* here is
between "your words" and "your word" respectively.] In some editions the lack of
vocalization indicates that there is a note on *qere*, and there is no need to make use of
the tiny circles customary in manuscripts of the Masora in order to refer to them.

However, that is not the case in the manuscripts. In all of the ancient manuscripts
of Scripture the vocalization is added to the *ketiv* form in the text itself and the note
on *qere* appears in the margins, usually without vocalization. Evidently the experts
who added the vocalization felt that all the vocalization should appear in the text
itself, even though it did not fit the letters to which it was added. The Masoretic note
outside the text completes the vocalization in the text, informing the reader how the
word should be read.[6] Most editions of the Tanakh – such as *Miqraot Gedolot*, Biblia
Hebraica and Breuer's edition – followed the style of the manuscripts, and vocalized
the *ketiv*, with the vowels that correspond to the *qere*, of course.

In some cases there is a special problem regarding adding vowels to the letters of
the *ketiv*. For example, in II Kings 18:27 the *ketiv* is שניהם and the *qere* is מֵימֵי רַגְלֵיהֶם.
The masorete who vocalized the Aleppo Codex made the effort of writing all the
vowels of both words of the *qere* beneath the single, relatively short word of the *ketiv*.
Of particular interest are the cases in which the order of letters is switched: In the
Aleppo Codex, an effort was made to add the vocalization to the letter to which it
belonged, and the result is, for example, הָאֵהֶל (I Kings 7:45, האלה קרי), וַיַּקְלֵהֻ (II Sam.
20:14, ויקהלו קרי), תְּבְשָׁלִי (Ez. 37:14, תשכלי קרי). In Ms. Leningrad, on the other hand, a
different practice was followed: the vowels appear in the correct order, but fall under
the wrong consonants: הָאֵהֶל, וַיִּקְלָהוּ, תְּכַשְׁלִי.[7]

---

ketiv, showing that in his opinion the qere was the truth and therefore he put the vocalization on it"
(Abravanel, Introduction to Jeremiah, Torah Vada'at ed., Jaffa 1954–1960, p. 299). "I have also discovered this, which is important to remember, that the Keri and Kethiv are never to be found on the
vowel-points and accents. That is to say, there is not a word to be found which is pointed in the text in
one way, and the marginal reading of which is in another way... And the reason of it is, because there
never was any difference of opinion among all Israel about the pronunciation of the words" (Elias
Levita [=Eliyahu Halevy Ashkenazi, Bahur], *Masoret Hamasoret*, Third Introduction, C.D, Ginsburg's
Edition with an English translation, London 1867, p. 112).

6 Here we should add: In the Koren and Dotan editions the *qere* form is given in the margin in the
same size letters as the text, without the word קרי. It looks like an alternate reading, which should
naturally be vocalized appropriately. In manuscripts that is not the case: The Masoretic note is written
in smaller print, intended to accompany the text and not to replace it. For that reason the vocalization
appears in the central text and the role of the Masoretic note is to resolve the dissonance created by
the inappropriate vowels added to a word in the text.

7 Cf. I. Yeivin, *The Aleppo Codex of the Bible: A Study of its Vocalization and Accentuation*, Jerusalem
1968 (Heb.), pp. 76–77.

Hidden *qere*

Qere notes are intended to alert the reader to unexpected *ketiv* that barely suits or entirely conflicts with the *qere*. In some cases there are no *qere* notes, but nevertheless it appears that the *ketiv* reflects a different form from the *qere*.

For example: In Song of Songs (3:4) the beloved says: אֲחַזְתִּיו וְלֹא אַרְפֶּנּוּ עַד שֶׁהֲבֵיאתִיו אֶל בֵּית אִמִּי ("I held him fast. I would not let him go till I brought him to my mother's house"). The spelling הביאתיו did not look exceptional to the expert who vocalized the text, and did not receive a Masoretic note. However, it is reasonable to presume that this *ketiv* reflected another reading, הֲבֵאתִיו, a form that appears elsewhere in the Tanakh. In the verbs וָאָשִׂם (Gen. 24:47), וָאָבֵא (Ex. 19:4), וָאַבְדִּל (Lev. 20:26), וָאַשְׁלֵךְ (Deut. 9:21), וָאֶצֹּל (Jos. 24:10) – it may be asserted that the *ketiv* form (without *yod* in the last syllable) reflects the jussive forms: וָאָשֵׂם, וָאָבֵא, וָאַבְדֵּל, וָאַשְׁלֵךְ, וָאָצֵל.[8] A linguist making such an assertion would have to present evidence based on the usage of *plene* and defective forms in Scripture. However such an examination is similar in principle to that of the Amora quoted above, who interpreted the *ketiv* ונסכה as reflecting the form וְנִסְכָּה. Yet it may be asked why did the Masoretes not write a note on such words as וָאָשִׂם and וָאָבֵא? The answer would be that the Masoretes only wanted to ensure the correct reading and writing of Scripture, and had no intention of interpreting or discussing the homiletic possibilities of grammatical forms. From the Masorete's point of view there was no gap between the *ketiv* and the reading of these forms, since *ḥiriq ḥaser* (without *yod*) is a very common occurrence in Scripture, and consequently there was no need for a Masoretic note here.[9]

Thus we see that the point of view of the homilist or the linguist is different from that of the Masorete: The former look for the meaning of the *ketiv* form, and in order to do so "reconstruct" it and "create" its vocalization. The Masorete, on the other hand, has no need to do so, and only wants to alert the reader (and the scribe as well) about the gap or dissonance between the spelling of the word and its reading.

Moreover: sometimes the Masora may comment in a *qere* note on one word, but interpretation of the *ketiv* – and restoration of its hypothetical vocalization – require reference to additional words. For example, regarding David it is said that he defeated Hadadezer [פְּרָת קרי ולא כתיב] בְּלֶכְתּוֹ לְהָשִׁיב יָדוֹ בִּנְהַר] ("when he was on his way to restore his

---

8 Cf. D. Talshir, "The Development of the Imperfect Consecutive Forms in Relation to the Modal System" (Heb.), *Tarbiz* 56 (1987), pp. 585–591.

9 Also Tannaim attributed to the *ketiv* different forms from the *qere* in a case where no Masoretic note was eventually added. For example, "Yohanan ben Dehabai said in the name of Rabbi Yehuda: One who is blind in one of his eyes is exempt from appearing [at the Pilgrimage festivals] as it is said יִרְאֶה (he will see) יֵרָאֶה (he will be seen) – just as he comes to see he comes to be seen. Just as he sees with both his eyes, he is to be seen with both his eyes." (Babylonian Talmud, Hagiga 2a; Rashi ad. loc.: "The *ketiv* is יִרְאֶה, but the reading is יֵרָאֶה"). Similar to that is the discussion of which is preferred – the text or the tradition (אם למקרא או אם למסורת – Sanhedrin 4a and parallel passages).

dominion on the [Euphrates] river", II Sam. 8:3). The word פרת (Euphrates) does not appear in the text itself and is added in the *qere* note. The *ketiv* would require the form בַּנָּהֵר (definite) rather than בִּנְהַר (indefinite, construct state; before a proper name).[10]

The Prophet Elisha says to the Shunamite woman: "Go sell the oil and pay your debt, and you and your children [וְאַתְּ וּבָנַיִךְ] **can live** [תִּחְיִי – Qal] on the rest (II Kings 4:7). In the *ketiv* form the conjunctive *waw* is missing, so it reflects another reading: וְאֵת בָּנַיְכִי תְּחַיִּי בַּנּוֹתָר "and you will **sustain** your children on the rest".[11]

On the basis of these occurrences we can go further and make a general statement: In every verse in Scripture one may suggest an interpretation that conformed to the letters of the text, but not the vocalization, claiming that he is interpreting according to the *ketiv* and not the *qere*. Of course the interpretation needs to be reasonable and convincing, since otherwise an explicit interpretation on the basis of the *qere* is better than a dubious interpretation that relies on the *ketiv*.

If this assertion seems too far reaching, it is in fact nothing new, and sages of the Talmud regarded *ketiv* and *qere* in this way. In their days there were no vocalization marks and obviously there were no marginal *qere* notes. They sensed the true conflict between *ketiv* and *qere*, i.e., between the written tradition and the reading tradition:

> Disciples asked R. Yehuda ben Ro'ez: I read שבעים ["seventy" – the *ketiv* for two weeks (שְׁבֻעַיִם) could be read as meaning seventy days] – could it be that she who gives birth to a female is impure for seventy days? He said to them. It both pronounced unclean and purified the male and both pronounced unclean and purified the female. That which it purified in the male was double for the female, so what it pronounced unclean in the male, in the female double.
>
> After they went out, he went out and brought them back: He said to them: You do not need that! The reading is שבועיים (=two weeks) and the reading tradition of the biblical text is authoritative!

The first approach of R. Yehuda ben Ro'ez was that the version of the *ketiv* should also be taken into account and not ignored, and that was also the opinion of R. Yehuda ben Dehabai,[12] who interpreted both the *ketiv* and the *qere*.

Returning to the main topic under discussion, interpretation derived from the *ketiv* for understanding the plain meaning of Scripture. This point must be stressed: The *ketiv* is always a reconstructed text, because it does not include a tradition of how it is to be read and is therefore essentially "not vocalized". However, when studying

---

10 The approach of the Masorete of the Aleppo Codex to this word is very interesting. As opposed to many manuscripts which note פרת קרי ולא כתב ("read Euphrates, but not in the text" – Mss. L, C, S1 and *Okhka We-Okhla*, par. 97), the Masorete of the Aleppo Codex noted: בנהר פרת קרי ("read at the Euphrates River" by which he hinted that the reading of the word *binhar* (at the river; indefinite) was different from that of the *ketiv*.

11 This last example I heard from Prof. Yoel Elizur. In the word בניכי there is an additional distinction between *ketiv* and *qere*, pertaining to the suffix כי-. Regarding such distinctions see below in the paragraph "Early and Late Linguistic forms".

12 See above, note 9.

Scripture, it should not be ignored, and a way should be sought to explain it. The Sages interpreted it and constructed homilies on it in their own ways in many occurrences, and Rabbi David Kimhi (Radak; Provence, twelfth and thirteenth centuries) outlined the method for interpretation of the simple meaning of the text, saying in his introduction to Prophets and Writings that he will make use of both *ketiv* and *qere* "when I can give meaning to both of them." And indeed Radak did so in many places in his commentary. Frequently his opinion is that there is no interpretative difference between the *ketiv* and the *qere* "and the meaning is the same" (e.g. his commentary on Jos. 4:18 – בעלות הכהנים - בבי"ת כתיב וקרי בכ"ף והענין אחד = "As soon as the priests came up" – the word בעלות is written with a *bet*, but read with a *kaf* [כַּעֲלוֹת], but the meaning is the same"). In other cases he suggests explanations for *ketiv* forms, even if they look surprising, as in his commentary on I Kings 7:45.

> ואת כל הכלים האהל ("and all those vessels") – it is written thus (האהל="the tent"), but read האלה (= those). The *qere* is clear. And the *ketiv* wants to say "like those vessels that were in the tent of congregation, thus did Hiram make them for King Solomon in the House of the Lord." And thus in *Targum Yonatan* (translation to Aramaic): "All those vessels, just as the Tabernacle vessels were made – thus made Hiram for King Solomon in the Temple of the Lord."

Another brief example is in a verse mentioned above (p. 86), Jer. 36, 15. Baruch son of Neriah pronounces Jeremiah's harsh prophecies in the House of the Lord, and their impact reaches the palace of the king. The officials summon Baruch to come and read the scroll before them, and the atmosphere is one of fear and anxiety. Baruch arrives at the palace and is requested: שב נא וקראנה באזנינו ("Sit down and read it to us"). Menahem Bula (The author of the commentary *Da'at Miqra*) says "the officials spoke to Baruch respectfully", and offered him a chair to sit down. However on the basis of the *ketiv*, it could be read שֵׁב (=repeat) instead of שֵׁב (=sit down) and interpreted as saying "please **repeat** and read", i.e. read again what you read in the House of the Lord. Possibly that was the understanding of *Targum Yonatan* which translated the word שב as תוב (=return) and not as תיב (=sit). At least that is the version of the *Targum* in printed editions. One can accept this interpretation or reject it, but in principle it is no different than the method of the Sages and of Radak regarding *ketiv* and *qere*. The Masoretes, in their technical approach, which refrained from interpretation, felt no need to comment here, since the reading *shev* conformed perfectly to the spelling of the word in the text.

Types of *qere* and *ketiv*

The notes on *qere* and *ketiv* can be categorized in a number of ways. The first attempt to do so was done by the Masoretes themselves, and its results are concentrated in the Masoretic compilation *Okhla we-Okhla*. That Masora cites ten words that are "*qere* and not *ketiv*" (ed. S. Frensdorff, par. 97), eight words that are "*ketiv* and not *qere"* (par. 98), words that are written as one word but read as two and the opposite (pars. 99-100), words that lack a final letter *he* or have a superfluous one (pars. 111-112) etc. About 70 Masoretic lists in this compilation deal with this subject (pars. 97-170), and these lists are arranged alphabetically according to the letter on which the *qere/ketiv* difference focused. However, the categorization in *Okhla we-Okhla* is not complete, and hundreds of additional occurrences were not included in it. In particular there is a large number of cases in which the letters *waw* and *yod* were interchanged, but only a small part of which were included in the categorization (pars. 135-148). Moreover the perspective of the Masora was technical and formal. The Masora did not suggest an explanation how and why these interchanges occurred, but only categorized them in order to preserve the text and prevent any deviation from it.

Other methods of categorization of the occurrences of *qere* and *ketiv* could be suggested in order to characterize and define the relation between the *ketiv* and the *qere* or to explain the discrepancy. Several scholars have attempted to do so.[13] Some of them suggested a systematic division and others a detailed categorization of occurrences of *ketiv* and *qere*, treating each one individually. Following their example, we shall suggest a systematic division into several main types.[14]

Qere as euphemism or respectful language

Two Talmudic passages characterize special categories of *ketiv-qere* occurrences:

> All of the scriptures that are written in the Torah in impolite language are read in language beyond reproach, such as [Deut. 28:30] ישגלנה ("ravish her") is read ישכבנה ("lie with her"); [Deut. 28:27] בעפלים ("with hemorrhoids") is read בטחורים; [II Kings 6:25] חריונים ("dove-droppings") is read דביונים; [II Kings 18:27] לאכול את חוריהם ולשתות את מימי שיניהם ("to eat their excrement and drink their urine") is read לאכול את צואתם ולשתות את מימי רגליהם ("to eat their excrement and drink the water of their legs"); [II Kings 10:27] למחראות ("latrines") is read למוצאות ("toilets").
>
> (Babylonian Talmud, Megilla 25b)
>
> Not as I am written am I read. I am written with *yod he* [the Tetragrammaton] and read with *aleph dalet* (*Adonay*).
>
> (Babylonian Talmud, Pesahim 50a)

---

13 See: R. Gordis, *The Biblical Text in the Making: A Study of Ketibh-Qere*, Philadelphia 1937 (New York 1971); S. Levin, "Qere – the Basic Text of the Tanakh", *Hebrew Thought in America*, I, Tel Aviv (1972), pp. 61–86 (Heb.); Maimon Cohen, *The Kethib and Qeri system in the Biblical Text: A Linguistic Analysis of the Various Traditions Based on the Manuscript 'Keter Aram Tsova'*, Jerusalem 2007 (Heb.); Breuer, "Ketiv and Qere" (above, note 1).
14 This description is based mostly on Breuer, "Ketiv and Qere" (above, note 1).

The first group includes euphemisms: the word written in the *ketiv* is considered vulgar or impolite and the *qere* refrains from pronouncing it explicitly, replacing it instead with a polite word, which suggests the exact meaning without saying it directly. In the second group – the Tetragrammaton – the *qere* refrains from pronouncing it as it is written because of its sanctity. Thus the two groups have something in common: The *ketiv* represents the precise intention of the word, but the *qere* bypasses it and refrains from pronouncing it explicitly. And this for opposite reasons, either because of the vulgarity of the word or its sanctity.

The group of euphemisms is small, and includes less than 20 words in all of Scripture. That is not the case regarding the second group – the Tetragrammaton pronounced either as *Adonay* or *Elohim*. This group includes over 6800 occurrences, i.e. four or five times more than all the other instances of *ketiv-qere* in the entire Tanakh. However regarding these names the Masora practiced "permanent *qere*", i.e. it does not cite a special note regarding each appearance of these names, since everyone knows how to read them.

Archaic and "modern" linguistic forms

Another type of *ketiv-qere* is related to the development of language. It is characteristic of the *ketiv* to retain archaic linguistic forms, and the *qere* to reflect later forms. The following examples belong to this category: [II Kings 4:16] אתי – read אַתְּ ("you", fem. sing.); [II Kings 4:2] לכי – read לָךְ ("you"); [I Kings 22:49] נשברה – read נִשְׁבְּרוּ ("were wrecked", pl.) and more.

In both of these categories – euphemisms and archaic forms – the role of *ketiv-qere* is clear: It is only natural that the explicit word be written, but the reader would find it difficult to read it aloud, in public, either because of its sanctity or because of its vulgarity. Likewise it is only natural that the archaic form be preserved in the text, but that the speakers would be influenced by changes in language and therefore pronounce the word in its "modern" form.

An interesting and exceptional occurrence is noteworthy:

אשר אנו [אנחנו ק'] שלחים אתך אליו ("to whom <u>we</u> send you" – Jer. 42:6)

In this case the "modern" form אנו (*anu* – we) which was used in the Mishnaic Hebrew, turns up in the tradition of the *ketiv*. The *qere* אנחנו (*anahnu*) is the usual form for the pronoun "we" in Scripture. In this case the *qere* reflects a tendency towards linguistic uniformity and refraining from divergent linguistic forms, whether early or late.

As for the question of the time when the gap between the two traditions developed, there are two possibilities and it is difficult to decide which is right: It may be that at the beginning of the writing of the book there were already two forms in use, i.e. the first scribe wrote the Tetragrammaton, and the first reader read *Adonay*; the scribe wrote ישגלנה, but the reader read יִשְׁכָּבֶנָּה; the scribe wrote אתי and the reader read אַתְּ.

Even today there are words that are written in "archaic, historical, spelling", but pronounced differently, such as the English word "laugh", which is pronounced "la:f".

The second possibility is that at first there was only the *ketiv*, but at some point the concept developed among the readers that it was inappropriate to read the sacred or vulgar word as it was written, or the reading tradition was influenced by contemporary usage at a particular time, and pronunciation of certain words changed. Deciding between these two possibilities is a subject for linguistic research, and in some cases it is difficult or even impossible.

Variants that reflect different linguistic dialects

Sometimes *ketiv-qere* reflects two different dialects, but it is difficult to determine which was the earlier and which the later dialect.

Biblical Aramaic deserves special attention. In the chapters of Ezra and Daniel that are written in Aramaic there are many occurrences of *ketiv-qere*, and examining them reveals that they reflect different dialects of Aramaic. For example [Dan. 2:29 and more] אנתה – read אַנְתְּ ("you"); [Dan. 3:12] עליך – read עֲלָךְ ("to you"); [Dan. 2:33 and more] מנהון – read מִנְּהֵין ("of it"). What is remarkable about Biblical Aramaic is the nearly total consistency of these changes, to the point that the Aramaic grammar reflected in the *ketiv* is to a degree different from that reflected in the *qere*.

According to Elisha Qimron, "It seems that each tradition reflects a different dialect of Aramaic, evidently the *ketiv* tradition reflects one of the royal Aramaic dialects, and the *qere* tradition a different dialect or dialects, the provenance of which is unknown" (*Aramit Miqrait* [Heb.], Jerusalem and Beer Sheva 1993, p. 7). Thus we may say that two different dialects of Aramaic reached the two parallel routes of tradition – written and oral – and in each of them one overpowered the other.

It is interesting to compare the distinction אנתה – read אַנְתְּ in Biblical Aramaic and אתי – read אַתְּ in Biblical Hebrew. In principle both cases are identical. The *ketiv* reflects an earlier linguistic phenomenon by which the second person pronoun was indicated by "a" for masculine and "i" for feminine. The *qere* reflects the disappearance of that final vowel. However there is a difference between them in terms of frequency. While the form אנתה appears in the *ketiv* of all 15 occurrences of the Aramaic word (except one – in Ezra 7:25), the form אתי appears in the *ketiv* six times, while nearly 50 times the form את appears in the *ketiv*.

Variants that are content-related

As opposed to the previous types of *ketiv-qere* occurrences, there are other occurrences in which one form appears as *ketiv* and another as *qere*, we can explain each form but we have no explanation why this specific form became *ketiv* while the other one became *qere*.

The difference between the two is sometimes a matter of content, and not of language, For example:

וַיְהִי יְשַׁעְיָהוּ לֹא יָצָא [חָצֵר קרי] הַתִּיכֹנָה וּדְבַר ה' הָיָה אֵלָיו II Kings 20:4 Before Isaiah had gone out of the middle *court*, the word of the Lord came to him". The word חצר ("court") is the *qere*, but the *ketiv* is העיר ("the city").

וַיְהִי הוּא מִשְׁתַּחֲוֶה בֵּית נִסְרֹךְ אֱלֹהָיו וְאַדְרַמֶּלֶךְ וְשַׂרְאֶצֶר [בָּנָיו קרי ולא כתיב] הִכֻּהוּ בַחֶרֶב II Kings 19:37 "While he was worshipping in the temple of his god Nisroch, *his sons* Adrammalech and Sarezer struck him down with the sword". The word בָּנָיו ("his sons") is given in the *qere* alone and not in the *ketiv*.

וַתֵּלֶךְ וַתַּעֲשֶׂה כִּדְבַר אֵלִיָּהוּ וַתֹּאכַל הוּא וָהיא [הִיא וָהוּא קרי] וּבֵיתָהּ יָמִים I Kings 17:15 "She went and did as Elijah had spoken, and *she and he* and her household had food for a long time". *Ketiv*: הוא והיא ("he and she"); *qere*: הִיא וָהוּא ("she and he").

וַתֹּאמֶר אֵלֶיהָ כֹּל אֲשֶׁר תֹּאמְרִי [אֵלַי קרי ולא כתיב] אֶעֱשֶׂה Ruth 3:5 "She replied 'I will do everything you tell *me*'". The word אֵלַי ("me") is in the *qere* only and not in the *ketiv*.

In these cases both the *ketiv* and the *qere* are equally suitable in context. Perhaps from the very beginning of the consolidation of the Book of Kings and the Scroll of Ruth there were two traditions regarding these verses, and finally one of them was accepted as the written tradition and the other the reading tradition. It is important to point out that there are not a great number of instances of this kind. The textual gap between the reading tradition and the written tradition is not that wide. For example, there is not one instance in the entire Scripture of an entire sentence that is read but not written or written but not read, and even the number of words in the category of כתיב ולא קרי (*ketiv* but not *qere*) or קרי ולא כתיב (*qere* but not *ketiv*) is no more than twenty in all of the Tanakh. This fact teaches us that the two traditions were not absolutely independent, but they were closely interrelated, since Scripture was read from the written text and not recited orally.

Variant linguistic forms in syntax, morphology and phonology

In many cases of *ketiv* and *qere* the differences are of variant grammatical forms or are related to the syntax of the sentence. Here are examples:

Different forms of nouns

המורשתי [מִיכָה ק'] מיכיה, "*Mica* the Morashtite" (Jer. 26:18). The *ketiv* is מיכיה (Michia).

יהודה מלך יהויקים בן [וְכָנְיָה ק'] יכוניה, "King *Jeconiah* son of Jehoiakim of Judah" (Jer. 27:20). The *ketiv* is יכוניה, but the qere is יְכָנְיָה (without the letter *waw*).

הָאָרֶץ מַמְלְכוֹת לְכֹל [לְזַוֲעָה ק'] לזועה וּנְתַתִּים, "And I will make them a *horror*" (Jer. 29:18). The word for horror is written לזועה, but read לְזַוֲעָה.

Different forms of verbs

[והיצא אל הכשדים יחיה [וחיה ק'], "but whoever surrenders to the Chaldeans *shall live*" (Jer. 38:2). The *ketiv* is יחיה ("shall live", future tense), but the *qere* is וחיה ('reversed past' tense [וקטל]).

אל תעש [תַּעֲשֵׂה ק'] אֶת הַדָּבָר הַזֶּה, "Do not *do* such a thing" (Jer. 40:16). *Ketiv* – תעש (jussive form); *qere* – תַּעֲשֵׂה ("do" – imperfect form).

Direct speech or indirect speech

כי מי עמד בסוד ה' וירא וישמע את דברו, מי הקשיב דברי [דברו ק'] וישמע, "But he who has stood in the council of the Lord and seen, and hear His word – He who has listened to *His word* must obey" (Jer. 23:18). *Ketiv* – דברי ("my word"), *qere* – דברו ("His word").

ותשלח ותקרא לסרני פלשתים לאמר: עלו הפעם כי הגיד לה [לי ק'] את כל לבו, "[Delilah] sent for the lords of the Philistines with this message: 'Come up once more, for he has confided everything *to me*'" (Jud. 16:18). The *ketiv* is לה ("to her"), but the *qere* is לי ("to me").

Differences in punctuation of the sentence

וַיֹּאמֶר דָּוִיד לִשְׁלֹמֹה בנו [בְּנִי ק'] אֲנִי הָיָה עִם לְבָבִי לִבְנוֹת בַּיִת לְשֵׁם ה' אֱלֹהָי, "David said to Solomon, '*my son*, I wanted to build a house for the name of the Lord my God'" (I Chr. 22:7; according to the *qere*). According to the *ketiv* the sentence should read: "David said to Solomon *his son*, 'I wanted' etc."

In all of these verses there is no significant difference between the two variants, and both are reasonable in the same degree.

Forms that were created as a result of a flaw in the transmission process

In our discussion this far we have refrained from trying to explain how the two channels of tradition split, and only tried to define the differences between the two parallel forms. But many instances of *ketiv-qere* may be explained as the product of a flaw in the long transmission process of Scripture. For example: Hundreds of instances of *ketiv-qere* are exchanges of the letters *waw* and *yod*. Examining the Dead Sea Scrolls, it is evident that one can hardly distinguish between these two letters in them. Thus it is possible that in the process of copying the books of Scripture the two letters were interchanged. Let us examine a few instances of this type:

וְעַל רִיב הֵמָּה יַעַמְדוּ לִשְׁפֹּט בְּמִשְׁפָּטַי ושפטהו [ישפטוהו ק'], "In lawsuits, too, it is they who shall act as judges; *they shall decide them* in accordance with My rules" (Ez. 44:24). For "they shall decide them" the *ketiv* is ושפטהו (*waw* instead of *yod*).

וְצָפַן [יִצְפֹּן ק'] לַיְשָׁרִים תּוּשִׁיָּה מָגֵן לְהֹלְכֵי תֹם, "He *reserves* ability for the upright and is a shield for those who live blamelessly" (Prov. 2:7). The word for "reserves" is written וצפן, but read יִצְפֹּן (*yod* instead of *waw*).

חוֹשֵׂךְ אֲמָרָיו יוֹדֵעַ דָּעַת וקר [יְקַר ק'] רוּחַ אִישׁ תְּבוּנָה, "A knowledgeable man is sparing with his words; a man of understanding is *reticent*" (Prov. 17:27). The words translated here as "reticent" are written וקר רוח, but read יְקַר רוּחַ (*yod* instead of *waw*).

וְאֵת אולי [אֵילֵי ק'] הָאָרֶץ הוֹלִיךְ גּוֹלָה מִירוּשָׁלַם בָּבֶלָה, "And the *notables* of the land were brought from Jerusalem to Babylon" (II Kings 24:15). The word written אולי is read אֵילֵי ("notables"), *yod* replacing *waw*.

שאי [שְׂאִי קרי] עֵינֵיכֶם וראי [וּרְאוּ ק'] הַבָּאִים מִצָּפוֹן, "*Raise* your eyes and behold those who come from the north" (Jer. 13:20). The word for "raise" is written שאי, but read שְׂאוּ, *waw* replacing *yod*.

וידו [וִידֵי ק'] אָדָם מִתַּחַת כַּנְפֵיהֶם, "They had human *hands* below their wings" (Ez. 1:8). The word for hands is written וידו, but read וִידֵי, *yod* replacing *waw*.

הִתְנַעֲרִי מֵעָפָר קוּמִי שְּׁבִי יְרוּשָׁלָם התפתחו [הִתְפַּתְּחִי ק'] מוֹסְרֵי צַוָּארֵךְ שְׁבִיָּה בַּת צִיּוֹן, "Arise, shake off the dust, sit [on your throne], Jerusalem! *Loose* the bonds from your neck, O captive one, Fair Zion!" (Is. 52:2). The word for "loose" is written התפתחו, but read הִתְפַּתְּחִי, *yod* replacing *waw*.

In all of these occurrences the *qere* is the more appropriate reading, and one could maintain that the *ketiv* is the product of scribal error. However in many verses the *ketiv* also makes sense, whether smoothly or with difficulty. For example:

וְעַל רִיב הֵמָּה יַעַמְדוּ לְשָׁפֹט בְּמִשְׁפָּטַי, וּשְׁפָטֻהוּ, "In lawsuits, too, it is they who shall act as judges accordance with My rules; *and they shall decide them*." the *waw* of the *ketiv*, ושפטהו, could be interpreted as changing past tense to future (וקטל tense).

וְצָפַן לַיְשָׁרִים תּוּשִׁיָּה, The *ketiv* וצפן could be interpreted as changing past tense to future (וקטל tense).

וְקַר רוּחַ אִישׁ תְּבוּנָה, The *ketiv* וקר רוח could mean "reticent".

In the last four other verses cited above it is more difficult to justify the tradition of the *ketiv*, but not impossible. The conclusion from these examples is that in many cases we have no sure way to explain why a gap developed between *ketiv* and *qere*. We may presume that in most cases it was connected to processes that occurred in the course of transmission, but when examining each case individually, there are few in which it can be said with certainty (or with great likelihood) that they are the product of a corruption.

It is a well-known rule that when trying to determine which of two variants is the original one, one must take caution and not prefer automatically the more comprehensible variant. It is possible that the more difficult version is the original, and the easier variant is the product of a correction made due to the difficulty (this rule is known in its Latin name, *Lectio difficilior potior*, meaning: "the more difficult reading is the stronger"). For example, in the verse below, in which the *ketiv* version diverges from the rules of syntactical conformity between the noun and adjective:

וְהָיָה לָכֶם דָּבָר הדבר [הַדָּבָר ק'] הַזֶּה, "That is why this happened to you" (Jer. 40:3) The *ketiv* is דבר, but the *qere* הדבר, with agreement in definition between the noun and the demonstrative pronoun.

If this variant is the result of the transmission process, there are two possibilities: Scribal error could have led to the omission of the definite article (the letter *he*) creating the difficult combination דבר הזה, but it could also have been the opposite. The difficult combination was the original form, and the readers corrected it, consciously or subconsciously, making the expression conform to accepted usage.

When and how was the difference created between the written tradition and the oral one?

In the light of all that we have seen the question clearly arises regarding the meaning of this phenomenon and when it occurred. It is appropriate to recall Radak's method, according to which *qere* and *ketiv* resulted from a disagreement between the books:

> It appears that these words are found thus, because in the first exile the books were lost and dispersed and the sages who knew Scripture died, so the men of the Great Assembly who restored the Torah found discrepancies in the books and followed the opinion of the majority, and when they did not agree clearly they wrote one variant, but did not vocalize it, or wrote it outside [in the margins], and did not write it inside [in the text] or they wrote one variant inside and the other in the margins.

On the other hand Abravanel (Portugal, fifteenth century) regarded the *qere* as a correction of the difficult *ketiv*:

> But the truth of the matter in my opinion is that Ezra and the Men of the Great Assembly found Torah scrolls that were complete and perfect as they were written. And before Ezra thought of adding vocalization and cantillation and punctuation he studied the Scripture, and when anything appeared strange linguistically or according to the context – and he thought it could be for one of two reasons, perhaps because the writer of those strange things intended [to transmit] one of the secrets of the Torah according to the height of his prophecy or the depth of his wisdom – and therefore he did not dare to erase anything from the Divine books [...] and thus left the text inside as it was written; and he wrote outside [in the margins] the *qere*, which is the interpretation of that strange written text according to the nature of language and the simple meaning of the matter.

> [...] It could also be that Ezra thought that there were in the holy books words that were not written strangely for a reason, but as a result of the careless speech of the one who said them, whether because of lack of knowledge of the Hebrew language or lack of knowledge of correct writing [...] and consequently he (=Ezra) had to interpret the true [meaning] of that word in context [...] and he put outside the *qere*, being his own interpretation, and there is no doubt that that is how he received it from the prophets and the sages of the previous generation. And indeed most of the *qere* and *ketiv* in this Book of Jeremiah, when you examine it, you will find that they are of this kind.

To define briefly the opinion of each of these exegetes regarding the source of the phenomenon, Radak speaks of *textual variants*, while Abravanel speaks of the *logical correction* of difficult expressions.

Maharal (Rabbi Judah Loewe ben Isaac of Prague, sixteenth century) in *Tiferet Israel*, Ch. 66 and Malbim (Rabbi Meir Leibush ben Yehiel Mikhel, nineteenth century) in his preface to Jeremiah offer a more conservative explanation. In their opinion both readings existed together from the beginning. Maharal said:

> If sometimes strange language is written, in order to hint at some wisdom or deep matter – this belongs to the writing. [...] but when it comes to reading in the book, it is appropriate to be read in clearer language because the former language was estranged from the way people read.

Malbim said:

> It was the intention of the Sages to interpret every case in which there is *qere* and *ketiv*. In their opinion the *qere* is always the simple meaning and the *ketiv* the homiletic meaning.

Objections could be raised against every one of these methods. As for Radak's method (textual variants), why did the Sages not decide which reading is correct, such as they decided in other places? How did they determine which version would be "inside" and which one "outside"? Did they never encounter more than two versions that they wanted to preserve? And what is the relation between the textual variants in the written Scripture and the reading instructions (in the *qere* notes)?

To Abravanel's method (and also that of Maharal and Malbim) one might object that there are occurrences in which the *ketiv* is more comprehensible than the *qere*, such as: הוצא (take out) – read הַיְצֵא (Gen. 8:17), בור (pit) – read בְּיִר (Jer. 6:7). Such cases are in fact few, but they present a serious objection to the method of these exegetes: How could they have corrected a reasonable and comprehensible form and written instead of it a strange and rare form? (Moreover, Malbim's claim that the *qere* is the simple meaning of Scripture could not apply here.) An additional difficulty is how to explain interchanged forms, such as: אסורי המלך (the king's prisoners) – read אֲסִירֵי (prisoners, Gen. 39:20) as opposed to בבית האסירים (prison house) – read הָאֲסוּרִים (Jud. 16:21). How could they correct in one place *asur* to *asir* and in the other *asir* to *asur*?

As mentioned above, in our opinion one should look at the *ketiv/qere* phenomenon from the perspective of the double way of transmitting the Bible, as both a written tradition and an oral one. Such a double transmission necessarily causes the gaps between its two components. These gaps were not created at once as an initiated action by one person or a group of people, as some of the commentators mentioned above suggested. Some gaps existed from the outset as early as the creation of the text, and some were created during the years as a result of the transmission processes. In the framework of this comprehensive explanation, the explanations of the commentators should be examined separately in relation to each case.

In certain cases it is possible that both forms existed from the original composition of the book, as suggested by Maharal and Malbim. In other cases corruptions may have taken place in the course of copying over centuries and millennia of transmission, as Radak presumed. And it could be that different books transmitted similar but not identical linguistic forms. Corrections may have also been made in the text of Scripture, consciously or sub-consciously, as suggested by Abravanel. And beyond any doubt the tradition of the *qere* tends to adopt the more comprehensible variant.

Moreover, from the perspective of generations, correction of the text and textual variants are not so far from each other, since any flaw in transmission creates variants, and any correction of a difficult text creates variants.

However, it must be stressed that we are not talking about a one-time initiated act of correction (as both Radak and Abravanel presumed) – such a reform does not suit the method of the Masoretes, who always tried to maintain the tradition and not change it. We are talking about processes of transmission that occurred in the course of many generations that preceded the Masoretes and the invention of vocalization signs.

And it should also be emphasized that both Radak and Abravanel focused on the version that was *written* "inside" and the version *written* "outside", ignoring the main reason for this phenomenon, the two parallel channels for transmission of Scripture, written and oral. These two exegetes allowed the external appearance on the page of scriptural codices to mislead them, and did not notice that the phenomenon had its antecedents in an earlier period that preceded the addition of vocalization and the writing of notes on the reading.

Throughout the years the Masoretes took great care with the text of Scripture. The difficult expressions, which might seem to be scribal error, are testimony to the care taken by the scribes with the text, since after all, what would be easier than to correct obvious errors?

However the continuous and cautious processes of transferring the written and oral text developed a gap between the two channels of transmission: the writing of Scripture and its reading tradition. If not for the double transmission process, we could presume that most disagreements would have been decided, by the Masoretes. But the double transmission of Scripture prevented that decision and led them to maintain both traditions, even when a lesser or greater conflict appeared between them. Determining the signs for vocalization was an important stage in revealing the gaps between the two traditions and bringing them to the fore – in the form of reading notes written in the margins of the codices.

Conclusion

The two parallel channels of transmission of Scripture led to the gap that we define as "*ketiv* and *qere*". In certain cases the gap may have existed from the origin of the book, and in other cases it may have been created in the long process of transmission, from the composition of the book until the completion of the activity of the Masoretes.

Some features revealed in the cases of *qere* and *ketiv* suit the special character of the two channels: Readers tend to prefer euphemisms and language of respect towards heaven, but scribes, on the other hand, can write things as they are; readers tend towards linguistic uniformity and reject deviant and archaic forms, while the scribe is more conservative; readers tend towards "smoother" versions, while the scribe may preserve deviant and unusual forms. But not all of the cases of *ketiv* and *qere* fit this characterization: The double route of transmission may create a situation in which in one of the channels one form was transmitted and in the other a different parallel one, which is not necessarily to be preferred. And in some cases the *ketiv* form is more comprehensible to us than that of the *qere*.

Both early and late commentators tried to explain the meaning of the matter of *ketiv* and *qere*, connecting it to different phenomena, such as a disagreement over the text and correcting a difficult reading according to grammatical rules. And in fact these subjects are related to *ketiv* and *qere*, but they are not the primary reason for its existence. The root of the matter of *ketiv* and *qere* is the double transmission of Scripture from generation to generation through both a written tradition and an oral tradition.

7 The Masora on Scripture as an "Error Correcting Code"

Introduction

In this chapter we shall look at the Masora from a novel perspective: We shall compare the activity of the Masoretes to the way modern communication transfers data efficiently and reliably. This comparison may give depth to our understanding of how masoretic notes work, and explain both the successes and the failures of the Masoretes in the course of generations.[1]

"Error Correcting Code" is the mathematical-engineering technique that enables data to be transferred reliably over a "noisy" channel that causes broadcast errors. The theory that deals with these methods and develops them is a sub-branch of information theory, and it concerns the construction of sophisticated and efficient methods in order to ensure with a high degree of probability that messages will be deciphered correctly even if errors occur in the course of the broadcast.

The classic problem with which this theory is concerned is as follows: The sender wants to transmit a series of signs, e.g. a series of bits 0 or 1 in a certain length, called **k**. Since in the course of the transmission errors are expected to occur, the sender will extend his message by a length of **n** (greater than **k**) that will enable the recipient of the message to identify, and even to correct, the errors.

There are two approaches to dealing with errors. According to the first approach, the data sent are coded in an "error detecting code". That is, additional information is added to each framework, enabling the receiving station to identify a flawed framework. When the receiving station identifies a flawed framework, it ignores it and requests the original station to transmit the framework again. According to the second approach the data is coded with an "error correcting code". In that case the information is added in every framework enabling the receiving station to locate the flawed bits and to correct them without a need for a second transmission. An error correcting code may also serve as an error detecting code, in case the number of errors that occurred is greater than the number than can be corrected. Practically, the activity for correcting errors is far more common. For example, a CD is manufactured in such a way that a scratch that harms the data will not preclude playing the music that was recorded; a message transferred over the telephone arrives and is deciphered correctly despite disturbances in communication.

---

1 This chapter is based on an article that I wrote together with Prof. Alexander Lubotzky of the Dept. of Mathematics at the Hebrew University of Jerusalem. Cf. Y. Ofer and A. Lubotzky, "The Masora as an Error Correcting Code", *Tarbiz 82 (2014), pp. 89–113* (Heb.)

https://doi.org/10.1515/9783110594560-007

A simple (but highly inefficient) example of an error correcting code is to send all the bits three times. In such a case, if a single error occurs, the recipient will be able to identify it and also to correct it. A more sophisticated example is the technique called the "Hamming Code", and specifically "Hamming Code (4, 7)": In order to transmit a series of 'words' of 4 bits each, add 3 bits to each word for control. This code guarantees that the recipient will be able to correct any error in an individual bit, and to identify a flaw if no more than two bits were damaged.

Note that while the naive way to repeat each letter 3 times costs 200% "overhead", the Hamming code (4,7) which makes it possible to correct a single mistake by sending 7 bits instead of 4, costs only 75% overhead. Researchers engaged in this area try to discover the most efficient ways to provide maximum protection for information transfer at minimum additional investment.

The Masora does for the biblical text exactly what an error correcting code does for a transmission: The purpose of the Masora is to protect the biblical text. For that purpose the Masora enlarges the original text, adding masoretic notes of different kinds, thus allowing the original text to be "broadcast" from one place to another and from generation to another and to correct it from errors that occur in copying it from one manuscript to the next.

In order to demonstrate this concept, the first five chapters of Joshua in the Aleppo Codex were examined.[2] The biblical text contains 8322 letters (including spaces), and counting the vocalization and cantillation signs - 13,885. In these chapters there are 38 Masora Magna notes, containing 2000 characters, and 210 Masora Parva notes, containing 910 characters. In this sample study, the Masora added 21% to the biblical text.

Error correcting code theory can help to understand the operation of the Masora. Discussing the Masora as an error correcting code may contribute to understanding the mechanism of the Masora and the reasons for its successes and failures. Naturally we are not using mathematical methods directly, but only the insights that may be derived from Information Theory.

Between electronic transmission of data and human transmission

A comparative examination of electronic communication and the Masora naturally reveals some essential differences between the two areas, resulting from the fact that the biblical text and the masoretic notes are transmitted by human beings.

The first difference between the two depends on the **reason for the mistake**. While in electronic communication the mistake is usually accidental, in human transmission of the biblical text the error may be intentional, from our point of view

---

2 For that purpose I used "Haketer" program of the *"Miqraot Gedolot Haketer"* project at Bar-Ilan University, edited by Menachem Cohen.

it may even be termed "malicious": An individual has a different tradition from that of the Masorete, and he may intentionally change the Masora in order to suit it to his tradition. This difference may require a different choice of protection.

The second difference is derived from the **location of the mistake**. Error correcting codes generally deal with accidental errors in the text that result in noise in the communication channel. These errors are totally oblivious to the content of the text, and they occur in different places completely unrelated to content. Scribal errors, on the other hand, with which the Masora is concerned, are highly content-dependent: The copyist will not usually change words accidentally. He may write the *plene* form rather than the defective form or vice versa (i.e. omit or add a *yod* or *waw*), add or omit the conjunctive *waw*, exchange similar letters or words, and the like. The Masora focuses on sensitive points in the text and most of its effort is devoted to their protection from error.

A third difference is related to the situation in which an error has already occurred and a dissonance was created: in modern codes such internal dissonance is maintained in transmission and revealed only in the course of examination and restoration. But in the case of human transmission, dissonance may be discovered quickly, and when discovered corrected immediately, leading to a corruption of the defense mechanism. This is particularly the case when the contradiction is local and immediate, such as lists that begin with the number of items, followed by their details. If one item is added or detracted, it causes an immediate dissonance. Anyone studying the list or copying it would notice the contradiction, and he might correct it by changing the number. If he does so, then the local defense mechanism of the Masora has failed. This consideration affects the resilience of the immediate local defense, and increases the importance of the more sophisticated and general defense provided by the Masora, that would maintain the dissonance more effectively, and protect the original text.

Nevertheless we can point out parallels between error correction codes in modern communication and the defense mechanism of the Masora: In fact the location of the damage in modern communication is not entirely accidental; the static that disrupts the transfer of data generally strikes a continuum of bits, and not random bits within the message. The transmitter who wants to protect himself from this kind of disruption, does not transmit word after word in order, but mixes the transmission and sends each time a group of bits belonging to different words. Consequently, if there is an eruption of error that destroys a large number of bits, the transmission can still be corrected, because in each word only one bit is destroyed. This is like the Masora, which matches the protection system to the nature of the potential strike (the second difference above) and to the awareness of the weakness of localized defense (the third difference above).

Below we shall discuss four defense mechanisms that were used to protect the text of Scripture: The first two failed, but the last two succeeded remarkably. The first mechanism deals with the verses of Scripture and includes the oldest masoretic notes. As we said above, this mechanism failed. The second defense mechanism deals with open and closed passages in the Torah, and it also failed. The third also deals with open and closed passages, and it had a great degree of success. The fourth mechanism includes all of the masoretic notes on *plene* and defective forms, and it was remarkably successful.

The first mechanism: Early masoretic notes

The Babylonian Talmud testifies on the activity of ancient Masoretes, who tried to protect the text of Scripture. This what it says in Tractate Qiddushin (30a):[3]

> Therefore the "first scholars" were called *soferim* [=scribes, lit. counters], because they counted the letters in the Torah. For they would said *waw* of "גחון" (Lev. 11:42) is half of the letters in the Torah scroll; "דרש דרש" (Lev. 10:16) half the words; "והתגלח" (Lev. 13:33) – of verses; "יכרסמנה" (Ps. 80:14) – the *'ayin* of יער is half of Psalms; "והוא רחום יכפר עון" (Ps. 78:38) half the verses.

In fact the Talmud reports here about two ways of protecting the text. One is the number, "because they counted the letters in the Torah". Indeed the following *baraitha* gives the total number of verses in the Torah, in Psalms and in Chronicles. The second way is finding the middle unit, the middle letter, the middle word or the middle verse – and data are provided here regarding the Torah and Psalms. And this is how the Amoraic discussion to clarify the expression begins:

> R. Joseph propounded: Does the *waw* of גחון belong to the first half or the second? Said they (=the scholars) to him, let a scroll of the Torah be brought and we will count them! Did not Rabbah b. Bar Hanah say, they did not stir from there until a scroll of the Torah was brought and they counted them? – They were thoroughly versed in the defective and *plene* words, but we are not. R. Joseph propounded: Does [the verse of] והתגלח belong to the first half or the second? Said Abaye to him, for the verses, at least, we can bring [a scroll] and count them! – In the (division of) verses too we are not certain. For when R. Aha b. Adda came (to Babylonia from Israel), he said: In the West (=Eretz Israel) the following verse is divided into three: "And the Lord said unto Moses, Lo, I come to you in a thick cloud" (Ex. 19:9)

---

3 It is difficult to determine precisely the date of the source quoted here. It looks like the continuation of the words of Rav Safra in the name of R. Yehoshua ben Hannanya in the previous lines in the Talmud. Rav Safra was an Amora of the fourth generation who lived in Eretz Israel and emigrated to Babylonia, while R. Yehoshua ben Hannanya was a second generation Tana, who lived between the destruction of the Temple and the Bar Kokhba revolt. In other words the report that Rav Safra gives was transmitted over generations by sages who remain unnamed. This source comes to describe the first scholars (*"rishonim"*), the generations that preceded the final version of the text, thus it should refer to the work of Masoretes of the first century C.E., towards the end of the Second Temple period. The Amoraim who discussed the issue, Rav Yosef and Abaye, of the third and fourth generations of Amoraim, were active in the early fourth century.

From the discussion in the Gemara we see that there were two problems – one regarding the text itself and the second regarding the defense mechanisms that were meant to protect it from corruption: regarding the text itself – the Amoraim admit that they were not sufficiently knowledgeable, either regarding letters or verses. The problem with letters is words that are spelled in *plene* or defective form, i.e. the letters *waw* and *yod* (and sometimes *he*), vowel letters that do not change the meaning of the text and are sometimes omitted and sometimes added. Another problem refers to the defense mechanism: it is unclear what is meant by the middle which the early Masoretes mentioned. Is the total number an odd number, or is it even number and, if so, is the middle the end of the first half or the beginning of the second half?

Thus the data given by the early scholars was already found in the Talmudic period inadequate for locating errors and correcting them. The Geonim of Babylonia also struggled with the meaning of the verses mentioned in the Gemara that do not suit the accepted version of Scripture.[4] In later generations we shall find that the indications for the middle mentioned in the baraitha also do not correspond to the accepted text.[5]

The masoretic literature includes data on the number of verses in every Torah portion and of every book in Scripture, and in some cases the number of words or letters. These are ancient and simple means of protection. The information is relatively minimal. It enables "error detection", i.e. determining that a scriptural text under discussion does not conform to the masoretic text; but in most cases it does not provide information for locating the "error" and consequently does not enable its "correction". In other words it is impossible to know what text the Masora was trying to maintain.

Another example of a mechanism that deals with the verses of Scripture is an ancient and venerable masoretic note, pertaining to the Babylonian tradition, and attributed to a long line of famous personalities from the period of the Tannaim and Amoraim, long before the known Masoretes. This note appears in numerous ancient sources and provides the total number of verses in Scripture: 22,747. Scholars who discussed this masoretic note have concluded that it goes back to the second century CE.[6]

---

4 Cf. Responsum of Rav Hai Gaon, in B.M. Levin, *Ozar Hageonim, Qiddushin*, Jerusalem 1940, Responsa, no. 191; Y. Ofer, *The Babylonian Masora of the Pentateuch, its Principles and Methods*, Jerusalem 2001, pp. 168–169 (Heb.).

5 Cf. S. Rosenfeld, *Mishpahat Soferim*, Vilna 1883, pp. 35–36 (Heb.); M.M. Kasher, *Torah Shelemah*, Vol. 28, pp. 286–289 (Heb.); E. Merzbach, "Half the words", weekly page of Bar Ilan University, no. 334 (*Parashat Shemini* 5760 =2000; Heb.).

6 The quotation is taken from *Okhla wa-Okhla*, Ms. Halle, at the end of the manuscript. The note and its sources are discussed in Ofer (note 4 above), pp. 169–170; 178–186. Regarding efforts to date the note and identify the personalities mentioned it, cf. *Ibid.*, p. 170.

This tradition which was transmitted by Dosa son of Elazar son of R. Afsi who received it from R. Yehuda HaBavli who received it from Shimon his father and Shimon his father received it from R. Ada and R. Ada was at that time a great expert in Scripture who received it from Rav Hamnuna who took it out in Nehardea and Rav Hamnuna and Rav Ada both received from Naqi who was exiled from Eretz Israel to Babylonia by Rufus, who did not [want] the Torah in Eretz Israel and they summed up the Torah and the Prophets and the Writings – twenty-four books – without error and without mistake as twenty thousand and two thousand and seven hundred and forty and seven verses, no less and no more.[7]

The text of Scripture before us contains 23,203 verses.[8] The difference is of hundreds of verses, precisely 456, which comprise 2% of the total number of verses. The tradition relating 22,747 verses is a Babylonian one, but nevertheless the extant manuscripts with Babylonian vocalization do not conform to this assertion at all. The division into verses in those manuscripts is very close to that of the Tiberian version and it differs in only a few individual cases.[9] There can be no doubt that the number of verses in this ancient counting is based on a **different, ancient version** of Scripture from that which was accepted in both Tiberias and Babylonia.[10] The same applies to masoretic notes from Babylonia on the middle verses of books of Scripture.[11] These masoretic notes on numbers are testimony of another version, but we have no way to reconstruct it. Thus we have here error detection, but without location, and moreover without any way to correct it. Consequently this is a very weak kind of protection.

Open and closed passages in the Torah

Now we shall take a look at the subject of open and closed passages in the Torah and describe one protection attempt that failed and another that succeeded. As we have already seen in Chapter 5, in the ancient Tiberian manuscripts we do not find uniformity in the placement of open and closed passages in the Torah or in the rest of

---

7 The text reads "and two thousand thousands", but should of course be read "and two thousand".
8 This number is mentioned in a masoretic note (cf. C.D. Ginsburg, *The Massorah Compiled from Manuscripts, Alphabetically and Lexically Arranged*, London 1880–1905, par. פ 215), and it was given the acronym זְכַר אָדָם (Cf. S. Baer and H.L. Strack, *Die Dikduke Ha-Teamim* des Ahron ben Moscheh ben Ascher, Leipzig 1879 [photographic reproduction, Jerusalem 1970], p. xxxi, quoting a manuscript from St. Petersburg, Russian National Library Ms. EVR. II C 144); the number 23,203 is taken as the sum of two other numbers: the 22,273 male first born (Num. 3:43) and the 930 years of Adam's life (Gen. 5:5).
9 Cf. my book cited above (note 6), pp. 154–166. Thirty cases are detailed there in which there is evidence for a different division into verses in manuscripts with Babylonian vocalization.
10 The ancient version was shorter, and it evidently lacked some passages that were accepted in the versions known to us. It may have also had other significant differences, such as a change in the order of passages in Scripture. However, the differences between the Tiberian version and the Babylonian that we know are "minor", such as differences in the vocalization and pronunciation of individual words.
11 Cf. Ofer (note 4 above), pp. 171–176.

Scripture, and the Tiberian Masora did not concern itself with that subject. However the Babylonian Masora does deal with passages, and various lists in Geniza detail the open and closed passages in the Torah; these lists are the second defense mechanism to be described here. The lists differ from each other both in content and in their descriptive techniques. However, one originally Babylonian list that has survived in the Geniza in a number of copies has had significant influence in both Ashkenaz and Italy. This list is connected in some sources to *"Sefer Tagi"*, and seems to have been a widespread and central list.[12] A short passage of this list can be seen in the Geniza fragment in Figure 7.1. This is the title of the list and the first passages included in it:

בשם יוי אל עולם. אתחיל לכתוב הפרשיות הסתומות והפתוחות שבתורה יגד'[לה] האלהים.
ממא דכר אנה נקל מן נסכה עתיקה בג'דאדיה.

In the name of the Lord, God of the world. I shall start to write the closed and open passages in the Torah, may God make it great, [from here on in Arabic]: from what is mentioned in that which was copied from an ancient version from Baghdad.

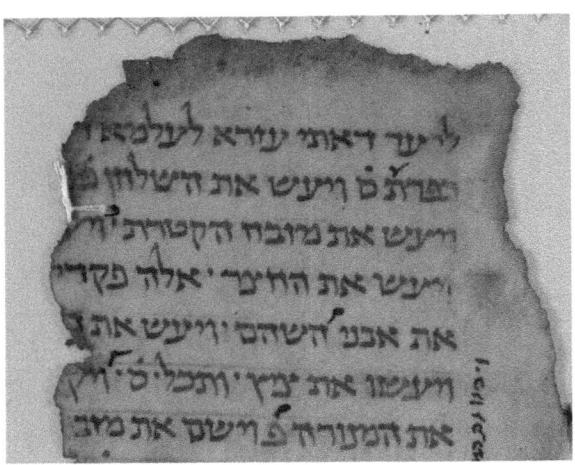

Figure 7.1: Detail from Geniza Fragment, Cambridge, UL, T-S D1,87, listing open and closed passages. With permission of the Syndics of the Cambridge University Library.

Genesis	ספר בראשית
Let there be an expanse (1:6)	יהי רקיע
Let the water below the sky be gathered (1:9)	יקוו
Let there be lights (1:14)	יהי מאורות

---

12 The list is discussed in my article "A Babylonian List of Open and Closed Parashiyot in the Pentateuch", in: M. Bar-Asher and C. E. Cohen (eds.), *Mas'at Aharon: Linguistic Studies Presented to Aron Dotan*, Jerusalem 2009, pp. 392–434 (Heb.). Additional lists of passages from the Geniza are mentioned in Ofer, *op. cit.*, pp. 140–150.

Let the waters bring forth swarms (1:20)	ישרצו
Let the earth bring forth (1:24)	תוצא
The heaven and the earth were finished (2:1)	ויכלו
Such is the story (2:4)	אלה תולדות
All open	כלן פת'
And to the woman (3:16)	אל האשה
To Adam (3:17)	ולאדם
closed	סת'
Now that the man (3:22)	הן האדם
open	פת'
Now the man knew (4:1)	והאדם ידע
In the course of time (4:3)	ויהי מקץ ימים
And Cain said "My punishment is too great" (4:13)	ויאמר קין דגדול
This is the record (5:1)	זה ספר
Seth (5:6)	שת
Enosh (5:9)	אנוש
Kenan (5:12)	קינן
Mahalalel (5:15)	מהללאל
Jared (5:18)	ירד
closed	סת'
Enoch (5:21)	חנוך
open	פת'
Methuselah (5:25)	מתושלח
closed	סת'
Lamech (5:28)	למך
open	פת'
etc.	וכו'

The descriptive apparatus is simple. The passages are listed consecutively as long as they are of the same kind. When the kind of passage changes, a sequence ends, and at its end a caption cites the type of passage listed in that sequence – open or closed. It is followed by a new sequence listing a different kind of passage from the previous one, and so on.

This technique has the advantage of brevity. By listing passages of one kind sequentially, there is no need to repeat each time what kind of passage is cited, but one caption at the end of the series suffices.

However, this apparatus is highly vulnerable. Some mistakes would be discovered readily. For example, if a caption of the kind "closed" were omitted, its lack would be apparent because two successive captions would read "open" one after the other. But other errors would not affect the formal structure of the list. For example, if one passage is omitted from the list of passages; or, on the other hand, if two consecutive sequences were omitted – which could happen as a result of *homeoteleuton* – the structure would not be affected, and only by checking in Scripture could the omission be discovered.

In fact, this list of passages did not achieve its intention. The success of a list is expressed by how it is maintained with stability and without changes. But that is not the case here: at least five copies of this list have survived – and each one is more or less different from the others. Despite the wide dissemination of this list, it does not have internal uniformity. Moreover the list does not confine itself to describing one system, but testifies to disagreements and adds appendices of passages regarding which the scrolls from Nehardea differ. Thus Maimonides was right when he described the situation of Torah scrolls in his day (*Laws of the Torah Scroll*, 8:4):

> And since I observed confusion in all of the scrolls that I have seen in these matters, and the Masoretes who write and compose to inform closed and open [passages] disagree in these matters like the scrolls on which they rely disagree.

Maimonides' way of determining the passages

Maimonides himself tried to solve the problem and succeeded; this is the third defense mechanism to be described here. Maimonides noticed that in his day there was an undecided controversy regarding the passages in the Torah. He did not give his support to an extant list of passages, but created a new list based on the most highly regarded and famous manuscript of the Tanakh. He relied on the Codex of Ben Asher, that was kept in Cairo, that which came to be known after a few generations as the Aleppo Codex. He said:

> The book that we relied upon in these matters is the well-known book in Egypt, which contains twenty-four books, that was in Jerusalem some years ago, to revise the books from it, and everyone relies on it since it was revised by Ben Asher, and he worked meticulously on it for many years, and corrected it many times according to tradition. And I have relied on it in the Torah Scroll that I wrote according to the Halakha.

Maimonides prepared a list on the basis of the passages in the Codex, and determined that all Torah scrolls should be written according to it. The list, included in Maimonides' code of law *Mishneh Torah*, was accepted in all Jewish communities in the course of generations, due to the authority of the "great teacher" Aharon Ben Asher in the area of the Masora and the halakhic authority of Maimonides. Hence Maimonides succeeded where his predecessors had failed.

However, in addition to the authority of Ben Asher and Maimonides, another, more important force also operated: When Maimonides drew up his list of passages, he did not confine himself to the protective techniques used by his predecessors. He created a new system for data protection – the first of its kind in this area, a system that can be defined as a modern error correcting code. It is based on the alternating description used in the Babylonian lists of passages described above.

But Maimonides added quantitative data – subtotals, for information protection. Below is a passage from his list:

Genesis	ספר בראשית
Let there be an expanse (1:6)	יהי רקיע
Let the water below the sky be gathered (1:9)	יקוו המים
Let there be lights (1:14)	יהי מאורות
Let the waters bring forth swarms (1:20)	ישרצו המים
Let the earth bring forth (1:24)	תוצא הארץ
The heaven and the earth were finished (2:1)	ויכלו
Such is the story of heaven (2:4)	אלה תולדות השמים
All open and they are seven passages.	כולן פתוחות והן שבע פרשיות
And to the woman (3:16)	אל האשה
To Adam he said (3:17)	ולאדם אמר
Both of them closed.	שתיהן סתומות
And the Lord God said (3:22)	ויאמר ייי אלהים
Open	פתוחה
Now the man knew (4:1)	והאדם ידע
This is the record (5:1)	זה ספר
When Seth had lived (5:6)	ויחי שת
When Enosh had lived (5:9)	ויחי אנוש
When Kenan had lived (5:12)	ויחי קינן
When Mahalalel had lived (5:15)	ויחי מהללאל
When Jared had lived (5:18)	ויחי ירד
When Enoch had lived (5:21)	ויחי חנוך
When Methusaleh had lived (5:25)	ויחי מתושלח
When Lamech had lived (5:28)	ויחי למך
And Noah was (5:32)	ויהי נוח
These eleven passages are all closed.	אחת עשרה פרשיות אלו כולן סתומות
The Lord saw (6:5)	וירא ה'
This is the line of Noah (6:9)	אלה תולדות נח
Both of them closed.	שתיהן פתוחות

An additional level of data protection is given at the end of each of the five books of the Torah. For example, at the end of Genesis:

מנין הפתוחות שלש וארבעים
והסתומות שמונה וארבעים.
הכל אחד ותשעים פרשיות

The total number of open passages forty-three
and closed passages forty-eight.
In total ninety-one passages.

And a third level of protection appears at the end of the Torah, in the form of a total sum of passages:

מנין הפתוחות של כל התורה מאתים ותשעים

ומנין הסתומות שלש מאות ושבעים ותשע.

הכול שש מאות וששים ותשע.

The total of open passages in the entire Torah – two hundred and ninety.

The total of closed passages – three hundred and seventy-nine.

The total [number of passages in the Torah] – six hundred and sixty-nine.

Maimonides used a very similar security system in his code of Law, the *Mishnehh Torah*: (1) Each of the fourteen books of the work was divided into *halakhot* (laws). At the beginning of the work the *halakhot* in that book are detailed and their number recorded, and at the end of the list the total number of *halakhot* in the composition is given.[13] (2) Each section of *halakhot* is divided into chapters. At the end of each book, the *halakhot* included in it are detailed and the number of chapters in each one is given and also the total number of chapters in each book. (3) In the case of every *halakha* the positive and negative commandments (prohibitions) are detailed. At the beginning of the composition, and also at the beginning of each of the fourteen books, Maimonides records the number of positive and negative commandments in each of the *halakhot*, summing up the number of commandments in that book: positive and negative.[14] The total number of commandments is 613: 248 positive commandments and 365 negative, as Maimonides wrote at the end of the preface to his book.[15]

Evidently Maimonides was very solicitous regarding the structure of his composition and wanted to avoid any damage to it.

The typological parallel between the description of the passages and the commandments is notable: the number of open and closed passages in each series is parallel to the number of commandments in each section of *halakhot*; the sum of the passages in each of the Five Books of Moses is parallel to the sum of the commandments in each book of the *Mishneh Torah*; the total sum of the passages is parallel to the total sum of the commandments.

Returning now to the number of passages and the protective measures that Maimonides added to them, and to what was said above regarding the difference between modern error correction codes and "human" codes like that of the Masora or

---

13 Cf. Rabbenu Moshe ben Maimon, *Sefer Mishneh Torah, Mif'al Mishneh Torah* edition, ed. Y. Makbili, Haifa 2008, pp. 23–32.

14 Rambam, *Ibid*. In some common editions the details of the *halakhot* and the commandments at the beginning of the book were omitted, perhaps because they were regarded as superfluous since they are listed at the beginning of each section of *halakhot*.

15 Rambam, *Ibid*., p. 6, Halakha 42.

Maimonides' lists. In modern codes the assumption is that the anticipated damage will be accidental, not intentional. Such damage may create internal dissonance, which will be revealed by examination and reconstruction. But when the transmission is done by humans, local protection is weak: omitting a passage or adding a passage, creates an immediate contradiction between the list of passages and the numerical sum adjacent to it. Anyone studying the list or copying it would surely notice the contradiction. And immediately he would confront a dilemma: he could correct the list of passages, or correct the number given at the end of the series, or leave the contradiction as it is, either because he does not know how to correct it or because he does not allow himself to change what he received. A copyist or Masorete who is confident in the tradition of passages he has received would most likely correct the number at the end of the series in accordance with the passages he had listed. If he does so, it means that the local defense mechanism of the Masora has failed. And then the two additional levels of defense prescribed by Maimonides would have to withstand the test: the total at the end of each book (of the Five Books of Moses) and the total sum at the end of the Torah.

In five places in the Torah some doubt has arisen regarding Maimonides' meaning in his list of passages (in other words, Maimonides' message incurred flaws): Ex. 8:1 (ויאמר – "And [the Lord] said"); Ex. 20:13ᵇ (לא תחמד – "You shall not covet"); Lev. 7:22 or 28 (וידבר – "And [the Lord] spoke"); Lev. 25:14 (וכי תמכרו – "When you sell"); Deut. 27:20 (ארור שוכב – "Cursed be he who lies"). J. Penkower discussed in detail these five places, examining Biblical manuscripts, manuscripts of *Mishneh Torah* and the writings of the disputants who debated Maimonides' intention.[16]

The accurate version that reflected Maimonides' original intention is reflected in Ms. Oxford Hunt. 80 of Mishneh Torah, authorized with Maimonides' signature. Finally, this version of the list of passages was fully accepted by all Jewish communities. Maimonides' defense mechanism managed to deflect all the other traditions that tried to infiltrate his list and change it. Moreover, in one place (Lev. 7:22 or 28), Maimonides' evidently omitted one passage by mistake, but reinforced his intention by means of the defense mechanism. Despite the difficulty and peculiarity this error created, it was accepted in all Jewish communities, even though a disagreement arose because Maimonides' words were not unambiguous.[17]

In conclusion: Maimonides' system of dividing the passages was not broken down in any one of the 669 passages in the Torah. There were some local "breakdowns" in certain manuscripts or printings, and there were some breakdowns of the individual "numerical defenses" – but the total defense of the books and the Torah – were never broken down!

And now we can go one step further and ask: How did Maimonides' tradition of passages spread throughout all the Jewish people and displace traditions of passages

16 J. S. Penkower, 'Maimonides and the Aleppo Codex', *Textus* 9 (1981), pp. 39–128.
17 For details of some of these instances, cf. Ofer and Lubotzky (note 1, above).

that had been accepted in various Diaspora? Its acceptance involved shelving (or burying) most of the Torah scrolls and writing new ones following a new tradition that differed from the accepted local traditions! How could such a change not have encountered opposition? In fact many of Maimonides' rulings in various areas of Halakha were not accepted in every community. As is well known, Rabbi Yosef Karo in his *Shulhan Arukh* took Maimonides' system into account, but also those of Rabbi Yitzhak Alfasi and Rabbenu Asher; Rabbi Moshe Isserles in his commentary on the *Shulhan Arukh* ("*Hamapa*" = the tablecloth on the table [*shulhan*]) detailed the places in which the Ashkenazi tradition differed, and these differences remain until today in every sphere of Halakha. How is it that with regards to the Torah scroll, all of the communities conformed to Maimonides' tradition?

In our opinion, the answer is that not only the authority of both Maimonides and Ben Asher was crucial here, but also the stability of the tradition: Maimonides' tradition was clear and unambiguous, and his sophisticated "error correction code" protected it and deflected any attempt to amend it or diverge from it. The other traditions were shaky, unstable and in dispute with one another in every detail. They could not stand up against Maimonides' clear and stable tradition!

In the course of the generations, the number of Torah scrolls that were written according to Maimonides' list gradually increased, while Torah scrolls written according to other traditions were gradually reduced until they ceased altogether. The old Torah scrolls wore out from usage and became invalid for public reading, so that only Torah scrolls based on Maimonides' list were left.

The Song of *Haazinu* and the Song at the Sea

The presentation of poetic sections, the Song of *Haazinu* (Deut. 32) and the Song at the Sea (Ex. 15) deserves separate attention since Maimonides' ruling regarding how they should be written was not accepted in entirety. Regarding *Haazinu* M. Goshen-Gottstein wrote at length. The tradition of Maimonides and the Aleppo Codex to write the song in 67 lines did not displace the more logical tradition in the communities of both Sefarad and Ashkenaz to write the poem in 70 lines, which was both easier to do and supported by Tractate *Soferim*. In this case Maimonides' system failed mainly because of the technical difficulty to execute it. Maimonides combined here a number of strong defense mechanisms: He cited the number of lines, listed the 67 words with which each line should begin and the 67 words with which the second hemistich should begin. However all of these measures were insufficient to protect the peculiar tradition that he upheld, and all of them were altered forcefully.[18]

---

18 Cf. Moshe Goshen-Gottstein, "The Authenticity of the Aleppo Codex", *Textus* 1 (1960), pp. 45–50. We shall quote here the words of R. Menahem di Lonzano, who pointed out the difficulty in writing

However, in the case of the Song at the Sea (Ex. 15:1-19) – Maimonides system failed because of a security problem, and not because of difficulty of execution. This is Maimonides' language:

> The Song at the Sea should be written in thirty lines: The first line, normally; the rest of the lines – one with one space in the middle, and the other with two spaces in the middle, dividing the line into three parts. Consequently, the space is below the writing and the writing below the space. And this is how it looks: [And here the song is copied with its spaces].

Maimonides described the song in two descriptions: a general verbal description and a detailed graphic description in which he copied the entire song, its words and the spaces between them. The verbal description is insufficient on its own. It describes the general form of the poem, but you cannot learn from it how to divide every line, i.e. what words should appear in each unit of text. Moreover, this description is also not entirely accurate, since you cannot discern from it that the second line in the poem should have two spaces and not only one. Likewise you cannot learn from it that the two last lines should be written with only one space each. And why? From a graphic perspective the last line should be divided into three and its last part contain only one word, like all the other even lines of this song; but from the point of view of contents a space cannot come between the last two words of the poem (בתוך הים – "into the sea") which are in a construct state, dividing בתוך ("into") from הים ("the sea")![19]

Haazinu in 67 lines: Someone who wants to write that way "must include in three places in one line what should be written in two lines according to the other opinion, and consequently in all three lines they will not be able to leave the space of a [closed] passage because there is not enough room. And if you say: he could do so… by making the column of the song much wider to begin with… that is not a solution, because if he did so the Torah scroll would be invalidated in another place, since above the song there are six lines, all of them short, and how can the scribe do it?" etc.

Thus someone took a stand and changed Maimonides' language making it conform to the 70-line system. By doing so he introduced ten changes in Maimonides' instructions: he moved three words and added six new words (בתו, זקניך – in the middle of the line instead of שאל, that was moved to the beginning of the line; על, ישאהו – in the middle of the line instead of יפרש, that was moved to the beginning of the line; ומחדרים, יונק – at the beginning of the line instead of גם, that was moved to the middle of the line), and also changed the number of lines from 67 to 70. This revised version of Maimonides' words was copied and disseminated, and then confronted with Maimonides' original version, and was finally accepted in the communities of Sefarad and Ashkenaz. Only the Yemeni tradition accepted Maimonides' system, writing the Song of *Haazinu* in 67 lines, as was done in the Aleppo Codex.

19 Regarding the writing of the Song at the Sea in different geographical locations, cf. J. S. Penkower, "A Sheet of Parchment from a 10th or 11th Century Torah Scroll: Determining its Type among Four Traditions (Oriental, Sefardi, Ashkenazi, Yemenite)", *Textus* 21 (2002), pp. 254–261; Y. Peretz, "The Layout of the Song of the Sea (Exodus 15: 1–19)", *Israel: Linguistic Studies in the Memory of Israel Yeivin* (ed. R. Zer and Y. Ofer), Jerusalem 2011, pp. 179–203 (Heb.); Orlit Kolodni, *The Pentateuch in Medieval Italian Bible Manuscripts and 'Tikkunei Soferim': Text, Open and Closed Sections, and the Layout of Songs*, Ph.D. Thesis, Ramat Gan 2008, pp. 221–257 (Heb.).

Why did Maimonides choose to copy the entire song rather than to give a detailed verbal description of its way of writing? Maybe he feared that a verbal description would be complicated and unclear. Consequently he decided to copy the song completely into his book, so that everyone could understand how it should be written. However, from the point of view of defense mechanisms that was a poor choice that proved ineffective. Copyists (and eventually printers), who were expected to copy the text and spaces accurately, faced complex graphic problems, and sometimes allowed themselves to make changes in order to fit the text into the available space. Furthermore, anyone copying a sketch should understand exactly what it demands, otherwise it will be distorted. In a short time scribes confused Maimonides' sketch. Some of them created a sketch that only illustrated writing a line with one space followed by a line with two spaces, without concern for how to divide the text, and even without consideration for the total number of lines. Others created a sketch of 30 lines, conforming only to Maimonides' verbal description. Others copied the Song at the Sea into manuscripts of Maimonides' work as they thought it should be written in the Torah. Penkower conducted a thorough examination of the manuscripts of *Mishneh Torah* and found that most of them do not conform to Maimonides' original (which is known from the Oxford manuscript). Maimonides' intention was to shape through his writing the uniform way in which Torah scrolls should be written in Jewish communities, but in fact the opposite occurred: The manner in which the Song at the Sea was written throughout the Jewish world shaped how it was copied into manuscripts of Maimonides' book![20]

Finally the technique for writing the Song at the Sea in the Aleppo Codex was adopted by most communities, except for the last line: This line was divided in Torah scrolls into three parts, although in the Aleppo Codex it was divided into two parts (In the Yemenite community this line is divided into two parts). Unlike the case of *Haazinu*, here there was no strong tradition that conflicted with the tradition of the Codex; thus we can presume that if Maimonides had used more effective measures of protection, such as describing verbally the special way in which the last line of the song should be written, he would have succeeded to implement the version of the Aleppo Codex in that line as well.

The conclusion that arises from this discussion is that sometimes what determined the acceptance of Maimonides' ruling was the defense mechanisms that he added to his ruling, rather than the contents of the tradition he transmitted or how reasonable or widespread it was.

---

20 J.S. Penkower, *New Evidence for the Pentateuch text in the Aleppo Codex*, Ramat Gan 1992 (Heb.); for the data regarding manuscripts of *Mishneh Torah*, cf. pp. 33–36.

The Apparatus of the Masora

Now we shall return to the apparatus of the Tiberian Masora – the *Masora Parva* and *Masora Magna*.[21] That is the fourth and last defense mechanism that will be dealt here.

First of all, placement of the notes of both the *Masora Magna* and the *Masora Parva* in the margins of a manuscript of Scripture heightened its status and testified to its accuracy. It should not be forgotten that in the period that preceded printing many hundreds of manuscripts were required for the use of young and old for reading and studying Scripture. Most of those who needed manuscripts of Scripture could not or did not want to invest great sums in their writing. They need popular copies, not written by expert scribes, and in those manuscripts extra care was not taken to ensure accuracy. Many books and fragments of such books were found in the Geniza.[22] Masoretic notes in the margins of a Scriptural manuscript create the impression that it is a revered and accurate copy.

Secondly, this technique itself granted a marketing advantage to the Tiberian Masora. The Masora transmits an aura of seriousness and accuracy, and is a status symbol, while manuscripts without a Masora were regarded as common, popular and inaccurate. Therefore any respectable community, or important individual, who wanted to own a highest quality copy of the Torah, Prophets or Writings, or of the entire Tanakh (Hebrew Bible) – sought out a scribe who was well-versed in the Masora, who could copy it for him and include in it masoretic notes as well. Consequently masoretic notes were widely disseminated since had these notes been written in separate books, they would have reached only the small pubic that engaged in Masora professionally. This trend continued into the age of printing: The widespread edition, *Miqraot Gedolot*, printed in Venice in 1524–1525 and reprinted many times over centuries, includes the masoretic apparatus, which was thus made available to the masses, even though only a few individuals take an interest in it and use it.

Not all of the Masoretes and scribes were alike: Some were experts, who tried to check that the masoretic notes they copied conformed to the version of the manuscript they were copying and corrected them when necessary. Others copied the

---

21 It is appropriate to point out that the apparatus of the Tiberian Masora was not the only way in which the Masora worked – the Babylonian Masora used a different method: It was not written in the margins of the text, but as a separate composition. This work was not limited in space like the margins of the manuscripts used by the Tiberian Masoretes and enabled the Babylonian Masoretes to write at length and give all of the information concerning a certain word in the discussion of the first verse in which it appeared. Regarding the Babylonian Masora cf. Ofer (note 6, above) pp. 26–29. This technique had its advantages, of course. However, it was the Tiberian Masora that has lasted for generations perhaps because of its intrinsic advantages, which are discussed in the body of this chapter.

22 Cf. For example the Geniza fragments in box A22 of the Taylor-Schechter Collection in the Cambridge University Library.

notes without checking that they matched the manuscript. However, both contributed to the dissemination of masoretic notes, and contributed to the reinforcement of their status.[23]

The apparatus of the Tiberian Masora may be defined as "close defense", but not "local defense" since masoretic notes appear "on the page" near the scriptural words they are meant to protect. However the protection is not local: Tiberian masoretic notes are characterized by the fact that they do not deal only with individual words that appear on the page. Usually you will not find notes such as אֹתוֹ – חסר (*oto* – him – defective) or מלא – אֹותוֹ (*oto* – him – *plene*). The area of reference is general, i.e. to the entire text of the Tanakh, to one of its three components, or to one of the books of the Bible. For example: The *Masora Parva* of the Aleppo Codex on Joshua 16:6 reads: אֹותוֹ – ד' מל'[א] בסיפ'[רא] (= the word *oto* occurs four times in *plene* form in the Book of Joshua; in all other occurrences it is defective). Even the very common masoretic note ל (= no other like it), which refers to an individual word, transmits knowledge regarding Scripture as a whole: this specific form is unique in Scripture.

What is the importance of this in the context of protecting the version? A "local" note attached to a particular word is superfluous and vulnerable. It is superfluous because the information already appears on the page. For example, when the word אֹתוֹ appears on the page, there is no point in adding a note that the word is in defective form. As opposed to the case of a code transmitted electronically, when copied by humans there is not much value in duplicating the information, since in a case of disagreement any copyist would notice the dissonance and correct either the text or the note. That is not the case when the note refers to all of Scripture. Here it would be more difficult to change the masoretic note, and the apparatus of both the *Masora Magna* and *Masora Parva* have impact as we shall see below.

It is worth remembering in this context a matter discussed above in the section on passages: Maimonides' local defense at the end of every series was damaged or

---

23 In many medieval manuscripts the version of the text is far from the masoretic version, even though many masoretic notes were copied in their margins. M. Cohen concluded that "in most masoretic codices from Ashkenaz there is no essential connection between the text and the Masora that ornaments it. The consonant image reflected in masoretic notes is that of the authorized version. [...] It seems that the high status attributed in general to the Masora in the Jewish world as "a fence around the Torah" led to the dissemination of the model of transmission of the 'codex of Scripture' also in areas that were beyond that of the authorized version, but in those areas the Masora was artificially appended to the local version" (M. Cohen, "Some Basic features of the consonantal text in Medieval Manuscripts of the Hebrew Bible", *Studies in Bible and Exegesis* I: Arie Toeg in Memorian, Ramat Gan 1980 [Heb.], p. 150). One may presume that the requirement, or the custom, of copying masoretic notes in the margins contributed to the dissemination of masoretic notes and to recognition of the position of the Masora, even in places where the Masora was not used efficiently or completely for creating a uniform text. Cohen (*Ibid.*), pp. 150–182, demonstrated by means of a sample how different Masoretes used masoretic notes, some more and some less, bringing the text of the manuscript they were entrusted to copy closer to the authorized version.

broken, in some cases. However his general defense was sustained and finally preserved the list of passages as he wrote it.

Masora Magna and *Masora Parva*

As described earlier, the *Masora Parva* gives numbers without detail and the *Masora Magna* details the verses. Why this double mechanism? Why split the information into two places? How was it created and how does it work?

One possible answer is developmental, and there were Masora researchers who thought of it in this way: The Masora developed in stages. First it was transmitted orally, and then written down in the brief notes of the *Masora Parva*, and only later did they begin to write the notes of the *Masora Magna*.[24] But this answer is not logical. It is difficult to see how the *Masora Parva* could exist without the *Masora Magna*, since how would the Masoretes operate on the basis of a number without the details it reflects? Could the Masoretes have recorded numbers without detailing their contents anywhere? And if they did so, why didn't they abandon the brief form once they had finally arrived at the *Masora Magna*? Why did the *Masora Magna* not replace the *Masora Parva* entirely?

The developmental claim has no solid textual basis. Indeed there are geniza pages on which there are notes from the *Masora Parva* without *Masora Magna*. But the manuscripts which contain detailed and intensive *Masora Parva* without any *Masora Magna* are rare. Moreover: the Masora is not a permanent text copied from one manuscript to another. Every Masorete created his collection of *Masora Magna* and *Masora Parva* according to his own selection and wording. Thus the *Masora Parva* cannot be regarded as a frozen relic of an earlier period. This Masora was re-created in every manuscript in which it was written, just like the *Masora Magna*. A close examination of the Aleppo Codex, for example, reveals that its masorete Aharon ben Asher wrote the *Masora Parva* and the *Masora Magna* in his manuscript, and for many years continued to correct and enhance them and added more and more new masora notes.

Thus we need to understand and explain how both of these apparatuses worked together as parts of one mechanism. We need to explain how the mechanism worked synchronically.

It seems that the Tiberian codices of Scripture were specifically designed to include both the *Masora Parva* and the *Masora Magna*. They were written in narrow columns, usually three columns to a page or two columns in the case of Job, Proverbs and Psalms (known as the books of ת"אמ = תהלים משלי ,איוב).[25] This layout allows

---

24 Cf., for example, M.H. Segal, *Mevo haMiqra (Intruduction to the Bible)*, Jerusalem 1977 (ninth edition; Heb.), p. 908: "The *Masora Parva* undoubtedly preceded the *Masora Magna*."

25 This differs from Babylonian manuscripts, which were generally written in one or two columns.

writing a great number of notes of the *Masora Parva* between the columns. Above and below the columns space was left for the notes of the *Masora Magna*. The number of notes of the *Masora Magna* on any page is limited, on the average six notes. The average number of notes of the *Masora Parva* is 50 per page.[26] Notes of the *Masora Magna* are much longer than notes of the *Masora Parva*, since detailing the verses takes up space, while the *Masora Parva* provides only a number, for which it is sufficient to write one or two letters ('ג, 'ד, ב"י, י"ג = 3, 4, 12, 13 respectively) and the like.

The relation between the two apparatuses is paradoxical: Even though the scribe leaves wide lines at the top and bottom of the page for the *Masora Magna* and only the tight space between the columns for the notes of the *Masora Parva*, the number of notes of the latter is at least five times greater than the former, and there still remains space for more. In effect, the space for the *Masora Parva* is essentially unlimited.

If for example a masoretic note mentions five occurrences of defective spelling, the details will appear only once in the *Masora Magna*, but the number will be cited in all five occurrences, or at least in most of them. If one encounters a note in the *Masora Parva* that concerns a topic that interests him, he can look for the relevant note in the *Masora Magna*. This may require effort, since the *Masora Parva* does not give references, and the note in the *Masora Magna* may not be found in the same manuscript as that in the *Masora Parva*. But if one looks enough, ultimately he will find it.

The *Masora Parva* may be regarded as a **mechanism for detecting errors**. It enables the Masorete to discern an error in the text, but does not point out their location or enable him to correct them, since it does not provide verse references. The *Masora Magna*, on the other hand, includes an apparatus for correcting errors since it says exactly where the word is written in defective spelling and where in *plene* form.

However, in our opinion the justification for the *Masora Parva* is otherwise. It disseminates the information of the masoretic note intensively. The number at the basis of the masoretic note is repeated again and again. This number will be engraved in the memory of people and written repeatedly, until it cannot be forgotten.

The great and random diffusion of masoretic notes, the fact that there is no permanent location for notes of the *Masora Magna* and that the number is repeated time and again in notes of the *Masora Parva*, give the Masora a force and stability and prevent Masoretes and scribes who have a divergent version from changing the masoretic notes and making them conform to their versions.

Let us imagine a scribe who encounters a conflict between the version he is copying and a masoretic note (whether of the *Masora Magna* or *Parva*), and tries to find a solution. In principle he has four options: (1) to leave the conflict as it is, without solving it; (2) to change the text and make it conform to the Masora; (3) to change the number in the *Masora Parva* or the number and the list of verses in the

---

26 The calculation is based on an analysis of the Book of Joshua in the Aleppo Codex. It contains 190 notes of the *Masora Magna* and 1500 notes of the *Masora Parva* in 29.5 pages.

Masora Magna, making them conform to the version he is using; (4) to try to resolve the conflict totally or partially in different ways (such as to say that two similar verses were counted as one, or that the number refers only to the word itself and not to the word when it occurs with a prefix).

Such a Masorete would have a dilemma: on the one hand, it is his responsibility to transmit that which he received faithfully and accurately. On the other hand, he sees that there is a conflict in the material before him, and he may feel responsible to resolve it. It is impossible to gauge which path he will choose: The first option, leaving the conflict in place, may be chosen by a less serious scribe, who wants to finish his job and receive payment, without struggling to find a solution to difficult problems. But even a professional Masorete may decide to give up and not change anything, leaving the problem for future generations to solve.

The wide dispersal of numbers in the Masora – particularly in notes of the *Masora Parva*, which repeat themselves in many places – made option 3 unappealing for Masoretes. Sometimes it is easier to find a tenuous justification for a surprising number than to change it. Here is where the power of the defense mechanism comes into play: the number preserved with such stability in many manuscripts for generations could often lead to the preservation of the original version it was intended to maintain.

The Masora as a convergence mechanism

The Masora on Scripture was created only after extensive activity for making a uniform text of Scripture, versions that did not conform to the accepted version were rejected and manuscripts that represented distant versions were shelved. However, it is difficult to imagine that the Masoretes arrived at **total agreement** regarding every letter in Scripture, and that only after an agreed text was determined, they began to write masoretic notes. That is an ideal situation, which it would be difficult to imagine ever existing anywhere, since the differences between Biblical manuscripts of which we know are quite numerous. Moreover, the Masora developed over many generations and was worded by many Masoretes. It would be hard to presume that everyone who made up masoretic notes had a uniform text of Scripture without textual differences.

We must conclude that the masoretic notes were based on a text that was **almost** agreed upon in every detail, but not totally uniform. It makes sense that the Masora did not operate solely as a **mechanism for preservation of the text**, but also as a **mechanism for deciding between differences of opinion** in order to arrive at a uniform version.

The appropriate term to use here is "Convergence Mechanism" and we need to try to understand how such a mechanism works. Let us presume that we have before us a great number of manuscripts that are close to each other, but not identical. Masoretes create notes that come to preserve the version they have and disseminate it. Generally notes coming from different Masoretes do agree and form a consensus that obliges later Masoretes. Sometimes conflicts do occur between versions and in different masoretic notes, and the Masoretes try to resolve them in different ways. Conflicting numbers may serve as an impetus to reveal discrepancies and to resolve them by reaching decisions, thus bringing the versions closer together – both the text and the contents of the notes. Thus masoretic notes led to a process of convergence that ultimately created a uniform version – **the masoretic text.**

8 The Aleppo Codex and its Discovery

Introduction

The Aleppo Codex is the most important manuscript from the period of the Masoretes. Its accuracy and its conformity to the Masora have been confirmed mainly in the last decades since its arrival in Israel (1958), and particularly since the publication of a facsimile edition in 1976.

The binding that is seen in Figure 8.1 was made after the manuscript was brought to Israel and deposited in the Ben-Zvi Institute. It was removed in 1986, in the process of restoration at the Israel Museum. Today the Aleppo Codex is kept in the Shrine of the Book of the museum. One quire is presented to the public in a special display table (Figure 8.2), the other quires are kept in a special cabinet, located in a protected warehouse (Figure 8.3).

Here are the conclusions of two of the experts who examined the Codex and described it, regarding the accuracy of the Aleppo Codex. Prof. Israel Yeivin asserted the following:

> This manuscript is vocalized and its cantillation signs were added most accurately, and it preserves purely all of the ancient characteristics of accentuation that were blurred and disappeared in later manuscripts; at any rate from these points of view it is the most accurate of all the Tiberian manuscripts of Scripture that I have examined in photographs (I. Yeivin, The Aleppo Codex of the Bible, Jerusalem 1968, Hebrew Introduction, p. י).

And Rabbi Mordechai Breuer declared:

> Anyone who examines the codex checking in principle and in detail is astonished by the ability of the vocalizer and Masorete to produce a perfect result, flawless and without error, in almost super-human perfection. He was familiar with defective and *plene* spellings, with vocalization and the secrets of the cantillation sings, and no mystery of the Masora escaped him. He was the only scribe, vocalizer, Masorete and editor who succeeded to write an entire copy of Scripture without departing from the rules and requirements of the Masora.

Examinations have demonstrated the nearly total conformity of details of vocalization, cantillation marks and accents in the Aleppo Codex to the opinion of Ben Asher, documented in the *Sefer Hahilufim*, a Masoretic treatise that represents the disputes between the two Masoretes Aharon ben Asher and Moshe ben Naphtali.

When the quality and importance of the Aleppo Codex became clear, efforts were made to learn more about it and its peregrinations over many generations. This research has two aspects, but they are interrelated: The first is an historical issue: Where was the Codex held, who had it in his possession, when was it moved from one place to another, who studied it and clarified its text?

The second aspect is related to the parts of the codex that were lost in the riots in late 1947, including all of the Torah except eleven pages (5 and a half folios), a few

https://doi.org/10.1515/9783110594560-008

Figure 8.1: The Aleppo Codex in its bound form.

Figure 8.2: The Aleppo Codex in the Shrine of the Book at the Israel Museum.

Figure 8.3: The Aleppo Codex in its special cabinet, divided to quires. Photographed by Michal Chelbin.

folios from Prophets, the end of Writings, and also the folios of Masora that were at the beginning and end of the manuscript. Scholars have tried to reconstruct in different ways data regarding the lost parts of the Codex, mainly on the basis of studies and copies made over generations.

And this is where the two aspects meet: When testimonies of copies made from the codex or clarifications of its version are revealed, they elucidate the status of the codex, the interest taken in it and the manners of those who inquired about it to find the answers to their questions. At the same time these testimonies offer information regarding the missing parts of the codex enabling a degree of reconstruction of those sections.

In this chapter we shall survey the history of the Aleppo Codex, and present some of these testimonies, most of which were discovered in the last decades.

While reading this chapter, the reader should examine the Aleppo Codex itself. A complete photograph of the extant manuscript is available in a website prepared by the Ben-Zvi Institute (which is entrusted with preserving and maintaining the manuscript) – in Hebrew and English. Besides the possibility of viewing the codex and examining the details of letters, vocalization, cantillation marks and masoretic notes with magnification – the site includes a survey of a wide range of topics related to the Aleppo Codex, and bibliographical references.

The URL of the site: http://www.aleppocodex.org/aleppocodex.html.

For further study

Books devoted to the description of the Aleppo Codex and its Masora:
Mordechai Breuer, *The Aleppo Codex and the Accepted Text of the Bible*, Jerusalem 1976 (Heb.); Israel Yeivin, *The Aleppo Codex of the Bible: A Study of its Vocalization and Accentuation*, Jerusalem 1968 (Heb.).

The creation of the Aleppo Codex

The manuscript known today as the Aleppo Codex (in Hebrew *Keter Aram Zova*), was written in the early tenth century in Tiberias, and received the title *keter* (in Arabic *taj* = crown) shortly after its writing by virtue of its great prestige. The appendage *Aram Zova* was added centuries later, when the manuscript was transferred to Aleppo, Syria, and preserved in the Jewish community there; the Jews referred to Aleppo by the biblical name *Aram Zova*.

The identity of the Masorete of the Keter may be derived from its **dedicatory inscription**, which was written about a century after the writing of the manuscript, when it was dedicated to the Karaite community in Jerusalem:

> This is the complete codex of twenty-four books... The one who vocalized it and added the Masora to it with the greatest care is the great learned... Rabbi Aharon ben Rav Asher, may his soul be bound in the bounds of life...

This inscription also relates that the letters of the Keter were written by the scribe Shlomo ben Buya'a, and that Aharon ben Asher added the vocalization and cantillation marks, and wrote the masoreteic notes. Writing the letters is mainly a technical job, which was delegated to an experienced scribe. However, responsibility for the version of Scripture was given to the expert Masorete Aharon ben Asher.

A tenth-century Masorete who studied the Keter and relied on it is the Masorete of Ms. **S1** (Sassoon 1053). He quoted a masoretic note from the Keter and gave testimony to his source: "And I found them in the work of the great scholar Aharon ben Asher in his works in the compilation called '*elTaj*'". *ElTaj* ("the crown") in Arabic is equivalent to *HaKeter* in Hebrew, thus we see that already in the tenth century Aharon ben Asher was renowned and his special Tanakh was called the Keter.

Regarding Aharon ben Asher's provenance we learn from the following inscription at the beginning of the book *Diqduqe haTe'amim*: "This is a book of *Diqduqe haTe'amim* (= "details of the cantillation marks"), that was written by R. Aharon ben Asher, **from Maaziah, called Tiberias**, on the western shore of the Sea of Galilee. May God grant him rest, and awake him with those who sleep in the earth" (A. Dotan (ed.), *The Diqduqe HaTe'amim of Aharon ben Moshe ben Asher*, Jerusalem 1967 [Heb.], Introduction, p. 105; regarding the book, its contents and author see below, chapter fourteen). The town Tiberias was also called Maaziah, after one of the ancient priests mentioned in the Tanakh, as the chief of the last of the 24 priestly clans (I Chr. 24:18).

An indirect testimony provides information regarding the date of the writing of the Aleppo Codex: In St. Petersburg (Leningrad) there is a manuscript of the Torah (Ms. SP NL II B 17) that was completed on "8 Kislev, in the year 1241 of the Seleucid era", i.e. 929 C.E. At the end of the Torah is a colophon stating: "[I] Shlomo Halevy bar Buya'a, disciple of Sa'id bar Fargoy, called Alquq, wrote this Torah of Moses thanks to my God's benevolent care for me (cf. Neh. 2:8)" etc. Shlomo ben Buya'a was the scribe who wrote the Aleppo Codex, thus it must have been written at approximately the same time. The calligraphy of

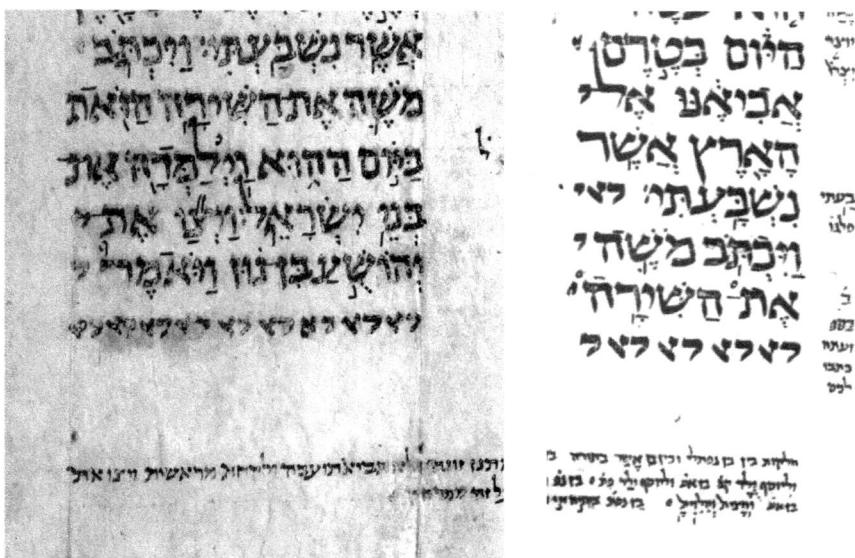

Figure 8.4: Right: some lines from Ms. St. Petersburg NL II B 17 written by Ben Buya'a. Left: Compare to the same text in the Aleppo Codex. Note the similarity of the filling signs in both manuscripts. See: M. Glatzer, "The Aleppo Codex: Codicological and Paleographical Aspects", Sefunot 19 (1989), pp. 227–229.

the two manuscripts shows that they were written by the same hand (see Figure 8.4; Pay particular attention to the similar filling signs in both manuscripts). The Masorete of the Leningrad manuscript was the scribe's brother, Ephraim ben Rabbi Buya'a.

The Peregrinations of the Keter

The Aleppo Codex underwent many peregrinations in the more than one thousand years since it was written. In some places it remained for only one or two generations, and in others it was held for many centuries. In some cases it was transferred from one place to another by its custodians, and in one case transferred by force, by a foreign conqueror.

The dedicatory inscription written at the end of the Keter tells about its transfer from Tiberias to Jerusalem. This occurred after the death of its distinguished creator, Aharon ben Asher. The Keter reached the hands of Israel ben Simha of Basra (who evidently purchased it from the heirs of Aharon ben Asher). He gave it to the heads of the Karaite community in Jerusalem, Yoshiyahu and Yeḥizqiyahu, for preservation, providing many conditions for its conservation and protection. Both Rabbanites and Karaites were to be allowed to examine the Keter in order to clarify textual questions, but not to read from it or study it (see Figure 8.5).

All these conditions did not help much. The Aleppo Codex reached Jerusalem in the middle of the eleventh century, and before the end of the century it was pillaged and reached Egypt. This occurred evidently in 1099, when the Crusaders conquered

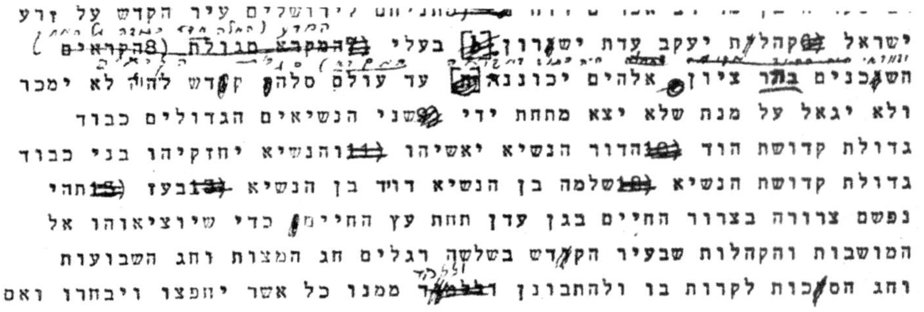
... לירושלים עיר הקדש על זרע
ישראל קהלות יעקב עדת ישרון בעלי המקרא מגלת הקראים
השכנים בהר ציון אלהים יכוננה עד עולם סלה קדש ליהוה לא ימכר
ולא יגאל על מנת שלא יצא מתחת ידי שני הנשיאים הגדולים כבוד
גדולת קדושת הוד ההדור הנשיא יאשיהו והנשיא יחזקיהו בני כבוד
גדולת קדושת הנשיא שלמה בן הנשיא דויד בן הנשיא בועז תהי
נפשם צרורה בצרור החיים בגן עדן תחת עץ החיים כדי שיוציאוהו אל
המושבות והקהלות שבעיר הקדש בשלשה רגלים חג המצות וחג השבועות
וחג הסכות לקרות בו ולהתבונן ממנו כל אשר יחפצו ויבחרו ואם

Figure 8.5: A section of the dedicatory inscription of the Keter. A copy made by Prof. M.D. Cassuto, who examined the Keter in Aleppo. The passage concerns conditions for use of the Keter by Karaites and Rabbanites.

Jerusalem. The conquerors did not damage the Keter, because they knew that they could receive a generous ransom for it from Jewish communities. Letters discovered in the Cairo Geniza tell about manuscripts that were redeemed from Crusaders in Ashkelon with the help of Jews from Egypt, and the Keter may have been one of them. At any rate the Keter was ransomed and reached the Rabbanite synagogue in Fustat (ancient Cairo).

In Egypt Maimonides saw it – as will be described at length below – and from Egypt it reached Aleppo, in Syria, evidently in the fourteenth century.

For further reading

Izhak Ben-Zvi "The Codex of Ben Asher", *Textus* 1 (1960), pp. 1–16

Damage to the Keter and Its Arrival in Israel

For a thousand years the Aleppo Codex was preserved in its entirety. Historical events had almost no influence on it, and it remained complete despite its peregrinations: Tiberias, Jerusalem, Egypt and Syria. For many centuries it was kept safe and unharmed by the Jewish community in Aleppo. It did suffer some of the ravages of time: on some pages the ink dried up and fell off and only its remnants could be seen, and some pages were cracked. Towards the end of the nineteenth century a fungus caused a red-purple stain in the external bottom corner, blurring some letters in the masoretic notes.

But nevertheless the Aleppo Codex remained the oldest complete copy of the Tanakh in the world. All of its 480 folios remained, and one could read in it from "In the beginning" to the last words of the Tanakh "Oh my God, remember it to my credit" (Neh. 13:31; in the Keter and in Tiberian manuscripts Chronicles appears at the beginning of Writings, and the last books are Ezra and Nehemiah).

In 1943 Prof. Umberto (Moshe David) Cassuto of the Hebrew University of Jerusalem visited Aleppo. He examined the Keter and described it in detail. According to Cassuto, it was kept "in a wooden box covered with red leather. The box opened into two parts and the book was tied to its two parts like to a normal binding."

Cassuto was one of the last to examine the Keter while it was still complete. Four years later it was damaged in an attack on the synagogue. On December 1, 1947, two days after the United Nations decision on the partition of Palestine, riots broke out in Aleppo. This is the testimony of the rabbi of the city, Rabbi Moshe Tawil:

> They took out forty Torah scrolls and burned them outside with kerosene and oil. The Jews were afraid to go out on penalty of death. The government warned against killing; plundering and destroying – were allowed... at the same time all the synagogues were set on fire, especially the bigger ones... after four days we entered the Great Synagogue and saw the ashes of books and small fragments... look and see the Keter lying in ashes. Its cabinet [a metal safe] was broken into pieces.

Most of the Keter was saved from the ashes and hidden in a safe place, with the intention of bringing it to the Land of Israel at the first opportunity. The hiding of the Keter and its secret dispatch to Israel were recorded briefly in a page attached to it:

> This Keter of the Torah was given by the Chief Rabbi of Aleppo, Rabbi Moshe Tawil and the Judge R. Shlomo Zafrani to Mr. Mordechai ben Ezra Hacohen Faham in the year 5718 [=1957], in order bring it to the Holy City of Jerusalem. Mr. Faham had the privilege to carry this out and agreed to endanger his life in order to save it and bring it to Jerusalem and gave it to the honorable President of the State, Mr. Izhak Ben-Zvi.

The Aleppo Codex was entrusted to the Ben-Zvi Institute in Jerusalem, and a committee of trustees appointed to supervise its care. The chairman of the committee was the chairman of the Ben-Zvi Institute; one of its members the Sefardi Chief Rabbi of Israel; and some of its members are representatives of the Aleppan community in Israel.

For further study

Yosef Ofer, "The Aleppo Codex according to the lists of M.D. Cassuto" (Heb.), *Sefunot* N.S. 4 (19) (1989), pp. 277–344.
Amnon Shamosh, *HaKeter – The Story of the Aleppo Codex*, Jerusalem 1987 (Heb.).

The extant parts of the Keter, their conservation and display to the public

The Aleppo Codex was not saved in its complete form. It lacks the first part, the last part and some pages from the middle. At the beginning of the Keter the Five Books of the Torah are missing, except for the end of Deuteronomy, from the word וּמִשְׁאַרְתֶּ֑ךָ (= "your kneading bowl", Deut. 28:17; derived from the root שא"ר) to the end of the book. The extant manuscript concludes with the word צִיּוֹן ("Zion", Cant. 3:11) and lacks some of the "Five Scrolls" (the end of Song of Songs, Ecclesiastes, Lamentations and Esther), and the books of Daniel and Ezra and Nehemiah. For that reason Rabbi Mordechai Breuer applied to it the verse "וְהָיָה הַנִּשְׁאָר בְּצִיּוֹן... קָדוֹשׁ יֵאָמֶר לוֹ" ("And those who remain in Zion ...shall be called holy", Is. 4:3).

In 1986 the Keter was transferred to the laboratory of the Israel Museum, Jerusalem, for restoration. The process took ten years, and in the course of it scotch tape and stains were removed, the ink was reinforced, and places where the parchment had started to disintegrate were repaired. After completion of the conservation, the Keter was put on display in the Shrine of the Book at the Israel Museum, where the Dead Sea Scrolls are displayed. In 2005 a special exhibit dealing with the Keter and its peregrinations was opened on the lower floor of the Shrine of the Book. In the same year, a photograph of the entire restored manuscript was placed on the internet in a special website devoted to it.

Locating and reconstructing the missing parts

Great efforts were made to locate the missing pages of the Keter, and from time to time rumors of such pages cropped up in different parts of the world. Some testified that they saw the Keter after the riots and only a few pages were missing from it, others claimed that they found pages and passed them on to others. The location of the missing pages troubled the writer Amnon Shamosh, who suggested an imaginary solution in his novel *Michel Ezra Safra and his Sons* (1978), which served as the basis for a controversial television series. According to the novel, the missing pages were placed in a secret safe in France, and were finally lost without leaving a trace. In his documentary book in Hebrew, *Haketer – The Story of the Aleppo Codex*, Shamosh devoted many pages to an attempt to clarify what exactly happened to the missing parts of the Keter.

Besides the 294 folios of the Keter that were brought to Israel in 1957, one entire folio and one small fragment have been located. The entire folio is one of those lost from the middle of the Keter, a part of Chronicles. A man from Aleppo lifted it from the floor of the Great Synagogue after the fire and passed it on to his mother. Some years later they went to the United States, and the folio was kept in a drawer for many years, as a kind of amulet, until it was brought to Jerusalem in 1981 and reunited with the Keter.

A small fragment of a page from Exodus was kept in the wallet of Samuel Sabbagh, native of Aleppo who lived in New York, as an amulet. He claims to have been the first person to enter the synagogue after the riots, and lifted the small parchment fragment from the floor himself. A photograph of the fragment was published in 1989 in the journal *Pe'amim*. After Sabbagh's death his family transferred the fragment to the Ben-Zvi Institute. Following delicate treatment in the Israel Museum laboratory, the fragment was put on display in the Shrine of the Book (see Figure 8.6).

Will more pages or fragments of the Keter ever be found? Only time will tell.

Figure 8.6: Fragment of the Aleppo Codex, Exodus, Ch. 8, dealing with the frogs plague.

For further study

Malachi Beit-Arié, 'A Lost Leaf from the Aleppo Codex Recovered', *Tarbiz* 51 (1982), pp. 171–173 (Heb.); Israel Yeivin, 'The vocalization and Accentuation of the Recently Recovered Leaf of Ms. Aleppo', *Tarbiz* 51 (1982), pp. 174–176 (Heb.); Yosef Ofer, "A Fragment of Exodus – From the Missing Part of the Aleppo Codex", *Pe'amim* 41 (Autumn 1989), pp, 41–48 (Heb.); Y. Ofer, "A Fragment of the Aleppo Codex (Exodus 8) that Reached Israel", *Textus* 26 (2016), pp. 173–198.

How much was the Keter damaged in the riots and where are the missing pages?

What exactly happened to the Keter in the riots? And what happened to it between the riots in 1947 and its arrival in Israel in 1958? And, above all, where are the missing pages?

Two books deal with the history of the Keter and tried to answer the questions about it. The first, *Haketer*, is by the writer Amnon Shamosh, published in 1987 by the Ben-Zvi Institute, in Hebrew (I served as Shamosh's research assistant in his work on the book). The other, *The Aleppo Codex*, is a book by the journalist Matti Friedman, published in 2012 (in English and Hebrew). Friedman claims that Shamosh's book was a smoke screen, a book from the point of view of the establishment, covering up something unclear.

Matti Friedman conducted a far-flung and serious study to gather documents and evidence. The major problem is that we are getting farther and farther from the events of the 1940s and 1950s. Many of the people whom Izhak Ben-Zvi questioned or might have questioned in the sixties were no longer available to Amnon Shamosh in the eighties, and many of those whom Amnon Shamosh spoke with passed away before Matti Friedman's investigation in this decade.

These are two of Matti Friedman's main conclusions: The first relates to the tension and disagreements within the Aleppan community in Israel and the representatives of the government of Israel: the Department of Immigration of the Jewish Agency for Israel, headed by Shlomo Zalman Shragai, and the President of the State of Israel Izhak Ben-Zvi, who received the Keter from the hands of the former. Friedman concludes:

> "The Crown of Aleppo was never given to Israel. It was taken. The government may have believed it was serving the interests of its people and of the book itself... the state took the sacred property of people who did not give it voluntarily..." (p. 138)

Regarding this question a lengthy trial was conducted in the Rabbinical court of Jerusalem in the 1960s. Representatives of the Aleppan community claimed that the messenger who brought the Keter to Israel betrayed his mission when he gave the Keter to agents of the Jewish Agency. From the documents it seems that the messenger, Mordechai Faham, was indeed unable to withstand the pressure of establishment representatives. His version – that the rabbis of Aleppo told him to give the Keter "to a religious person, whom he deemed worthy" – was essentially refuted in court. But finally the sides reached a compromise, and the court was left only to approve it. The Aleppo Codex was entrusted to the Ben-Zvi Institute in Jerusalem, and a board of trustees was appointed to supervise it, consisting many representatives of the Aleppan community in Israel.

But my main interest here regards Friedman's second conclusion, which he calls "explosive":

> If the Crown was intact in Aleppo in 1952 ... it meant the missing pages were not "lost." They were not burned, looted by rioters or picked up as souvenirs. The missing pages were missing... (p. 210).

Freidman presents in his book several testimonies of people from the community of Aleppo. Before the discussion I must say a few words regarding human memory: People do not remember much. I have a practice of transcribing important telephone conversations immediately after they occur. A year or two later I read them, thinking: Very interesting, I do not remember that at all. One famous Hebrew scholar, whose mind is clear and sharp despite his age, well over 90, told me once "At our age, our memory improves: We even remember things that did not happen". The point is clear: Someone who saw the Keter as a child of ten, and fifty years later remembers exactly what it included and what it did not, his memory may be suspect.

I cannot address all the testimonies cited in the book, but only the most important of them, that of Rabbi Itzjak (Yitzhak) Chehebar (1912–1990), a leading rabbi of Aleppo, who was eventually the Chief Rabbi of the Aleppan community in Buenos Aires. In 1989, he was interviewed by an investigator named Rafi Sutton, together with a television crew from Israel's Channel One program "A Second Look" doing a report on the Aleppo Codex (see Figure 8.7). Rabbi Chehebar saw the Keter in Aleppo in 1952, five years after the riots and five years before it was smuggled to Israel.

Figure 8.7: Rabbi Chehebar: From "A Second Look", Israel Channel One (Courtesy of the Israeli Public Broadcasting Corporation "Kan").

"I opened it in the storeroom of Ibrahim Effendi Cohen, and I saw it," the rabbi said. "It was missing a few pages that perhaps fell to the ground and were burned, but not to this extent, Not hundreds of pages."

SUTTON: Missing are Genesis, Exodus, Leviticus, Numbers and half the book of Deuteronomy. And parts of other books are missing.

CHEHEBAR: I saw that it was missing a few pages. Not that many pages.

SUTTON: You mean individual pages?

CHEHEBAR: Individual pages. Not even dozens were missing.

(M. Friedman, *The Aleppo Codex*, p. 209)

Rabbi Chehebar said that it was not missing so much. Not even dozens of pages. In my opinion, the interviewer tried to put words in Rabbi Chehebar's mouth, that hundreds of pages were not missing, only "individual" pages.

But in the archive of Ben-Zvi there is a detailed four-page account written by Rabbi Itzjak Chehebar, entitled "Details on the Tanakh manuscript known as the Aleppo Codex as written from my memory". The document bears a stamp with the date April 24, 1960, but I think it was written some years earlier, because Rabbi Chehebar testifies that the Keter was still in Aleppo, and we know that the Keter was smuggled from Aleppo in 1957. Rabbi Chehebar writes (Figure 8.8):

> Thus because of sins, all those books were lost in the riots, and none of them remained except one ancient one (i.e. the Keter) and we did not know how it survived the destruction, but pages were missing from it in different parts of the Tanakh, and it was missing nearly one quarter....

> This precious remnant is held by one merchant in Aleppo.

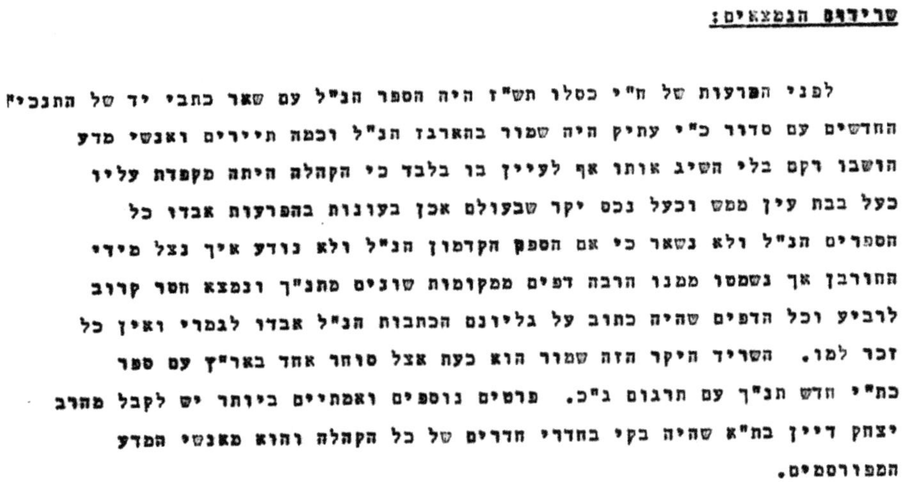

שרידים הנמצאים:

לפני הפרעות של ח"י כסלו תש"ז היה הספר הנ"ל עם שאר כתבי יד של התנכ"ים
החדשים עם סדור כ"י עתיק היה שמור באהרגז הנ"ל וכמה תיירים ואנשי מדע
הושבו רקם בלי השיג אותו אף לעיין בו בלבד כי הקהלה היתה מקפדת עליו
כעל בבת עין ממש וכעל נכס יקר שבעולם אכן בעונות בהפרעות אבדו כל
הספרים הנ"ל ולא נשאר כי אם הספף הקדמון הנ"ל ולא נודע איך נצל מידי
החורבן אך נשמסו ממנו הרבה דפים ממקומות שונים פתנ"ך ונמצא חסר קרוב
לרביע וכל הדפים שהיה כתוב על גליונם הכתבות הנ"ל אבדו לגמרי ואין כל
זכר למו. השריד היקר הזה שמור הוא כעת אצל סוחר אחד באר"ץ עם ספר
כת"י חדש תנ"ך עם תרגום ג"כ. פרטים נוספים ואמתיים ביותר יש לקבל מהרב
יצחק דיין בת"א שהיה בקי בחדרי חדרים של כל הקהלה והוא מאנשי המדע
המפורסמים.

Figure 8.8: Rabbi Chehebar's written testimony on the Aleppo codex.

That is to say, when the document was written the Keter was still in Aleppo, and already missing about one quarter.

In my opinion this testimony is far stronger than what Rabbi Chehebar said decades later to an interviewer, who tried to extract from him that hundreds of pages were not missing.

This document was in the hands of Izhak Ben-Zvi, as may be seen in a notation in his notebook from 1958 (Figure 8.9).

In my opinion Rabbi Chehebar's description, "it was missing about one quarter" led Izhak Ben-Zvi to the conclusion that there were about 380 folios in the Keter. When

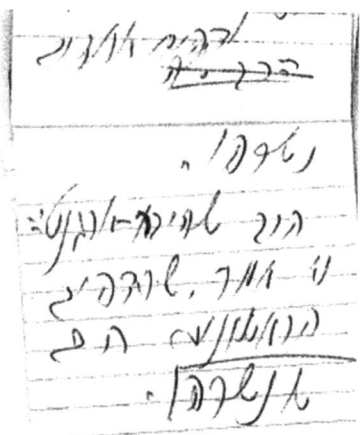

Figure 8.9: A note about the Keter in Izhak Ben-Zvi's notebook from 1958: "A few pages were burned. Rabbi Chehebar – Argentina, did not say that the first pages were burned".

I began to study the Keter, I calculated the total on the basis of the extant pages, and easily found that it in the Keter was much greater – at least 480 folios, one hundred more than Ben-Zvi's estimate. And I was surprised how Izhak Ben-Zvi arrived at an erroneous estimate. I believe the answer is that he relied on Chehebar's testimony.

Izhak Ben-Zvi's annotation is noteworthy: Chehebar spoke of a quarter of the pages of the Keter as missing, but did not stress that the Torah was missing. Perhaps a hint may be found here that some pages of the Torah did exist when he saw the Keter in Aleppo in 1952.

To conclude this section: I do not believe that somewhere in the world there may be a suitcase containing the hundreds of missing pages from the Keter. The Keter was damaged in the riots and that accounts for most of the missing pages. Individual pages or fragments of pages may be discovered yet. Unfortunately the chances of that are getting lower from year to year. The generation that was active 70 years ago has passed on, but maybe something was given to its sons. However, sometimes the passage of generations may lead to discovery of things that were hidden in the preceding generation. Who knows?

Photographs of the Aleppo Codex

Considering the mystery of the fate of the missing pages of the Aleppo Codex, another question must be asked: Were the missing pages ever photographed?

The fact is that some of them were, and we know today of two photographs in which three of the missing pages of the Keter appear. One page was photographed towards the end of the nineteenth century, and two more pages in one photograph from the beginning of the twentieth. A single page from Genesis 27 was published in 1887 at the beginning of a book on cantillation marks by William Wickes. Amnon Shamosh found in the archive of the Alliance in Paris a letter from 1873, speaking about four photographs of the Aleppo Codex. Apparently the photograph published by Wickes is one of them, but the location of the other photographs is unknown. A photo of two pages was published in 1910 in a book on the travels of the missionary Joseph Segall, and it shows verses from the Ten Commandments in Deuteronomy 5.

It should be noted that U. Cassuto intended to photograph the Keter, or at least its first part. However after making contacts in Aleppo he learned that it would be difficult to obtain film and the quality of the photography would not be high. It would be difficult to convince the heads of the community to allow the photography. For these reasons he gave up the idea and made do with copying details from the manuscript.

For further study

M. H. Goshen-Gottstein, "A Recovered Part of the Aleppo Codex", *Textus* 5 (1966), pp. 53–59 (Heb.);
    A. Shamosh, *Ha-Keter: The Story of the Aleppo Codex*, Jerusalem 1987 (Heb.), pp. 50–52; 104–105.

Maimonides and the Aleppo Codex

The status of the Keter was reinforced in the twelfth century by Maimonides' assertion in his halakhic masterpiece, *Mishneh Torah*. In the section regarding laws of the Torah scroll, discussing the spaces between passages (open and closed), he points out that he had encountered doubts and disagreements between all those engaged in the issue. In order to solve the problem Maimonides decided to include in his book a list of the 669 passages in the Torah, and a precise description of how the "Song at the Sea" (Ex. 15) and the "Song of *Haazinu*" (Deut. 32) should be written. As the source for his list Maimonides chose the famous manuscript that was in Egypt. These are his words:

> And the book we relied upon in these matters is the well-known book in Egypt, which contained twenty-four books, that was in Jerusalem some years ago, to revise the books from it, and everyone relied on it, since it was revised by Ben Asher, and he worked meticulously on it for many years and revised it many times, according to tradition. And I have relied on it in the Torah Scroll that I wrote according to the Halakha. (Laws of the Torah Scroll, 8:4).

Maimonides describes here a manuscript of the entire Tanakh ("twenty-four books") that was revised by Ben Asher again and again over many years. Maimonides prefers this Tankah to all the other Torah scrolls and manuscripts and all the lists of Masoretes, and asserts that Torah scrolls should be written according to it. Maimonides' authority was so great that within a few generations the Jewish communities accepted his ruling, and all the Torah scrolls throughout the Jewish world were written according to his list, which is based on the book revised by Ben Asher.

But was that book indeed the Aleppo Codex? In fact the tradition in the Aleppan community was that Maimonides referred to this Codex that was in their possession. This tradition is documented from the fifteenth century by Sa'adya ben David Ha'Adani, who visited Aleppo and viewed the Keter.

It would seem to be easy to confirm or refute this tradition. We only have to compare the Torah in the Keter with Maimonides' detailed list and see if the two sources conform to each other in every case. However, the matter is not that simple. As mentioned above, most of the pages of the Torah in the Keter were lost, and only eleven pages containing seven chapters remain.

One scholar, who examined the Keter when it was still complete, concluded that it was **not** the book Maimonides relied upon. That was Umberto Cassuto, who examined the Keter in Aleppo in 1943, and gave his opinion several times without explaining it, before his death in 1951. In 1946 Cassuto published the Book of Jonah as an example of the Tanakh he intended to publish, and the following appears at the beginning of the volume (in Hebrew):

> Accepted opinion regards the book on which Maimonides relied as the "Keter" of Aharon Ben Moshe Ben Asher, preserved today in the city of Aleppo; but after a precise examination of the Keter by the aforementioned scientific director [= Cassuto], who went to Aleppo in 1943, it became clear to him that this opinion was erroneous.

It would seem that there is no choice but to accept this negative conclusion. However, Moshe Goshen-Gottstein was able to reverse this conclusion shortly after the Keter arrived in Israel. Goshen presumed how Cassuto arrived at his negative conclusion. The key to the puzzle is what Maimonides said about the "Song of *Haazinu*". This is what is written in the common printed editions of Maimonides' *Mishneh Torah* (*Ibid.*):

> The Song of *Haazinu* – every line has in the middle a space like a closed passage, and every line is divided into two, and it is written in **seventy** lines.

The "Song of *Haazinu*" appears in the few pages at the end of the Torah that remained from the Aleppo Codex. Examining these pages reveals a remarkable phenomenon in the way it is written: three of the lines are very long, and they contain a text that was usually written in two separate lines: Consequently the total number of lines of the song in the Keter is **sixty-seven** and not seventy.

However a comprehensive examination of the manuscripts of the *Mishneh Torah* holds a surprise: In the oldest and most reliable manuscripts of the *Mishneh Torah* the number of lines prescribed for this text is not seventy, but sixty-seven! The list of words with which each line should begin also conforms perfectly to the text in the Aleppo Codex. Moreover, the Torah scrolls of the Jewish communities of Yemen are written according to the tradition of sixty-seven lines, as was Maimonides' original opinion. The writing of the "Song of *Haazinu*" in sixty-seven lines is unknown from any other codex of Scripture before the time of Maimonides, and thus beyond any doubt it was the Keter on which Maimonides relied.

How then was the printed version of Maimonides created, prescribing writing the song in seventy lines? Evidently the background to its creation was the difficulty to write those three long lines in the "Song of *Haazinu*". It can only be done if the song is written in extra-wide columns, leaving a very large space between the two parts of all the other lines. Moreover, this tradition of writing was not accepted in most communities, and thus aroused opposition. In order to solve the problem, someone revised Maimonides' words making them conform to the accepted way of writing, which itself was an ancient tradition, documented in "Tractate Soferim" (Ch. 12) from the Geonic times.

Most of Goshen's conclusions were proven correct many years after he asserted them when Cassuto's notes from his examination of the Keter were given to me for study. The main reason for Cassuto's assertion was indeed related to the "Song of *Haazinu*". Thus we may conclude that the Aleppo Codex was in fact the book on which Maimonides relied and the ancient tradition regarding his use of the Keter has been validated.

For further study

Moshe Goshen-Gottstein, "The Authenticity of the Aleppo Keter", *Textus* 1 (1960), pp. 17–58; Y. Ofer, "M.D. Cassuo's Notes on the Aleppo Codex", *Sefunot* 19 (1988), pp. 325–330 (in Heb.)

Testimonies on the missing sections

Reconstruction of many important details from the missing sections of the Aleppo codex has been carried out on the basis of testimonies and lists by scholars who viewed the codex before it was damaged. As mentioned, the reputation of the Keter had spread far and wide in the Jewish world for centuries, and it was known among those dealing with the Masora as the most accurate work of Aharon ben Asher, and as the Tanakh on which Maimonides relied when he wrote the "Laws of the Torah Scroll" in his *Mishneh Torah*. Consequently many of the specialists in the Masora and the writing of Torah scrolls wanted to examine the Keter to find answers to problems they had regarding the accurate text of Scripture. Writings and lists made on the basis of the Keter can help today to reconstruct the missing parts.

Here are four of those testimonies.

1. At the end of the sixteenth century Yishai ben Amram Hacohen 'Amadi, from 'Amadiya in Kurdistan revised the Torah on the basis of the Aleppo Codex. His corrections were made in the margins of a printed Pentateuch from 1490, and discovered in New York, in the library of the Jewish Theological Seminary of America. 'Amadi wrote at the end of Leviticus: "this is my codex, which I the young and small servant of Israel, Yishai bar Amram Hacohen, may he rest in peace, revised using the Keter that ben Asher of blessed memory, revised." Similar inscriptions appear at the end of other of the Five Books of Moses. From this copy important conclusions may be derived regarding open and closed passages in the Keter and the way in which the "Song at the Sea" was written in Exodus.

2. As mentioned above. U. Cassuto examined the Aleppo Codex in 1943. He found a note attached to it, recording the differences between the Torah scrolls of Aleppo and the version of the Keter. One of the sages of Aleppo, Rabbi Menashe Sitthon, had prepared the list, and Cassuto copied it into his notes. On the basis of these notes, it is possible to reconstruct with a high degree of accuracy the version of the Keter with regard to the letters of the Torah.

3. Yaakov Sapir, one of the Ashkenazi sages of Jerusalem, sent in the 1850s a list of more than 500 notes on the orthography, vocalization and cantillation marks in different parts of the Keter (from the Torah, *Haftarot* [=the readings from the Prophets that correspond to each weekly reading of the Torah] and the Five Scrolls). This list was sent to Rabbi Menashe Sitthon, mentioned above, regarding whom Sapir testified, "head of [the Jews] in Aleppo, and also a great expert in the Masora". He asked Sitthon to look in the Keter and write **yes** or **no** regarding each question. This list reached Jerusalem and was copied many times. A passage from one of these copies is presented in Figure 8.10.

For example, one of the questions regarded vocalization of the word זכר (memory) in the verse "blot out the memory of Amalek" (Deut. 25:19). For generations there was some doubt regarding the correct vocalization of the word זֵכֶר (the first letter with a *zere*, to be read in the Ashkenazi pronunciation: *zeikher*) or זֶכֶר (the first letter with a *segol*, to be read *zekher*), and in some Ashkenazi communities the verse is read twice on the special Sabbath before Purim on which the passage is read in the synagogue, in order to satisfy both opinions. From Sapir's testimony we learn that the word was written with a *zere* in the Keter (זֵכֶר).

Figure 8.10: Testimony on the vocalization of the word זכר in the Aleppo Codex in reply to Yaakov Sapir's question (New York, JTSL MS L729, fol. 7v). Courtesy of The Library of The Jewish Theological Seminary.

4. Rabbi Shalom Shachna Yellin (1790–1874) was an expert scribe of Torah scrolls, living in the town of Skidel in Lithuania. He was engaged throughout his life in writing Torah scrolls, tefillin and mezuzot and in the study of the Masora in order to clarify the correct text of the Tanakh. In 1855 he began preparations to move to the Land of Israel, and on route was asked to check Torah scrolls in communities through which he passed. Rabbi Shalom Shachna's son, Rabbi Aryeh Leib Yellin, was the rabbi of the town of Bielsk, and is known for his composition *Yefe 'Einayim*, printed in the Vilna Talmud. Here is what Rabbi Shalom Shachna wrote to his son:

> And now I am on my way to travel to the Holy Land with God's help. And there in Aleppo is a Tanakh written on parchment with Masorot which was revised by Ben Asher over a long time, on which Maimonides relied... and my intention with God's help is to reach it and edify my eyes by resolving doubts... regarding the spelling [of some biblical words] and the Masora comments.

Rabbi Shalom Shachna arrived in Jerusalem and obtained recommendations from the most important rabbis of Jerusalem, both Ashkenazim and Sefardim. However, in the end he did not have the strength to make the difficult trip to Syria, and sent his son-in-law, Moshe Yehoshua Kimhi, giving him a printed Tanakh and in its margins a list of doubts and disagreements that required clarification. The emissary wrote in the margins the version found in the Keter in each case. All of these facts were known from contemporary testimonies, but the whereabouts of the Tanakh itself containing the evidence from the Keter – was unknown.

In 1987 an old house in the Kiryat Moshe neighborhood of Jerusalem was about to be knocked down. In the attic were many old books and documents. Some of the books were removed from the attic before the house was destroyed, among them a small, old Tanakh with annotations in tiny script in its margins. The Tanakh was given to a bookseller, who was about to send it to be buried with other worn out, sacred books. At the last minute the nature of the Tanakh was discovered by me, and it was saved: This was Yellin's Tanakh, and the marginal annotations contained exclusive data regarding the Keter (see Figure 8.11).

In the margins of the Tanakh all of the places in the books of Prophets and Writings in the Keter in which there was a space (open and closed passages), were noted, including in parts of the Keter that have not survived. Editions of the Tanakh published in recent years – including 'Horev', 'Keter Yerushalayim' and 'Miqraot Gedolot HaKeter' editions – rely on this old Tanakh regarding that matter. Yellin's Tanakh was donated to Ben-Zvi Institute by the Yellin family and is displayed in the Shrine of the Book together with the Keter.

For further study

Jordan S. Penkower, *New Evidence for the Pentateuch Text in the Aleppo Codex*, Ramat Gan 1992 (Heb.).
Rafael Y. Zer, "R. Ya'aqov Sappir's *Meoroth Nathan*", *Leshonenu* 50 (1986), pp. 151–213 (Heb.).
Yosef Ofer, "The Aleppo Codex and the Tanakh of R. Shalom Shachna Yelin" *Mordechai Breuer Festschrift*, Jerusalem 1992, pp. 295–353 (Heb.).

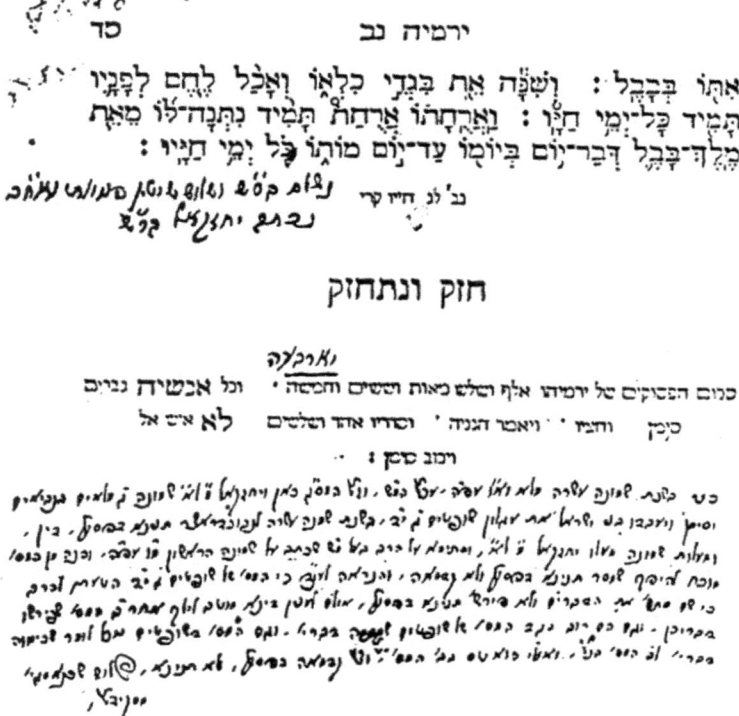

Figure 8.11: A page from the Kimhi Tanakh, with annotations from the Aleppo Codex.

Additional ways to reconstruct the missing parts

Despite all of these testimonies, there remain parts of the Tanakh that did not survive in the Keter and for which there is no evidence. Can the version of the Keter be reconstructed in other ways? This goal is not just an intellectual exercise by scholars. It is essential for any edition of Scripture based on the Aleppo Codex. After all, it would be absurd to print an edition of the Tanakh, leaving the pages that are lacking in the Keter blank!

Scholars have tried to reconstruct the version of the Aleppo Codex in two ways. One way relies on the Keter itself, learning from the extant parts about the missing parts. For example, in the "Miqraot Gedolot HaKeter" of Bar-Ilan University, edited by Menachem Cohen, the editor made a thorough study of how the Keter dealt with cantillation marks and stress marks ("ge'ayot"), using the conclusions of his study to reconstruct the missing parts. Another example: Notes in the Masora Magna are intended to establish rules that apply to the entire Tanakh. Masoretic notes in the Keter concerning orthography, for example, refer to the spelling of many words in Scripture, among them words in the parts that are missing today.

The second way is to find other manuscripts that are close to the system of the Keter. These are usually manuscripts from the tenth or eleventh centuries, that have been examined and found to be close to the Keter in various areas: orthography, vocalization and cantillation marks.

By using both techniques it is possible to arrive at a satisfactory approximation of the text of the Aleppo Codex: internal testimony from the Keter, learning from parts that have survived regarding missing parts and comparison with other manuscripts close to the Keter. Experts on the Masora today may disagree regarding details for achieving the best result. However they all agree that the Aleppo Codex is the most accurate of all the Masoretic manuscripts, the work of an expert and highly skilled Masorete. Many scholars think that it should serve as the basis of every edition of the Masoretic text.

For further study

Menachem Cohen, "Introduction to the Keter Edition" in *Miqraot Gedolot HaKeter*, I, Joshua and Judges and introduction to the Keter edition, Ramat Gan 1992, pp. 1*-82* (Heb.).

9 The Babylonian Masora and Its Influence

The familiar vocalization signs in use today are the Tiberian signs. The cantillation marks in printed Pentateuchs and volumes of Hebrew Scriptures are also Tiberian. The system of vocalization and cantillation developed in Tiberias, evidently in the seventh and eighth centuries CE, and over generations was accepted by Jewish communities the world over. That is the system used in the manuscripts of Scripture discussed in the previous chapters – the Aleppo Codex, Ms. Leningrad and other similar manuscripts – and also in contemporary printed editions of Hebrew Scripture.

However in ancient times, the Tiberian system was not the only one in use. In other parts of the Jewish world systems of vocalization and cantillation were created, each one reflecting the reading and recitation tradition in its provenance. We know about these systems from remnants of ancient manuscripts and from Geniza fragments.

The two main areas Jewish presence in the period of the Talmud and the Geonim were Eretz Israel (Palestine) and Babylonia (Iraq). The major works of the Oral Law – The Babylonian Talmud and the Jerusalem Talmud – were created in these two regions. The Babylonian system is the most important of all the non-Tiberian vocalization systems, and it will be discussed in this chapter. It should be noted that in addition to the Tiberian and Babylonian systems, there were additional systems: the Palestinian system, the 'extended' Tiberian system and Samaritan vocalization.[1]

In order to understand the situation with regards to the transmission of Scripture in Eretz Israel and Babylonia in the Masoretic period, we may use an analogy to Jewish communities today: In all communities the Torah is read, but the reading tradition is not uniform: the pronunciation of vowels in the Yemeni community differs from that in the Sephardi communities, both of which differ from that of Ashkenazi communities. The same applies to the manner of cantillation, in which each community maintains its own special melody. A person hearing for the first time recitation of the Torah in an unfamiliar way would encounter difficulty in identifying the words and comprehending them. All this despite the fact all of the communities read from the same Torah scrolls, and all of them use printed Pentateuchs with identical vocalization signs and cantillation marks!

Similarly, we may presume that in the period of the Talmud and the Geonim (i.e. the fifth to eighth centuries CE) there were different reading traditions in Eretz Israel and in Babylonia. This was the period before the systems of transcribing vocalizing and cantillation were developed, that is to say, the reading traditions were entirely oral, and signs for reading and chanting had not yet been created. Consequently evidence on the Babylonian pronunciation tradition is sparse. However, once the Babylonian vocalization signs were established, these reading traditions were preserved in writing, and from an analysis of ancient manuscripts with Babylonian vocalization we can assert

---

1 On the vocalization Systems see: S. Morag, 'Niqqud', *Encyclopaedia Biblica* V (Jerusalem 1968), pp. 837-857 (Heb.).

https://doi.org/10.1515/9783110594560-009

that the differences in the reading tradition between Babylonia and Eretz Israel were greater than the differences between communities today. This may be discerned by a study of the Babylonian system and the Babylonian cantillation system.

Babylonian Vocalization

Here is a page from the Book of Jeremiah with Babylonian vocalization (Figure 9.1):

In this Geniza fragment with Babylonian vocalization the signs of vocalization and cantillation appear above the words (and are therefore called "upper vocalization"). The vocalization is partial, i.e. not every word is completely vocalized. Generally the scribe does not vocalize common words regarding which the pronunciation is unambiguous.

Babylonian vocalization uses six signs for vowels: The signs for *hiriq* (i) and *zere* (e) are like those in the Tiberian system, but appear above the word (cf. right column, line 3: *hiriq* above the word וְשָׁכַנְתִּי; line 2: *zere* above the word אֲחֵרִים). The *holam* (o) is two dots arranged vertically (l. 5, above the word בֹּטְחִים), and the *shuruq* (u) is a vertical line above the word (left column, l. 11: וּבַחֲצֹות). The signs for *qamaṣ* (å, a vowel between a and o) and *patah* (a) are like the sign ⊥ (a horizontal line intersected by a vertical line), but the *patah* is horizontal and the *qamaṣ* leans towards the right (cf. right column, l. 3: בְּמָקוֹם).

Thus far we have presented differences in form alone: The Babylonian signs differ graphically from their Tiberian counterparts. But there are also differenced of essence. The Babylonian symbol that is parallel to the Tiberian *segol* is the *patah*, as in the word וּבָאתֶם (l. 10; = וּבָאתֶם). From this we may conclude that in the Babylonian pronunciation there was no distinction between *segol* and *patah*. However, this description is from the Tiberian perspective, in which *segol* is a separate vowel. From the non-Tiberian perspective, this matter could be phrased differently: In the Babylonian system there were only six vowels and only in the Tiberian system a seventh vowel developed, the *segol*. It should be kept in mind that even in today's Yemeni pronunciation there is no differentiation between *segol* and *patah*. This similarity is not coincidental, and also in other cases the influence of Babylonian pronunciation is apparent among the Jews of Yemen. Moreover, manuscripts with Babylonian vocalization were widespread in Yemen till the twentieth century.

Some words reflect grammatical differences between the two language traditions. For example: In the words וְלַאֲבוֹתֵיכֶם (left column, l. 2) the conjunctive *waw* at the beginning of the word is vocalized with a *hiriq*. In the Babylonian punctuation a conjunctive *waw* before a *shewa* is vocalized with a *hiriq*, like the letters *bet*, *kaf* and *lamed* before a *shewa* in the Tiberian tradition: וְדָבָר like בִּדְבָר). In the Tiberian Masora this word is vocalized with a *shewa* and *patah*: וְלַאֲבוֹתֵיכֶם (Jer. 7:14).

Here are a few more linguistic differences on the page reproduced above (the Babylonian vocalization is depicted in the explanation by Tiberian signs since the

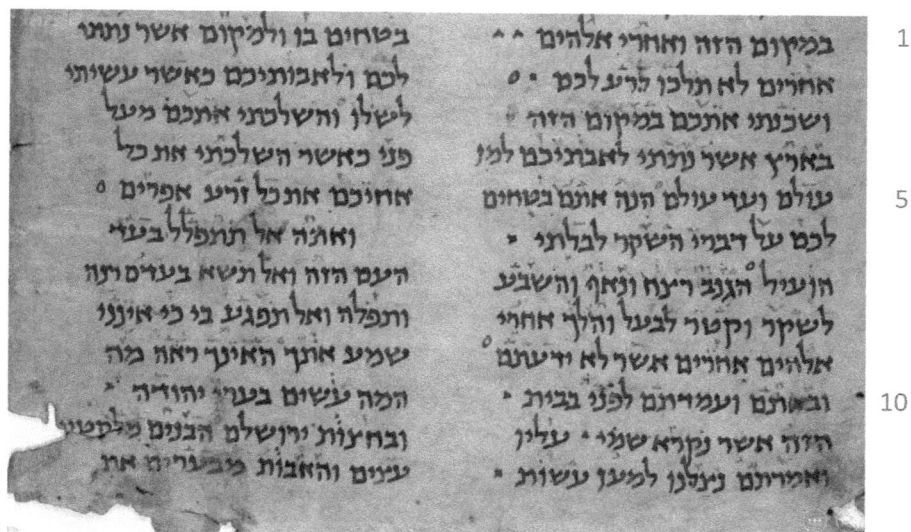

Figure 9.1: Ms. Cambridge T-S A39, 9 p. 1r; Jer. 7:6–10,14–18. With permission of the Syndics of Cambridge University Library.

Babylonian ones are unavailable on contemporary keyboards). אֶתְכֶם (right column, l. 3) versus והשבע אֶתְכֶם (7:7); והשבע (right, l. 7) versus וְהִשָּׁבֵעַ (7:9); נצלנו (right, l. 12) versus נִצַּלְנוּ (7:10).

The cantillation signs in the Babylonian system also differ from the Tiberian ones. The verse is divided into two parts by a sign called *sihfa*, equivalent to the Tiberian *etnahta*. In many cases the *sihfa* itself is not written, but only the preceding sign, *rimiya*, indicated by a "v" above the word, equivalent to the Tiberian *tipha*. For example על דברי השקר (right column, l. 6; Jer 7:8) – the sign *rimiya* appears above the word על, indicating that the word השקר should be chanted with a *sihfa* (i.e. *etnahta*). Many cantillation signs are indicated by letters, such as *zayin* for *zaqef* and signs in the form of *het*, *tav* and *tet*. Only the signs that indicate pauses are written, and not the auxiliary signs (conjunctive accents) as in the Tiberian system.

We will not elaborate here on the Babylonian punctuation and the Babylonian accentuation, because our main concern is the Babylonian masora. Let us suffice with a reference to several books dealing with the punctuation and cantillation of the Babylon tradition.

For further study

Shai Heijmans, "Babylonian Tradition", in: W.R. Garr and S.E. Fassberg (eds.), *A Handbook of Biblical Hebrew*, Indiana: Eisenbrauns 2016, Vol. I, pp. 133–145

Ronit Shoshani, *The Biblical Accentuation in the Babylonian Tradition, Compared to the Tiberian Tradition* (in press; Heb.)

How the Babylonian Masora is Written

In many manuscripts of Scripture with Babylonian vocalization there are no masoretic notes, as can be seen, for example, in the page from Jeremiah we examined above. The technique for writing the Masora in Babylonia was different from that in Tiberias: The Masora was not written in the margins of the text, but in a separate composition: the Babylonian Masora.

This technical difference dictated a number of additional differences: In compositions of the Babylonian Masora the beginnings of verses are cited, as a way of organizing the data. After the first word in a verse, the masoretic notes pertaining to that verse are given. These are followed by the citation of the next verse and its notes, etc.

The Babylonian Masora on the Torah has survived only partially. 45 pages or fragments of pages from the Geniza are extant, originating in 15 different manuscripts. These fragments enable us to reconstruct about one sixth of the composition, containing masoretic notes on various passages in the Torah. On the basis of these fragments we can evaluate the size of the entire composition, and determine that it was expansive, about three times longer than the Masora Magna in the Aleppo Codex or Ms. Leningrad.

The Babylonian Masora had a standard version. This may be discerned by a comparison of manuscripts in which the same sections appear. For example: On Gen. 10:15–25, identical passages survived in two manuscripts of the Babylonian masora. This fact is all the more remarkable in comparison to Tiberian manuscripts: Each one of them gives a different choice of Masoretic notes, phrased differently and presented differently.

And another interesting principle may be observed in the Babylonian Masora. In almost every case "the principle of the first verse" is implemented: Every masoretic note is given in the context of the first verse to which it applies. This technique also differs from the Tiberian Masora, in which the notes may be cited in the context of any verse to which they apply.

Here is an example of a passage from the Babylonian Masora (Figure 9.2), followed by an edited version of the text in which references have been added (Figure 9.3):

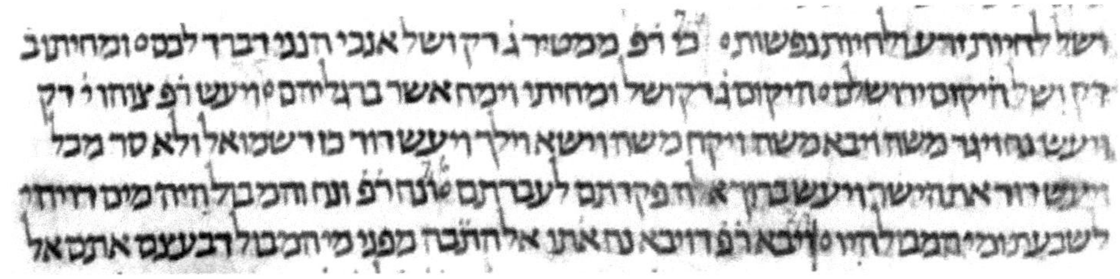

Figure 9.2: MS11, from Ofer, *The Babylonian Masora*, p. 316: Gen, 7:4–6.

בר' ז, ה	וִיעש ר"פ			
צ85	צָוָּהוּ י' דק			
בר' ז, ה	ויעש נח	בר' ז, ד	כי ר"פ
שמ' ד, כח	ויגד משה		ממטיר ג' דק ושל'
שמ' יט, ז	ויבא משה	בר' ז, ד	אנכי
במ' כ, ט	ויקח משה	שמ' ס, יח	הנני דברד
שמ"א יז, כ	וישא וילך	שמ' טז, ד	לכם °
שמ"ב ה, כה	ויעש דוד כן דשמואל		וּמָחִיתִי ב' דק ושל'
מל"א טו, ה	ולא סר מכל	מ273	היקום
דה"א יד, טז	ויעש דוד	בר' ז, ד	ירושלם °
מל"א טו, ה	את הישר[187]	מל"ב כא, יג	
יר' לו, ח	ויעש ברוך	ל בר' ז, כג; י545	הַיְקוּם ג' דק ושל'
° דה"א כד, יט	° אלה פקדתם לעבדתם	בר' ז, ד	ומחיתי
בר' ז, ו	ונח ר"פ	בר' ז, כג	וימח
בר' ז, ו	ונח	דב' יא, ו	אשר ברגליהם °
	וְהַמַּבּוּל הָיָה מַיִם		
בר' ז, ו	דויהי לשבעת		
	וּמֵי הַמַּבּוּל הָיוּ °		

Figure 9.3: The same passage, edited, *Ibid.*, p. 354.

The passage deals with three verses from the passage about Noah (Gen. 7). Identify the notes that refer to the beginning of the verses: ויעש ר"פ (v. 5), כי ר"פ (v. 4); and ונח ר"פ (v. 6). Before each note on the beginning of a verse (ר"פ = ראש פסוק) there is a circle, dividing the notes one from another.

The first masoretic note on verse 4 opens with the title ממטיר ג' דק ושל'. It is followed by a list of references to scriptural verses in which the word מַמְטִיר (= "will make it rain") occurs. The first is of course our verse, Gen. 7:4, following the principle of the first verse in the Babylonian Masora.

Two terms from the Babylonian Masora, which need to be explained, are used in this note: The term דק is an abbreviation of דְּקָרֵן, meaning "which is read", i.e. the word under discussion is read in this form a certain number of times (in this case ג' = 3). If the word דְּקָרֵן were omitted here, it would not change the meaning of the masoretic note. However this term has an additional use in the Babylonian Masora: it points out a unique occurrence, such as וַיִּתְגַּל דק (Gen. 9:20: "and he uncovered himself"). In this use it is parallel to the term ל' (לית דכוותיה = "none like it") in the Tiberian Masora.

The term שׁל׳ is an abbreviation of שָׁלֵם, indicating *plene* orthography, parallel to the expression מל׳ (= מלא) in the Tiberian Masora. Thus the Masora asserts that the word מַמְטִיר occurs three times in Scripture, and in every case it is written in *plene* form with the letter *yod* after the *tet*.

The next three masoretic notes are much like the first one. They assert that the word וּמָחִיתִי (= "I will blot out") occurs twice in Scripture, both times in *plene* form with the *yod*; the word הַיְקוּם (= "existence") occurs three times, also in *plene* form, with the letter *waw*; and the word צִוָּהוּ (= "commanded him") ten times. Every note has a corresponding number of references to verses. The last note is of the kind called "comparative Masora", citing two similar verses and indicating the difference between them. In the first verse it says: וְהַמַּבּוּל הָיָה מַיִם עַל הָאָרֶץ (= "when the Flood came, waters upon the earth") and in the other: וּמֵי הַמַּבּוּל הָיוּ עַל הָאָרֶץ (= "the waters of the Flood came upon the earth"). Incidentally, the Tiberian vocalization in the edited list of Babylonian masoretic notes is not found in the manuscript, of course. It was added by the editor to facilitate reading.

In terms of content, all of the masoretic notes we have seen suit the Tiberian version of the Scripture just as they do the Babylonian version, and they do not differ from the Tiberian notes except in the terminology they use. That is the case with regards to most of the notes in the Babylonian Masora. However, we shall see below that some of the notes in the Babylonian Masora reflect Babylonian language traditions and Babylonian versions of Scripture, and they do not correspond to the Tiberian version of Scripture.

Let us take another look at the way in which the Babylonian masoretic notes are arranged. The composition of the Babylonian Masora, which is independent of the text of Scriptures, allows the Masorete to present his masoretic material in a permanent order. The fact that each note appeared in the first verse in which it was mentioned meant that a great number of masoretic notes were concentrated in the first chapters of the Torah, and relatively few in the later books of the Torah and in the books of Prophets and Writings. The Tiberian Masora preferred writing the notes in the margins of the page, and every Masorete devoted the upper and lower margins of the page to the Masora Magna that pertained to verses on that page. In every copy of Scripture (i.e. in every codex), the pages are divided differently, and the space devoted to the Masora was limited and differed in extent. For that reason the Masorete had to decide which masoretic notes he would include on a given page, and was also free to determine the style and wording of the notes. In Tiberias the common practice was to write the books of Scriptures in three narrow columns, which facilitated inclusion of many notes of Masora Parva between the columns. In Babylonia on the other hand, Scripture was written without masoretic notes (consigned to a separate composition), and consequently they preferred to write the Biblical text in only one or two columns.

An interesting phenomenon in the Babylonian Masora is that of cross references. This is a likely phenomenon in a composition with a permanent text copied from one manuscript to another. On the other hand, most of the manuscripts of the Tiberian Masora – such as the Aleppo Codex and Ms. Leningrad – do not have cross references since each manuscript is unique and unlike the others.

Below are two examples of references taken from the Babylonian Masora:

בראשית ו, יד: "אֹתָהּ חס', ושלמי מסר בוירא בלק"

Gen. 6:14 – "אֹתָהּ defective, and for *plene* cf. 'And Balak saw'"

The note appears in reference to the first occurrence of the word אֹתָהּ (= "her") in Scripture (Gen. 6:14). It says that the word appears in defective spelling, and refers the reader to the Torah portion "Balak", where the same word first occurs in *plene* spelling (אוֹתָהּ), in the verse כי עתה גם אתכה הרגתי וְאוֹתָהּ הַחֱיֵיתִי (= "you are the one I should have killed, while sparing her", Num. 22:33). Consequently, the Babylonian Masora details there all of the verses in Scripture in which this word occurs in *plene* form.

ויקרא כז, ב: "נַפְשֹׁת חס', מ]סר ב]השכם"

Lev. 27:2 – "נַפְשֹׁת defective; cf. 'Early'"

This verse is one of two in which the word נַפְשֹׁת occurs in defective spelling. The Babylonian Masora refers the reader back to the verse ולקח הוא ושכנו הקרב אל ביתו בְּמִכְסַת נְפָשֹׁת (= "let him share one with a neighbor who dwells nearby, in proportion to the number of persons", Ex. 12:4), the first verse in which the word appears in defective form, where, of course, the masoretic note on this word appears.

A notable feature of this reference is that it refers to the weekly Torah portion as השכם (= "Early") rather than בא אל פרעה (= "Go to Pharaoh"), as we might expect. This note, and many others, reflect an ancient Babylonian tradition according to which the third portion in Exodus was called השכם בבקר (= "Early in the morning"), beginning with Ex. 9:13. The 23 verses describing the plague of hail do not belong to the previous portion (וארא = "I appeared", beginning with Ex. 6:2), as is the common custom, but to the following portion.

For further study

Yosef Ofer, *The Babylonian Masora of the Pentateuch, its Principles and Methods*, Jerusalem 2001: Ch. 2 (Basic Principles), Ch. 5 (References), Ch. 9 (The Portion *Hashkem*) (Heb.).

Ms. L^M – A Unique Manuscript

Ms. L^M is a unique codex of the Torah written in the early eleventh century. Its scribe and Masorete was Shmuel ben Yaaqov, the scribe and Masorete of the well-known

Leningrad Codex (Ms. **L**). The manuscript is Tiberian in terms of vocalization and writing style – three columns to a page, with marginal notes from the Masora Magna and Masora Parva. Nevertheless, the manuscript contains significant remnants of Babylonian masoretic material, making it an important source for knowledge of that Masora.

At the beginning of the twentieth century Ms. **L**ᴹ was held in the Karaite synagogue in Cairo and described by Richard Gottheil in 1905. Towards the end of the twentieth century the manuscript was transferred to the United States and purchased by Dr. Manfred Lehmann. Rabbi Mordechai Breuer examined the manuscript in the U.S., and in 1992 published a scientific edition of its Masora Magna.[2]

How can we tell that a certain masoretic note comes from Babylonia? The clearest case is when the note refers explicitly to a Babylonian source, and does not conform to the Tiberian version of the text of Scripture. For example:

בר' מא, א 1: חלם ג' לנהר' – ופרעה (כאן), ויזכר יוסף (בר' מב, ט), חלם
נבוכדנצר (דניאל ב, א).
וסור' חלֶם והנה חמש. ונרדע' חָלַם חמש.

Gen. 41:1a – "חלם 3 according to Nehardea – 'Pharoah dreamed' (ad loc.), 'Joseph remembered' (Gen. 42:9), 'Nebuchadnezzar had a dream'" (Dan. 2:1).

According to Sura חלֶם והנה (="dreams and behold"), חמש (="five"). According to Nehardea חָלַם (= "dreamed"), חמש (="five").

As in most cases, the first word in the masoretic note (חלם [= "dreamed", Gen. 41:1]), the subject under discussion, is given in the manuscript without vocalization – but its vocalization may be inferred from the continuation of the note. Following the initial word three verses are cited. The last two verses וַיִּזְכֹּר יוֹסֵף אֵת הַחֲלֹמוֹת אֲשֶׁר חָלַם לָהֶם (= "And Joseph remembered the dreams that he had *dreamed* about them", Gen. 42:9) and חָלַם נְבֻכַדְנֶצַּר חֲלֹמוֹת ("Nebuchadnezzar *had a dream*", Dan. 2:1) give the verb in past tense, from which we conclude that the reading in our verse (Gen. 41:1) should also be חָלַם (= "dreamed") and not חֲלֹם (= "dreams") as in the accepted text of the Torah. This version is attributed in the note to the Masora of נהר', i.e. the school of Nehardea. In the continuation of the note it states explicitly that the school of Sura, reads חֹלֵם in the present tense, as in the accepted masoretic version. The term חמש (= "five") which occurs twice in the note refers evidently to an additional disagreement about the punctuation between the schools of Sura and Nehardea elsewhere in the Torah (probably in Ex. 26:3).

---

2 Regretfully, the location of this important manuscript today is unclear, and a photocopy of it is unavailable.

Sura and Nehardea were towns in Babylonia (Iraq) where the central yeshivot of the Talmudic scholars were active. The Amora Rav founded the Yeshiva of Sura, and his counterpart Shmuel the Yeshiva of Nehardea. This masoretic note teaches that in the two towns there were also schools of Masoretes, who were in disagreement on some matters.

Returning to the masoretic note from Ms. L^M, it does not specify the Tiberian version, from which we may conclude that it is a Babylonian Masora, referring to the two schools that were active there. Such masoretic notes are extremely rare in Tiberian manuscripts, but there are a few such notes in this manuscript.

From a linguistic point of view, the Nehardea reading "Pharaoh dreamed" (in the past tense) is no less suitable to the language of Scripture than the reading "Pharaoh dreams". Cf. ויהי בחצי הלילה וה' הִכָּה כל בכור (= "In the middle of the night, the Lord struck down all the first-born" Ex. 12:29) or ויהי בעת ההיא וירבעם יָצָא מירושלים (= "During that time Jeroboam went out of Jerusalem", I Kings 11:29). After expressions of time that begin with the word ויהי, the past tense is usually used.

In many additional cases masoretic notes of Babylonian origin may be discerned, even if they are not ascribed to that origin explicitly. In order to understand the next example it should be noted that the word בָּר meaning "produce" occurs 13 times in Scripture, and in all cases but three it is vocalized with a *qamaṣ*. That is how it appears in the accepted version, following the Tiberian Masora. However, in the Babylonian manuscripts there is evidence of three verses in which the word is vocalized with a *patah*: ויצברו בר תחת יד פרעה (= "Let the *grain* be collected under Pharoah's authority", Gen. 41:35), לשבר בר בארץ ("to get *rations* in Egypt", Gen. 42:3), יהי פסת בר בארץ (= "Let abundant *grain* be in the land", Ps. 72:16). Of course we do not know with certainty the Babylonian version of all the books of Scripture. The evidence that has survived in manuscripts was studied and described in detail in a book by Israel Yeivin (*The Hebrew Language Tradition as reflected in the Babylonian Vocalization*, Jerusalem 1985 [Heb.]). However, there is not clear evidence for every verse. Nevertheless Yeivin says (p. 798), that there are some places in which the Babylonian version also vocalizes the word with a *qamaṣ*, such as the verse מנע בר יקבהו לאום (= "He who withholds *grain* earns the curses of the people", Prov. 11:26).

Against this background, here is a masoretic note from Ms. L^M on Gen. 42:25:

בר ו' וסימנהון ויצו יוסף (בר' מב, כה) ומלאו גרנות (יואל ב, כד) והשבית
דעמוס (עמ' ח, ה) לבשו כרים (תה' סה, יד) מנע בר (מש' יא, כו) אבוס (מש' יד, ד)

The import of the note may be described as follows:

בר [with a *qamaṣ*] 6 occurrences, Gen. 42:25, Joel 2:24, Amos 8:5, Ps. 65:14, Prov. 11:26, Prov. 14:4

In all six verses the word בר occurs with *qamaṣ*, according to the Tiberian version. However, it is clear that this Masora note does not conform to the Tiberian tradition, because it has ten such occurrences and not only six. However, the note does conform well to the Babylonian tradition, since it does not include the three verses in which we know that the Babylonian tradition vocalized the word with a *patah* rather than a *qamaṣ*.

The nature of this masoretic note is noticeable only if the data throughout Scripture is analyzed carefully. The Masorete of this ancient manuscript copied the masoretic note from a Babylonian source that he was using, and evidently did not realize that the note does not conform to the Tiberian version of Scripture. He clearly knew that the composition was Babylonian, and he took care to omit the Babylonian masoretic terminology (such as דק or של') or to exchange it for parallel terms used in the Tiberian Masora. However, in cases that required in-depth clarification, he did not always filter and revise the Babylonian material correctly. For that reason this manuscript is an important source for study of the Babylonian Masora. It is reasonable to presume that a great part – maybe even the majority – of masoretic notes in the manuscript were copied from the compilation of Babylonian Masora on the Torah. As we pointed out above, only one sixth of the Babylonian Masora has survived. Thus the indirect testimony of Ms. **L**^{M} complements the direct testimony of Babylonian manuscripts.

Here is another brief and "innocent" masoretic note from Ms. **L**^{M}, concealing an interesting grammatical and exegetical issue. In the Masora Magna on Ex. 5:1, it says:

ויפץ ב' וסימנהון העם בכל ארץ (שמ' ה, א) העם מעליו (שמ"א יג, ח)

The import of the note may be described as follows:

ויפץ 2 occurrences: Ex. 5:1 and I Sam. 13:8

Here are the two verses to which the Masora refers:

וַיָּפֶץ הָעָם בְּכָל אֶרֶץ מִצְרָיִם לְקֹשֵׁשׁ קַשׁ לַתֶּבֶן.

[= "Then the people scattered throughout the land of Egypt to gather stubble for straw" (Ex. 5:12).]

וייחל [וַיּוֹחֶל ק'] שִׁבְעַת יָמִים לַמּוֹעֵד אֲשֶׁר שְׁמוּאֵל וְלֹא בָא שְׁמוּאֵל הַגִּלְגָּל וַיָּפֶץ הָעָם מֵעָלָיו.

[= "He waited seven days, the time that Samuel [had set]. But when Samuel failed to come to Gilgal and the people began to scatter" (I Sam. 13:8).]

So far, so good. But a careful examination shows that the form וַיָּפֶץ occurs in the Tiberian version in an additional verse, not mentioned in the masoretic note:

וַיָּפֶץ ה' אֹתָם מִשָּׁם עַל פְּנֵי כָל הָאָרֶץ וַיַּחְדְּלוּ לִבְנֹת הָעִיר.

[="Thus the Lord scattered them from there over the face of the whole earth; and they stopped building the city" (Gen. 11:8).]

Why wasn't this verse cited in the masoretic note? How did it differ from the other two verses? In the previous two verses the people are described as scattering, and the verb

ויפץ is intransitive. But in the verse from Genesis God scattered the builders of the Tower of Babel, and the verb ויפץ is transitive in the *hif'il* conjugation. Judging from the masoretic note it appears that the reading in the two verses mentioned in the note was וַיָּפָץ (*wa-yafotz*) in *qal* conjugation! This may be compared with these pairs of verbs: וַיֵּשֶׁב (="dwelled", intransitive verb in *qal* conjugation) as opposed to וַיָּשֶׁב (="restored", intransitive verb in *hif'il* conjugation); וַיָּקָם as opposed to וַיָּקֶם; וַיָּמָת as opposed to וַיָּרֶם; וַיָּרֶם as opposed to וַיָּרֶם. And indeed there is evidence from a manuscript with Babylonian vocalization for the form ויפץ using a *holam* in the verse from Exodus. We should point out that in the linguistic tradition of Babylonia the *qamaṣ qatan* was not used, and its equivalent was either a *holam* or a *shuruq*.

The Influence of the Babylonian Masora on the Tiberian Masora

As we have seen, the Masora of Ms. L^M reflects Babyonian linguistic traditions and the few examples given here are only a small part of a broad phenomenon. However it should be stressed that the manuscript is Tiberian; the vocalization and cantillation signs are Tiberian, and the text of Scripture in the manuscript is Tiberian and not Babylonian. Nevertheless its masoretic notes do reflect extensive use of Babylonian masoretic notes.

This phenomenon raises the question of whether this was an exceptional and unique occurrence or part of a broader phenomenon of the influence of the Babylonian Masora on the Tiberian. It is important to emphasize that no other Tiberian manuscript approaches L^M in the extent of Babylonian influence on its Masora. However, there are many indications of a certain degree of Babylonian influence in many other manuscripts. In some cases the Masorete of a Tiberian manuscript mentions the Babylonian Masora explicitly. In other cases terminology of the Babylonian Masora appears in Tiberian manuscripts, and sometimes there are other indications of Babylonian influence on the style of a note or the way it was revised.

Here is an example of explicit mention of the Babylonian Masora in the Masora Magna of Ms. **S** (Jerusalem, National library, Heb. 24° 5702) on Deut. 34:12:

'הגדול ח' מל' בתו' וסימ'.'... המאור הגדול (בר' א, טז) מלי לנהרדעי חסי לסוראי, ונהרדעי מסירין ט' מל.

הגדול (="the great") – 8 occurrences in *plene* in the Torah, which are...

המאור הגדול (="the greater light", Gen. 1:16) *plene* in Nehardea, defective in Sura, and in Nehardea they list 9 occurrences in *plene*.

This masoretic note has three parts: The first part lists eight instances of the word הגדול (=" the great") in *plene* form according to the Tiberian Masora. In the second part it reports on the disagreement between schools of Masora in Babylonia as to how the word should be written in the verse את המאור הגדול לממשלת היום (="the greater light to dominate the day", Gen. 1:16). This verse is not listed among the eight verses which according to the Tiberian tradition were to be written *plene* form, and the school of Sura, concurred. The school of Nehardea, however, disagreed with this and asserted that nine verses should have been listed. That is the gist of the third part of the masoretic note.

Here is another note that resembles the Babylonian Masora in style, but comes from the most representative Tiberian manuscript – the Aleppo Codex. In a note on the word אֵיל in Ezekiel's prophecy regarding Pharaoh, King of Egypt: וָאֶתְּנֵהוּ בְּיַד אֵיל גּוֹיִם עָשׂוֹ יַעֲשֶׂה לּוֹ כְּרִשְׁעוֹ גֵּרַשְׁתִּהוּ [="I delivered it into the hands of the mightiest of nations, They treated it as befitted is wickedness. I banished it" (Ez. 31:11)], the Masora Parva of the Aleppo Codex reads:

ביד איל גוים של בטעותא

That is to say: The word איל in this verse refers to idolatry, foreign gods (in Aramaic: טָעֲוָתָא); of all the occurrences of the word איל / אל with that meaning, this is the only one in *plene* form. The masoretic term של (=*shlam*, i.e. full) is a Babylonian term, and the phrasing of the note also resembles the Babylonian Masora. If the note had been "translated" into Tiberian terminology and style it should have been phrased ל' מל' בעבודה זרה (="no other occurrence in *plene* meaning idolatry"), and such a note does appear in one of the Tiberian manuscripts (Ms. **L20** = SP NL Evr. II B 9).

Here is another note from the Aleppo Codex with Babylonian characteristics, a note of the Masora Magna on Jer. 24:8. This long note lists thirty verses that open with the words כי כה אמר ה' [="For thus said the Lord" – without the addition of the word אלקים or אלקי ישראל (="God" or "the God of Israel")] , and due to its length it is presented here with omissions:

כי כה אמר יי' כ"י - לא תראו (מל"ב ג, יז) אכל (מל"ב ד, מג) נירו לכם (יר' ד, ג)
שממה (יר' ד, כז) [...] כחזקת היד (יש' ח, יא) אשקוטה (יש' יח, ד) [...]

The title of the note says that this opening occurs כ"י (20 + 10) times, i.e. 30 [the Masorete refrained from using the letter *lamed* to indicate 30, because it was used in the Tiberian Masora to abbreviate the term לית (="no other occurrence")]. Following the title the note lists all thirty verses in order: two verses from Kings, eighteen verses from Jeremiah, nine verses from Isaiah and one from Amos.

What is peculiar here is the order of the books cited. Why do the verses from Jeremiah precede those from Isaiah? In Tiberian manuscripts, including the Aleppo Codex itself, the Book of Isaiah precedes the Book of Jeremiah. Placing Jeremiah before Isaiah conforms to the Babylonian Masora since that was the order accepted in Babylonia. This is the customary order in notes of the Babylonian Masora, and conforms to the order of the books in Babylonian manuscripts and to the Babylonian

Talmud in Tractate Baba Batra (14b). Thus it seems that the Masorete of the Aleppo Codex was using Babylonian masoretic material here. As an expert Masorete he checked carefully that the contents of the note conformed to the Tiberian version of the text, but he did not regard the order of the verses as important and did not rearrange them to follow the Tiberian order.

Evidences of Antiquity in the Babylonian Masora

In many cases, within the Masora and outside it, an ancient tradition discusses the total number of verses in Scripture. This tradition is reminiscent of a very long list of sages who transmitted the number of verses from one generation to the next:

> The tradition transmitted by Dosa b. Elazar son of R. Afsi who received it from Yehudah the Babylonian, who received it from Shimon his father and Shimon his father received it from R. Ada and R. Ada was at the time a great master of Scripture who received it from Rav Hamnuna who took it from Nehardea and R. Hamnuna and R. Ada both received it from Naqi, who was exiled from the land of Israel to Babylonia, whom Rufus exiled so that there would be no Torah in the land of Israel. They [count and] combined the [number of verses of] Torah and the Prophets and the Writings, twenty-four books without error, and made no mistake twenty-two thousand and seven hundred and forty seven verses, no less and no more (*Okhla we-Okhla*, Ms. Halle, end of the manuscript).

It seems that some of those mentioned here by name were Amoraim from Babylonia (such as Rav Yehuda and Rav Ada [bar Ahava]), and that we have here a very ancient tradition, according to which Masoretic activity in Babylonia began in the first generations of Amoraim. It should also be pointed out that the number of verses in the accepted text of Scripture is 23,203, nearly 500 more verses than the number given in this tradition (22,747). Evidently that number is based on a significantly different text of Scripture from the Masoretic version, which is like some features discovered in the Dead Sea Scrolls and the Septuagint.

Conclusion: The Relations between the Tiberian Masora and the Babylonian Masora

The beginning of the Babylonian Masora stems from a very ancient period. It seems that masoretic activity developed and flourished in Babylonia at an early stage, perhaps even earlier than the Tiberian Masora. The latter used Babylonian masoretic material in a variety of ways. Expert Masoretes revised material from that Masora and adapted it well to the Tiberian character of their own Masora. But there were Masoretes who did not take such care with every masoretic note, leaving traces of their use of Babylonian masoretic material.

For further study

Mordechai Breuer, *The Masorah Magna to the Pentateuch by Shemuel ben Ya'aqov (Ms. למ)*,
    New York 1992 (Heb.).
Yosef Ofer, *The Babylonian Masora of the Pentateuch its Principles and Methods*, Jerusalem 2001,
    Ch. 8 and Ch. 13 (Heb.).
Yosef Ofer, "Aharon ben Asher's Masorah in the Aleppo Codex", in: M. Bar-Asher (ed.), *Language
    Studies V–VI – Israel Yeivin Festschrift*, Jerusalem 1992, pp. 495–499 (Heb.).

The General Descriptive Method of the Babylonian Masora

The Babylonian Masora has a characteristic way of counting that differs from that of
the Tiberian Masora. Both Masora Schools strive to present the data with the greatest
brevity possible, and prefer to list the fewest examples from each book or section of
Scripture. However, The Babylonian method differs from the Tiberian, and is called
the general description. Here is an example:

מס11 בר' ו, ו: אֶל לִבּוֹ ד' דק - ויתעצב (שם) וירח ייי (בר' ח, כא) ונביי וכתיבי
בר מן ב' אתם זכר (יר' מד, כא) וישם דניאל (דנ' א, ח).

MS11[3] Gen. 6:6: אֶל לִבּוֹ (="to his heart") occurs 4 times – "And he was saddened" (Ibid.), "And
the Lord smelled" (Gen. 8:21) and [all] Prophets and Writings except for 2 occurrences "He
remembered them" (Jer. 44:21), "Daniel resolved" (Dan. 1:8).

The combination אל לבו appears twice in the Torah and seven times in the Prophets
and Writings. However the combination על לבו occurs twice in the Torah and twice in
the Prophets and Writings. This masoretic note lists the two occurrences of אל לבו in
the Torah and the two occurrences of על לבו in the Prophets and Writings.
    In table form:

	אֶל לִבּוֹ	עַל לִבּוֹ
Torah	2	2
Prophets and Writings	7	2

According to the method of the Tiberian Masora, we would expect to find two separate classifications of the two areas of reference: one classification for the Torah and

---

3 MS11 is the name given to a "manuscript" of the Babylonian Masora. Complete manuscripts of
that Masora have not survived, but various Geniza fragments containing pages from manuscripts
that included the composition have survived, and they were described and numbered by Y. Yeivin in
his book *The Hebrew Language Tradition as reflected in the Babylonian Vocalization*, Jerusalem 1985,
pp. 204–211.

another one for Prophets and Writing. However, the Babylonian Masora lists only **four**, which is the total number of אל לבו in all of Scripture: Two of the four are the two verses from the Torah, and the two others are two units: Prophets and Writings (except for the two exceptions cited). In this general description there is no use for the word דכותהון (=like them) which serves to link the two separate areas of reference, since the whole Bible is referred to as one big area.

Here is a masoretic note that is found in both a Babylonian source and a Tiberian source. There is no disagreement between the Masorot regarding the correct version of the Scriptural text they describe, and essentially there is no difference between their descriptive methods, which refer separately to the Torah and the Book of Jeremiah. The only difference is the way the data is presented. For the sake of brevity I did not cite the words referring to the verses and wrote instead only the number of verses and their area. This is the note from the Babylonian source:

מסו11 במ' ד, יט: כולה אוריתא. [1 משמואל]. ירמיה בר מן [1]. [2 מכתובים] - הלין יָמֻתוּ דחס' בע

MS11 Num. 4:19: all of the Torah. [1 verse from Samuel]. Jeremiah except for [1]. [2 verses from Writings] – These are all occurrences of ימתו with defective spelling.

This Masora describes the orthography of יָמֻתוּ-יָמוּתוּ (="they will die"), and it lists all occurrences in defective form, following the order of the books of Scripture: All of the Torah, one verse from Samuel, all of Jeremiah except for one verse and two verses from the Writings. This is a general description of the occurrences with defective spelling; this note does not include a general number.

Here is the parallel passage in the Tiberian Masora, taken from the Aleppo Codex on II Sam. 18:3:

יָמֻתוּ ג' חס'... וכל אוריתא וירמיהו **דכותהון** בר מן חד...

יָמֻתוּ 3 occurrences in defective spelling... and all of the Torah and Jeremiah like them except for one...

As opposed to the Babylonian note, the Tiberian note differentiates between the two areas of reference. In the first area the spelling is *plene* except for three verses, and in the second the spelling is defective except for one verse. In every area a number is given. The areas of reference are intertwined and connected by the term דכותהון (="like them").

Below is a table that presents the data:

	יָמֻתוּ [+שֶׁיָּמֻתוּ]	יָמוּתוּ
Torah	**9**	–
Samuel	1	**2**
Jeremiah	5	**1**
Ezekiel and the Twelve Minor Prophets	–	**3**
Writings	2	**6**

Here are additional examples of the general description from the Babylonian Masora. The numbers at the beginning of the note include verses and groups of verses defined in different ways:

1. MS11, Gen. 8:13: מִכְסֵה ט' באור' - [8] + וכל דגבי בי
   The word מִכְסֵה ("cover") occurs 9 times in the Torah: [8 verses] + in all occurrences in which the letter *bet* precedes this word.

2. MS11 Lev. 13:3: הוא י' בפרשתא - [8] + וכל "טמא" וכל "טהור" הוא
   The word הוא ("he") occurs 10 times in this weekly portion (*tazri'a*): [8 verses] + in all occurrences in which the word טמא ("impure") or the word טהור ("pure") precedes the word הוא.

3. MS11 Deut. 7:7: מְעַט י"א - [9] + וסיחפי וסוף פסוקי
   The word מְעַט ("few") occurs 11 times: [9 verses] + in all occurrences that are chanted with *sihfa* (parallal to the Tiberian accent *etnahta*) or *sof pasuq* ("the end of the verse").

4. MS11 Lev. 12:6 (and Ms L[M]): [1] + וכול נשיאים + [3] - עולה דקדים לחטאת ה' דק
   The word עוֹלָה ("burnt offering") precedes the word חטאת ("sin offering") 5 times: [3 verses] + all the chieftains' sacrifices (in Num. 7) + [1 verse]

5. Ms L[M] Gen. 3:13b (and MS3 there): ".בד ונחלת" עד "בגוים שם לך ויצא" ומן + [4] - עָשִׂית ה'
   The word עשית ("you [fem.] did") occurs 5 times: [4 verses] + from Ez. 16:14 to Ez. 22:16.

In these examples the general number includes a sub-group of forms from the group of words under discussion (1) or combinations that include the word under discussion (2), Babylonian cantillation marks with which the word is to be chanted (3), a group of verses dealing with one topic (4) or a scriptural passage defined by its beginning and end (5).

Conversion of the all-inclusive Description

The difference in methods of presenting the data of the Masora may lead the masoretes to process the masoretic notes and transfer them from one style to another. Such process may lead to strange phrasing. Below is one example of this phenomenon and the interested reader will be referred to additional studies of other examples.

The Masora Magna of Ms. **S** on Num. 28:27 discusses the *plene* and defective spelling of the word עוֹלָה (="burnt offering") throughout Scripture. The language of the Masora is presented in the right column of the table, and the data from Scripture in the other columns:[4]

---

4 The data and the masoretic note are based on: M. Breuer, *The Aleppo Codex and the Accepted Text of the Bible*, Jerusalem 1976, p. 219 (Heb.). The numbers in the table refer to the word עוֹלָה also when it appears with prefixes (e.g. הָעוֹלָה, לָעוֹלָה, וְעוֹלָה, וְהָעוֹלָה).

Plene - עוֹלָה	Defective - עֹלָה		Masoretic note from Ms. **S**
1	About 100	Torah	עולה דבכורים שלמ' באורית'
3	1	Joshua	יהושע כל חס' בר מן ג' מלי ...
1	5	Judges	שפטים כל חסי בר מן חד ...
3	6	Samuel	שמואל כל חסי' בר מן ג ...
0	9	Kings	מלכים כל חסי'
2	0	Isaiah	ישעיהו כל חסי בר מן ב'...
3	1	Jeremiah	ירמיהו כל מלי בר מן חד ...
10	5	Ezekiel	יחזקאל כל מלי בר מן ה' חסי'...
0	0	Minor Prophets	תרי עשרה כל חסי'
9	15	Chronicles	כתובייא כל חס' בר מן י"ב מלי ...
			[9 פסוקים מדברי הימים]
3	0	Psalms	וכל תלים
1	0	Job	ואיוב
1	0	Ezra	ועזרא
0	3	The rest of Writings	

In most cases the presentation is logical and conforms to the data in the table. But there are a few problems:

(1) **Joshua:** The Masora says that all occurrences are defective except for 3, but in fact there is only one defective occurrence.

(2) **Isaiah:** The Masora says that the entire book is defective except for 2 occurrences, but in fact there are no defective occurrences at all in Isaiah, and the only two occurrences of עֹלָה are the two *plene* ones listed.

(3) **The Minor Prophets:** According to the Masora all of the Minor Prophets are defective, but in fact there are no occurrences of the word in the Minor Prophets in either form.

It is important to point out that from a purely mathematical point of view there is no contradiction between the Masora and the data (e.g. in the book of Isaiah the entire book is really defective except for 2 occurrences, even though the number of the defective occurrences is zero!). But the way in which the Masora presents the data contradicts human logic, according to which the general rule given regarding a book should reflect the predominant reality in that book, and the exceptions should reflect the minority.

It is not difficult to guess how the peculiar phrasing of these notes came about: The Masorete revised the masoretic material before him, drawing conclusions from them, and rephrased them without checking directly each and every verse involved. For example, if he had a list of verses in the Prophets in which the word appeared in *plene* form, and the Masorete checked and found that there is no verse from the Minor Prophets in this list of *plene* occurrences, he could have concluded that all of the Minor Prophets are defective. This is a "mathematical" conclusion, but the Masorete did not check and did not realize that the word עֹלָה does not occur at all in the Minor Prophets.

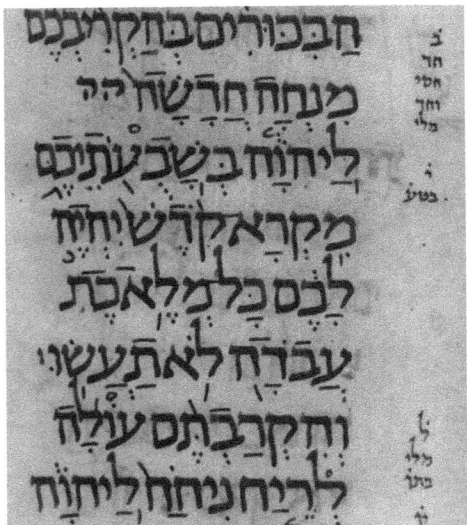

Figure 9.4: Notes of Masora Magna and Masora Parva of Ms. **S** (Ms. Jerusalem NL Heb. 24° 5702) on Num. 28:27.

However, in the light of our knowledge regarding the Babylonian Masora and how it worked, and its influences on the Tiberian Masora we can move one step further in understanding the process. First of all, the note itself carries evidence of its Babylonian source. It begins with the words 'עולה דבכורים שלמ' באורית (= "the word עולה in the passage on the day of the first fruits is [the only case of this word that is] שלמ' [*plene*] in the Torah"). The term שלמ' is a Babylonian usage for *plene*, and in fact the phrasing of the entire sentence conforms to Babylonian style. The Tiberian usage would be: ל' מל' בתורה [*leita male baTorah* = "no other *plene* case of this word in the Torah"], as in the note in the Masora Parva in Ms. **S** [see above, Figure 9.4], or ל' מל' וכל נביאים וכתובים דכוותהון [="this word is the only case of *plene*, and all the Prophets and Writings are the same"].

We may presume that the Babylonian Masora gave here an all-inclusive description of the *plene* occurrences in Scripture, and that it also included a general number, detailed with individual verses and books.[5] The Masora that gave this general description preferred for some reason to detail the two verses in Isaiah rather than listing the entire book in the number of *plene* occurrences, and also preferred to detail the

---

5 A remnant of the total number remained at the end of the masoretic note, which cites 12 *plene* forms in the books of Writings. This number includes nine verses and three books: Psalms, Job and Ezra.

three verses in Joshua rather than listing the entire book except for one exception. But the Masorete of Ms. **S** had a different style. He dismantled the comprehensive rule into individual rules, each of them referring to one of the books of Scripture.

For further study

Mordechai Breuer, *The Aleppo Codex and the Accepted Text of the Bible*, Jerusalem 1976, pp. 193–231 (Heb.).
Yosef Ofer, *The Babylonian Masora of the Pentateuch, its Principles and Methods*, Jerusalem 2001: Ch. 6 (Heb.).

10 The Masoretic Text and its Role in the History of the Text of Scripture

Introduction

Having discussed at length the Tiberian masoretic text, the question arises what is its place among texts of Scripture? And in more detail: What can be said regarding the versions of Scripture that **preceded** the work of the Masoretes? How different were books of Scripture from one another before the Masoretes established an accepted version? And another question: What happened in the Jewish world in the centuries **subsequent** to the work of the Masoretes? Did their version reach all of the Diaspora Jewish communities, or did conflicting versions continue to exist in some parts of the Diaspora?

These are broad questions, and a complete answer to them would include nearly the entire history of the biblical text. In order to answer them all, every testimony regarding the text and every ancient and later manuscript would need to be consulted. For the purpose of this study, we shall confine ourselves to an outline providing a general description of the rise of the Tiberian masoretic text and its spread to Jewish communities in the centuries after its formulation.

The "Masoretic Version" and its Role at the End of the Second Temple Period

The three most important ancient sources for the text of Scripture are the Dead Sea Scrolls, the Septuagint and the Samaritan version of the Torah. We shall give some examples of special scriptural versions that are reflected in each of these three sources. The Dead Sea Scrolls, which were discovered in the middle of the twentieth century, and published gradually since then, revealed a great variety of scriptural versions, some closer to the accepted masoretic text, and some different from it. Already in the 1950s the complete Isaiah scroll from the Dead Sea Scrolls (on display in the Shrine of the Book at the Israel Museum, Jerusalem) was published. In the same cave at Qumran in which it was discovered, another, partial scroll of Isaiah was discovered. Below is a comparison of the two versions of Isaiah 58:4–6 in the Dead Sea Scrolls with the masoretic text (See also Figure 10.1 and Figure 10.2):

Masoretic Text:	להשמיע במרום קולכם: הכזה יהיה צום אבחרהו יום ענות אדם נפשו
1st Isaiah Scroll:	לשמיע במרום קולכמה: הכזה יהיה צום אבחרהו יום ענות אדם נפשו
2nd Isaiah Scroll:	להשמיע במרום קולכם: הכזה יהיה צום אבחרהו ויום ענות אדם נפשו

Masoretic Text:	הלכף כאגמן ראשו ושק ואפר יציע הלזה תקרא צום ויום רצון ליהוה:
1st Isaiah Scroll:	הלכוף כאוגמן רואשו שק ואפר יציע הלזה תקראו צום יום רצון ליהוה:
2nd Isaiah Scroll:	הלכף כאגמן ראשך שק ואפר יציע הלזה תקרא צום יום רצון ליהוה:

https://doi.org/10.1515/9783110594560-010

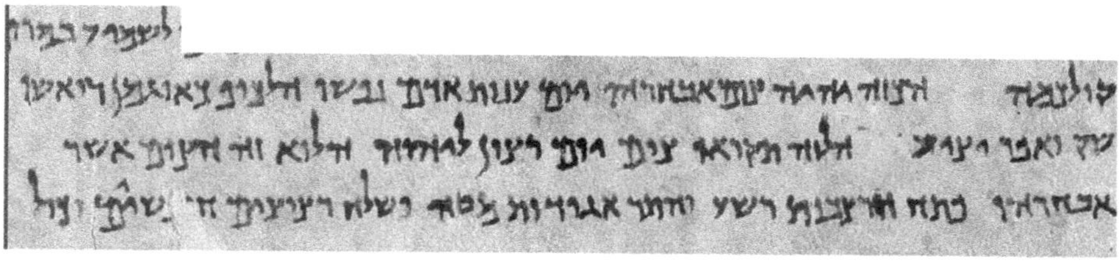

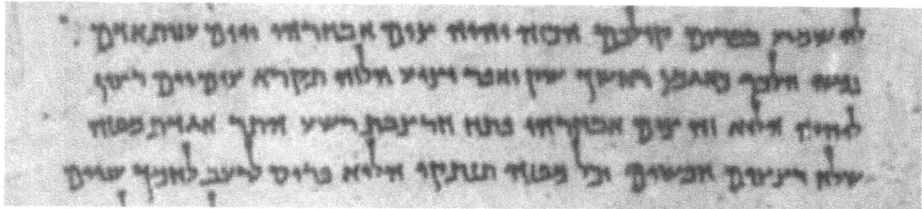

Figure 10.1: A passage from the complete Isaiah scroll – Is. 58.

Figure 10.2: A passage from the second Isaiah Scroll – Is. 58.

Masoretic Text: פתח חרצבות רשע התר אגדות מוטה ושלח רצוצים חפשים   הלוא זה צום אבחרהו

1st Isaiah Scroll: הלוא זה **הצום אשר** אבחרהו פתח חרצבות רשע **והתר אגדות** מטה ושלח רצוצים

חפשיים

2nd Isaiah Scroll: הלוא זה צום אבחרהו   פתח חרצבת רשע התר **אגד מטה שלח רצים** חפשים

In the table each line is presented three times: (1) according to the masoretic text; (2) according to the complete Isaiah scroll; (3) according to the other fragmentary Isaiah scroll from the same cave. The passage contains 36 words, and the differences in the two scrolls from the masoretic text are indicated in bold letters. Comparing the text of the first Isaiah scroll to that of the masoretic text, we find no less than 14 differences of various kinds: special language forms (קולכמה instead of קולכם [= "your voice"], לשמיע instead of להשמיע [="make heard"]; כאוגמן instead of כאגמן ["bulrush"]); changes of person (תקראו instead of תקרא ["call", plural instead of singular]); adding or omitting the conjunctive *waw* (שק [="sack"], יום [="day"], והתר [="untie"]); adding a definiteness *he* and a relative pronoun (הצום אשר אבחרהו [="the fast **that** I desire"]); *plene* spelling (הלכוף instead of הלכף [="bowing"], אגודות instead of אגדות [="cords"]); defective spelling (מטה instead of מוטה ["yoke"]); and exceptionally *plene* spelling (רואשו instead of ראשו [="his head"]).

The version of the second Isaiah scroll is closer to that of the masoretic text, and in this sample there are only nine differences between the two. Although the two scrolls were discovered in the same cave, they have no less than 15 differences in this sample, from which we may deduce that at the time these scrolls were written, about 2000 years ago, there was no uniform text of Scripture as there is today.

Before the discovery of the Dead Sea Scrolls, the most ancient and important witnesses for the text of the Bible were the Septuagint and the Samaritan Pentateuch. Scholars studied the Septuagint methodically, trying to reconstruct the Hebrew version of the Scripture that was used by the translators to Greek. It seems that that version was very different from the masoretic text: in some cases the Greek translation reflects the absence or omission of sentences, verses and even entire passages, or a difference in the order of the passages. In other places the translation reflects changes of a word or two, and researchers have tried to reconstruct the Hebrew words reflected in the Greek translation. When the Dead Sea Scrolls were discovered, some passages in their Hebrew version conformed to the text reflected in the Septuagint, as reconstructed by scholars.

For example, in the story of the birth of Samuel and his consecration the masoretic text reads: ותעלהו עמה כאשר גמלתו בפרים שלשה... וישחטו את הפר (="she took him up with her along **with three bulls** ...and they slaughtered the bull", I Sam. 1:24–25). The Septuagint reflects the reading בפר משולש ("with a three-year-old bull"), which better fits the continuation, "and they slaughtered the bull". In one of the fragments from the Dead Sea Scrolls such a reading was indeed found,[1] from which two conclusions may be made immediately: First of all, the reconstruction suggested on the basis of the Greek translation is correct. Secondly, this variant was not the work of the translator, but reflects an ancient Hebrew version of Scripture, which was in use in the Land of Israel towards the end of the Second Temple period. That, of course, does not deny the existence of a version such as that of the Masora, "three bulls", in other copies of Scripture. The question of which version is the original remains open.

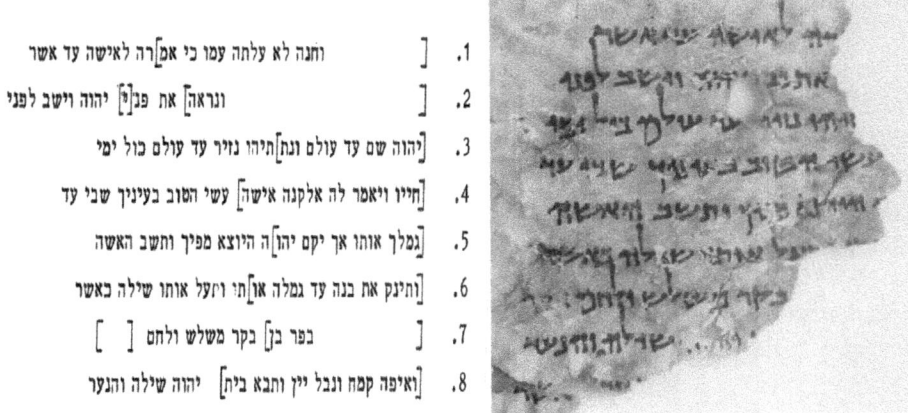

] .1 וחנה לא עלתה עמו כי אמ[ר]ה לאישה עד אשר

] .2 ונראה[את פנ[י] יהוה וישב לפני

] .3 [יהוה שם עד עולם ונת[תיהו נזיר עד עולם כול ימי

] .4 [חייו ויאמר לה אלקנה אישה] עשי הטוב בעיניך שבי עד

] .5 [גמלך אותו אך יקם יהו]ה היוצא מפיך ותשב האשה

] .6 [ותינק את בנה עד גמלה או[תי] ותעל אותו שילה כאשר

] [.7 [   ] בפר בן[בקר משלש ולחם

] .8 [ואיפה קמח ונבל יין ותבא בית] יהוה שילה והנער

Figure 10.3: Photograph and reconstructed transcription from a fragment of Samuel from Qumran, 4QSamᵃ, supporting the reading בפר משלש (="a three-year-old bull"). The reconstruction was made by Emanuel Tov.

---

1 The fragment from Samuel (4QSamᵃ), found in Cave 4 of Qumran, reads [בפר בן] בקר משלש ולחם (= "a three-year-old bull and bread"). Cf. F. M. Cross, BASOR 132 (1953), pp. 15–26. See also Figure 10.3.

The most notable feature of the Samaritan Pentateuch is "duplication of passages". For example, in Deuteronomy, Moses says "I cannot bear the burden of you by myself" (1:9) after which the appointment of judges is described. However, in Exodus 18 we find that Jethro's advice led to the appointment of chiefs of thousands and hundreds to judge the people. This difficulty is resolved in the Samaritan Pentateuch by the insertion in Exodus of verses identical to those in Deuteronomy regarding the appointment of judges: "וישמע משה לקול חתנו, ויעש כל אשר אמר. ויאמר משה אל העם לא אוכל אנכי לבדי שאת אתכם" וכו' (="Moses heeded his father-in-law and did just as he had said. And Moses said to the people: I cannot bear the burden of you by myself" etc., amalgamation of Ex. 18:24 and Deut. 1:9). See Figure 10.4. This phenomenon occurs dozens of times in the Torah, and its harmonizing intention is apparent: adding a command before its execution or an execution of a command after its giving, complementary completion of parallel stories and the like.

Figure 10.4: Exodus 18: the masoretic text (on the right) compared to the Samaritan version (on the left). The photograph is taken from the edition by Abraham and Razon Zedaka, Tel Aviv 1963.

A similar phenomenon is found in the Dead Sea Scrolls as well. These texts may be called "pre-Samaritan" or "proto-Samaritan", but they have no direct connection to the Samaritans. Evidently the tendency for harmonization existed among Jewish groups during the Second Temple period, and the Samaritans adopted Scriptural texts of this kind.

In conclusion: The textual reality at the end of the Second Temple period was highly varied. It included different kinds of texts. They belonged to different "types of versions": Some were closer to the "masoretic type", some to the "Septuagint type" and some similar to the harmonizing "Samaritan type". In terms of orthography they also differed from each other: Some of the scrolls reflect the extremely "*plene*" Qumran spelling, and others have spelling closer to that of the Masora.

In an article from 2016, Emanuel Tov looks at the various branches of the Torah that are reflected in all the textual witnesses, including the findings of the Judean Desert. He points to a special status of the 'Masoretic type' within the entire range of texts and testimonies. According to him, the Masoretic type is an independent textual branch, which differs textually from the second branch, that of the Septuagint, the Samaritan version, and the 'rewritten' Torah texts found in Qumran. The textual branch of the Masora is less exposed to processes of unification and harmonization, and is characterized by greater internal uniformity.

In light of these findings, the question arises: When and how did the Masoretic text merit exclusivity? What caused the Masoretic text to be adopted throughout the Jewish world, rejecting the other versions until they disappeared? We shall try to answer this question below.

For further study

E. Tov, "The Development of the Text of the Torah in Two Major Text Blocks", *Textus* 26 (2016), pp. 1–27.

The dominance of the Masoretic text after the destruction

An examination of the biblical scrolls from the Judean Desert led to an interesting finding: the scrolls found outside Qumran – in Masada, Naḥal Murba'at, Naḥal Ḥever, Naḥal Arugot and En Gedi – belong to the Masoretic type. These are generally findings from the years following the destruction of the Second Temple (70 CE).

Thus, for example, a burnt scroll of the Torah was discovered in En Gedi in the 1970s, and due to its condition it could not be opened or read. In 2015, a computerized scan of the scroll was performed, which enabled the reading of parts of the first two columns of Leviticus. According to the tests, the scroll was written in the second or third century CE. It turned out that the spelling and the *parashiyot* in this passage are identical to that of the Masoretic text (see Figure 10.5).

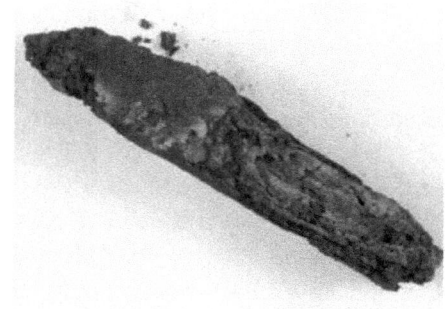

1	¹ויק[רא אל משה וי]דבר יהוה אליו מא[הל]הל
2	מוע[ד לאמר ²ד]בר אל בני ישראל ואמ[רת]
3	אלה[ם אדם] כי יקריב מכם קרבן ליהוה [מן]
4	הבהמה מן הבקר [ו]מן הצאן תקריבו את
5	קרבנכם ³אם עלה קרבנו מן הבקר זכר
6	תמים יקריבנו אל פתח אהל מועד יקריב
7	אתו לרצנו לפני יהוה ⁴וסמך ידו על ראש
8	הע[ל]ה ונרצה לו לכפר [עליו ⁵ושח]ט את בן

Figure 10.5: The burnt scroll from En Gedi (Courtesy of the Leon Levy Dead Sea Scrolls Digital Library, IAA, photo taken by Shai Halevi) and the text of its first lines (by M. Segal).

For further study

Z. Talshir, "Biblical Texts from the Judaean Desert", *The Qumran Scrolls and their World*, Jerusalem 2009, pp. 113–114 (Heb.)

M. Segal et al., "An Early Leviticus Scroll from En-Gedi: Preliminary Publication", *Textus* 26 (2016), pp. 29–42.

The Silent Period (From the Third Century to the Eighth)

The Dead Sea Scrolls include nearly 200 biblical scrolls (most of them fragmentary) that contain sections from every book of Scripture (except Esther).[2] Many additional scrolls quote verses from biblical books. The earliest scrolls were written in the third century B.C.E. and the latest in the second century C.E.[3]

The discovery of the scrolls created an anomalous situation: The earliest dated manuscripts of Scripture are from the tenth century. Among the Geniza fragments there are evidently Scriptural passage from the ninth century. Thus a gap of about 600 years exists in the documentation of the text of Scripture: There is almost no evidence from the third century to the eighth.

---

2 Emanuel Tov (*Textual Criticism of the Hebrew Bible*, 3rd ed., rev. and expanded, Minneapolis, MN: 2012, p. 95) gives accurate numbers: the remains of 210–212 biblical scrolls were found in Qumran, including 224–226 copies biblical books (since several scrolls contain the remains of more than one book). However, in footnote 157, Tov says that establishing a clear and absolute number is not easy, for several reasons: (a) Sometimes it is not clear if separate fragments belong to one scroll; (b) sometimes it is difficult to determine whether a particular manuscript represents the Bible itself or any processing of it; (c) The boundaries of the biblical corpus in the eyes of the people of Qumran are unclear.

3 E. Tov, *Textual Criticism*, pp. 98–99.

In 2004 the existence of an ancient fragment of a Torah scroll, known as the "Ashkar-Gilson Manuscript" was made known. It presents some columns from the book of Exodus (13:19–16:1) and contains the oldest documentation of "The Song at the Sea" in Exodus in the masoretic version and format. It was dated as stemming from the seventh or eighth century. Dr. Mordechai Mishor and Dr. Edna Engel identified this manuscript as the continuation of the "London Manuscript" in the Stephan Leventhal Collection, New York, which also contains a passage from Exodus (9:18–13:2); both were once part of the same Torah scroll. Both manuscripts were exhibited at the Israel Museum, Jerusalem in 2010. The version of this scroll is very close to the Masoretic text.

From this finding, as well as from the Leviticus Torah Scroll from En Gedi described above, it can be seen that the Masoretic text, as far as the letters are concerned, was already fixed in a relatively early period. However, of course, these few findings cannot provide a comprehensive picture of the distribution of all the biblical manuscripts during the "period of silence".

As for the period from the ninth century onwards, this is the period of Masoretic manuscripts, and it is rich in findings. Manuscripts from the Masoretic period are much more alike. Most of the differences are between *plene* and defective spelling. Differences in morphology are uncommon, and cases of addition or omission of words are rare. However these differences are very slight in comparison to the variety found in the first centuries C.E. We may conclude that all the manuscripts from the ninth century on belong to the "masoretic type".

Let us recall that biblical manuscripts from the third to the eighth century are very rare, but it seems that already during this period, manuscripts of the 'Masoretic type' were used primarily and perhaps exclusively.

For further study

P. Sanders, "The Ashkar-Gilson Manuscript: Remnant of a Proto-Masoretic Model Scroll of the Torah", *Journal of Hebrew Scriptures* 14, article 7 (2014, 26 pp.)

A Model to Explain the Processes of the Masora

Prof. Menachem Cohen proposed a model that describes the mutual relations in the course of generations between the accepted masoretic text and the other versions. We shall present his ideas in brief.

We find a variety of versions in the Dead Sea Scrolls. All three types of text that are known from different witnesses – the "masoretic type", the "Septuagint type" and the "Samaratin type" (for the Torah) – are represented in the scrolls, and there may even be additional types and sub-types. But already in the first century C.E. there started to be a rejection of the texts adopted by sectarian groups and the acceptance of the "masoretic type" alone. The types rejected carried clear signs of their identity, and thus it is relatively easy to identify them. A fragment in which Mount Gerizim is mentioned in the Ten Commandments is clearly Samaritan – and disqualified. If in Numbers we find a citation of the description of Moses' spies identical to that in Deuteronomy – it is also disqualified. And so forth. This process of rejection is reflected in the scrolls found outside Qumran and also in the testimonies that stem from some Bible translations and from Talmudic literature.

At a later stage the sages acted to unify the text of Scripture **in terms of its letters**. In the Mishna and the *Baraithot* we hear of this ideal – that every single letter in Scripture must be written with precision, "If you omit one letter or add one letter, you are found destroying the entire world" (*Baraitha* in Babylonian Talmud, Eruvin 13a). But the practical solution for the lack of uniformity was found only centuries later, in the period of the Masoretes, who established the masoretic text and protected it with thousands of masoretic notes. At that time they had to decide regarding hundreds of places in Scripture, about which there were disagreements within the masoretic type itself. These are orthographical differences, changes of prefixes, different grammatical forms and the like. The results of this enterprise are found in the accurate manuscripts of the Masora from the tenth century, and above all in the Aleppo Codex. Complete manuscripts (or nearly complete manuscripts) that precede the tenth century have not survived, and consequently it is difficult to determine exactly when the "masoretic text" was first created and when the Masoretes started their intensive efforts of writing masoretic notes to preserve that text. Nevertheless it is clear that the masoretic notes reflected in the Aleppo Codex and related manuscripts were the product of a continuous development of decades and centuries. So we can assume that the intensive creation of the Masora Comments began roughly in the eighth century.

For further study

Menachem Cohen, "Some basic features of the consonantal text in medieval manuscripts of the Hebrew Bible", *Studies in Bible and Exegesis* [I], Ramat Gan 1980, pp. 123–182 (in Hebrew).

Evidence on the Text of Scripture in the Middle Ages: Manuscripts and Citations of Verses

What happened in the period following the Masoretes? An examination of the available data regarding the text of Scripture in the Middle Ages reveals a variety of different versions in terms of spelling, vocalization and cantillation. There are cases of more significant differences, some of which have an impact on the meaning of the text.

Two kinds of sources testify to the versions of Scripture that were extant in the Middle Ages. The first is direct testimony: medieval codices of Scripture that have survived until today. The second is indirect testimony: the citation of verses quoted in the writings of medieval exegetes. We shall discuss first the citations and then the manuscripts.

It should be pointed out that we are discussing writings that were written one or two hundred years after the period of the Tiberian Masoretes. For example, Aharon ben Asher, the Masorete of the Aleppo Codex, was active in the early tenth century, and he is considered one of the latest Masoretes, who framed the Tiberian Masora in detail. Rashi, the famous exegete of Scripture, lived in northern France between 1040 and 1105; R. Abraham Ibn Ezra, was born in Spain in 1089 and wandered in Europe until 1164; R. Hizqiya ben Manoah, author of the commentary called *Hizquni* – was active in Provence (southern France) in the thirteenth century.

We shall discuss here two examples in which the writings of commentators reflect a text that differs from the Masoretic text. The first example is the passage on the Tabernacle. In the description of the Ark and the cherubim the text says: ונועדתי לך שם, ודברתי אתך מעל הכפרת, מבין שני הכרבים אשר על ארון העדת, את כל אשר אצוה אותך אל בני ישראל (="There I will meet with you, and I will impart to you – from above the cover, from between the two cherubim that are on top of the Ark of the Pact – all that I will command you concerning the Israelite people", Ex. 25:22).

Rashi comments ad. loc:

> ואת כל אשר אצוה אותך אל בני ישראל "**and** all that I will command you concerning the Israelite people" – The *waw* is superfluous, the likes of which there are many in Scripture. And this is how to interpret it: **And all that I will impart to you**, is all that I will command you concerning the Israelite people.

Rashi addresses a problem and suggests two solutions. The problem is the superfluous *waw* on the word ואת, that comes between the verb ודברתי ("and I will impart to you") and its direct object – "and all that I will command you".

According to Rashi's first solution, the *waw* should be ignored, and the verse should be interpreted as if it were not there. There are additional examples of such a phenomenon in Scripture. Rashi first noted this principle in his commentary on Gen. 36:24: *"The sons of Zibeon were these: **and** Aiah and Anah – a superfluous waw. And there are many such instances in Scripture: the sanctuary be surrendered and the [heavenly] host be trampled [Dan. 8:13 – the *waw* between תת and וקדש superfluous]; horse and chariot lay stunned [Ps. 76:7 – superfluous waw in the word ורכב]").*[4]

Rashi's second solution is to explain the letter *waw*. He suggests a different understanding of the syntax of the entire verse. It should not be understood as a simple

---

4 ואלה בני צבעון ואיה ואנה ועבה - וי"ו יתירה. והוא כמו 'איה ועבה'. והרבה יש במקרא: תת וקדש וצבא מרמס (דנ' ח, יג) נרדם ורכב וסוס (תה' עו, ז)

sentence, but one comprising two parts, linked by the *waw* in the word ואת. The verb ודברתי in the first part has no object; and the second part is an incomplete sentence: "and [what I will impart to you] is all that I will command you".

At any rate, the problem and both solutions are based on a version of Scripture that differs from the accepted version. The text before us today reads את כל אשר אצוה without the problematic *waw*, and thus no solution is needed!

A study of Ibn Ezra's longer commentary reveals that he also had before him the version ואת:

"And the reason for the *waw* in the expression ואת כל אשר אצוה is that: The word ודברתי is used twice, as if were written *and I will impart to you* from above the cover, from between the two cherubim, but without mentioning what was said, and the meaning is that I shall speak to you to make known my secret and answer your question, *and I will impart to you* all that I will command you concerning the Israelite people."[5]

The solution that Ibn Ezra suggests is a syntactical solution similar to Rashi's second proposal. He also sees here a compound sentence in which the two parts are joined by the letter *waw*. However, according to Rashi the second sentence serves to explain the first, but according to Ibn Ezra the second adds to it: the speaking in the first sentence deals with different matters that are not mentioned explicitly in the written text (such as "to make known my secret and answer your question"); the speaking in the second sentence concerns a different subject (the command to Israel).

Hizquni also interpreted the phrase ואת כל אשר אצוה much like Ibn Ezra. His commentary on the verse may stem from Ibn Ezra's, but at any rate he must have had a text that read ואת, since otherwise he would not have quoted Ibn Ezra without any comment on the text of Scripture.

As we said above, Rashi, Ibn Ezra and Hizquni all lived in different periods and were active in different places in Europe. Consequently, we may conclude from the commentaries of these three exegetes on this verse that in the Middle Ages the text ואת כל אשר אצוה was widespread in Europe, in different countries and periods.

Additional confirmation of this phenomenon may be found in the apparatus of textual variants in the Kennicott Bible from the eighteenth century (about which see below). The occurrence of the variant ואת כל אשר אצוה is documented there in 14 manuscripts (see Figure 10.6).

A second example may be detected in Rashi's commentary on the "Covenant between the Pieces". On the verse ידע תדע כי גר יהיה זרעך בארץ לא להם (="Know well that your offspring shall be strangers in a land not theirs", Gen. 15:13), Rashi says:

---

5 "וטעם וי"ו ואת כל אשר אצוה ככה הוא, מלת ודברתי משרת בעבור אחרת, כאילו כתוב ודברתי אתך מעל הכפרת מבין שני הכרובים, ולא הזכיר הדבר המדובר, והטעם שאדבר אתך להודיע סודי ולהשיב על שאלתך, ודברתי את כל אשר אצוה אותך אל בני ישראל".

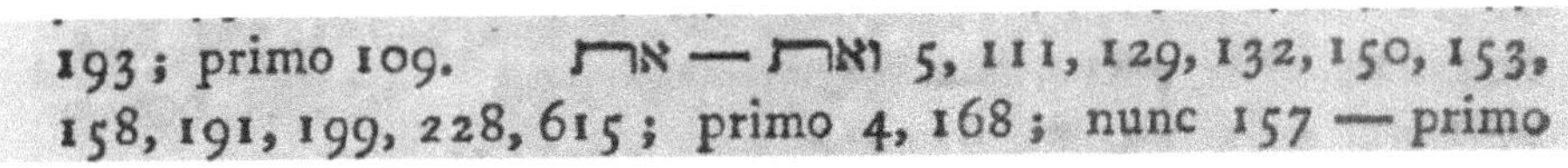
193; primo 109. ואת — את 5, 111, 129, 132, 150, 153, 158, 191, 199, 228, 615; primo 4, 168; nunc 157 — primo

Figure 10.6: A section from the textual variants in the Kennicott Bible (Ex. 25:22).

> "In a land not theirs" – it does not say "in the land of Egypt", but "not theirs". Since the birth of Isaac: "Abraham sojourned" [Gen. 21:34], and Isaac "Isaac sojourned in Gerar" [cf. Gen. 26:6], "Jacob sojourned in the land of Ham" [Ps. 105:23], "we have come to sojourn in this land" [Gen. 47:4].[6]

Rashi addresses the well-known problem of 400 years of Diaspora that were decreed in the "Covenant between the Pieces". In his opinion the counting begins during Abraham's lifetime. The decree "your offspring will be strangers" begins to take effect with the birth of Isaac, and he cites a series of verses proving that in the days of the Patriarchs there was a decree of sojourning, that is, the Patriarchs did not settle in the land, but wandered from place to place, as expressed in the verb גור (=sojourn), attributed to all the Patriarchs.

However, the verse concerning Isaac is problematic in Rashi's version, and both manuscripts and printed editions present his words differently: The verse ויגר יצחק בגרר does not appear in Scripture at all! Gen. 26:3 says וישב יצחק בגרר (="Isaac stayed in Gerar") – and clearly that text does not fit Rashi's interpretation here, since it does not demonstrate sojourning and wandering on the part of Isaac! The reading in the first printing of Rashi, ויגר בגרר (="and he sojourned in Gerar") does appear in Scripture (Gen. 20:1), but it speaks of Abraham not Isaac! Some versions of Rashi's commentary read גור בארץ הזאת (="sojourn in this land", Gen. 26:3), which is the most appropriate to prove Rashi's point. However, it also poses a problem: it is not a description of what Isaac did, but of what he was commanded to do.

This variety of versions is testimony to a problem that students and copyists encountered, and which each tried to solve in his own way. The original text of Rashi *ad loc.* was ויגר יצחק בגרר, as is found in the most reliable manuscripts of Rashi's commentary, and also from the logical consideration of *lectio difficilior*: the difficulty inherent in this version can explain the variety of versions of Rashi's commentary here; the problem was sensed, and different attempts were made to resolve it.

How can the reading ויגר יצחק בגרר be explained? It is difficult to determine its source. Maybe Rashi was citing from memory and exchanged the two verses concerning a stay in Gerar, ויגר בגרר in the case of Abraham and וישב יצחק בגרר regarding Isaac. It is also possible that ויגר יצחק בגרר was the reading he had before him for Gen. 26:3. It is difficult to determine unequivocally which opinion is correct, but the fact that we have not found such a reading in other commentaries or in the textual

---

6 בארץ לא להם - לא נאמר "בארץ מצרים" אלא "לא להם". משנולד יצחק: "ויגר אברהם" (בר' כא, לד), ויצחק "ויגר יצחק בגרר" (ראה בר' כו, ו) "ויעקב גר בארץ חם" (תה' קה, כג) "לגור בארץ באנו" (בר' מז, ד).

variations in Kenicott's book – leads us to conclude cautiously that we have here an erroneous citation from memory.

After these two examples, a much more general perspective is called for: There are many hundreds of cases in which we find citations of verses by Biblical exegetes that do not match the Masoretic text. The phenomenon is widespread in most manuscripts, and in the case of every exegete. However, not all of the cases are the same. Most of them **do not** reflect a different version that the exegete had in his possession. There are many other explanations for the inaccurate citation phenomenon: With regards to orthographic matters, and mainly the use of *plene* spelling, the exegete – or the scribe who copied his commentary – did not insist on following the orthography of the Masora, intentionally in order to facilitate the reading, as is done by some writers today as well.

In other cases, the exegete cited from memory and did not sense the inaccuracy of his quotation. In most cases the difference between the version quoted and the Masoretic text has no impact on the exegete's intent. In many cases it is not easy to distinguish between a citation from memory or use of a version of Scripture that was regarded to be authoritative. If we can find additional witnesses to a certain reading – in other quotes by this exegete or others or in manuscripts – it will reinforce the opinion that the exegete indeed knew a different version of the verse, and was not quoting erroneously.

Of particular importance are the cases in which the commentary is based on an exceptional reading, and could not be suggested on the basis of the Masoretic text. Here the fault should not be attributed to the copyist since the version is derived from the commentary itself. In some cases – such as Rashi's comment on ואת כל אשר אצוה – it is apparent that he found this reading in the books he used, and was not quoting from memory.[7]

For further study

J. S. Penkower, "The Text of the Bible Used by Rashi as Reflected in His Biblical Commentaries" in: A. Grossman and S. Japhet (eds.), *Rashi: The Man and His Work*, Jerusalem 2009, I, pp. 99–122 (in Hebrew).

Shnayer Z. Leiman, ואת כל אשר אצוה אותך: *Critical analysis of Rashi's commentary on Exodus, chapter 25, verse 22*, Kew Gardens Hills, N.Y. 2003

---

7 It is interesting to see how the *Miqraot Gedolot Haketer* (editor: M. Cohen, Bar Ilan University) treats "inaccurate citations" of Scriptural verses by medieval commentators. Unlike many earlier editions the citation of verses in the commentaries is verbatim and not corrected according to the Masoretic text. The reader's attention to the difference is attested by a parenthetical note. For example, in Rashi Gen. 41:55 - ואשר (בנוסחנו: אשר) יאמר לכם תעשו – the absence of the *waw* at the beginning of the word ואשר is pointed out in parenthesis; Gen. 41:19 – דלות – weakness, as in (כבה דל) מדוע אתה דל ככה (בנוסחנו: ככה דל) (=Why are you dejected so [in our version: so dejected]) regarding Amnon (II Sam. 13:4).

Direct Examination of Medieval Manuscripts

The primary source for data on the variety of texts of Scripture in the Middle Ages is direct examination of biblical manuscripts that have survived to this day. The findings are very rich, and they include many hundreds of complete manuscripts and fragmentary ones, written in different times and in different places throughout the Jewish world. This enormous corpus requires analysis regarding a number of aspects: script, orthography, vocalization, cantillation signs, stress marks, masoretic notes and more.

There are two problems that arise here: The first is a problem of abundance: The great number of manuscripts makes it difficult to make a detailed description of each one. Dissertation-length studies have been made on individual manuscripts, and there are hundreds of manuscripts that have not been described yet.

On the contrary the second problem is that the differences between the manuscripts are not outstanding: Many differences concern spelling, details of vocalization and the system of secondary stress marks (*ge'ayot*) – all subjects that interest only specialists. There are almost no differences that have impact on the meaning of the text. There are very few cases in which words or sentences are added or omitted or passages appear in a different order. Uniformity is the predominant characteristic.

For these two reasons there has been very little research into medieval biblical manuscripts. Anyone who needs to clarify a certain version and find out whether it is found in manuscripts makes use of eighteenth-century studies, those by Kennicott and De Rossi.

Kennicott, a learned scholar from Oxford, published an edition of the Tanakh between 1776 and 1780 with a critical apparatus of textual variants.[8] See Figure 10.7. Kennicott and his assistants examined hundreds of manuscripts, and each one was given an abbreviation. In the Pentateuch, the Masoretic Text is given on the right side of each page (without vocalization and cantillation signs) and the Samaritan version on the left. For the Prophets and Writings the Masoretic Text alone appears. The textual variants give a certain picture of the manuscripts: Some variants are supported only by one or two manuscripts, while others are supported by dozens.

The Kennicott edition has a number of failings: First of all, it deals only with the letters in the text and not with vocalization or cantillation of the words. Secondly, some have claimed that the examination carried out by Kennicott and his staff of assistants was incomplete. An additional disadvantage is that the edition does not include a description or evaluation of the manuscripts. Using the edition it is difficult to locate

---

8 B. Kennicott, *Vetus Testamentum Hebraicum cum variis lectionibus*, 1–2, Oxford 1776–1780. A digital version of this work is available online.

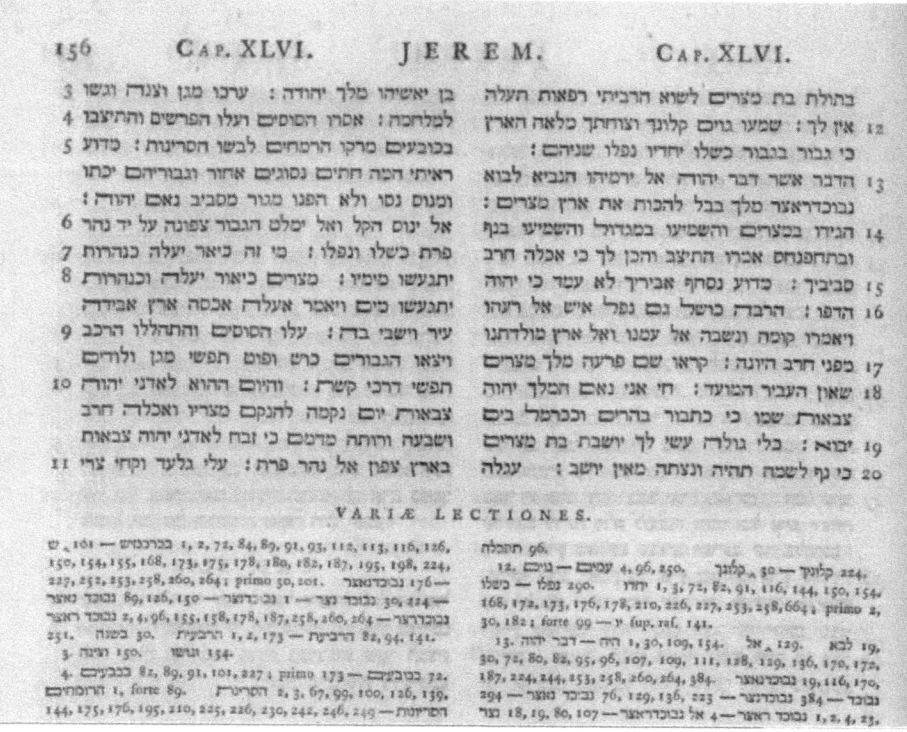

Figure 10.7: A page from the Kennicott edition (Jer. 46:3–20).

a particular manuscript, to find out its date and provenance, and most importantly, to know if it is an important manuscript reflecting an ancient version, or perhaps the popular work of a careless scribe. Nevertheless the Kennicott edition is the most available tool for obtaining a first impression of the degree to which a certain version of a given textual passage was widespread in the Middle Ages. A cursory glance at the edition can determine whether a reading is documented, and if so whether it is rare or widespread.

C. D. Ginsburg tried to make up for the failings in the Kennicott edition in his critical edition of the Tanakh. Ginsburg examined dozens of manuscripts and early printed editions, and checked their special versions in orthography, vocalization and cantillation signs. His second edition (1908–1920) includes extensive variant readings, although he compared far fewer manuscripts than did Kennicott.[9] Ginsburg

---

9 Ginsburg's second edition was published in London during the years 1908–1920. On this Bible edition see also Chapter 12, pp. 207–208.

described at length the manuscripts that he used in a separate book that constitutes an introduction to his edition.[10]

The edition of the Bible Project of the Hebrew University of Jerusalem also presents (in its third apparatus) partial data on the variations in some of the manuscripts, based on the Kennicott collection.

Yet there is still much work to be done. It is peculiar to rely on an eighteenth-century research project in the twenty-first century.

The Role and Influence of the Tiberian Manuscripts

The Aleppo Codex was a landmark in the history of the Masora, and it represents the stage at which the Masoretes arrived at an agreed version in all its details. The codex demonstrates a remarkable uniformity between the letters of the Tanakh and the masoretic apparatus, in which thousands of masoretic notes represent the choices made by the Masoretes.

But the success of project at a certain point in time did not mean that the Masoretic text spread and became the exclusive version in Jewish communities from that time on.

In the centuries after the creation of the Aleppo Codex masoretic notes were disseminated and copied in the margins of codices of Scripture. This form of writing came to be the accepted way of writing Biblical manuscripts. However, despite the writing of masoretic notes, and despite the recognition in principle of the authority of the Masora, in many cases the text of Scripture remained different from the Masoretic text. Many scribes did not know how to implement the notes, or how to interpret obscure notes, or notes that appeared to be corrupt or contradictory. On the other hand there were local traditions regarding orthography, particularly in the Torah, which the scribes believed were accurate and did not agree to change them in order to conform to masoretic notes (for an example, cf. a responsum by Rashba, which will be dealt with at length in Chapter Thirteen below). The masoretic notes served in many cases as a decorative element, and only occasionally were they implemented for their original purpose, mainly when they explicitly contradicted a version that appeared on the same page on which they were written. The degree of use of masoretic notes differed from one place to another and from one scribe to another. But it was known that "the accurate books of Sefarad (=Spain)" were closer to the Masoretic text than those of Ashkenaz (=France and Germany).

What was the source of the versions that differed from the Tiberian text, which were widespread in Spain, Italy, France and Germany in the Middle Ages? Some

---

10 C.D. Ginsburg, *Introduction to the Massoretico-Critical Edition of the Hebrew Bible*, London 1897 (a second edition with Prolegomenon by Harry M. Orlinsky, New York 1966). Cf. I. Yeivin, *The Biblical Masorah*, Jerusalem 2003 (Heb.), pp. 28–31.

scholars regarded them as corrupted versions of the Tiberian text (since they are vocalized in the Tiberian system), corrupted by the carelessness of scribes. However M. Cohen has shown that these versions preserve ancient characteristics that are also found in manuscripts that preceded the Tiberian ruling. In other words, later European manuscripts "sidestepped" the decisions of the Tiberian Masora, and continued to preserve ancient traditions that were rejected in Tiberias. They did so despite the fact that they adopted the Tiberian vocalization system, copied Tiberian masoretic notes, and recognized the authority of the Masora!

Cohen proved his claim by a comparison of manuscripts. He first compared the Aleppo Codex with a fragment of the book of Joshua in Palestinian vocalization (Ms. Oxford Heb. d 29), evidently older than the Aleppo Codex. 117 differences were found, most of them orthographic, but some more significant, such as the addition of the word כלב (=Kaleb) in Jos. 15:19 and the addition of the conjunctive *waw* before the words בית צור in 15:58. In the second stage Cohen checked these 117 differences in nine medieval biblical manuscripts: six Ashkenazi and three Sefardi. It was readily apparent that most of the manuscripts are closer to Ms. Oxford than to the Aleppo Codex. 92 differences are shared by the Oxford manuscript and all or at least most of the Ashkenazi manuscripts. The Sefardi manuscripts demonstrate a lower ratio: 60 differences are shared by the Oxford manuscript and the Sefardi manuscripts or most of them.

The conclusion to be drawn from this examination is that the Ashkenazi manuscripts preserve ancient traditions of the text that were rejected by the Masoretes of Tiberias, but continued to be maintained in different parts of the Jewish world.

For further study

M. Cohen, "Some basic features of the consonantal text in medieval manuscripts of the Hebrew
  Bible", *Studies in Bible and Exegesis*, [I], Ramat Gan 1980, pp. 123–182.

Processes of Textual Unification in Later Periods

The process of determining the Masoretic text in all its details – the division into passages, orthography, vocalization, cantillation marks and stress signs – was long and complicated. Ramah – R. Meir Halevy Abulafia (Spain, 1170–1240) – wrote a book devoted to the decision on *plene* and defective spelling in the Pentateuch, entitled *Masoret Seyag laTorah* (="The Masora is a Fence around the Torah"). When writing a Torah scroll, only the issues of passages and orthography are relevant, not the other factors, but nevertheless Ramah described in his introduction the difficult situation that existed in his day regarding the writing to the Torah scrolls:

> "Your heart shall murmur in awe, where is one who could count? Where is one could weigh? Where is one who could count the towers?" (after Is. 33:18). A scribe (סופר, the root also means to

count) who counts all the letters in the Torah. [...] And moreover for our sins [the prophecy] has been fulfilled "Truly, I shall further baffle that people with bafflement upon bafflement; and the wisdom of its wise shall fail, and the prudence of its prudent shall vanish" (Is. 29:14). And if we come to rely upon the corrected books that we have, they also have many disagreements, and if not for the Masorot that make a fence around the Torah, no one could find his way in the disagreements. And even the Masorot were not spared disagreements as even they disagree in certain places, but not as many as the scribes. And if a person wants to write a Torah scroll properly, he will debate about defective and *plene* [spelling], and he will be like a blind man stumbling in the dark of the disagreements and he will not be able to find his way and "though a wise man think to know it, yet shall he not be able to find it" (after Eccl. 8:17).

Ramah needed old manuscripts and masoretic notes, and used them to clarify the text of the Torah. We do not know what manuscripts were available to him. It is hard to imagine that he had ancient manuscripts from the period of the Masoretes that were written in the East, like the Aleppo Codex and the Leningrad manuscript. Nevertheless Ramah was able to determine a text nearly identical in every point to the orthography found in these ancient manuscripts and their masoretic notes. The text established by Ramah was accepted in most Jewish communities, and by so doing he had a great impact on the uniformity of Torah scrolls.

The Printing Revolution

The most important historical turning point that influenced the dissemination of the Masoretic text was the invention of printing. The edition of the Tanakh printed in Venice in 1524–1525, which is called *"Miqraot Gedolot"* (and also 'Second Rabbinic Bible'), is the most important edition, even though it was not the first. The printer, Ya`akov ben Haim Adoniyahu, made use of manuscripts and masoretic notes in order to determine the text, and included in his edition both Masora Magna and Masora Parva comments, which he collected from several manuscripts. This edition is important for two reasons:

1. **A common basis** – Even though the edition itself does not conform totally to the Masora in every point, and even though it has more than a few typographical errors, its wide dissemination provided everyone concerned with the text of Scripture a common basis. Scholars of the Masora from now on could point out errors in the printed edition, and took exception in some cases with the printer's choice. The text as corrected by some Masora scholars came to be the accepted text of Scripture throughout the Jewish world.

2. **The Masora** – The masoretic notes published in this edition became the basis for further discussion of the Masora. The masoretic material included in the edition was very rich, some of it printed in notes in the margins of the text, and other material in the lengthy alphabetical appendix at the end of the book (entitled *"Masora Rabati"* or *"Masora Finalis"*).

The most important scholars of the Masora who commented on this edition were Menahem di Lonzano and Yedidya Shelomo Norzi. The former wrote the book *Or Torah*, on the text of the Torah, and the latter *Minhat Shai*, which deals with the entire text of the Tanakh.

The Discovery of Ancient Manuscripts and their Study

In the course of the twentieth century and the beginning of the twenty-first, four important developments have advanced the study of the masoretic text of the Tanakh in all its details and determining the correct version:

1. **Discovery of manuscripts of the Masoretes** – Two manuscripts that stem from the Ben Asher family were discovered towards the end of the nineteenth century. The first one – the well-known Leningrad Codex – is a complete manuscript of the Tanakh copied "from books revised by the learned Aharon Ben Moshe Ben Asher". The second manuscript was found in Cairo and contains the Prophets, and according to its colophon it was written by Aharon's father, Moshe Ben Asher. These two manuscripts joined the most important manuscript, the Aleppo Codex, the existence of which was known generations earlier, but the possibilities of examining and studying it were limited. During the twentieth century many more – complete and partial – manuscripts were revealed, which are close to the Aleppo Codex in their time, their place of writing and their version.

2. **Photography** – The invention of photography made the ancient manuscripts much more available, and enabled intensive research into the text of Scripture. Manuscripts related to the Tiberian Masora were the basis of many studies, and subsequently editions of Scripture based on ancient manuscripts were printed. In comparison to earlier editions, these editions were much closer to the version established by the Tiberian Masoretes. These editions of Scripture will be discussed below, in Chapter Twelve. Here we shall only mention the names of six main editions. Three of them are based on Ms. Leningrad: *Biblia Hebraica* (BH³, BHS and BHQ), the Dotan edition and the new JPS edition. Another three are based on the Aleppo Codex: the Breuer editions (including *Keter Yerushalayim* of the Hebrew University), the edition of the Hebrew University Bible Project and *Miqraot Gedolot Haketer* edition of Bar-Ilan University (edited by Cohen).

3. **Scanning manuscripts and making them available on the internet** – Recently, many manuscripts have undergone digital photography, and their photographs have been made available to the public on the internet. This process began in the beginning of the twenty-first century, and it continues to expand. Digital photographs of the Aleppo Codex and many other manuscripts are available online. Geniza fragments from libraries throughout the world were photographed and catalogued and made available to scholars as part of the Friedberg Genizah Project.

4. **The computer revolution** – Towards the end of the twentieth century software containing the text of Scripture was developed. Most of these programs included vocalization and some of them even cantillation signs. The development of these programs and their refinement give researchers into the text of Scripture powerful tools for examining the Masoretic text and determining correct readings.

Editors of editions of Scripture have disagreed regarding the methodology for arriving at the correct version. But as the techniques are refined and research into the text of many manuscripts advances – the disagreements have been reduced to very minor details (such as secondary stress marks and semi-vowels), and these disagreements have been documented and clearly defined.

11 Secondary Stress Marks (*Ge'ayot*) – in Manuscripts and in Printed Editions

What are *Ge'ayot*?

The *ga'ya* is the sign of a secondary stress in a word. It is indicated by a perpendicular line beneath a letter, also called a *meteg*. There are different kinds of *ge'ayot* (pl. form of *ga'ya*), each one appearing in different circumstances. Breuer counted ten different kinds in his book.[1] We will limit ourselves to a detailed presentation of two kinds, and a brief presentation of three more.

Manuscripts and printed editions of Scripture differ significantly regarding the degree to which they use *ge'ayot*, thus an examination of the system of *ge'ayot* implemented in a certain manuscript or printed edition, may indicate its provenance or time, and its degree of conformity to Ben Asher's system, as will be explained below in this chapter.

The Light *Ga'ya*

This is the formula of the light *ga'ya*:

1. Stressed syllable	2. Separation [by means of sounded *shewa* or a semivowel or a vowel or more]	3. Open syllable

(Read the table from right to left, even though the numbering is from the stressed syllable backwards!)

The light *ga'ya* is a stress that comes on an open syllable, separated from the primary stressed syllable, by a sounded *shewa* at least. These are a few words that suit the formula of the light *ga'ya*:

כִּי-אָמַר ,יַעַבְדוּהוּ ,הַחֲוִילָה ,אָנֹכִי ,יַעֲשֶׂה ,שָׁמְרוּ

Here are the same words separated into three parts to illustrate the three parts of the formula:

כִּי-אָ-מַר ,יַ-עַבְ-דוּהוּ ,הַ-חֲוִי-לָה ,אָ-נֹ-כִי , יַ-עֲ-שֶׂה ,שָׁ-מְ-רוּ

---

1 Mordechai Breuer, *The Biblical Accentuation in the Twenty-one Books and in the Three 'emet' Books*, Jerusalem 1982, pp. 173–208 (Heb.). See also: Israel Yeivin, *The Biblical Masorah*, Jerusalem 2003, pp. 209–226 (Heb.).

https://doi.org/10.1515/9783110594560-011

It is easy to observe how the formula of the light *ga'ya* is fulfilled in every word. In the word שָׁמְרוּ (="they kept") a sounded *shewa* separates the open syllable *sha* and the primarily stressed syllable *ru*. In the word יַעֲשֶׂה (="he will do") a semivowel separates the first syllable from the last; the word אָנֹכִי ("I") – contains a separation by a vowel (i.e. a syllable that includes a vowel – *no*), and in the word הַחֲוִילָה (= "the [land of] Havila") the separation is by a semivowel and a vowel. The word יַעַבְדֻּהוּ (="they will serve him") carries a penultimate primary stress (on the syllable *du*), but two syllables before it there is an open syllable (*ya*), therefore this word also conforms to the formula for the light *ga'ya*. Two hyphenated words are treated as one word for the subject of *ge'ayot*, so that the formula also applies to the combination כִּי־אָמַר (="as he said").

With practice the reader can easily identify in a given text all the places in which the light *ga'ya* formula exists, and he will notice that they are very common, on the average more than one word to a verse.

In popular printed editions of the Tanakh (such as the Bible editions of Letteris, Ginsburg or Koren) the light *ga'ya* is indicated in every case in which the formula exists. In these editions the reader can make use of the *ga'ya* in order to differentiate between a sounded *shewa* and a silent *shewa* in the middle of a word. Thus he will see, for example, the *ga'ya* in words such as הֹלְכִים or יֵצְאוּ and will know to sound the *shewa* after the *holam* or *zere*. This is particularly important after the vowel *qamaṣ*. If the reader notes the *ga'ya* on the letter *shin* in the word שָׁמְרָה, he will know that the *qamaṣ* beneath the letter *shin* is a *qamaṣ gadol*, and the *shewa* beneath the letter *mem* is a sounded *shewa* (as in the verse שָׁמְרָה נַפְשִׁי עֵדֹתֶיךָ [Ps. 119:167] – "My soul has obser-ved Your testimonies"; pronounced *shamera*). However if there is no *ga'ya*, he can conclude that the *qamaṣ* is a *qamaṣ qatan* and the *shewa* is silent (as in the verse שָׁמְרָה נַפְשִׁי וְהַצִּילֵנִי [Ps. 25:20] – "Keep my soul, and deliver me"; pronounced *shomra*).

However an examination of manuscripts of the Tanakh from the period of the Masoretes (such as the Aleppo Codex and Ms. Leningrad) shows that the system used in the manuscripts regarding the light *ga'ya* is different, and it is indicated only in some of the cases in which the formula exists. If the word carries a cantillation sign that does not indicate a pause (i.e. a conjunctive accent) the *ga'ya* appears only rarely. And also in words with disjunctive accents the *ga'ya* comes only in some of the cases. With the accent called *pashta* the *ga'ya* will appear in most of the words in which the formula exists; with other accents the *ga'ya* is less frequent.

Moreover, the appearance of the *ga'ya* in manuscripts is not uniform, and in many cases one manuscript indicates a light *ga'ya* while another does not. For that reason some researchers have called this *ga'ya* "an optional *ga'ya*". This, as opposed to other types of *ge'ayot*, regarding which the manuscripts agree, and therefore they are regarded as "obligatory *ge'ayot*".

It is interesting to point out that the significant difference between the manu-scripts and the printed editions regarding *ge'ayot* was not known to some important scholars in the nineteenth century (such as Isaac Seligman Baer and William Wickes), who thought the system applied in the printed editions was the system of Ben Asher and the other Masoretes. Ancient manuscripts (such as the Aleppo Codex) were not available to these scholars, and they did not know the system they used.

The Heavy *Ga'ya*

The formula for the heavy *ga'ya* is slightly more complicated than that for the light *ga'ya*:

1. Stressed syllable	2. Sounded shewa or semivowel	3. Additional syllable	4. Closed syllable

(Again: Read the table from right to left)

The heavy *ga'ya* appears on a closed syllable (as opposed to the light *ga'ya*!). It is followed by an additional syllable (usually with a short vowel), and then a sounded *shewa* or a semivowel, concluding with the stressed syllable.

This formula exists in mainly three patterns: *mitpaʻᵃlim, mitpalpᵉlim, mitqattᵉlim* (מְתְקַטְּלִים, מְתְפַּלְפְּלִים, מִתְפַּעֲלִים). These examples serve to illustrate the structure of the syllables alone (without relation to the grammatical form *hitpaʻel*).

These are some words in which the formula for the heavy *ga'ya* applies: וַיִּשְׁמְעוּ, אֶל-הַבְּאֵר, אֶת-יַעֲקֹב, וּלְכָל-מְלָאכֶת, וַיִּשְׁתַּחֲווּ, הִתְעַשְּׁקוּ, וַיְשַׁלְּחֶהָ.

The word וַ-יִשְׁ-מְ-עוּ conforms to the pattern of מְתְפַּלְפְּלִים: a closed syllable, another closed syllable with a silent shewa, a sounded shewa and finally the stressed syllable. The word וַיְ-שַׁ-לְּ-חֶהָ conforms to the pattern of מְתְקַטְּלִים, which includes a closed syllable with a *dagesh* forte.[2] The hyphenated expression אֶת-יַ-עֲ-קֹב conforms to the pattern מִתְפַּעֲלִים, in which the syllable before the stress has a semivowel. The reader should try to define the appropriate pattern for the remaining words: אֶל-הַבְּאֵר, וּלְכָל-מְלָאכֶת, וַיִּשְׁתַּחֲווּ, הִתְעַשְּׁקוּ.

Since this formula is more complicated than that of the light *ga'ya*, it rarely appears in the text. There is more uniformity among the manuscripts related to the Aleppo Codex in this case: When a word appears with a *ga'ya* in the Aleppo Codex, it usually will appear as such in the related manuscripts as well; when there is none in the Aleppo Codex, it does not appear in the other manuscripts either. Consequently this *ga'ya* is called an "obligatory *ga'ya*".

In most cases, if a word conforms to the formula for the heavy *ga'ya* and carries a disjunctive cantillation sign – a *ga'ya* is indicated; In cases in which the cantillation sign is not disjunctive – no *ga'ya* appears.

Regarding both elements of this rule there are exceptions, that is, sometimes the *ga'ya* does appear even when the cantillation sign on the word is conjunctive, and sometimes there is no *ga'ya* even though the sign is disjunctive. Similarly a heavy *ga'ya* occurs also on words that diverge slightly from the formula presented above. In

---

2 In determining the structure of a word, one should ignore the syllables that follow the stressed syllable.

most of these cases, there is generally agreement among the manuscripts, since this is an obligatory *ga'ya*, appearing according to a firm tradition like most of the vocalization and cantillation signs.

The Source of the System of Mutiple Light *Ge'ayot*

Returning to the light *ge'ayot*, which are *ge'ayot* on an open syllable, we noted already that there is a serious quantitative difference between the number of *ge'ayot* in printed editions (like the Letteris or Ginsburg) and the manuscripts (like the Aleppo Codex and Ms. Leningrad). The printed editions give a *ga'ya* in every word that conforms to the formula, but the manuscripts give a *ga'ya* only in a minority of occurrences. How did the system used by the printers develop?

M. Cohen checked and found that the system of multiple *ge'ayot* characteristic of the printed editions is also found in manuscripts from Italy and Ashkenaz, and in his opinion the system may have originated in Eretz Israel. These manuscripts are different in their system from the notable manuscripts of the Tiberian Masoretes who created manuscripts close to the Aleppo Codex. Many of these manuscripts differed in the system of vocalization from the Aleppo Codex. Their system is called "Expanded Tiberian Vocalization", because it indicates the *dagesh* and the *shewa* more than is usual.

R. Menahem di Lonzano (seventeenth century) described, in his work *Or Torah* (end of the first portion in Genesis), his impression from Ashkenazi manuscripts that implemented multiple (light) *ge'ayot*: "I am tired of the multiple, superfluous and useless *ge'ayot* that the Ashkenazim inserted in their books, calling them *meteg*, and I call them *meteg laḥamor* (="a bridle for a donkey" – after Prov. 26,3), they have become a burden for me, I cannot endure correcting them, because they have multiplied like locust beyond number" (after Jer. 46,23).

To illustrate the distribution of various types of *ge'ayot* in manuscripts and in printed editions, M. Cohen examined a passage from the book of Kings (II Kings 13:1–14:21),[3] and we shall briefly review it here.

Let's begin with *light ge'ayot*: 63 words in the sample section fulfill the formula. Only six of them have *light ga'ya* in the Aleppo Codex (all of them in the accent '*pashta*'). In three ancient Tiberian manuscripts, including the Leningrad Codex, the number of *light ge'ayot* ranges from 6 to 15. In contrast, in all the printed editions examined – of Venice, Letteris, Koren, and Breuer – each of the 63 words have a *ga'ya*. This is also the case in two Ashkenazi Manuscripts from the 13th Century: The British Library Add. 15451 and Paris 1.

---

3 M. Cohen, "Introduction to the Book of Kings", *Miqraot Gedolot Haketer*, Kings I & II, Ramat Gan 1996, pp. 12*–20* and the tables on pp. 17*–18* (Heb.).

As for the heavy *ge'ayot*, there are nine words in the sample section that conform to the formula of heavy *ga'ya* in disjunctive accents. The Aleppo Codex and the Leningrad Codex have a ga'ya in all of them. Other manuscripts and printed editions – such as Ms. Paris 1 and the Venice and Letteris printed editions – do not mark this ga'ya at all or almost at all. These are the same sources that contained multiple light *ge'ayot*, and evidently this caused the omission of the other kinds of *ge'ayot* almost entirely.

Indicating *Ge'ayot* in Modern Editions of the Hebrew Bible

New editions of the Tanakh have been published in the last decades, based on early manuscripts of the Masoretes (see below Chapter Twelve). We shall survey briefly their approach to *ge'ayot*.

The *Biblia Hebraica* editions since 1937 (BH³, BHS and BHQ) as well as Dotan's editions (the Hebrew edition of 1973 and the English edition, *Biblia Hebraica Leningradensia* of 2001) are based on Ms. Leningrad and give the *ge'ayot* as they appear in that manuscript. The *Hebrew University Bible Project* edition (1973 onward) and *Miqraot Gedolot Haketer* edition of Bar Ilan University (edited by M. Cohen, 1992 onward) are based on the Aleppo Codex (the "Keter") and give the *ge'ayot* found there. However, as opposed to the Leningrad manuscript which survived completely, in the Keter most of the Torah and certain parts of the Prophets and Writings are missing. An editor using it as the basis for an edition of the Tanakh is confronted by a problem – how to treat the missing sections. M. Cohen tried to solve the problem by means of reconstruction.[4] He investigated the system of the Keter regarding *ge'ayot*, and implemented it in the missing sections. That is relatively simple in the case of heavy *ge'ayot*, which are obligatory, but more complicated with light *ge'ayot*, which are optional. Nevertheless Cohen demonstrated that following the tendency of indicating *ge'ayot* in the Keter in various constructions and with different cantillation signs makes it possible to reconstruct them in such a way that is not far from what appeared in the Keter.

M. Breuer used a different approach (in the various editions he edited, detailed below in Chapter Twelve). He copied the *ge'ayot* from the Keter, and in the sections missing in the Keter – from Ms. Leningrad. In addition he gave the light *ge'ayot* as they appear in printed editions, but in a different form from the *ge'ayot* taken from the manuscripts. By doing so he enabled the reader to make use of the *ge'ayot* to differentiate between a sounded *shewa* and a silent *shewa*, as explained above.

---

4 A similar method was also introduced in the Bible Project edition, but most of the books missing in the Aleppo Codex have not yet been published in this edition.

Cohen and Breuer argued about the appropriate way to indicate *ge'ayot* in contemporary editions of the Tanakh. More information about this disagreement and the detailed justification of both systems may be read in the sources cited at the end of this chapter.

Additional Kinds of *Ge'ayot*

Here are three additional kinds of *ge'ayot*, of special interest:

Ga'yat ha-domot (the *ga'ya* of similar letters) – When two consecutive identical letters appear in a word, and the first is vocalized with a *shewa* (not at the beginning of the word, and without a *dagesh*) – it is unclear whether the *shewa* is mobile (sounded) or quiescent (silent). For example, the words: הַמְלַקְקִים, רְבָבוֹת, קִלְלָתְךָ, הַלְלוּ, הִנְנִי. If the *shewa* is silent, no vowel separates the two identical consonants, and they would seem to merge into one. The word הִנְנִי (=‟here I am") would be pronounced as if it were vocalized הִנִּי (*hinni*) with a *dagesh forte* in the letter *nun*.

Elia Levita, a Renaissance Hebrew grammarian (1469–1549), solved the problem by determining that in all of these cases, the *shewa* under the first of identical letters is mobile. To this day his five rules for the mobile *shewa* are taught in schools, and the last of them is the rule of "*ha-domot*" (the similar letters).

However, from writings of the Masoretes it seems that the *shewa* in this case is not always mobile. According to Rabbi Mordechai Breuer, the *shewa* is mobile if the vowel adjacent to it is stressed (such as מְחַלְלֶיהָ, ‘those who desecrate it' – Ex. 31:14); it is quiescent when it stands between two unstressed vowels (such as קִלְלָתְךָ, ‘your curse' – Gen. 27:13). This rule has several exceptions. For example, the *shewa* is quiescent in the words הִנְנִי ‘I am', הִנְנוּ ‘we are', הַרְרֵי, ‘the mountains' (Ps. 133: 3), יְבָרֶכְךָ ‘May he bless you'.

In cases where the *shewa* is mobile, a Ga'ya can precede the shewa to indicate its mobility. This Ga'ya is called "*Ga'yat ha-domot*". For example: הַלְלוּיָהּ, מְחַלְלֶיהָ. This kind of *ga'ya* is optional, and consequently does not appear in all of the manuscripts, in every case in which the *shewa* of similar letters is mobile.

The vocalizers also had another means for indicating the mobile *shewa*: sometimes they replaced it with a semivowel (*hataf-patah*). This sign did not change the pronunciation of the *shewa*, since the Tiberians pronounced most mobile *shewa*s like a *hataf-patah*. The purpose of the sign was therefore to indicate that the *shewa* should be sounded. This was also an optional addition, not an obligatory one. The vocalizer of the Aleppo Codex made much use of this alternative, writing: חֲנֲנֵנִי, קֲנֲנוּ, קֲלֲלַת, עֲלֲלוֹת.[5]

---

5 For further study see: M. Breuer, *The Biblical Accentuation in the Twenty-one Books and in the Three 'emet' Books*, Jerusalem 1982, pp. 200–201 (Heb.).

One who reads Scripture in a Sephardi-Israeli pronunciation and wants to read a word of this kind that has a *hataf-patah* beneath a non-guttural letter, should read it with a normal mobile *shewa*, pronounced 'e' (not 'a'!). This is because, in this case, the *hataf-patah* is appropriate for the pronunciation of the Tiberians (and of the Yemenite community today), but not for the Sephardi (or "Israeli") pronunciation.

A *ga'ya* that causes a *shewa* to be mobile – Sometimes a *ga'ya* appears after a conjunctive *waw* vocalized with a *shuruq* or after the interrogative *he* or the definite article *he*, or in other circumstances after a short vowel, causing the *shewa* that follows it to be mobile. For example:

וְשָׂדֶה ,וְשָׁבֶה ,וּלְהַבְדִּיל ;הַמִּדְבָּר ,בַּמְסִלָּה ,הַמְצָאתַנִי ,לְקָחָה-זֹאת ,וַתְּאַלְּצֵהוּ ,חֲשָׁרַת-מַיִם

In all of these cases there are manuscripts in which the *shewa* is replaced by a *hataf-patah*, indicating that the *shewa* is sounded. And in all of them the *ga'ya* is obligatory, following an established tradition in the accurate manuscripts.

It should be emphasized that in the case of this kind of *ga'ya*, and in the *ga'ya* of the similar letters – the *ga'ya* indicates that the following *shewa* is mobile. That is not the case regarding the heavy *ga'ya*. The heavy *ga'ya* appears in a closed syllable, and the *shewa* following it is silent. The mark only serves to stress and lengthen the closed syllable in which it appears. Consequently it is impossible to formulate a simple rule connecting the *ga'ya* to the *shewa* that follows it, because it depends what kind of *ga'ya* it is.

Sometimes it is difficult to determine with certainty what kind of *ga'ya* occurs because the structure suits two kinds. For example: The word הַמְדַבְּרִים (="who spoke") appears twice in Scripture, and in both cases there is a *ga'ya* beneath the letter *he*. It may be regarded as a heavy *ga'ya* (of the pattern מִתְקַטְּלִים), and if so, the *shewa* is silent. But it could also be understood as a *ga'ya* on the letter *he* that causes a *shewa* to be mobile. According to a passage in masoretic literature included in the book *Diqduqe HaTe'amim*, it is possible to determine that there is a difference between the two occurrences of the word in Scripture. In Ex. 6:27 the stress mark is a heavy *ga'ya* and the *shewa* is silent, but in II Chr. 33:18 it is a light *ga'ya* and the *shewa* is mobile. This distinction finds support in the vocalization of manuscripts, in which the letter *mem* is vocalized with a *hataf-patah* in Chronicles and with a *shewa* in Exodus. There is some logic to this distinction. In Exodus the word carries a disjunctive cantillation sign, thus a heavy *ga'ya* should be expected, but in Chronicles, it is not expected since the word carries a conjunctive cantillation sign.

Ga'ya of a *shewa* – In this special kind the *ga'ya* does not appear with a vowel, but with a *shewa*, and always at the beginning of a word. The *ga'ya* of a *shewa* indicates that the reader should slow down and virtually extends the semivowel to a full vowel. This kind of *ga'ya* is especially common in Job, Proverbs and Psalms. Examples:

בְּעֵינֵיכֶם ,כְּהוֹצִיאָם ,וְעַד-הַנָּהָר

There are no clear rules regarding this *ga'ya*, but it is nonetheless obligatory. It appears as a stable tradition common to the vocalizers of the accurate manuscripts.

"The Book of Differences" between Ben Asher and Ben Naphtali

Sefer Hahilufim ("The Book of Differences") is a work in Arabic, and its main subject is the points of dispute between the two Masoretes, Ben Asher and Ben Naphtali. It was written by Mishael ben Uziel, who lived in Jerusalem at the end of the tenth century or the beginning of the eleventh. The early translation to Hebrew (in which the influence of Arabic is apparent) was made in the twelfth century and included in a work called *Adat Devorim.*

And this is the opening passage in the book:

> You requested, may God give you strength, to write for you the differences between the two scholars, Aharon ben Moshe ben Asher and Moshe ben David ben Naphtali, may God have mercy on them. And I shall do so as you requested and trust in God.[6]

The work follows the order of the books of Scripture, and it refers to the entire Tanakh. At the beginning it cites seven issues regarding which Ben Asher and Ben Naphtali disagreed in many places in Scripture. The first of them is the vocalization of the name Issachar:

> Know, Sir, may God give you strength, that the scholar Abu Said ben Asher, may God have mercy on him, vocalized only the first letter *shin* in the word יששכר (Issachar), reading it *sin*, omitting the vocalization of the second letter and not pronouncing it, as follows: יִשָּׂכָר, and throughout [Scripture] he did so.

> And Ben Naphtali differed from him in that, because he vocalized both letters, the first as a *shin* and the second *sin*, as follows: יִשְׁשָׂכָר, and throughout he did so.

> And Moshe Mohe would vocalize both reading them as *sin* as follows: יִשְׂשָׂכָר. And this is their difference regarding this word.

Ben Asher's system is the one accepted today. The first *shin* is read as a "left *shin*" (pronounced *s*) with a *dagesh forte*, and the additional letter is not read at all. In this way wherever the word appears in the Tanakh it is treated like a case of *qere/ketiv*, but not marked as such. According to Ben Naphtali the reading is different: a *shin*, followed by a *sin*. Exceptionally, a third system is presented here, that of an early Masorete named Moshe Mohe. His system is close to that of Ben Asher, but it does not treat the second shin as superfluous, and evidently he read the two identical consonants ($s + s$) with a slight separation between them.

---

6 L. Liphschütz (ed.), *Kitāb Al-Khilaf: Mishael Ben Uzziel's Treatise on the Differences Between Ben Asher and Ben Naphtali*, Jerusalem 1965 (in Arabic), p. ג.

Following the seven general differences the book details 867 differences in Scripture between Ben Asher and Ben Naphtali, and also 406 "agreements", i.e. places in which Ben Asher and Ben Naphtali agreed, but evidently disagreed with unnamed Masoretes. Mishael ben Uziel lists all of these places following the order of Scripture, Torah portion after Torah portion and book after book in the Prophets and Hagiographa. Mishael also details all the *sedarim* of the Tanakh, indicating the *sedarim* that are included in every portion in the Torah and in every book of the Prophets and Hagiographa.[7] Perhaps he saw detailing the *sedarim* as important, or maybe he listed them in order to facilitate finding the differences that he discussed.

This long list reflects an interesting picture: At the beginning of the tenth century, when the two Masoretes were active, the Tiberian Masoretic text was already formulated and highly uniform. There were nearly no disagreements regarding orthography, or the basic principles of vocalization and cantillation. The points of dispute were mainly minor issues, such as the conjunctive cantillation signs in Job, Proverbs and Psalms, hyphenation and secondary stress marks. Thus it would seem that Ben Asher and Ben Naphtali were among the last Masoretes who framed the Tiberian Masoretic text. Decisions regarding the text, finalizing the vocalization and cantillation signs and their rules – these projects were completed before the time of Ben Asher and Ben Naphtali. The issues that remained open for decision concerned minor details and miniscule distinctions.

This list also reflects the meticulousness with which the Masoretes regarded these minor details, to which a reader of Scripture today does not pay any attention, and of which even experts in reading the Torah in public are generally unaware, such as the precise location of a secondary stress mark in a word.

As we have said, most of the disagreements in *Sefer Hahilufim* are about *ge'ayot*. An examination of the list of disagreements reveals a surprising fact: The list does not include disagreements regarding the light *ga'ya*. Most of the disagreements concern the *ga'ya* on a closed syllable (heavy ga'ya) and the *ga'ya* of a *shewa*. This may be taken as evidence that the light *ga'ya* was regarded as optional, regarding which there are no obligatory rules, and therefore it made no sense to discuss disagreements about indicating it on a certain word or not.

Figure 11.1 is a passage from the original version of *Sefer Hahilufim* (in Judeo-Arabic), concerning the Torah portion *Toledot* (Gen. 25:19-28:9).

The writer begins by detailing the three *sedarim* included in the portion, points out the number of verses in the portion (106), and gives a textual equivalent for the

---

7 The division of the Torah into about 170 *sedarim* indicates the weekly reading of the three-annual reading cycle used in Eretz Israel, while the division into 53 Portions indicates the Babylonian one-year reading cycle. The division of the Prophets and Hagiographa into *sedarim* was perhaps used for some reading-cycle of these parts of the Bible. See: Y. Ofer, "The Masoretic Divisions (*sedarim*) in the Books of the Prophets and Hagiographa", *Tarbiz* 58 (1989), pp. 155–189 (Heb.).

ז   כתאב אלכלף

פרש ואלה תולדת יצחק תלתה אסדאר כאמלה· ואלה תולדת יצחק א

(25. 19) ויהי כי זקן ב (27. 1) ויתן לך אלהים ג (28. 27)· ועדד פואסיקהא

מאיה וסתה קו יואזיה יהללאל ופיהא מן אלכלף סבעה כלמאת ויהי

אשר   נפתלי

אשר	נפתלי
וַיִּתְרוֹצְצוּ [3] הבנים בקרבה	וַיִּתְרוֹצְצוּ הבנים בקרבה (25. 22)
ולָמֶּה-זה לי בכורה	ולָמֶּה-זה לי בכורה בגעיה (25. 32)
כי עתה הרחיב במקף	כִּי עתה הרחיב בשופר (26. 22)
שנאתם אתו וַתְּשַׁלְּחוּנִי	וַתְּשַׁלְּחוּנִי מאתכם בגעיה (26. 27)
עלי קללתך בני	קִלְלָתְךָ בני אך שמע [4] (27. 13)
ריח [5] בגדיו וַיְבָרְכֵהוּ	וַיְבָרְכֵהוּ ויאמר ראה [6] (27. 27)
ועל-חרבך תחיה	ועל-חרבך תחיה [7] (27. 40)

ואלתי ליס בכלף כלמתין והי ורבקה אמרה אל-[8]יעקב (27. 6) ואהרגה

את-[9]יעקב אחי (27. 41)·

Figure 11.1: The Torah Portion *Toledot Izhak* – from *Sefer Hahilufim*, p. 7.

number (the biblical name יהללאל, that appears in I Chr. 4:16). Following that he details seven differences and two agreements.

The first disputed word is וַיִּתְרֹצֲצוּ (Gen. 25:22 – "struggled"). The word conforms to the formula for the heavy *ga'ya* (but not according to the examples mentioned above; it suits the pattern of מִתְבָּרְכִים, in which a long vowel precedes a mobile shewa). The word carries an conjunctive cantillation sign (*mahpakh*), and we should not expect it to be given a secondary stress mark. That is how Ben Asher treats the word, but Ben Naphtali does put a *ga'ya* beneath the letter *yod*.

In the word וַיְבָרֲכֵהוּ (Gen. 27:27 – "and he blessed him") the disagreement is the opposite: Ben Asher adds a *ga'ya*, but Ben Naphtali does not. The structure of the words is the same as the previous one, but it carries the disjunctive cantillation sign *etnaḥta*. Consequently Ben Asher gives it a secondary stress mark. But Ben Naphtali did not do so, evidently because the structure of the word does not conform to the notable patterns of the heavy *ga'ya*.

One of the disagreements concerns hyphenation. Ben Asher adds a hyphen to the expression כִּי-עַתָּה (Gen. 26:22 – "for now"), but Ben Naphtali gives the word כִּי a conjunctive cantillation sign (*munaḥ*). The disagreement regarding the word קִלְלָתְךָ (Gen. 27:13 – "your curse") concerns the *ga'ya* of similar letters: Ben Naphtali adds a *ga'ya*, sounding the *shewa* beneath the letter *lamed*; Ben Asher does not indicate a *ga'ya*, and in his opinion the *shewa* is silent.

The rest of the disagreements and both of the agreements concern *ge'ayot* in closed syllables (heavy *ge'ayot*). The reader can try to determine whether in each case the word conforms or is close to the formula for the *ga'ya*, and whether it is cantillized with a conjunctive cantillation sign or a disjunctive one. It should be emphasized that regarding *ge'ayot* there are no strict rules, but only preferences. Nevertheless, each of the Masoretes had a clear reading tradition for every word in Scripture as to the obligatory ge'ayot.

Mishael lived about one century after Ben Asher and Ben Naphtali. He did not know them personally, and mentions them in his book with the blessing for the deceased. We do not know how Mishael collated his list of disagreements. He may have received some of the information orally, he may have relied on lists of differences that were written earlier, and he may have compared two codices of Scripture himself, each codex coming from one of these two Masoretes.

"The Book of Differences" as a Tool for Categorizing Scriptural Manuscripts

With the help of *Sefer Hahilufim* we can examine manuscripts of Scripture and determine to what degree they conform to the system of Ben Asher or Ben Naphtali. Israel Yeivin conducted such an examination and his findings regarding some of the manuscripts are summarized in the following table[8]:

Manuscript	Correspondence to Ben Asher (in disagreements)	Correspondence (in agreements)
A (Aleppo Codex)	94%	90%
L (Ms. Leningrad)	92%	90%
B (British Library)	80%	73%
C (Ms. Cairo, Prophets)	33%	75%
S (Ms. Sassoon 507, Torah)	52%	76%
S1 (Ms. Sassoon 1053, Tanakh)	40%	60%

It is easy to see that the Aleppo Codex conforms best of all the manuscripts to Ben Asher's system as reflected in *Sefer Hahilufim*. This may serve as evidence for the attribution of the manuscript to Aharon Ben Asher, but the question still remains why, if Ben Asher vocalized and added the cantillation signs himself, the correspondence is not 100%. There are a few possible answers to this question, and they may all be correct: (1) The text of *Sefer Hahilufim* that has survived may not be perfect itself, because the scribes who copied it did not understand the book from which they were

---

8 Based on Israel Yeivin, *The Biblical Masorah*, Jerusalem 2003, pp. 13–19 (Heb.).

copying and did not copy meticulously the *ga'ya* signs and other signs that indicated the differences; (2) Mishael's sources were not perfect, and he could not transmit Ben Asher's system perfectly; (3) Ben Asher changed his mind in certain cases, and the system reflected in the Aleppo Codex is not identical to that in the manuscript Mishael used.

The degree of accuracy of the Leningrad Manuscript is nearly as good as that of the Aleppo Codex. However, that is the case only if the final version of the manuscript is examined. Ms. **L** contains numerous corrections, including erasure of *ge'ayot*. When it was written, the manuscript was not that close to Ben Asher's system, and only the anonymous "second hand" who corrected it, brought the system of *ge'ayot* in the manuscript so close to that of Ben Asher.

The findings regard the Cairo Prophets manuscript are very surprising because the colophon attributes the manuscript to Moshe Ben Asher, the father of Aharon Ben Asher. Different sources of the Masora relate the genealogy of the Ben Asher family of Masoretes, and we would have expected members of this family to belong to the same school having one system that was transmitted from one generation to another, as opposed to another school represented by Ben Naphtali. However, not only is the Cairo manuscript closer to Ben Naphtali's system than Ben Asher's, it is closest to Ben Naphtali's system of any manuscript known! This problem is one of the strongest arguments of scholars who have cast doubts regarding the authenticity of the colophon of Ms. Cairo, asserting that it was not vocalized by Moshe Ben Asher. Some of these scholars presumed that the colophon was copied verbatim from another manuscript that was written by Moshe Ben Asher.

The Distinction between *Qamaṣ Qatan* and *Qamaṣ Gadol*

When a *qamaṣ* appears followed by a *shewa*, the question sometimes arises whether it is a *qamaṣ gadol* (and the *shewa* is mobile) or a *qamaṣ qatan* and the *shewa* is silent. The doubt arises when both forms are possible grammatically, as when Jeremiah describes the conquest of Egypt by its enemies. The verse says: כָּרְתוּ יַעְרָהּ נְאֻם ה' כִּי לֹא יֵחָקֵר (Jer. 46:23 – "**Cut** down the forest! [or: **They** shall cut down the forest] – declares the Lord – though it cannot be measured"). Is the prophet calling upon the enemies of Egypt to cut down the forest (כָּרְתוּ – *qamaṣ qatan*, imperative), or is he describing what he saw in his prophecy: enemies who came and cut down the forest (כָּרְתוּ – *qamaṣ gadol*, past tense)?

R. David Qimhi (Radaq) considers both options in his commentary *ad loc.*:

> There is a disagreement regarding this word: Some read כָּרְתוּ, imperative (="cut down"), like חָרְבוּ מְאֹד (Jer. 2:12 – "be horrified") – as if he is addressing the army. And others read כָּרְתוּ, past tense like שָׁמְרוּ (="they observed"), זָכְרוּ (="they remembered").

> And in a few accurate books the letter *kaf* has a *ga'ya*. And that is the correct reading according to the context.

ⅅ 395

And some say that it could not be past tense, because it says afterwards ה' נאם (="declares the Lord"), and it is not customary for the expression "declares the Lord" to come after a past tense verb in prophecy. But they forgot [the verses] ירדו לטבח נאם המלך ה' צבאות שמו (Jer. 48:15 – "[young men] have gone down to the slaughter – declares the King whose name is Lord of Hosts") and the words of rebuke כלכם פשעתם בי נאם ה' (Jer. 2:29 – "you have all rebelled against me – declares the Lord").

And he said כרתו in past tense even though it deals with the future as was the practice in many places in prophecy that the future in prophecy is described as if it had already occurred.

If a light *ga'ya* appears beneath the letter *kaf*, it could solve the disagreement. Radaq says that he found a *ga'ya* in some of the accurate books, and he decided to rely on them, concluding that the verb is in the past tense. After that he considers the context, claiming that the past tense suits the context in this verse.

If we examine the accurate manuscripts known to us, we find a similar situation to that which Radaq found. In Ms. **C** there is a *ga'ya* beneath the letter *kaf*, as in "a few accurate books" of Radaq. However, in Ms. **A** and **L** there is no *ga'ya*. Breuer cites these data in "The Text and its Sources" (appendix to the commentary *Da'at Miqra*), and says: "In text **C** the *qamaṣ* is a *qamaṣ gadol*; and there is no doubt that it is such according to the masoretes of **A** and **L**; however they omitted the *ga'ya* as was their practice in many words that carry a conjunctive cantillation sign." In other words, V # 326, # 331 the *ga'ya* proves that the *qamaṣ* is a *qamaṣ gadol*, but its omission is not an argument because the light *ga'ya* is optional.

This is evidently the reason that some vocalizers, among them the one who vocalized the Aleppo Codex, looked for another way to indicate the *qamaṣ qatan*: They replaced it with a *hataf-qamaṣ*. This sign was not used consistently in the Aleppo Codex, but only in five words, regarding which the reader may have some doubt. For example: שֹׁמּוּ שָׁמַיִם עַל זֹאת וְשַׂעֲרוּ חָרְבוּ מְאֹד נְאֻם ה' (Jer. 2:12 – "Be appalled, O heavens, at this; be horrified, utterly dazed! – says the Lord"); קוּמוּ עֲלוּ אֶל קֵדָר וְשָׁדְדוּ אֶת בְּנֵי קֶדֶם (Jer. 49:28 – "Arise, march against Kedar and ravage the Kedemites!"). Similarly Ez. 15:4; 32:20; II Chr. 6:42.[9]

For further study

M. Breuer, "The *Ga'ya*", *The Biblical Accentuation in the Twenty-one Books and in the Three 'emet' Books*, Jerusalem 1982, pp. 173–208 (Heb.).

M. Breuer, "Insoluble Problems", *Leshonenu* 58 (1995), pp. 283–288 (Heb.).

---

9 We have ignored in this discussion some points that need clarification: (1) *qamaṣ gadol* and *qamaṣ qatan* are not distinguished in the Tiberian Masora by the quality of the vowel. Evidently the two types of *qamaṣ* were differentiated by length rather than quality. (2) According to the sources of the Tiberian Masora the *shewa* in such words as שָׁמְרוּ (past tense) or שׁוֹמְרִים is silent, not mobile.

M. Cohen, "Introductory Chapters: On the System of Ben Asher in marking *ge'ayot* and a reconstruction of missing sections in the Keter" in *Mikra'ot Gedolot 'Haketer'*: Kings I & II, Ramat Gan 1995, pp. 1*-26* (Heb.).

M. Glatzer, 'The Aleppo Codex: Codicological and Paleographical Aspects', *Sefunot* 19 (1988), Ch. 12: The Authenticity of MS Cairo of the Prophets, pp. 250–259 (Heb.)

L. Liphschütz (ed.), *Kitāb Al-Khilaf: Mishael Ben Uzziel's Treatise on the Differences Between Ben Asher and Ben Naphtali*, publications of the Bible Project of the Hebrew University, II, Jerusalem 1965.

J. S. Penkower, "A Tenth Century Pentateuchal MS from Jerusalem (MS C3), Corrected by Mishael ben Uzziel", *Tarbiz* 58 (1988), pp. 49–74 (Heb.).

Israel Yeivin, *Introduction to the Tiberian Masorah* (Translated and edited by E.J. Revell), Missoula, Montana 1980, pp. 240–264; 141–144

M. Wilensky (ed.), *Sefer HaRiqma* (Kitab Al-Luma') by R. Jonah Ibn Janah translated by Yehuda Ibn Tibbon, Jerusalem 1963, Chapter 30 (29) – on the issue of *qamaṣ gadol* and *qamaṣ qatan*.

12 Published Editions of the Hebrew Bible – and Their Relation to the Masora and the Aleppo Codex

How do contemporary editions of the Tanakh differ? Uniformity or multiple differences?

Many editions of the Tanakh are available today. This chapter will discuss some important editions, pointing out the distinctions between them. Are there genuine differences between them? Should a student or a teacher of Scripture care what edition he is using, or are they all equivalent as far as he is concerned?

First of all there are no significant differences in content between the different editions. There is no reason to be concerned: anyone studying or teaching the Book of Exodus will find in all of the editions the Ten Plagues, the Exodus from Egypt, the Giving of the Torah, the Golden Calf and the building of the Tabernacle. He will not find one single verse in the book of Exodus that appears in one edition and not in the others. He will not find even one word or even one letter that changes the reading![1]

We may presume that even veteran Bible teachers have not encountered a disagreement in the classroom because of a difference between editions of the Tanakh used by the students. If the teacher is not an expert on matters of secondary stress marks and semivowels, it is highly unlikely that he would accidentally come across any lack of uniformity between the editions.

What is the reason for this "boring" uniformity? If the reader maintains that the sages over generations took great care about the version of the Torah, and were very meticulous about the accuracy of the text, that would be correct. Note the comment of Rabbi Ishmael to Rabbi Meir in the Babylonian Talmud (tractate Eruvin 13a): "My son,

---

[1] Such cases are very rare in the entire Tanakh. Some cases will be dealt with here. The *Biblia Hebraica* edition of Kittel and Kahle (1937), prints after Jos. 21:35 two verses in small letters (in which the cities of refuge of the tribe of Reuven are specified), and marks them as verses 36–37, even though they do not appear in the Leningrad manuscript. This is also the case in *Biblia Hebraica Stuttgartenensia* (1969–1970). In Ginsburg's Bible editions (that of 1894 and that of 1926), verses 36–37 appear in the body of the Bible in regular letters. Another verse appears in the textual variants apparatus after Nehemiah 7:67. Even in Dotan's *Biblia Hebraica Leningradensia* (2001), the two verses from Joshua and the verse from Nehemiah do appear, not in the main text but at the bottom of the page, without numbering, and with a remark: "A few other manuscripts include here two additional verses". In Breuer's editions, following the Aleppo Codex and the manuscripts that are close to it, all these verses are not mentioned at all.

Another example: At the end of Koren's Hebrew edition there is a list of significant textual variants between printed editions of the Tanakh. In only two instances is there an addition of an entire word that is not a preposition (אבי in II Chr. 10:14; ואו in II Chr. 10:16), and few are the instances in which one word replaces another (such as צדק in place of ארץ in Prov. 8:16). The number of differences between editions printed subsequently is even lower than in that list.

https://doi.org/10.1515/9783110594560-012

what is your profession? I told him I am a scribe. He said to me: My son take care because your work is the work of heaven. If you omit one letter or add one letter, you will be found destroying the entire world!"

And now we shall examine this matter from the opposite perspective, making a converse assertion: There are **thousands** of differences between the editions in use today and even many **tens of thousands** of differences. They can be found in every verse, if you know how to look for them! These differences are not apparent to the ordinary reader, because they involve minor matters that do not attention ordinarily: *ge'ayot* (secondary stress marks – discussed in chapter 11), some semivowels, some cantillation signs and the like. And there is another area in which there are differences, more noticeable, which is design: the font of the letters, the layout of the page, how verses are numbered and *qere/ketiv* notations. These matters are also of importance concerning the most sacred book of the Jewish People, the Book of Books. And they are very important when examining modern editions of the Tanakh.

If we would like to examine and find the differences between various editions, we can implement what we have learned in previous chapters regarding the various witnesses of the Tanakh and the manuscripts that were used in the Middle Ages, the Aleppo Codex and both Tiberian and Babylonian Masora. We shall also make use of what we have learned about secondary stress marks. Below is a survey of some important printed editions of the Tanakh and their characteristics. The starting point for the discussion will be one of the first editions of the Hebrew Bible: the *Miqra'ot Gedolot* edition of 1524–1525 (known also as the second rabbinic Bible).

The *Miqraot Gedolot* Edition and the Subsequent Editions

The Masoretes of Tiberias basically arrived at a uniform edition, which is reflected in the masoretic notes. But the uniformity characteristic of the accurate manuscripts from the East does not pertain to other Jewish centers. Research has shown that in the Middle Ages there were many manuscripts of Scripture that differed significantly from the masoretic text – throughout the Jewish world, but particularly in Italy and Ashkenaz (central and western Europe). This situation – that was described and discussed in chapter 10 – continued until the sixteenth century, when the printed edition of *Miqraot Gedolot* appeared and brought about an essential change in the situation of the versions of Scripture.

In the sixteenth century, the printing press of the Christian printer Daniel Bomberg operated in the city of Venice, Italy, where important basic books of Judaism were printed. A Jewish scholar from Tunisia, Yakov ben Haim Adoniyahu, highly knowledgeable in Judaica in general and the Masora in particular, arrived in Venice. He began work in the important Bomberg printing house, and was involved in the printing of the Jerusalem Talmud. But his most important project was the edition of Scripture called *Miqraot Gedolot* ("Great Scriptures"), published in 1524–1525. This was an edition of the entire Tanakh, printed with the Aramaic translation, and the commentaries of medieval exegetes: Rashi, Ibn Ezra and Radaq on the same page as the text. This design of *Miqraot Gedolot* was repeated over the course of many generations and is still in use today. In some of the editions improvements and additions were added, but the basic pattern designed in Venice is still in use today. It is difficult to understand how they were able to carry out this complicated project in the course of about two years.

From the perspective of the text of Scripture and the Masora, Adoniyahu's project has enormous importance because he decided to implement the Masora, to include it in his edition and to use it for establishing the text of Scripture.[2] He took several accurate manuscripts of Scripture that contained masoretic notes, used them to establish the text for his edition, edited the masoretic notes he found in the margins of the manuscripts and printed them in his edition. It was an impressive achievement and totally revolutionary: Copies of this Bible edition were distributed in hundreds and even thousands of copies throughout the Jewish world, all of them identical. Indeed this edition of *Miqraot Gedolot* contains many typographical errors, unacceptable versions and failures to conform to the Masora. But from then on anyone concerned with the Masora had a uniform edition, and it could be a common point of departure for further discussion, enabling its correction and arriving at a better text. The wide distribution of this edition of *Miqraot Gedolot* led to its acceptance in the course of generations as "the accepted Jewish text of Scripture" (*textus receptus*).

About a hundred years later, at the beginning of the seventeenth century, two scholars were active, who made important contributions to the accuracy of the text of Scripture. These two scholars were R. Menahem di Lonzano (circa 1550–1626), who was active in Turkey, Eretz Israel and Europe, and wrote a book entitled *Or Torah*, dealing with the Torah versions, and R. Shlomo Yedidya Norzi from Italy (circa 1560–circa 1630), who wrote the book *Minhat Shai* on the entire Tanakh. Lonzano compared the editions printed in Venice to manuscripts with masoretic notes, and wrote hundreds of corrections on the basis of the manuscripts. Norzi undertook a similar project using Lonzano's book intensively and essentially incorporating it into his work. In addition he created a collection of thousands of testimonies regarding textual differences that do not conform to the Masora and are reflected in homiletic writings, rabbinic literature, grammatical works, sermons and the like.

The influence of *Or Torah* and *Minhat Shai* on subsequent printed editions of Scripture was extensive and highly significant. *Or Torah* was printed in 1618 (in Venice), during the writer's lifetime. Norzi's work, on the other hand, went to print more than 120 years later: Norzi completed his work in 1626, and prepared it for

---

2 An earlier edition of *Miqraot Gedolot* was printed in the same printing house in 1517, corrected by Felix Pratensis. However, it did not include the Masora, which was the great innovation in Adoniyahu's edition, and the main reason for printing it. Cf. J. S. Penkower, *Jacob ben Hayyim and the rise of the Biblia Rabbinica*, Ph.D. dissertation, Hebrew University of Jerusalem, 1982 (Heb.).

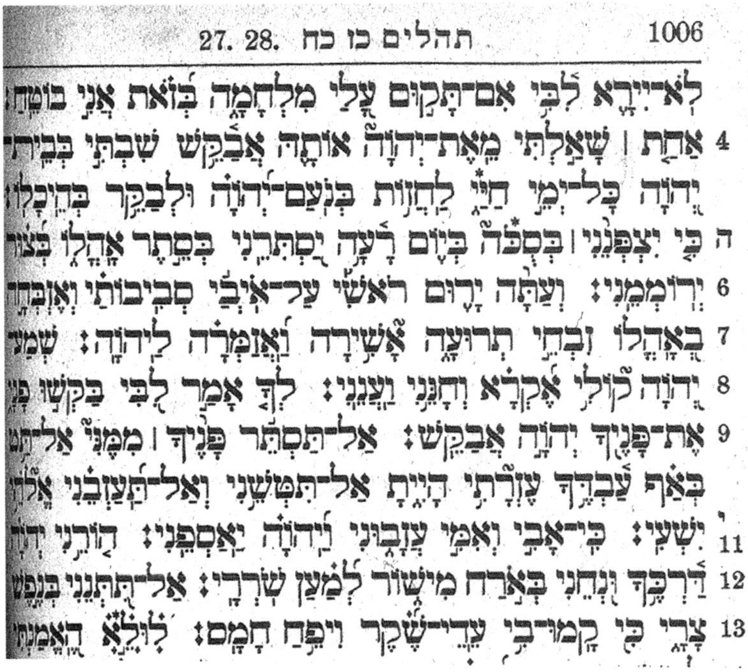
27. 28. תהלים כז כח 1006

לא־יירא לבי אם־תקום עלי מלחמה בזאת אני בוטח:
4 אחת | שאלתי מאת־יהוה אותה אבקש שבתי בבית־
יהוה כל־ימי חיי לחזות בנעם־יהוה ולבקר בהיכלו:
ה כי יצפנני | בסכה ביום רעה יסתרני בסתר אהלו בצור
6 ירוממני: ועתה ירום ראשי על־איבי סביבותי ואזבחה
7 באהלו זבחי תרועה אשירה ואזמרה ליהוה: שמע־
8 יהוה קולי אקרא וחנני וענני: לך אמר לבי בקשו פני
9 את־פניך יהוה אבקש: אל־תסתר פניך | ממני אל־תט
באף עבדך עזרתי היית אל־תטשני ואל־תעזבני אלהי
11 ישעי: כי־אבי ואמי עזבוני ויהוה יאספני: הורני יהוה
12 דרכך ונחני בארח מישור למען שוררי: אל־תתנני בנפש
13 צרי כי קמו־בי עדי־שקר ויפח חמס: לולא האמנתי

Figure 12.1: A page from the Letteris Tanakh, Psalm 27.

printing with great care, even writing instructions to the printer. But he was unsuccessful, and his treatise was published only in 1742.

In the years between the publication of *Or Torah* and that of *Minhat Shai*, some dozens of editions of the Torah were printed by printers all over Europe: Amsterdam, Venice and other cities. Many of the publishers used the corrections and choices in Lonzano's version. However, since 1742 *Minhat Shai* has been the predominant influence, to this day many hundreds of editions have used it.[3]

Over centuries editions of the complete Tanakh were printed based mainly on the Venice edition of *Miqraot Gedolot* with corrections by Lonzano and Norzi. One of the most widespread editions was that of Letteris, printed in Europe in the middle of the nineteenth century (Vienna, 1862), under the supervision of the Hebrew Poet Meir Halevy (Max) Letteris (1800–1871). See Figure 12.1. This edition was distributed extensively and many photographic editions of it were printed in different parts of the world for many years. In some of these editions the printers did not cite the source, and deleted the name Letteris. In some cases

3 The enormous influence of *Minhat Shai* is evident from the bibliography prepared by J. S. Pankower, citing the hundreds of editions of the Tanakh based on it. Cf. J. S. Pankower, "*Minhat Shai* by R. Yedidiah Norzi: Printed Editions of the Work and Printed Bible Editions that were Corrected According to it (circa 1725–2006)", *Italia* 19 (2009), pp. 53–98 (Heb.).

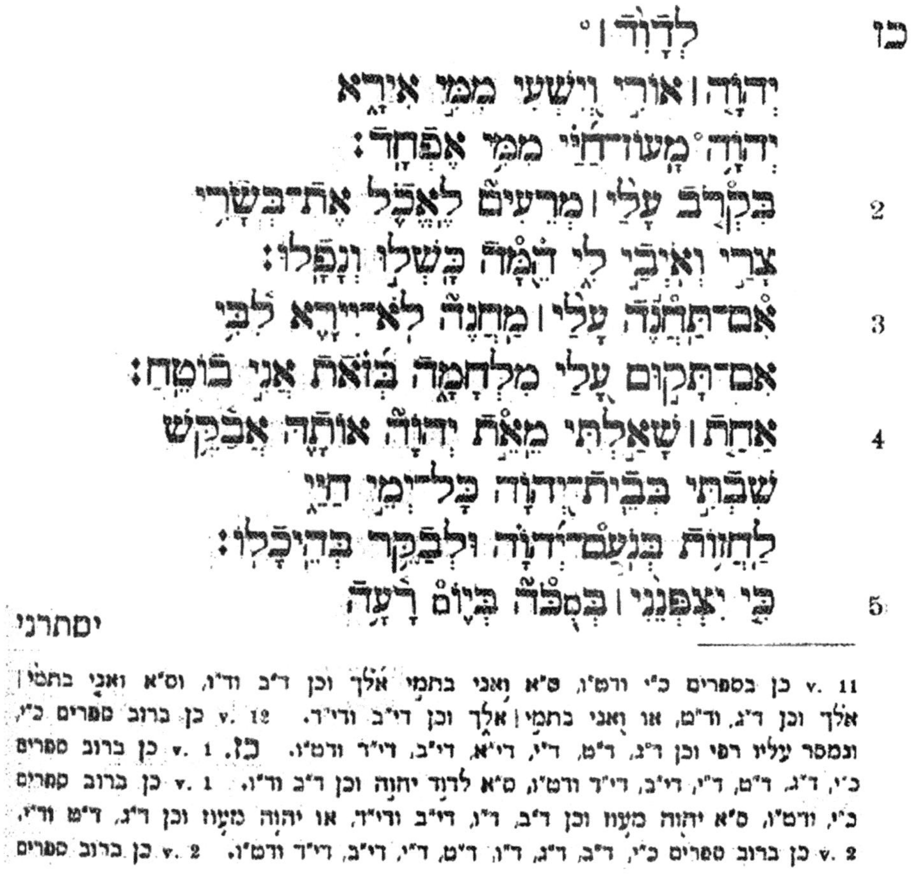

כו

לְדָוִ֡ד ׀

יְהֹוָ֤ה ׀ אוֹרִ֣י וְ֭יִשְׁעִי מִמִּ֣י אִירָ֑א

יְהֹוָ֥ה מָֽעוֹז־חַ֝יַּ֗י מִמִּ֥י אֶפְחָֽד׃

בִּקְרֹ֤ב עָלַ֨י ׀ מְרֵעִים֮ לֶאֱכֹ֢ל אֶת־בְּשָׂ֫רִ֥י   2

צָרַ֣י וְאֹיְבַ֣י לִ֑י הֵ֖מָּה כָשְׁל֣וּ וְנָפָֽלוּ׃

אִם־תַּחֲנֶ֬ה עָלַ֨י ׀ מַחֲנֶה֮ לֹֽא־יִירָ֢א לִ֫בִּ֥י   3

אִם־תָּק֣וּם עָ֭לַי מִלְחָמָ֑ה בְּ֝זֹ֗את אֲנִ֣י בוֹטֵֽחַ׃

אַחַ֤ת ׀ שָׁאַ֣לְתִּי מֵֽאֵת־יְהֹוָה֮ אוֹתָ֢הּ אֲבַ֫קֵּ֥שׁ   4

שִׁבְתִּ֣י בְּבֵית־יְ֭הֹוָה כׇּל־יְמֵ֣י חַיַּ֑י

לַחֲז֥וֹת בְּנֹֽעַם־יְ֝הֹוָ֗ה וּלְבַקֵּ֥ר בְּהֵיכָלֽוֹ׃

כִּ֤י יִצְפְּנֵ֨נִי ׀ בְּסֻכֹּה֮ בְּי֢וֹם רָ֫עָ֥ה   5

ימתרני

v. 11 כן בספרים כ"י ודט"ו, ס"א וְאָנִי בתמִי אֵלֵךְ וכן ד"ב וד"ו, וס"א וַאֲנִי בתמֹי
אֵלֵךְ וכן ד"ג, וד"ם, או וַאֲנִי בתמִי אֵלֵךְ וכן די"ב ודי"ד. v. 12 כן ברוב ספרים כ"י,
ונמסר עליו רפי וכן ד"ג, ד"ם, ד"י, די"א, די"ב, די"ד ודט"ו. v. 1 כז. כן ברוב ספרים
כ"י, ד"ג, ד"ם, ד"י, די"ב, די"ד ודט"ו, ס"א לְדָוִד יהוה וכן ד"ב וד"ו. v. 1 כן ברוב ספרים
כ"י, ודט"ו, ס"א יהוה מֵעוֹ וכן ד"ב, ד"ג, די"ב ודי"ד, או יהוה מָעוֹ וכן ד"ג, ד"ם וד"י,
v. 2 כן ברוב ספרים כ"י, ד"ג, ד"ב, ד"ו, ד"י, ד"ם, די"ב, די"ד ודט"ו. v. 2 כן ברוב ספרים

Figure 12.2: Ginsburg first edition, 1894.

the few masoretic notes included in the Letteris edition were also deleted, presumably because they thought that the average reader did not have the expertise to understand these notes and was not interested in the small print. However, many of these notes were *qere* notes, and since they were omitted, the reader finds it difficult to know how to read words that had *qere* and *ketiv*.

Christian David Ginsburg (1831–1914) published two editions of the Tanakh (Figures 12.2 and 12.3). These editions include textual variants, and *ketiv/qere* notes, variants from manuscripts and printed editions, and also variants reflected in the Greek and Syriac translations.[4] Two innovations in Ginsburg's edition are particu-

---

4 Ginsburg's first Bible edition was published in 1894 by the Trinitarian Bible Society, based on old printed editions of the Bible. His second edition was published in 1908–1911 by The British and Foreign Bible Society, and included textual variants from dozens of biblical manuscripts. This edition included only the Torah and the Prophets; Writings appeared later, in 1920, some years after Ginsburg passed away.

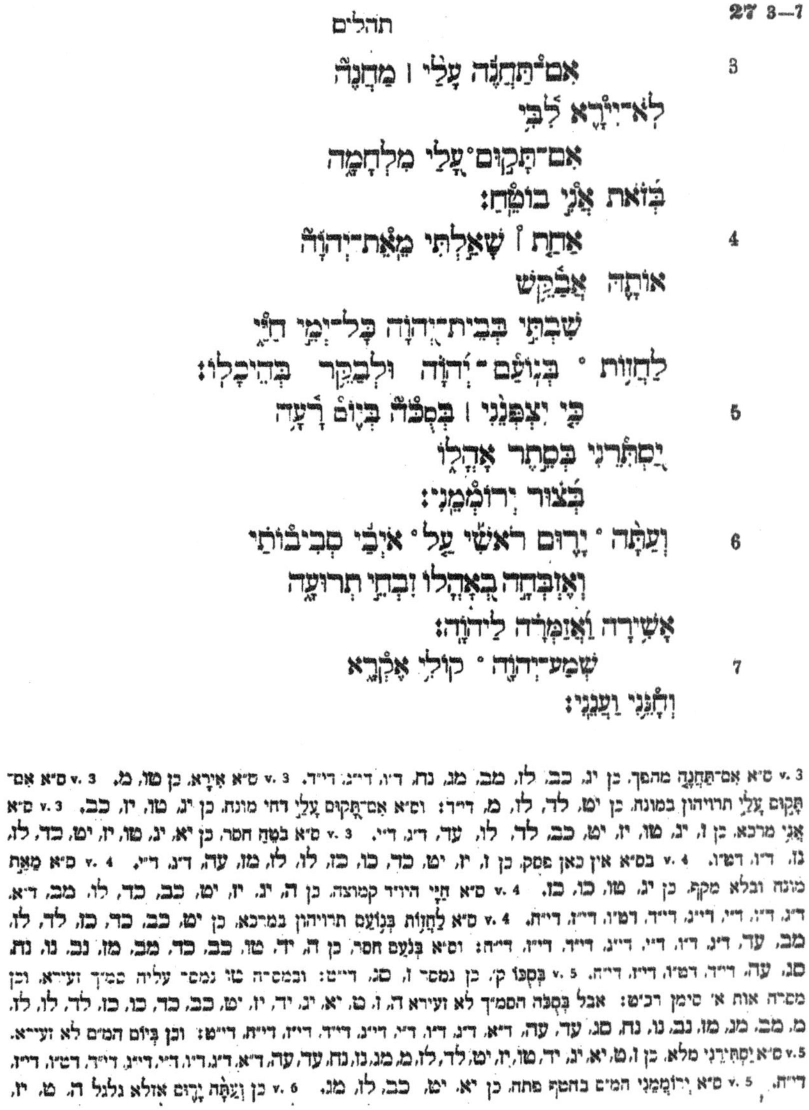

תהלים

27 3—7

3
אִם־תַּחֲנֶה עָלַי ׀ מַחֲנֶה
לֹא־יִירָא לִבִּי
אִם־תָּקוּם עָלַי מִלְחָמָה
בְּזֹאת אֲנִי בוֹטֵחַ׃

4
אַחַת ׀ שָׁאַלְתִּי מֵאֵת־יְהוָֹה
אוֹתָהּ אֲבַקֵּשׁ
שִׁבְתִּי בְּבֵית־יְהוָה כָּל־יְמֵי חַיַּי
לַחֲזוֹת בְּנֹעַם־יְהוָה וּלְבַקֵּר בְּהֵיכָלוֹ׃

5
כִּי יִצְפְּנֵנִי ׀ בְּסֻכֹּה בְּיוֹם רָעָה
יַסְתִּרֵנִי בְּסֵתֶר אָהֳלוֹ
בְּצוּר יְרוֹמְמֵנִי׃

6
וְעַתָּה יָרוּם רֹאשִׁי עַל אֹיְבַי סְבִיבוֹתַי
וְאֶזְבְּחָה בְאָהֳלוֹ זִבְחֵי תְרוּעָה
אָשִׁירָה וַאֲזַמְּרָה לַיהוָה׃

7
שְׁמַע־יְהוָה קוֹלִי אֶקְרָא
וְחָנֵּנִי וַעֲנֵנִי׃

ע. 3 ס"א אִם־תַּחֲנֶה מהפך. בן יג, כב, לו, מב, מג, נת, דיו, דיי"ג: דיי"ד.   3 ע. ס"א אִירָא, כן טו, מ.   3 ס"א אִם־
תָּקוּם עָלַי תרויהון במונה. בן יט, לה, לו, מ. דיר: וּסֵא אִם־תָּקוּם עָלַי דחי מונה. כן יג, טו, יו, כב.   3 ע. ס"א
אֲנִי מרכא. בן ו, יג, טו, יו, יט.   ע. 3 ס"א בֹּטֵחַ חסר. כן יא, יג, טו, יו, יט, כד, לו,
נג. דיו, דטו.   4 ע. בס"א אין כאן פסק. כן ו, יו, יט, כד, כו, כז, לו, לז, מו, עה, דיג, דיי,   4 ע. ס"א מֵאֵת
מונה ובלא מקף. כן יג, טו, כד, כו.   4 ע. ס"א חַיַּי היויד קמוצה. כן ה, יג, יט, יט, כב, כד, לו, מב, דיא,
דיג, דיי, דיי"ג, דטו, דיי"ד, דיי"ה.   4 ע. ס"א לַחֲזוֹת בְּנֹעַם תרויהון במרכא. כן יט, כב, כד, כו, לה, לו,
מב, עד, דיג, דיו, דיי, דיי"ג, דיי"ד, דיי"ה: וּסֵא בְּנֹעַם חסר. כן ה, יד, טו, כב, כד, מב, מו, נב, נג, נת
סג, עה, דיי"ד, דטו, דיי"ג, דיי"ה.   5 ע. בְּסֻכֹּה ק', בן נמסר ו, סג, דיי"ט: ובמסו"ה טו נמסר עליה סמיך זעירא. וכן
מסי"ה אות א' סימן רכיט: 5 ע. ס"א בְּסֻכֹּה הסמיך לא זעירא ה, ו, ט, יא, יג, יד, יו, יט, כב, כד, כו, לד, לו, לז,
מ, מב, מג, מו, מז, נב, נג, נו, נח, סג, עד, עה, דיא, דיג, דיו, דיי, דיי"ד, דיי"ג, דיי"ה, דטו: וכן בְּיוֹם הַמִּים לא זעי"א.
ע. 5 יַסְתִּרֵנִי מלא. בן ו, טו, יא, יג, יד, טו, יו, יט, כב, כו, לד, לו, מ, מג, מו, נו, נת, עד, עה, דיא, דיג, דיו, דיי"ג, דטו,
דיי"ה.   5 ע. ס"א יְרוֹמְמֵנִי המים בחטף פתח. כן יא, יט, כב, לו, מג.   6 ע. ס"א וְעַתָּה יָרוּם אזלא נגלגל ה, ט, יו,

Figure 12.3: Ginsburg second edition, 1920.

larly noteworthy: In his first edition he used the *rafe* sign, a horizontal line above the letters *bet, gimmel, dalet, kaf, pe* and *tav* without a *dagesh* and for the letters *aleph* and *he* when they are not consonants. This sign was used in manuscripts, but not in printed editions before. He introduced a special innovation when dealing with

---

Ginsburg wrote a detailed introduction to his edition of the Tanakh, describing the manuscripts and printed editions, and dealing with masoretic terminology and masoretic phenomena: Cf.: C.D. Ginsburg, *Introduction to the Massoretico-Critical Edition of the Hebrew Bible*, London 1897.

words that have *ketiv* and *qere*: The word appears in the text without vocalization, and in the textual variants it is vocalized twice: both according to the *ketiv* and according to the *qere*.

The Discovery of Manuscripts Related to the "Ben Asher" Family

At the end of the nineteenth century and the beginning of the twentieth, ancient manuscripts of Scripture were discovered in various parts of the world; they were published and research into them started. It became clear that there existed manuscripts related to the Ben Asher family and to Aharon Ben Asher, who was regarded by many ancient experts of the Masora as the greatest authority who had the final word regarding the text of Scripture.

Three important manuscripts relating to the Ben Asher family were known at the end of the nineteenth century: The Aleppo Codex in Syria, attributed to Aharon Ben Asher himself; Ms. Leningrad (B19a), also a complete Tanakh, written according to Ben Asher's system; Ms. Cairo of the Prophets alone, and attributed to Aharon Ben Asher's father Moshe Ben Asher ("Ben Asher" is the family name, stemming from one of the ancient progenitors of this dynasty of Masoretes). Researchers gave these manuscripts code names: **A** = The Aleppo Codex; **L** = Ms. Leningrad; **C** = Ms. Cairo. We discussed these manuscripts and what is known about them in previous chapters. However, here we shall discuss them in the context of the history of printed editions of Scripture.

One of the leading scholars of the Masora in Europe, Paul Kahle, decided to base the new scientific edition of the Tanakh, *Biblia Hebraica* (BH³), on these ancient and authoritative manuscripts. First and foremost – the Aleppo Codex. For that purpose he made contacts with the Jewish community of Aleppo, and offered to purchase the manuscript for cash, or at least to borrow it for a few months in order to use it to prepare his edition of Scripture. However the community in Aleppo rejected his offer entirely.

Consequently Kahle had to make do with Ms. Leningrad (which was not vocalized or corrected by Ben Asher himself, but only according to his method). He approached the authorities in Russia, who agreed to lend him that complete manuscript of the Tanakh, Ms. Leningrad, and in 1937 he based his new edition of *Biblia Hebraica* on it (Figure 12.4).[5] The primary text in that edition is Ms. Leningrad, and the Masora Parva from that manuscript was also included in the edition. This is the scientific edition of Scripture, in use in European and American universities. Additional editions (BHS and BHQ) appeared in the following years, in which the primary text is Ms. **L**. Some

---

5 This is the third edition of *Biblia Hebraica*. R. Kittel published the first edition in 1905–1906 and the second in 1913; the primary text in both of them was based on the Venice 1524 edition. The 1937 edition, based on Ms. **L**, was edited by R. Kittel and P. Kahle.

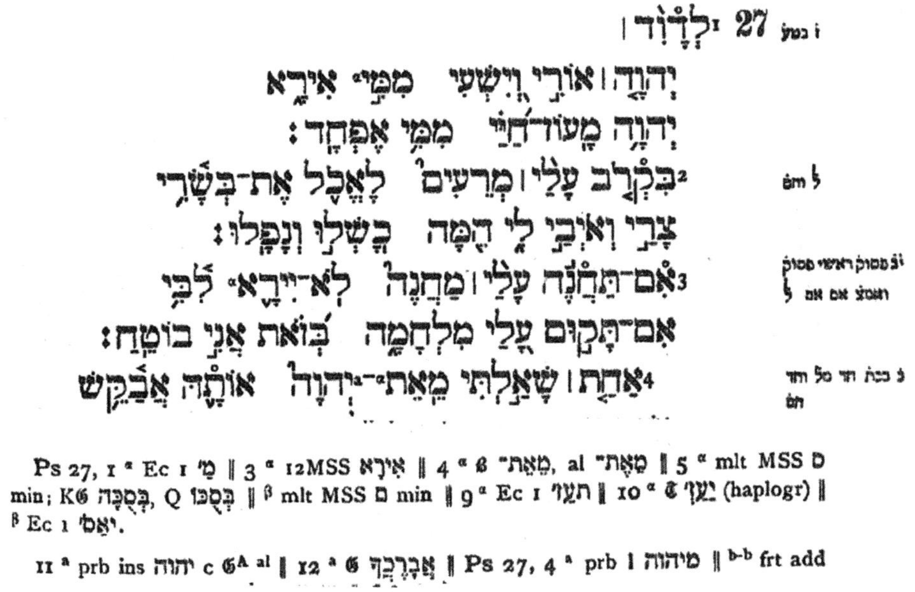

ּ i בנ"ע **27** יְלְדָוִד ׀

יְהוָה ׀ אוֹרִי וְיִשְׁעִי מִמִּי אִירָא

יְהוָה מָעוֹז־חַיַּי מִמִּי אֶפְחָד׃

בִּקְרֹב עָלַי ׀ מְרֵעִים לֶאֱכֹל אֶת־בְּשָׂרִי

צָרַי וְאֹיְבַי לִי הֵמָּה כָּשְׁלוּ וְנָפָלוּ׃

אִם־תַּחֲנֶה עָלַי ׀ מַחֲנֶה לֹא־יִירָא לִבִּי

אִם־תָּקוּם עָלַי מִלְחָמָה בְּזֹאת אֲנִי בוֹטֵחַ׃

אַחַת ׀ שָׁאַלְתִּי מֵאֵת־יְהוָה אוֹתָהּ אֲבַקֵּשׁ

Ps 27, 1 ᵃ Ec ᵇ מ׳ ‖ 3 ᵃ 12MSS אִירָא ‖ 4 ᵃˉᵃ 𝕭 מֵאֵת, al מָאֵת ‖ 5 ᵃ mlt MSS D min; K𝕲 בְּסֵפָה, Q בְּסֻכּוֹ ‖ ᵇ mlt MSS D min ‖ 9 ᵃ Ec ᵇ תֵּעֵז ‖ 10 ᵃ 𝕭 𝕵 יַעַז (haplogr) ‖ ᵇ Ec ᵇ יֹאסֵף׳.

11 ᵃ prb ins יהוה c 𝕲ᴬ ᵃˡ ‖ 12 ᵃ 𝕲 אֲבָרְכֶךָ ‖ Ps 27, 4 ᵃ prb l מֵיהוה ‖ ᵇˉᵇ frt add

Figure 12.4: One page from *Biblia Hebraica*, ed. Kittel & Kahle.

reference books for the Masora were written on the assumption that the student uses the *Biblia Hebraica* edition and is familiar with the Masoretic annotations of Ms. **L**.

For further Study

Page H. Kelley, Daniel S. Mynatt, Timothy G. Crawford, *The Masorah of Biblia Hebraica Stuttgartensia: introduction and annotated glossary*, Grand Rapids, Mich.: W.B. Eerdmans, 1998; Edson de Faria Francisco, *Manual da Bíblia hebraica: introdução ao texto massorético, guia introdutório para a Biblia Hebraica Stuttgartensia*, 3. edição revisada e ampliada, São Paulo: Edições Vida Nova, 2008 (in Spanish).

The Hebrew University Tanakh (1943–1953)

In this context it is interesting to describe the history of one edition of Scripture that was printed in Israel. All of the editions we described above were printed in Europe by Christian printers. When the Hebrew University of Jerusalem was established in the late 1920s, the heads of the university took steps to print a new edition of the Tanakh in the Eretz Israel and by Jews – an *accurate* text in a *new* and attractive layout. The President of the University, Dr. J. L. Magnes held a festive press conference in 1943 to announce the plan. The head of the project was Professor Moshe David (Umberto)

Cassuto, the rabbi of Florence, Italy, who immigrated to Eretz Israel in order to teach Tanakh at the Hebrew University of Jerusalem.

The project operated on two levels: In order to design the Tanakh, a committee was set up to choose the right font, and it approached an expert typographer named Eliyahu Korngold, to design the selected font. Regarding the text, Cassuto wanted to base the text on the Ben Asher manuscripts, and made contacts to obtain photographs of three such manuscripts: the Aleppo Codex, Ms. Leningrad and the Cairo Prophets manuscript. First he received photographs of Ms. Cairo, and afterwards photographs of Ms. Leningrad arrived from Russia. Regarding the Aleppo Codex he had partial success: Cassuto traveled to Syria, and was allowed to view the Keter. In fact he was not permitted to photograph it, and Cassuto viewed it over only a few days, but that was much more than Kahle had been able to achieve.[6]

In 1946 a small brochure of the book of Jonah appeared as an example of the projected edition. The font was designed on the basis of medieval Sephardic script, and the text based on the Cairo manuscript of Moshe Ben Asher. But these were tough days of wartime, and the project progressed slowly. When Cassuto died in 1951, the project was endangered. They decided to forfeit the idea of a new design. Instead they chose Ginsburg's second edition (1908–1920), and this edition was photographed and changes were introduced on the basis of the lists that the late Prof. Cassuto and his assistants had prepared.[7] This edition was published in 1953. Researchers and experts were highly critical, finding in it a mixture of methods and too many errors. The failure was a double one: both in terms of design and from a textual point of view.

The Koren, Dotan and Breuer Editions

However, the effort was not for naught. Korngold did not give up. Eliyahu Korngold, later known as Eliyahu Koren, produced a new edition of the Tanakh, published by his own firm, Koren Publishers Jerusalem Ltd. The first edition appeared in 1962 (see Figure 12.5). In terms of design, this Tanakh is very close to what Cassuto and his colleagues had in mind: It uses a new font, in the style of Sephardic manuscripts; the division of the text follows the Masora, indicating open and closed passages in the masoretic style, and not according to the chapters of Christian Bibles, which had a strong influence on the division of the text in editions of the Tanakh printed in Europe.

The Koren Bible Edition with an English translation appeared in 1983 (*The Holy Scriptures*, English text revised and edited by Harold Fisch). It is known today as "The Koren Jerusalem Bible".

---

6 Regarding Cassuto's lists and what can be learned from them about the Aleppo Codex, see above, Chapter Eight.

7 Only the text of Scripture was included; the apparatus of textual variants at the bottom of the page were omitted.

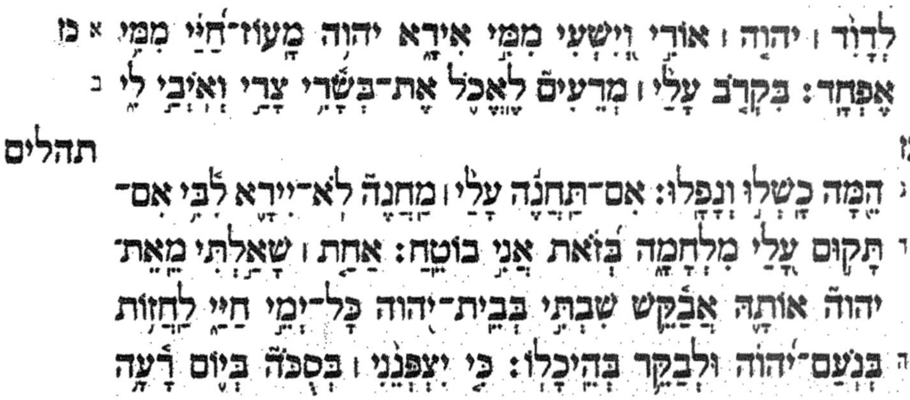

לְדָוִד ׀ יְהֹוָה ׀ אוֹרִי וְיִשְׁעִי מִמִּי אִירָא יְהֹוָה מָעוֹז־חַיַּי מִמִּי א כז
אֶפְחָד: בִּקְרֹב עָלַי ׀ מְרֵעִים לֶאֱכֹל אֶת־בְּשָׂרִי צָרַי וְאֹיְבַי לִי ב

תהלים נז

הֵמָּה כָשְׁלוּ וְנָפָלוּ: אִם־תַּחֲנֶה עָלַי ׀ מַחֲנֶה לֹא־יִירָא לִבִּי אִם־ ג
תָּקוּם עָלַי מִלְחָמָה בְּזֹאת אֲנִי בוֹטֵחַ: אַחַת ׀ שָׁאַלְתִּי מֵאֵת־ ד
יְהֹוָה אוֹתָהּ אֲבַקֵּשׁ שִׁבְתִּי בְּבֵית־יְהֹוָה כָּל־יְמֵי חַיַּי לַחֲזוֹת
בְּנֹעַם־יְהֹוָה וּלְבַקֵּר בְּהֵיכָלוֹ: כִּי יִצְפְּנֵנִי ׀ בְּסֻכֹּה בְּיוֹם רָעָה ה

Figure 12.5: Psalm 27 in the Koren edition.

And what about the text? Here the editors took an entirely different path from that of Cassuto. The three editors of the edition, M. Medan, D. Goldschmidt and A.M. Haberman – decided to follow the "later authorities", i.e. the Jewish Masoretic authorities of recent generations. They relied primarily on the edition of the Torah by R. Wolf Heidenheim from the early nineteenth century, and the rulings of *Minhat Shai* (of the seventeenth century) regarding the Prophets and Writings. By doing so they expressed basically the opinion of prevalent Halakha: They preferred the rulings of the latest authorities in the chain of generations, and not to return and seek out ancient manuscripts for which there is no continuous tradition of agreement or living communities that relied on them.

The Koren edition introduced several innovations not found in manuscripts in order to help the reader. For example: In cases of *ketiv/qere* the *ketiv* appears in the text without vocalization, and the *qere* is vocalized in the margin. In the case of words carrying the cantillation signs *zarqa*, *segol* and *telisha qetana*, the sign is repeated if the penultimate syllable should be stressed.

Other editions printed in Israel at a later date were based on manuscripts stemming from the Ben Asher family. In 1973 a Tanakh newly typeset in Israel was published by Adi Publishers (Tel Aviv). See Figure 12.6. The editor was Prof. Aron Dotan, and he based the

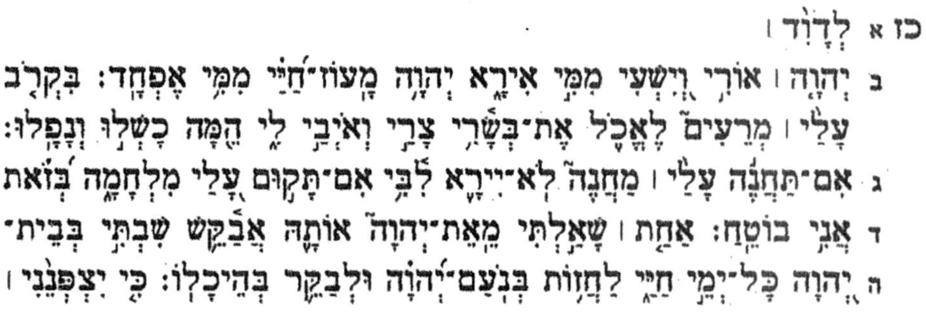

כז א לְדָוִד ׀

יְהֹוָה ׀ אוֹרִי וְיִשְׁעִי מִמִּי אִירָא יְהֹוָה מָעוֹז־חַיַּי מִמִּי אֶפְחָד: בִּקְרֹב ב
עָלַי ׀ מְרֵעִים לֶאֱכֹל אֶת־בְּשָׂרִי צָרַי וְאֹיְבַי לִי הֵמָּה כָשְׁלוּ וְנָפָלוּ:
אִם־תַּחֲנֶה עָלַי ׀ מַחֲנֶה לֹא־יִירָא לִבִּי אִם־תָּקוּם עָלַי מִלְחָמָה בְּזֹאת ג
אֲנִי בוֹטֵחַ: אַחַת ׀ שָׁאַלְתִּי מֵאֵת־יְהֹוָה אוֹתָהּ אֲבַקֵּשׁ שִׁבְתִּי בְּבֵית־ ד
יְהֹוָה כָּל־יְמֵי חַיַּי לַחֲזוֹת בְּנֹעַם־יְהֹוָה וּלְבַקֵּר בְּהֵיכָלוֹ: כִּי יִצְפְּנֵנִי ׀ ה

Figure 12.6: Psalm 27 in the Dotan edition.

text on Ms. Leningrad (deviating from it regarding only some matters such as open and closed passages, for which he followed the rulings of Maimonides for writing a Torah scroll – see above, Chapter 5). The edition is highly popular to this day. The font used in it, FrankRuehl, was a very popular font, to which the vocalization and cantillations signs were added.

In 2001 Dotan published another edition of the Bible, based also on the Leningrad Codex: *Biblia Hebraica Leningradensia*: prepared according to the vocalization, accents, and masora of Aaron ben Moses ben Asher in the Leningrad Codex, edited by Aron Dotan, Peabody, Mass.: Hendrickson Publishers, 2001

An edition of the Prophets appeared in Madrid between 1979 and 1992 based on Ms. Cairo, which also includes masoretic notes from the manuscript: *El Codice de profetas de el Cairo:*[edicion de su texto y Masoras], [dirigida] por Federico Perez Castro et al., introductory vol. & v.1–8, Madrid 1979–1992.

In 1958 the Aleppo Codex (the "Keter") arrived in Israel and was given to the President of the State, Izhak Ben-Zvi. He entrusted it to the Bible Project of the Hebrew University of Jerusalem. The Keter arrived incomplete because it was damaged in the riots that occurred in Syria towards the end of 1947. The Torah is almost completely missing, and also the end of Writings, but most of the Tanakh survived. The staff of the Bible Project decided to use it as the basis for a new edition of the Tanakh that could compete with the European edition, *Biblia Hebraica*, i.e. a Tanakh with a detailed apparatus of textual variants from all the known sources, the Dead Sea Scrolls, rabbinic literature, ancient translations and a variety of manuscripts of Scripture from different periods and various venues. This edition has been appearing slowly because of the great extent of textual investigations required. To this day (2018) only the books of the Later Prophets have appeared.

At the same time Rabbi Mordechai Breuer started work, at the behest of the Mossad Harav Kook Institute, on an edition of the Tanakh with a scientific-traditional commentary, entitled *Da'at Miqra*. Breuer did not accept the approach used by Tanakh Koren of adopting the rulings of "later authorities". He maintained that all of the scholars of the Masora – both early and late – tried to decide on the basis of the Masora in general and of Ben Asher in particular. Consequently, since ancient manuscripts from the period of the Masoretes that transmit the accurate text of Scripture and masoretic notes as well have been identified and made available, they should be examined thoroughly and decisions regarding the text should be made in accordance with them. He claimed that had they been available to the later authorities of the Masora, they too would have followed them.

In theory this system resembles that which Cassuto proposed. However Breuer added and developed a method for clarifying the text by combining the information from the text of the manuscripts and from the masoretic notes in them. Breuer's method for determining orthography in Scripture was described in principle above in Chapter 3, and there we saw that the technique led to a surprising conclusion. All of the manuscripts and the masoretic notes lead to one clear conclusion – the accurate text of the Masora is that found in the Aleppo Codex! That is the case at least in so far as orthography is concerned. But also in other areas the superiority of the Keter and of its Masorete, Aharon Ben Asher, is apparent. In other words: Until now the reputation of the Aleppo Codex was based on its attribution to Aharon Ben Asher and the testimony of Maimonides regarding it. From this point the manuscript itself was examined and found to be far better than all other manuscripts.

However one major problem remained: What could be done regarding the parts of Scripture that are missing in the Keter, such as the Torah and some of the books in the Writings? Rabbi Breuer found solutions to this problem, basing himself primarily on manuscripts close to the Keter and on the masoretic notes of the Keter itself.

The Three Breuer Editions

Rabbi Breuer published three different editions using this method: the Mossad Harav Kook edition (1977–1982; see Figure 12.7); the Horev edition (1998) and the Keter Yerushalayim (Jerusalem Crown) edition (2000). In principle all three editions used the same method, but nevertheless there are certain differences between the three, which are elucidated here.

The main innovation in the Horev edition pertains to the missing parts of the Aleppo Codex and to open and closed passages. Strange as it may be, the Masoretes were unable to achieve consensus and uniformity regarding this, and there are more than a few differences between the manuscripts. For example: There are places in which the Aleppo Codex has an open passage but Ms. **L** a closed passage, or the Aleppo Codex has a passage and Ms. **L** no space at all and the like.

Nearly 200 years after the writing of the Keter, Maimonides tried to solve this problem that the Masoretes had failed to solve. He took the Aleppo Codex, which at the time was in Egypt, and was regarded as an accurate and authoritative manuscript – and created a list of open and closed passages throughout the Torah as they appeared in it, proscribing that Torah scrolls be written according to it. Maimonides' ruling was not adopted instantly by all the Jewish communities the world over, but gradually it was implemented. New Torah scrolls were written according to Maimonides' program, and finally the tradition of passages in the Torah from the Aleppo Codex was accepted everywhere.

But what about the Prophets and Writings? Here the situation remained undecided for centuries to this day. In fact only a few communities read the *haftarot* (weekly readings from the Prophets) from parchment scrolls written according to the strictures of Halakha. Since the discovery of the Aleppo Codex, Rabbi Breuer printed the Prophets and Writings according to the division of passages in it, and slowly but surely scribes began to write books of the Prophets (and guide books for scribes) according to it.

However a difficult problem still remained: What should be done regarding the sections of the Keter that were lost? Should a different tradition be copied, such as that of Ms. **L**, for lack of choice and with the knowledge that it was not identical to the Keter? Breuer did so in his first edition, the one published by Mossad Harav Kook.

A few years later a surprising solution to this problem was found. It turned out that in the middle of the nineteenth century Rabbi Shalom Shachna Yellin sent an emissary to Aleppo in order to copy the passages from the Keter in the margins of a printed Tanakh (that was printed in London in these years) and using these notations scribes in Jerusalem wrote scrolls of the Prophets. Thus we may conclude that before Kahle and the other European scholars, the scholars of Jerusalem made sure to have in their possession accurate books of the Prophets based on the most accurate and authoritative manuscript – the Aleppo Codex. The letter of recommendation from Jerusalem was signed by the rabbi of Jerusalem, Rabbi Shmuel Salant, along with other important rabbis of the city, both Ashkenazi and Sephardi.

This Tanakh was left in an attic in Jerusalem, and its whereabouts were unknown. One day, when the house was about to be torn down, the books in the attic were passed from one hand to another and the Tanakh was nearly cast aside for burial (*geniza*). At the last minute it was identified by me, and saved from being lost forever. In the Horev edition (see Figure 12.8) Breuer arranged the open and closed passages in those parts that are missing from the Aleppo Codex according to this Tanakh, and thus it is the first printed Tanakh in which the passages completely conform to the Keter.

The Keter Yerushalayim edition (2000) is designed in a special way: On every page there are three columns, as in the Aleppo Codex. This is not a decision based on Halakha, but a choice made by the designer. The community of readers is left to determine if this layout is attractive and convenient for reading. However, this layout did involve another decision, which is related to Halakha. The open and closed passages were indicated in a special way, resembling that of the ancient manuscripts and unlike contemporary Torah scrolls. An open passage is always indicated by a blank line, like the blank lines before and after the Song at the Sea, regarding which there is agreement, and as done in manuscripts and in some ancient Torah scrolls.

The most important innovation in the Keter Yerushalayim edition relates to the layout of the books of Psalms, Proverbs and Job (which are called "*Sifrei Emet*" – אמ"ת being initials of איוב, משלי, תהלים). The Masora does not indicate how to divide the lines, except for the titles of individual psalms. But the scribes who wrote the manuscripts used to leave a blank space in every line. In the Mossad Harav Kook edition the lines were divided into hemistiches in accordance with the cantillation signs. However the ends of the lines do not create a justified left margin, which is unacceptable according to Halakha. For that reason, in the Horev edition Rabbi Breuer refrained from division into hemistiches, except in the case of titles of Psalms. But in the Keter Yerushalayim edition, he found a satisfactory solution to the problem: the lines are wide, justified both on the right and the left, and the division of every line conforms to the cantillation signs (see Figure 12.9).

The three ways in which the Psalms appear in the Breuer editions are illustrated in the following photographs:

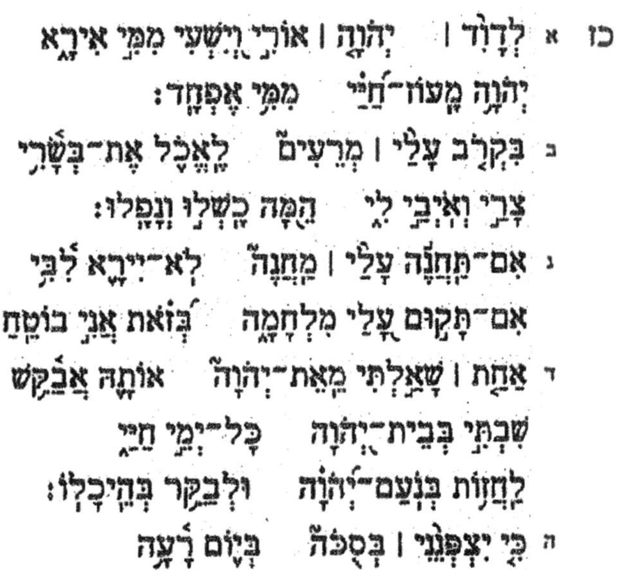

כז א לְדָוִ֨ד ׀ יְהֹוָ֤ה ׀ אוֹרִ֣י וְ֭יִשְׁעִי מִמִּ֣י אִירָ֑א
יְהֹוָ֥ה מָֽעוֹז־חַ֝יַּ֗י מִמִּ֥י אֶפְחָֽד׃
ב בִּקְרֹ֤ב עָלַ֨י ׀ מְרֵעִים֮ לֶאֱכֹ֢ל אֶת־בְּשָׂ֫רִ֥י
צָרַ֣י וְאֹיְבַ֣י לִ֑י הֵ֖מָּה כָשְׁל֣וּ וְנָפָֽלוּ׃
ג אִם־תַּחֲנֶ֬ה עָלַ֨י ׀ מַחֲנֶה֮ לֹֽא־יִירָ֢א לִ֥בִּי
אִם־תָּק֬וּם עָלַ֨י מִלְחָמָ֑ה בְּ֝זֹ֗את אֲנִ֥י בוֹטֵֽחַ׃
ד אַחַ֤ת ׀ שָׁאַ֣לְתִּי מֵֽאֵת־יְהֹוָה֮ אוֹתָ֢הּ אֲבַקֵּ֥שׁ
שִׁבְתִּ֣י בְּבֵית־יְ֭הֹוָה כׇּל־יְמֵ֣י חַיַּ֑י
לַחֲז֥וֹת בְּנֹעַם־יְ֝הֹוָ֗ה וּלְבַקֵּ֥ר בְּהֵֽיכָלֽוֹ׃
ה כִּ֤י יִצְפְּנֵ֨נִי ׀ בְּסֻכֹּה֮ בְּי֢וֹם רָ֫עָ֥ה

Figure 12.7: Psalm 27, Breuer, Mossad Harav Kook edition.

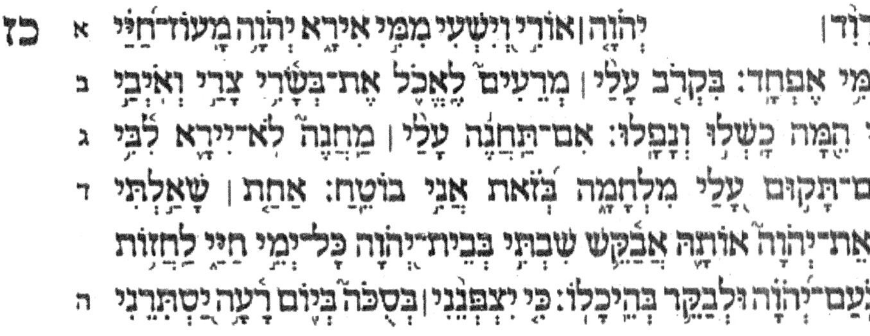

כז א לְדָוִ֨ד ׀ יְהֹוָ֤ה ׀ אוֹרִ֣י וְ֭יִשְׁעִי מִמִּ֣י אִירָ֑א יְהֹוָ֥ה מָֽעוֹז־חַיַּ֗י
מִמִּ֥י אֶפְחָֽד׃ ב בִּקְרֹ֤ב עָלַ֨י ׀ מְרֵעִים֮ לֶאֱכֹ֢ל אֶת־בְּשָׂרִ֥י צָרַ֣י וְאֹיְבַ֣י
לִ֑י הֵ֖מָּה כָשְׁל֣וּ וְנָפָֽלוּ׃ ג אִם־תַּחֲנֶ֬ה עָלַ֨י ׀ מַחֲנֶה֮ לֹֽא־יִירָ֢א לִ֥בִּי
אִם־תָּק֬וּם עָלַ֨י מִלְחָמָ֑ה בְּ֝זֹ֗את אֲנִ֥י בוֹטֵֽחַ׃ ד אַחַ֤ת ׀ שָׁאַ֣לְתִּי
מֵֽאֵת־יְהֹוָה֮ אוֹתָ֢הּ אֲבַקֵּ֥שׁ שִׁבְתִּ֣י בְּבֵית־יְהֹוָה כׇּל־יְמֵ֣י חַיַּ֑י לַחֲז֥וֹת
בְּנֹעַם־יְהֹוָ֗ה וּלְבַקֵּ֥ר בְּהֵֽיכָלֽוֹ׃ ה כִּ֤י יִצְפְּנֵ֨נִי ׀ בְּסֻכֹּה֮ בְּי֢וֹם רָ֫עָ֥ה יַסְתִּרֵ֗נִי

Figure 12.8: Psalm 27, Breuer, Horev edition.

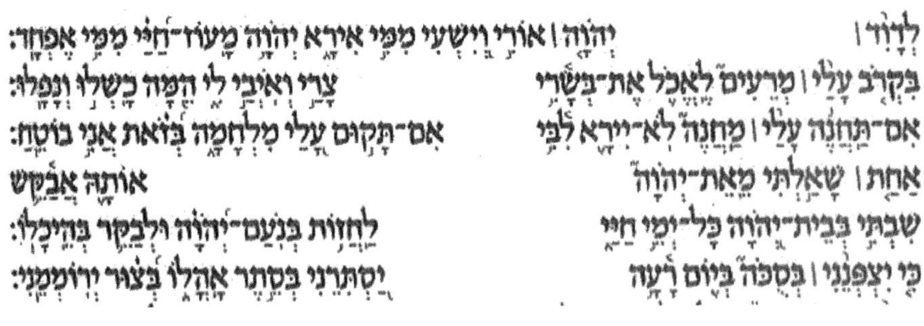

כז א לְדָוִ֨ד ׀ יְהֹוָ֤ה ׀ אוֹרִ֣י וְ֭יִשְׁעִי מִמִּ֣י אִירָ֑א יְהֹוָ֥ה מָֽעוֹז־חַיַּ֗י מִמִּ֥י אֶפְחָֽד׃
ב בִּקְרֹ֤ב עָלַ֨י ׀ מְרֵעִים֮ לֶאֱכֹ֢ל אֶת־בְּשָׂרִ֥י צָרַ֣י וְאֹיְבַ֣י לִ֑י הֵ֖מָּה כָשְׁל֣וּ וְנָפָֽלוּ׃
ג אִם־תַּחֲנֶ֬ה עָלַ֨י ׀ מַחֲנֶה֮ לֹֽא־יִירָ֢א לִ֥בִּי אִם־תָּק֬וּם עָלַ֨י מִלְחָמָ֑ה בְּ֝זֹ֗את אֲנִ֥י בוֹטֵֽחַ׃
ד אַחַ֤ת ׀ שָׁאַ֣לְתִּי מֵֽאֵת־יְהֹוָה אוֹתָ֢הּ אֲבַקֵּ֥שׁ
שִׁבְתִּ֣י בְּבֵית־יְהֹוָה כׇּל־יְמֵ֣י חַיַּ֑י לַחֲז֥וֹת בְּנֹעַם־יְהֹוָ֗ה וּלְבַקֵּ֥ר בְּהֵֽיכָלֽוֹ׃
ה כִּ֤י יִצְפְּנֵ֨נִי ׀ בְּסֻכֹּה בְּי֢וֹם רָ֫עָ֥ה יַסְתִּרֵ֗נִי בְּסֵ֣תֶר אׇהֳל֑וֹ בְּצ֥וּר יְרוֹמְמֵֽנִי׃

Figure 12.9: Psalm 27, Breuer, Keter Yerushalayim edition.

Editions of the Tanakh as a Tool for Clarifying Issues of Text and Masora

The *Mikraot Gedolot Haketer* edition of Bar-Ilan University (edited by Menachem Cohen) began appearing in 1992 and is nearing completion.[8] This edition seeks to be totally faithful to the Aleppo Codex. In those parts of the Keter that are extant, the text of the Keter is copied precisely, and in those parts that are missing an effort was made to reconstruct it as much as possible. This in contradistinction to Rabbi Breuer's method, which rejects some aspects of the vocalization in the Keter (on the difference between this edition and Breuer's with regards to secondary stress marks, see Chapter 11).

Now we can summarize the characteristics of the editions of the Tanakh discussed in this chapter: Both *Biblia Hebraica* editions (BH³, BHS and BHQ) and the Dotan editions are based on Ms. **L**. The Breuer editions, the edition of the Hebrew University Bible Project and the *Mikraot Gedolot Haketer* edition are based on the Aleppo Codex. All of these use to some degree or other Ms. **L** and additional manuscripts in order to make up for the missing parts of the Keter and also to determine the text.

The Dotan and Breuer editions of the Tanakh present the text of Scripture alone. Other editions add additional information related to the Masora and to other textual witnesses of Scripture. The *Biblia Hebraica* edition gives the notes of the Masora Parva from Ms. **L**, and its latest edition (BHS, Stuttgart 1967) and the one that is currently being completed (BHQ, since 2004) – also refer to notes of the Masora Magna in Ms. **L**.[9] Both the Bible Project edition and *Mikraot Gedolot Haketer* give the notes of the Masora Magna and Masora Parva from the Aleppo Codex (In its missing parts, both use the masora of Ms. L). In *Mikraot Gedolot Haketer* an additional apparatus called *Ein Hamasora* briefly elucidates the masoretic notes giving references to the verses they mention.

Both *Biblia Hebraica* and the Bible Project editions provide textual variants. *Biblia Hebraica* cites variants from ancient translations, various manuscripts and even provides reasonable suggestions for correcting the text. The Bible Project edition contains five apparatuses of textual variants, and refers to translations, rabbinic literature, the Dead Sea Scrolls, manuscripts that are unrelated to the Ben Asher text and manuscripts that are close to it. Both of these editions make use of a wide range of abbreviations, which require study and practice in order to use them to their full advantage.

---

8 To date (2018) all of the books of the Torah and Prophets and half the books of Writings have appeared.

9 The BHS edition refers to the notes of the Masora Magna that were published in a separate book by G. E. Weil. In the BHQ edition the notes of the Masora Magna appear in the margins of the text.

Finally we shall point out two differences between the editions discussed, that need to be noted in order not to read them incorrectly: In the editions based on manuscripts (such as *Biblia Hebraica*, *Mikraot Gedolot Haketer* and Breuer's or Dotan's editions) there is no sign for the stressed syllable, in words accented with a *segol*, *zarqa* or *telisha*. For example in an expression such as טֶ֫רֶם֩ יִשְׁכָּ֔בוּ ("They had not yet lain down", Gen. 19:4) in which both words have penultimate stress, only one *zarqa* and one *segol* appear at the end of the words, unlike Koren's method, which doubles the signs. In the editions based on manuscripts, such as Biblia Hebraica, *Mikraot Gedolot Haketer* and Dotan's editions, generally a secondary stress mark is not given in words such as: הוֹלְכִים, שָׁמְרוּ. Breuer adds a short *ga'aya*, to help the reader, even though there is none in the manuscripts (see above, Chapter 11).

Conclusion

Throughout generations the sages of the Masora tried to arrive at an accurate and authoritative text of Scripture. In the period of manuscripts the Masoretes did so with the help of sophisticated and complex systems of vocalization and cantillation as well as masoretic notes. In the period of printing, this new technology contributed much to the accuracy of Scripture, to distribution of an accurate text and the aesthetic aspect of the books. In our generation, the computer generation, both means of control and printing techniques have advanced, and contemporary scholars of the Masora use them, adding an additional, important layer to research on the text of Scripture, its accuracy and its dissemination to the general public.

For further study

C. Rabin, *"Miqra, defusei HaMiqra"* (=Printed Bible Editions) *Encyclopaedia Biblica* 5, 1968, cols. 368–386 (Heb.).

M. Breuer, "Three Editions of the Bible", *Leshonenu* 64 (2002), pp. 33–50 (Heb.).

Y. Ofer, "The Preparation of the Jerusalem Crown Edition of the Bible Text", *Hebrew Studies* XLIV (2003), pp. 87–117.

Part III: **The Masora in Interaction with Other Disciplines**

13 The Masora and Hebrew Grammar

Masoretes and grammarians are two distinct groups of scholars, who operated in different venues and periods, and with different aims. The early Masoretes established the vocalization and cantillation signs and created the first masoretic notes. The later Masoretes wrote the ancient codices of Scripture that are known today, which include vocalization and cantillation signs, notes of the Masora Magna and Masora Parva on the same page as the text, masoretic notes that appear in appendices at the beginning or end of the codices, and separate masoretic collections such as *Okhla weOkhla*. The important group of later Masoretes flourished in Eretz Israel, and their center was Tiberias. They were most active in the ninth and tenth centuries and included such outstanding exponents as Aharon Ben Asher and his father Moshe, as well as his adversary Moshe Ben David Ben Naftali.

The grammarians flourished all over the Jewish world: the first grammarian is thought to have been Saadia Gaon (882–942), who was active in Egypt and Iraq, and wrote a dictionary (the *Agron*) and a book of grammar. In the tenth century, the Karaite lexicographer David Alfasi operated in Eretz Israel; Menahem ben Saruq, author of the dictionary *Mahberet Menahem* (in Hebrew) worked in Spain as did the grammarian Yehuda Hayyuj and (later on) Yona ibn Janah. In later generations R. Abraham Ibn Ezra and R. David Kimhi and others continued that work in Spain and Provence.

Both groups made use of Scripture, which stood at the center of their activity. The Masoretes' intention was to preserve the accurate text of Scripture: its writing, pronunciation and cantillation. The grammarians dealt with the language of Scripture: They described it grammatically, revealed its rules and inflections and categorized its vocabulary and roots lexicographically, clarifying the connections between words that stemmed from the same root, and detailing the different meanings included in every root.

What then were the relations between these two groups of scholars? Did the Masoretes engage in grammar and the grammarians in Masora? Did they cooperate and exercise mutual influence or was there tension and disagreement between them? Were the borders between the Masoretic area and the grammatical unequivocal, or were they sometimes blurred? We shall try to answer these questions and related ones in this chapter.

The Masora as the Basis for Grammar

The accurate transmission of Scripture – in essence the work of the Masoretes – is the basis and the foundation of all grammatical investigation of Scripture, since determining the linguistic facts enables their analysis and description. This is particularly important regarding vocalization signs: The description of the vowels is an essential part of the grammatical description, and every such description requires categorizing and listing the vowels in a given word. Thus the grammarians made use of the signs established by the Masoretes and based their compositions on them.

https://doi.org/10.1515/9783110594560-013

This is what the grammarian Yona ibn Janah (c. 990 – c. 1050) said, when dealing with a linguistic matter (*Sefer Hariqma*, ed. Wilensky, p. 253, translated from R. Judah ibn Tibbon's Hebrew translation):

> And I said it is possible [to assimilate similar letters, like the letters *tet* and *taw* in the words וְהַעֲבַטְתָּ or וּשְׁחַטְתֶּם] without saying so unequivocally since I have not encountered until today anyone with a clear pronunciation whose tradition I could trust entirely on hearing Scripture. But I do rely on checking the words in accurate books, and I have seen a book of Scripture from Jerusalem and another from Iraq... and I also rely on the *Masoret*. And what I said about never encountering a scholar of tradition whose tradition I could trust – was not for sloth on my part to investigate, because you know my investigations and my attempts and my perennial diligence for investigating since my youth, but we have grown up in this distant and far-removed corner of the world, and by necessity I have not seen anyone of this description.

Ibn Janah reveals his sources here. He relies on accurate books of Scripture for his grammatical study. In order to know accurately how a word should be pronounced he relies on its vocalization: both the Tiberian vocalization that was used in Eretz Israel (which he found in a "Scripture from Jerusalem") and the Babylonian vocalization used in Iraq (which he found in "another [Scripture] from Iraq"). Ibn Janah also relied on *"Masoret"*, i.e. masoretic notes and masoretic compositions. But all of this was insufficient for him. He looked for someone with clear speech, from whom he could receive Scripture orally, i.e. an individual who could read Scripture to him, and whose oral tradition was authoritative, stable and clear. Certain questions of pronunciation, such as how to pronounce the letters *tet* and *taw* when they appear together in words like וְהַעֲבַטְתָּ or וּשְׁחַטְתֶּם – were unclear to him, and he could not solve the question from written sources, so he wanted to find a living oral tradition, but could not find a suitable informant.

Thus the Masora is the basis for grammar, and it is clear that it preceded it. First there was a tradition of writing Scripture and how it should be read. The Masoretes came along and wrote the tradition down (adding vocalization and cantillation signs), and stabilized the written tradition with masoretic notes. After them came the grammarians who tried to describe the text that the Masoretes had established.

This is a simplified description, which is correct in general, but not entirely accurate and requires clarification and refinement. Below we shall see that certain grammatical concepts were already known to the early Masoretes. Moreover the later Masoretes operated after the first grammarians, and it is unimaginable that they were not influenced by them and that their influence is not evidenced in the Masoretes' writings.

Similarities and Differences in the Work of the Grammarian and the Masorete

Here we return to what we have already observed in Chapter Two, which dealt with the descriptive techniques and ways of classification used by the Masora: The early grammarians regarded Scripture as the exclusive source for their description of the

Hebrew language and almost entirely ignored post-Biblical Hebrew. Obviously Scripture is the area of operation of the Masorete. Both the grammarian and the Masorete dealt with the words of Scripture and tried to describe them in general, which is what they have in common.

However there is a basic difference between the intent of the grammarian and that of the Masorete (also discussed in Chapter Two, see above): The grammarian seeks to describe the *rules of language* and explain them, while the Masorete wants to relate the *textual facts*, doing so as efficiently and briefly as possible. The Masorete may make use of the rules of language or style in order to describe the text of Scripture. He may point out the connection between the penultimate stress of the word אנכי (=I) and its cantillation accent, or the different distribution to the forms יונתן and יהונתן (=Jonathan) in two parts of the Book of Samuel. But for the Masorete discovering the grammatical rules is not a goal in itself, but only a means. He makes use of the rules, details precisely exceptions to them, arriving at an accurate description of the findings in every verse of Scripture. The grammarian, on the other hand, regards the grammatical rules revealed as his main goal, and will try to express them and explain them. He does not discuss exceptions to the rule, if they are not too many, since they do not undermine the rule itself.

Sometimes the Masorete makes use of a distinction that is of no importance to the grammarian, such as the fact that in a certain book of Scripture a particular word appears in *plene* form more often than in defective, and vice versa in another book. In other cases, the Masorete's description is notably grammatical, such as:

מ"ג-א יח' טז, לט: אוֹתָךְ י"ו מל' לשון נקבה...

(=Masora Magna of the Aleppo Codex, Ez. 16:39 – אוֹתָךְ [=you (object)] – 16 *plene* occurrences in feminine form...)

מ"ג-ל יר' יט, י: אוֹתָךְ ט' מל' בלשון זכר...

(=Masora Magna of Ms. Leningrad, Jer. 19:10 – אוֹתָךְ – 9 *plene* occurrences in masculine form [pausal form of אוֹתְךָ])[1]

Here the Masorete decided to make use of the distinction between masculine and feminine forms in order to describe the occurrence of different forms efficiently. From this we may deduce, of course, that he was familiar with the grammatical distinction between masculine and feminine forms, and also had sufficient knowledge of grammatical terminology to express that distinction.

---

1 An example of the feminine form is the words of Yosef to Potiphar's wife about her husband "וְלֹא חָשַׂךְ מִמֶּנִּי מְאוּמָה כִּי אִם אוֹתָךְ בַּאֲשֶׁר אַתְּ אִשְׁתּוֹ" ('he has withheld nothing from me except **yourself**, since you are his wife – Gen. 39, 9); an example of the masculine pausal form is God's words to Ezekiel "קוּם צֵא אֶל הַבִּקְעָה וְשָׁם אֲדַבֵּר אוֹתָךְ" ('Arise, go out to the valley and there I will speak **with you**' – Ez. 3: 22).

Rudiments of Grammar in the Masora

Complete and sophisticated Hebrew grammar developed on the basis of Arabic grammar. The first grammarians were familiar with the grammatical literature of Arabic and implemented it, modifying to the needs of Hebrew. Early grammars of Hebrew were written in Arabic, applying the grammatical terminology used to describe Arabic for the sake of Hebrew, and many of the grammatical rules created for the Arabic language were adapted for use in Hebrew grammar.

However Prof. Aron Dotan demonstrated in an important article that even in the early period that preceded the influence of Arabic grammar, rudiments of grammatical distinctions and grammatical thinking may be found in Hebrew masoretic literature. Here are two examples of such distinctions:

Above, in Chapter Four, mention was made of list no. 5 in the collection *Okhla weOkhla* (ed. Frensdorff) entitled:

א"ב מן חד וחד, חד מלעיל וחד מלרע דלוג ולית דכוותי'

> (=Alphabet, i.e., an alphabetical list, containing pairs of words, one *mil'el* and the other *milra'*, the alphabetical list is not complete, and there are none like them, i.e. unique words.)

The terms *mil'el* and *milra'* as used in this list carry a special meaning, and they represent a contrast between the vowels in the words listed. For example, in the first pair אָמַר-אֹמֶר, the contrast is between *holam* and *qamaṣ* (*qatan*); in the second pair, אָרְחוֹת-אֹרְחַת between *holam* and *patah*, etc. This use refers to a theoretical scale of vowels, rating the vowels used in the Hebrew language from top to bottom. The *holam* is regarded as higher on the scale than the *qamaṣ* and the *qamaṣ* higher than the *patah* and the *zere*.

Another example of grammatical awareness is the use of abstract terms for generalization. When the Masoretes wanted to speak of a group of words from one root that had a certain characteristic, or all the words from a certain root, they exemplified the group by use of a gerund (verbal noun) derived from the root. The concept of root (שורש) was not yet in use by the Masoretes, and we use it here in order to clarify their intention for ourselves in terms we use.

Here are a few examples of masoretic notes that use abstractions of verbal nouns:

מ"ג-ב שמ' יג, יז: נחימה אלהים ג' וסימנ' ויהי בשלח פרעה את העם (שם – ולא נָחָם א-להים).
מי יודע ישוב (יונה ג, ט – וְנִחַם הא-להים). ושלאחריו (יונה ג, י – וַיִּנָּחֶם הא-להים).

> (=Masora Magna, Ms. **B.**, Ex. 13:17 – נחימה אלהים [=an artificial construct meaning "relenting" + G-d] 3 occurrences, which are: "Now when Pharaoh let the people go [*God did not lead* them...]", *Ibid.*]. "Who knows [but that *God may* return and *relent*", Jonah 3:9]. And in the following verse [Jonah 3:10 – "And *God renounced* the punishment"].)

מ"ג-ב שמ' כט, מב: דבירא שם ד' וסימנה' עלת תמיד (שם – לְדַבֵּר אליך שם). ואצלתי מן הרוח
(במ' יא, יז – וְדִבַּרְתִּי עמך שם). הנה עודך מדברת דמלכים (מל"א א, יד – מְדַבֶּרֶת שם). רד בית
מלך יהודה ודברת שם (יר' כב, א).

(=Masora Magna, Ms. **B**, Ex. 29:42 דבירא שם – [=an artificial construct meaning "speaking there"] – 4 occurrences, which are: "a regular burnt offering [... and *there* I will *speak* with you", *Ibid.*]. "I will draw upon the spirit" ["I will come down and *speak* with you *there*, and I will draw upon the spirit", Num. 11:17]. "While you are still talking" in Kings ["While you are still *there talking* with the king", I Kings 1:14]. "Go down to the palace of the king of Judah *where* you shall *utter* this word" [Jer. 22:1].)

מ"ג-ב ו'י' ח, טז: המזבחה ה'... וכל הקטרה דכות' בר מן ג'...

(=Masora Magna, Ms. **B**, Lev. 8:16 – "the form המזבחה ("on the altar") has 5 occurrences" ... "and all הקטרה [= "burning"] like that except 3 occurrences...)

In the first note the *artificial* abstract term נחימה represents the three verbs derived from the 'root' *nun, ḥet, mem* (נָחַם, וְנִחָם, וַיִּנָּחֶם), which mean respectively led, relented and renounced. In the second the abstract term דבירא represents four forms of the verb דבר (to speak). In the third note all of the verses containing verbal forms related to the abstract term הקטרה (burning) – הִקְטִיר, יַקְטִיר, וְהִקְטַרְתָּ, וְהִקְטִיר, וַיַּקְטֵר – are regarded as one category from the perspective of the Masora.

Furthermore, it should be noted that the words נחימה and דבירא do not exist in the language, and were coined here in order to express an abstract concept. The inclusion of the verse "God did not lead them..." (Ex. 13:7) in the category of נחימה is particularly interesting since the term נָחָם there is not derived from the root *nun, ḥet, mem*, but is constructed from the verb נחה (=to guide, lead) with the addition of the objective suffix *mem*. It is difficult to determine whether the inclusion of the word here was purely technical, or whether the Masorete understood the word as expressing a change of mind (an interpretation to be found in a midrash).

For further study

Aron Dotan, "From Massora to Grammar – The Beginnings of Grammatical Thought in Hebrew", *Leshonenu* 54 (1990), pp. 155–168 (in Hebrew).

Aron Dotan, "De la Massora à la grammaire: les débuts de la pensée grammaticale dans l'hébreu", *Journal Asiatique* 278, 1–2 (1990), pp. 13–30 (in French).

Yosef Ofer, "The Relation of Different Masora Types to Grammar", in M. Bar-Asher (ed.), *Hebrew Through the Ages: In Memory of Shoshanna Bahat*, Jerusalem 1997, pp. 51–69 (in Hebrew).

David Lyons, "Abstract Nominals in the Tiberian Masora: a Collection of Annotations from the London British Library MS. Or. 4445 Pentateuch", *Studies in Bible and Exegesis 3: Moshe Goshen-Gottstein – In Memoriam*, Ramat Gan 1993, pp. 231–265 (in Hebrew).

The Concept of Roots and the Accumulative Masora Lists

Determining the root of a given word is one of the essential and central issues in Hebrew grammar. According to the perspective accepted today most roots in the Hebrew language constitute three consonants, but there are some weak consonants that drop out in inflection, and consequently the roots that include them are divided into different conjugations according to the weak consonant and its placement in the root, such as נ"פ (the letter *nun* as the first letter), פ"י (the letter *yod* as the first letter), ע"ו (the letter *waw* as the second letter), ל"י (the letter *yod* as the last letter), the double conjugation, ע"ע (The second letter and the last letter are identical) etc. This grammatical perspective was the innovation of R. Yehuda Hayyuj, towards the end of the tenth century.

However, before Hayyuj other grammarians suggested other methods for determining the root. Saadya Gaon did not choose an abstract skeleton of letters, but an actual form, the basic noun form from which he derived all the other forms. Another group of grammarians from the ninth and tenth centuries, among them Yehuda ben Quraysh, Menaham ben Saruq, Dunash ben Labrat and David ben Avraham Alfasi – subscribed to the "minimal root". According to that system the root is comprised of the letters that occur in every inflection and conjugation.

Aron Dotan, in his book *The Awakening of Word Lore* (2005), points out a connection between the minimal root concept and the lists of accumulative Masora. In his opinion, the Masoretes who created these lists did not operate in a vacuum: A deep basic knowledge of grammar in general and the concept of the root in particular was clearly imbedded in them. This concept is readily apparent in their linguistic practice even thought they did not write it down or express it – and perhaps could not express it – in clear and explicit rules.

Here are some examples of groups of unique words that were combined in the accumulative masoretic notes in various manuscripts: וָאֹהֲבֵם, אֹהֲבֶם, כְּאָהֲבָם, כְּאַהֲבַת, תְּאֵהֲבוּ, בְּאַהֲבִים, וְאָהוּב, אֲהַבְךָ (the root אה"ב; masoretic note in Ms. **Cairo** on Hosea 14:5); נָשׂוּי, וּמַשָּׂא, וּמְשִׂאֹתוֹ, וּמַשָּׂאֲכֶם, וּמַשָּׂאֵת, וּמַשָּׂאתְ, וּנְשָׂאתַנִי, נְשָׂאתַנִי, וְאֶשָּׂאֶנּוּ, אֶשָּׂאֶנּוּ (the root נש"א or perhaps the common letters *sin* and *aleph*, Ms. **Cairo** on Jer. 10:19); שִׁיבַת, שְׁבִיתֶם, שְׁבִיתֵנוּ, שְׁבִיתַיִךְ, שְׁבִיתָהֶן (forms derived mainly from *shin* and *bet* from the roots שו"ב and שב"י, Ms. Cairo on Ez. 16:53); כָּלוּ, וַיִּכְלוּ, וַיָּכְלוּ, וַתֵּכֶל, מַאֲכָל, הֶאֱכַלְתָּם, הֶאֱכַלְתָּם, אָכָל, יְכַלְכֵּל, וְכִלְכְּלוּ, וּלְכַלְכֵּל, כָּל, וְכֹל [בשליש], יָכֵל etc. (forms derived mainly from *kaf* and *lamed*, from the roots כל"ל, כו"ל, בל"י, אכ"ל; Ms. P [St. Petersburg – Russian National Library Evr. I B 3: Codex Babylonicus Petropolitanus] on Is. 40:12); בְּמֹסֶרֶת, לְמֹסֵר, וּמֹסְרוֹת, מִמֹּסְרוֹת, בְּמֹסְרוֹת, וּבְמֹסְרָם (detailed masoretic note in Ms. **L**^M based on the Babylonian Masora on Num. 31:16).

In the last note, the Masorete finds a common element in all of the words, *mem-sameh-resh*. This in contradiction to Menaham's system that does not include in the root letters that serve the pattern, such as the letter *mem* in the word וּמֹסְרוֹת (Job 39:5). Menaham lists that word under the root ס"ר.

For further study

Aron Dotan, *The Awakening of Word Lore: From the Masora to the Beginnings of Hebrew Lexicography*, Jerusalem 2005, pp. 61–72 (in Hebrew);

Yosef Ofer, "The Accumulative Masorah and Word Study" (on: Aron Dotan, *The Awakening of Word Lore*, Jerusalem 2005), *Leshonenu* 67 (2005), pp. 403–405 (in Hebrew).

Chapters of Grammar in the Masora

Some of the codices of Scripture have at the beginning or the end chapters of "Grammar of the Masora". These chapters contain rules and descriptions of the letters of the alphabet, vocalization and cantillation signs, secondary stress marks (*ge'ayot*) and the relations between them.

This material is essentially different from ordinary masoretic notes. It does not concentrate on the number of occurrences of a given form, or descriptions of orthography, but in a broad description of phenomena and rules. Consequently it is a step in the direction of a grammatical description.

These chapters do not have a standardized order, and in each manuscript a different collection appears. The edition of *Diqduqe HaTe'amim* edited by Aron Dotan (Jerusalem 1967) presents 26 chapters, which Dotan attributes to the Masorete Aharon Ben Asher himself. A much broader collection of masoretic grammatical chapters was collected in the edition of *Diqduqe HaTe'amim* by Baer and Strack (Leipzig 1879), arranged in the order determined by the editors. We shall return to these two editions below.

One of the characteristic phenomena of these chapters is *examples*. Ordinary masoretic notes usually list the verses that are exceptions from the rule, and include all of the exceptions in order to provide a description that covers all of Scripture. But in the grammatical chapters we find verses that illustrate the rule, preceded by the word כמות (= "such as"). That is the case, for example, in one of the masoretic chapters in an appendix to the Aleppo Codex, which was meant to describe the condition in which the letter *bet* carries a *dagesh* at the beginning of a word that starts with two *bet*s:

כאשר יהיה שוא תחת האות הראשון יהיה דגש **כמות** זה: "וַיְהִי בְּבוֹאָם" (שמ"א טז, ו)

חוץ משבא יהיה רפי **כמות**: "והוא אִשָּׁה בִבְתוּלֶיהָ" (וי' כא, יג)

(When there is a *shewa* beneath the first letter it has a *dagesh*, such as: וַיְהִי בְּבוֹאָם [= "When they arrived", I Sam. 16:6].

Except when the first letter is vocalized with another vowel it is soft (without *dagesh*), as in: והוא אִשָּׁה בִבְתוּלֶיהָ [= "He may marry only a woman who is a virgin", Lev. 21:13]).

Some of the chapters try to explain a particular phenomenon, and do not make do with only a description. For example the chapter that clarifies the use of the *paseq* (ed. Dotan, chapter 16; ed. Baer and Strack, par. 28):

הפסק יהיה לה' (=לחמישה) דברים, כאשר תקנו החזים הישרים. האחד, להפריד את (=אות) מחברתה שהיא כמוה... כמו "להגדיל | למעלה" (דה"א כב, ה) "וברזל | לרב" (דה"א כב, ג)...

שנית, שתי תיבות, זו לעומת זו כתובות, כגון: "ד' | ד'" (שמ' לד, ו) "יום | יום" (בר' לט, י ועוד)...

השלישית, ליראה שלא יסמכו שתי תיבות, זו לעומת זו חצובות, והם לא יתכנו להתחבר, ובמלה

אחת לדבר, כגון: "אלוה | רשע" (תה' קלט, יט), "יודוך עמים | אלהים" (תה' סז, ד)...

The *paseq* [which is marked as a vertical line: |] serves five purposes, as established by the honest prophets. One, to separate one letter from the next that is like it [when the last letter in the first word is the same as the first letter in the next]... such as להגדיל | למעלה (= "excee-dingly great", I Chr. 22:5) or וברזל | לרב (= "much iron", I Chr. 22:3); [...] second, two [identi-cal] words, written one after the other, such as ד' | ד' (= "The Lord! The Lord!", Ex. 34:6) or יום | יום (= "day after day", Gen. 39:10 etc.); [...] third, lest they put two words together that come one after the other that cannot be combined and pronounced together, such as: אלוה | רשע (= "God | the wicked", Ps. 139:19) or יודוך עמים | אלהים (= "O God | Peoples will praise you", Ps. 67:4)...

This is not a masoretic rule, since one cannot derive from it where a *paseq* should occur and where it should not. The purpose of the rule is to explain the phenomenon called *paseq*, which is in principle a grammatical issue.

One of the chapters (ed. Baer and Strack, par. 36, entitled שער נקודות אומץ המקרא [= "Chapter on the vowels, 'Courage of Scripture' (?)"]) is clearly grammatical in cha-racter. It discusses the changes that occur in vowels when a word is transferred to another by inflection: plural, possessive form or changes of tense. The chapter is very similar to a chapter in the grammar by Saadya Gaon, and scholars have debated the question of its origin: Does it reflect an unusual development within the Masora, which Saadya Gaon adopted and developed further, or vice versa: Saadya's grammati-cal teachings reached one of the Masoretes, who translated it to Hebrew [Saadya's grammatical work was written in Judeo-Arabic] and framed it in verse as a chapter of Masora, abbreviating it and simplifying it.

Here is a section from this chapter:

כי הדבר הנמשך להצטרפה, כאשר יצא מנטעו בשפה, הוא שלשה ענינים להאליפה:

(1) או קבוץ יתקבץ בו השם המאוחד בניבו כאשר תדבר בשם מיוחד בקבצו תאמר דָּבָר מֶלֶךְ חֵפֶץ יוֹם וכדומה להם, וכאשר תקבץ אותו תאמר דְּבָרִים מְלָכִים חֲפָצִים יָמִים.

(2) או דבר יומשך אליו השם המיוחד תאמר דָּבָר, וכאשר תוציא אותו אל קונה תאמר דְּבָרִי דְּבָרֶנוּ דְּבָרְךָ דְּבָרוֹ [...]

(3) או זמן יפול על השם ויעשה פועל, ויבדיל בו עבר מן הנצב ומן העתיד

For the matter pertains to inflection, when the form of the word changes for three reasons:

(1) Either the noun undergoes declension, when you speak in the singular, you say דָּבָר, מֶלֶךְ, חֵפֶץ, יוֹם and the like, but when you speak in plural you say דְּבָרִים, מְלָכִים, חֲפָצִים, יָמִים. [*Note how the vowels change from singular to plural form.*]

(2) Or the noun is in possessive form: You say דְּבָר, and when the possessor is indicated you say דְּבָרִי, דְּבָרֶנוּ, דְּבָרְךָ, דְּבָרוֹ.

(3) Or the verbal form differentiates between past, present and future tense.

The reader should pay attention to the special grammatical terminology that the author uses, creating new Hebrew terms: the word צירוף refers to declension of a noun. נטעו בשפה is the basic form of the word. קבוץ השם המאוחד is making a plural noun from a singular form, דבר יומשך אליו השם refers to the possessive form.

Quasi 'Masoretic Notes' from *Mahberet Menahem*

When the Masoretes started their activity it was long before the development of Hebrew grammar. But the earliest extant dated manuscripts of the Masora are from the tenth century, by which time Hebrew lexicographers and grammarians were already working on lexicons and grammars. Consequently, the Masoretes who prepared these manuscripts may have been aware of the new grammatical teachings of that time.

Did the new findings of the grammarians influence the Masoretes in their work? In many cases the answer is negative: The Masorete was only interested in the quintessential area of the Masora, revising the masoretic notes he received, and even if he knew the lexicons and grammars, he did not use them in writing the codices of Scripture.

However some of the Masoretes may not have confined themselves in that way, and did create masoretic notes or chapters of "Grammar of the Masora" under the influence of grammatical literature. Above we noted the possibility that a Masorete knew the grammatical teaching of Saadya Gaon, and that he wrote under its influence a chapter of "Grammar of the Masora". Here we shall see a different case, in which the influence is beyond doubt.

Ms. L^S (St. Petersburg, National Library of Russia, Evr. II C1), is a manuscript of the Torah that includes Saadya Gaon's translation to Arabic. The scribe of the manuscript was Shmuel ben Yaakov, the scribe who also wrote Ms. **L**, the complete manuscript of the Tanakh, the writing of which was completed in Egypt in 1009. Ms. L^S includes a special kind of masoretic notes. These are lexical notes that refer to the different meanings of a given Hebrew root. There are more than one hundred such notes in this manuscript, and they do look different from the rest of the normal masoretic notes.

The source of these notes is the dictionary of Menahem ben Saruq, *Mahberet Menahem*, written in the mid-tenth century. The Masorete refers to a word in Scripture, determines its root and the number of meanings the root carries, and then lists the different meanings. The details are given in accordance with space available: In short notes, the Masorete cites the number of meanings of the root under discussion, and illustrates each one with one or more Scriptural verses taken from the *Mahberet*. In longer notes the Masorete establishes first that the root has many meanings (and does not indicate their number), and then details each one by use of one or two verses for each meaning, as much as the space on the page allows.

Here is an example of a short entry in Mahberet Menahem and its revision by the Masorete of Ms. L^S:

מנחם: ירד מתחלק לשני ענינים: האחד,

יוצאי ירך יעקב   שמות א, ה

ועד ירכים   שמות כח, מב

תחת ירכי   בראשית כד, ב

השני, לירכתים ימה   שמות כו, כז

ולירכתי המשכן ימה   שמות כו, כב

ענין זויות המה

Menahem: The root ירך is divided into two matters (=has two meanings):
The *first*:
"from Jacob's *loins*" (Ex. 1:5)
"to the *thighs*" (Ex. 28:42)
"under my *thigh*" (Gen. 24:2)
The *second*:
"of the wall of the Tabernacle *at the rear* to the west" (Ex. 26:27)
"the corners of the Tabernacle *at the rear*" (Ex. 26:22)
      The meaning (of the second group of verses) is 'edges'

מ"ג-לס שמות לו, כז:

וּלְיַרְכְּתֵי ב'   שמות לו, כז [+כו, כב]

ועיקרו ירך ויש לו תרין עיני'

יצאי ירך יעקב   שמות א, ה

ממתנים ועד ירכים   שמות כח, מב

שים נא ידך תחת ירכי   בראשית כד, ב

הענין השני

ולירכתי המשכן   שמות כו, כב

לירכתים ימה: שמות כו, כז

<u>Masora Magna, Ms. L^S – Ex. 36:27</u>

וּלְיַרְכְּתֵי – This word has two occurrences in the bible (Ex. 36:27 & 26:22)
And its root is ירך, which has two meanings:

"from Jacob's *loins*" (Ex. 1:5)
"from the hips to the *thighs*" (Ex. 28:42)
"Put your hand under my *thigh*" (Gen. 24:2)
      And the second meaning:
"the corners of the Tabernacle *at the rear*" (Ex. 26:22)
"of the wall of the Tabernacle *at the rear* to the west" (Ex. 26:27)

The masoretic note begins with a brief masora note, "Two", without details, as in the Masora Parva. Afterwards he cites the root, ועיקרו ירך, noting that the root has two meanings (ענינים = "matters"), and finally quotes the verses for illustration from the *Mahberet* for each meaning. In this case the lexical entry is very brief, and the Masorete cites it nearly completely, omitting only the definition of the second meaning.

     In the second example the lexical entry is longer, and the Masorete had to abridge it:

מ"ג-לס בראשית לז, א

מְגוּרֵי

עיקרו גר ויש לו דרכים הרבה כמות

מגורי אביו	בראשית לז, א
גר ותושב:	בראשית כג, ד
דרך אחר והגרתי לגי	מיכה א, ו
נגרות ביום אפו:	איוב כ, כח
דרך שני גורו לכם מפני	איוב יט, כט
מתגרת:	תהלים לט, יא
דרך שלישי יגורהו בחרמו	חבקוק א, טו
דברי אגור:	משלי ל, א
דרך רביעי גרה לא יגר:	ויקרא יא, ז
דרך חמיש' [קרא בגרון]	ישעיה נח, א
[ו]גרונך מצמ[אה]	ירמיה ב, כה
דרך שישי(ת) גור אריה:	בראשית מט, ט
דרך שביעי מגררות במגרה	מל"א ז, ט

Masora Magna, Ms. **L**[S] – Gen. 37:1

מְגוּרֵי

Its root is גר and it has many meanings, such as:
"the land where his father had *sojourned*" (Gen. 37:1)
"resident *alien*" (Gen. 23:4)
Another meaning: "I will *tumble* [her stones] into the valley" (Micah 1:6)
"*Spilled out* the day of his wrath" (Job 20:28)
A second meaning: "*Be in fear* of the [sword]" (Job 19:29)
"[your] *blows*" (Ps. 39:11)
A third meaning: "*pulled* them *up* in trawl" (Hab. 1:15)
"The words of *Agur* (=the one who collected the wisdom)" (Prov. 30:1)
A fourth meaning: "it does not *chew the cud*" (Lev. 11:7)
A fifth meaning: ["cry with full *throat*"] (Is. 58:1)
"*your throat* from thirst" (Jer. 2:25)
A sixth meaning: "a lion's *whelp*" (Gen. 49:9)
A seventh meaning: "*sawed with saws*" (I Kings 7:9)

In the extant *Mahberet Menahem* the root גר has eleven sections, and here only seven are numbered (and eight cited). The verse to which the masoretic note refers (Gen. 37:1 – "the land where his father had *sojourned*") is inserted in the appropriate place, given as the first meaning here. The verse is not listed in Menahem's book.

In Ms. **L**[S] there are masoretic notes with grammatical characteristics. Here is an example of one of them:

אֶחָד	במדבר לא, לט
כל לשון זכר אֶחָד קמ'	
כמות אחָד וששים	במדבר לא, לט

אחד מן הנערים	מל״ב ד, כב	
הַאִישׁ אֶחָד יֶחֱטָא:	במדבר טז, כב	
וכל לשון נקבה אַחַת		
מדה אַחַת	שמות כו, ב ועוד	
חקה אחת	במדבר ט, יד ועוד	
וכבשה אחת:	במדבר ו, יד	

אחד [one – masculine singular] (Num. 31:39)
In masculine form always אֶחָד with *qamaṣ*
Such as "sixty-*one*" (Num. 31:39)
"*one* of the servants" (II Kings 4:22)
"when *one* man sins" (Num. 16:22)
And in feminine form always אַחַת
"the same measurement" [מדה אַחַת] (Ex. 26:2 and more)
"*one* law" (Num. 9:14 and more)
"*one* ewe lamb" (Num. 6:14)

Here the Masorete wanted to point out the grammatical phenomenon according to which the form אֶחָד is used in the masculine and the form אַחַת in the feminine (the form in absolute state with a *qamaṣ* in the masculine and a *patah* in the feminine). He does not suggest an explanation for the difference between the two forms, but only points out the fact and illustrates it. His perspective is clearly grammatical, but he ignores the form of the masculine in the construct form (אַחַד) and the pausal form of the feminine (אֶחָת), in contradistinction to the norm in masoretic notes, which generally ignore grammatical distinctions and center on the appearance of אֶחָד-אַחַד or אֶחָת-אַחַת and describe them (See, for example, the Masora Magna of MS L on Gen. 26,10 and to Ex. 16,33).

Finally here is a list of grammatical characteristics that are not customary in masoretic notes. When at least one of these appears in a masoretic note, that is a sign that the Masorete is coming close to the area of grammar, either under the direct or indirect influence of the grammarians, or as part of an internal development in the world of the Masoretes:

1. Reference to grammatical pattern or conjugation (even if it is not defined using the accepted terminology);
2. Reference to the grammatical inflection of a word, such as reference to the relation between absolute state and construct state.
3. Reference to theoretical forms that do not appear in Scripture;
4. Determining a general rule, without citing its exceptions precisely;
5. Pointing out a trend in the text without explaining exactly when it occurs;
6. Attempts to explain a phenomenon, when the explanation is not required by the description itself;
7. Posing questions without solutions;
8. Using grammatical terminology.

Between Masoretes and Grammarians – Respect and Tension

Some of the grammarians stressed the greatness of the Masoretes and the importance of their work. R. Yona ibn Janah in the introduction to his grammar, *Kitab Al-Luma'* (Hebrew Name: *Sefer HaRiqma*), described the importance of both the Masora and grammar:

> And those who are slothful in the this respect should learn from the Masoretes and follow them in their great efficiency and research and their enormous effort in counting *plene* and defective and knowing ultimate and penultimate stress, until they cited verses in which the entire alphabet appears, and beyond that the care they have given to make these holy books accurate. And no less this valuable and honorable study [=grammar], that enables us to understand the words of God, helping us to fulfill his commandments, bringing us closer to his reward and distancing us from his punishment.
>
> (R. Yona ibn Janah, *Sefer Hariqma*, translated from the Hebrew translation of R. Yehuda ibn Tibbon, ed. Wilensky, Introduction, p. 15).

But there were grammarians who regarded the science of Masora as inferior to that of grammar, because the Masora dealt with mainly technical questions like *plene*/defective spelling, and not with essential matters. R. Abraham Ibn Ezra was opposed to homilies based on the Masora and says in the introduction to his commentary on the Torah:

> And I shall not mention the explanations of the Masoretes for why a word appears in *plene* form in one place and defective in another, because all of their reasons are homiletic, as Scripture writes the word once in full for clarity, and once lacking a letter and abbreviated. And after the homiletic explanation for *plene* and defective forms, may they instruct us how the books should be written. And Moses wrote without the letter *waw* ד' ימלך ("the Lord will reign", Ex. 15:18), and the scribe copying Proverbs wrote with a *waw* תחת עבד כי ימלוך ("a slave who becomes king", Prov. 30:22), and many years passed between them. These explanations are appropriate only for children.

And at the beginning of his book *Yesod Mora weSod Torah* (ed. Yosef Cohen, Ramat Gan 2002, pp. 64–65) Ibn Ezra criticizes the Masoretes even more severely for engaging in preserving the text alone and not concerning themselves with its contents:

> And a Masorete who has not learned another discipline is like a camel carrying silk, who neither does the silk any good, nor does the silk benefit him.

The Controversy of Saadya Gaon with the Masoretes

The controversy between Saadya Gaon, the grammarian, and the Masoretes regarding an important issue should be mentioned here. The Masoretes discussed at length the question of whether a *dagesh* should occur in the letters *bet, gimmel, dalet, kaf, pe, taw* when they appear at the beginning of word, stating a rule called סימן אוי"ה ובגדכפ"ת (=mnemotechnical note: *aleph, waw, yod, he* and *bet, gimmel, dalet, kaf, pe, taw*). This basic rule determines that when the aforementioned letters at the beginning of a word will be pronounced without a *dagesh* if the previous word ends with the letters *aleph, waw, yod* or *he*. Saadya Gaon formulated the rule differently: It does not depend on the final *letter* of the previous word, but the last *vowel*. If the previous word ends with a vowel, the letters בגדכפ"ת at the beginning of the following word will occur without a *dagesh* even if the letters אוי"ה do not appear at the end of the previous word (e.g. אֵלֶיךָ פָרָה [Num. 19:2] or וְעָשִׂיתָ בַדֵּי [Ex. 25:13]), and if it does not end with a vowel, the letters בגדכפ"ת will have a *dagesh* even if the previous word ends with the letters אוי"ה (e.g. בְּצִדָּהּ תָּשִׂים [Gen. 6:16], עֵינַי תָּמִיד [Ps. 25:15], וְיָדָיו תְּבַצַּעְנָה [Zech. 4:9]).

Saadya says:

> And this is the rule that I established for the letters בגדכפ"ת, by which I mean that if the [previous] word ends in a vowel [these letters are without a *dagesh*], is more appropriate for scholars to use as a rule, than the rule that says: Whenever the letters אוי"ה come before the letters בגדכפ"ת the latter are without a *dagesh* except in the case when *waw, yod* or *he* are pronounced as consonants... and except when the letters *kaf* or *taw* are vocalized with a *qamaṣ*... since these are wearisome ways, but the value of my formulation is that it is more comprehensible for the masses.
>
> (Saadya Gaon, *The Dawn of Hebrew Linguistics: The Book of Elegance of the Language of the Hebrews by Saadia Gaon*, ed. Aron Dotan, Jerusalem 1997, Ch. 4, text 2, p. 422)

> And in this chapter many people have abandoned the issue of whether a *dagesh* occurs or not, and turned to the chapter on בגדכפ"ת, thinking that it contains everything they need to know about language. They (=The Masoretes) gave their rule the title אוי"ה, by which they refer to the four letters, but these are not the pertinent factors!
>
> (*Ibid.*, Ch. 4, text 1, p. 410)

Saadya looked for the essential grammatical reason that influenced the occurrence of the *dagesh* and also wanted to formulate a simpler rule that had no exceptions. The Masoretes, devoted to preserving the text, did not have to explain the rule, but only to describe the situation in Scripture, so for them Saadya's rule is not preferable. It seems that they preferred to attribute the rule to the letters אוי"ה, because in that passage of the Masora they elaborated on the qualities of these letters.

For further study

A. Dotan, "Vestiges of Masora in the Grammar of Rav Saadya Gaon", *Proceedings of the Eleventh Congress of the International Organization for Study of the Masora* (IOMS), Jerusalem 1994, pp. 7*-16* (in Hebrew).

Sefer Diqduqe HaTe'amim – Its Attribution and Editions

זה ספר מדקדוקי הטעמים שהחביר ר' אהרן בן משה בן אשר שממקום מעזיה הנקראת טבריה, אשר על ים כנרת מערבה, אלהים יניחהו על משכבו ויקיצהו עם ישני אדמת עפר, המשכילים והמזהירים יזהירו כזהר הרקיע בגן עדן.

This is a book of *Diqduqe HaTe'amim* that was written by Aharon ben Moshe ben Asher, of Ma'aziya, called Tiberias, on the western shore of the Sea of Galilee, may God grant him to rest in peace, and awake him with those who sleep in the ground, the enlightened and splendid who will be as bright as the firmament in paradise.

This passage presents the book *Diqduqe HaTe'amim* (="The Grammar of the Cantillation Signs") and its author. From it we may learn that the author of the book was the famous Masorete Aharon ben Moshe of the Ben Asher family that lived in Tiberias. It is also clear that when the passage was written Aharon Ben Asher was no longer living.

But where is the book to which this passage refers? Surprisingly enough, the solution to this question is not simple.

We have already mentioned the practice of copyists of manuscripts of Scripture to include at the beginning or the end of their books collections of masoretic material. This masoretic material is highly varied, but two primary genres may be discerned: The first consists of lengthy lists, such as lists of *paseqim*, controversies between *madinhai* (=the Eastern Jews, the Babylonian Jews) and *ma'arvai* (the Western Jews, The Jews of the land of Israel), controversies between Ben Asher and Ben Naftali, etc. The second includes chapters of "Masoretic Grammar", which deal with letters, vocalization, cantillation signs and secondary stress marks (*ge'ayot*), and the rules related to them.

There is no standard order by which the chapters on grammar appear in the manuscripts. In that way they resemble notes of the Masora Magna and Masora Parva in the Tiberian manuscripts, which appear in a different order and in different formulation in every manuscript. But in a minority of manuscripts (and not necessarily the earliest ones) the aforementioned opening passage does appear, attributing all their Masora chapters to Aharon Ben Asher.

Thus two questions arise:

1. Should we accept the testimony of the manuscripts that Aharon Ben Asher wrote or edited the masoretic composition entitled *Sefer Diqduqe HaTe'amim*, or should we regard that as a later attribution of masoretic material to the famous and important Masorete Aharon Ben Asher?
2. If there indeed was a masoretic composition by Aharon Ben Asher, can it be identified in the manuscripts and can we know its extent and the order of its chapters?

As mentioned above, two, essentially different, editions of *Sefer Diqduqe HaTe'amim* have been published, and the reason for the difference between them is the approach of their editors to these two questions.

S. Baer and H. L. Starck published their edition at the end of the nineteenth century (Leipzig 1879). The Hebrew and the German title of their edition said: "The Book of *Diqduqe HaTe'amim* by Rabbi Aharon ben Moshe ben Asher with other ancient traditions. From the title itself, it is clear that Baer and Strack answered the first question affirmatively and the second negatively. In their opinion there was once a book "written" by Ben Asher, but today we have no way to identify its extent or the order of the chapters in it. The editors collected with care as many manuscripts as they could that included "masoretic grammar". They treated every chapter separately on the basis of the manuscripts in which it appeared. They determined the order of the chapters themselves on the basis of their grammatical logic: chapters dealing with letters, vocalization, cantillation, secondary stress marks (*ge'ayot*) etc.

But on careful consideration Baer and Strack's work was misleading: They inserted the passage attributing the book to Aharon Ben Asher at the beginning of their edition! In that way they created the impression that the entire book, as presented in their edition, was by Ben Asher. This superficial impression misled many readers and researchers who used the book, allowing themselves to be misled by its form. Even though the editors did not hide their methodology, the "small print" did not overcome the superficial impression that the book created.

The other edition of the book is that of Aron Dotan, whose approach was the opposite. Dotan answered both questions affirmatively. In order to understand how he identified the original work of Aharon Ben Asher, we should examine a comparative table he presents in his book (Figure 13.1).

We see here two multi-columned tables, and each column presents the order of the chapters is one manuscript. Each chapter is designated by a number or letter. The opening passage is marked by the letter פ, and it appears in three manuscripts from the group marked א (on the left). The order of the chapters in those three manuscripts is basically identical, containing twenty chapters and six more. According to Dotan the testimony of those three manuscripts should be accepted, and their example should be followed. They represent the complete work arranged by Aharon Ben Asher!

Aharon Ben Asher was not the author or originator of the grammatical material included in *Diqduqe HaTe'amim* . This material crystallized in a long process, starting generations before him. But it was Ben Asher who "compose" the book, that is, edited it and arranged it out of this masoretic material into a well-thought-out composition with a standardized order and text. After his death an anonymous writer added the opening passage that conveyed the identity of the author, creating the text reflected in the three manuscripts of group א, on which Dotan based his edition.

In the other manuscripts, cited in the table as group ב (on the right) – different combinations of chapters appear, in an order that may have preceded Ben Asher's editing, or may have come later. These are, no doubt, important and ancient masora materials, and they should be examined and understood. But Dotan's edition restricts itself to the twenty six chapters included in the collection edited by Aharon Ben Asher, and marked them as nos. 1–26 (כו-א). In every chapter Dotan cites parallel passages from the other manuscripts, and analyzes the material in depth and thoroughly.

However, another, entirely different, opinion should not be ignored. D. S. Loewinger presented it in his critique of Dotan's edition. Loewinger answers both questions posed above in the negative. He contends that the attribution to Ben Asher is late, evidenced by the fact that the passage on which it is based does not appear in the ancient manuscripts from the East, but only in later manuscripts of European

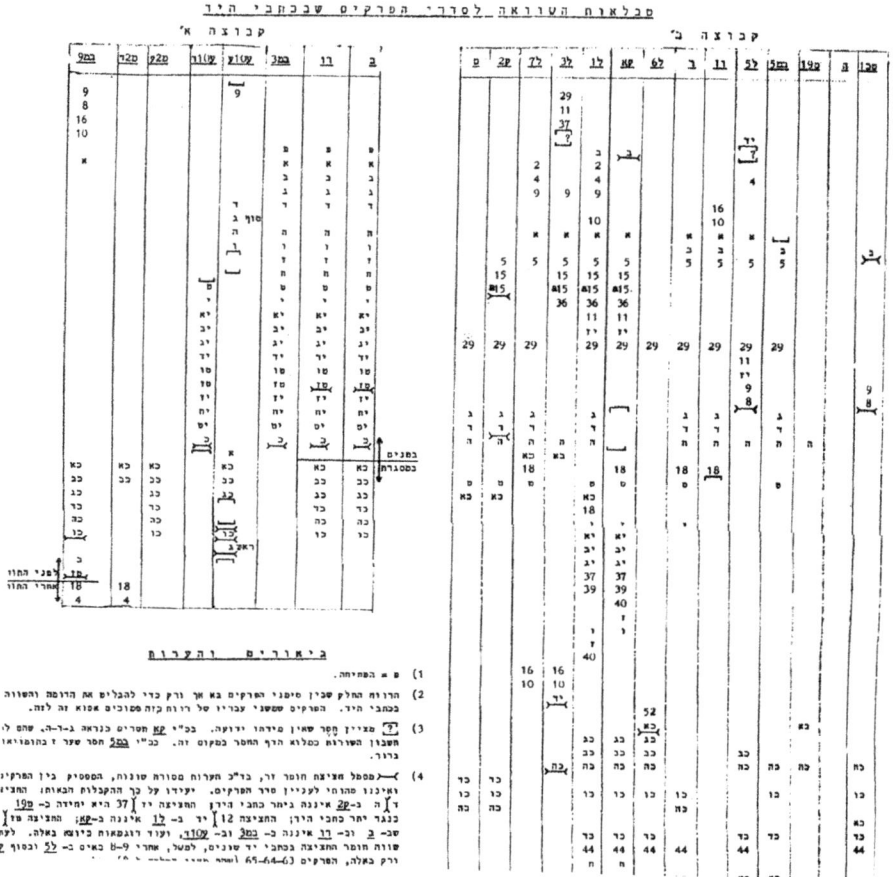

Figure 13.1: *Diqduqe HaTe'amim*, ed. A. Dotan, p. 2 (Courtesy of the Academy of the Hebrew Language).

provenance. In that case, there is no special value to the group of chapters that is presented in Dotan's edition, and their crystallization only took place at a later date.

In this context attention should be paid to the Aleppo Codex. According to testimony regarding the codex, it included at the beginning eight folios that contained a collection of passages of "masoretic grammar". This collection is not at all like Dotan's edition of *Sefer Diqduqe HaTe'amim* . If indeed the Aleppo Codex was "the personal copy of the Tanakh" used by Aharon Ben Asher, how could the collection at the beginning of the codex not be identical to *Sefer Diqduqe HaTe'amim* that Ben Asher wrote?

Several solutions may be suggested to solve this problem. Perhaps *Sefer Diqduqe HaTe'amim* was not the work of Ben Asher, as Loewinger maintained; on the other hand, one may doubt the attribution of the Aleppo Codex to Ben Asher, although it is supported today by a number of solid pieces of evidence. And there are also solutions that resolve the contradiction: Maybe Ben Asher wrote the collection of "masoretic grammar" at the beginning of the Aleppo Codex before he edited *Sefer Diqduqe HaTe'amim* . It is also possible that the collection of chapters that was at the beginning of the Aleppo Codex was not Ben Asher's work, but was appended to the codex at a later date after its completion under his supervision.

For further study

Aron Dotan, *The Diqduqe HaTte'amim of Aharon Ben Moshe Ben Asher: with a critical Edition of the original Text from new Manuscripts,* Jerusalem 1967 (in Hebrew), pp. 15–25.

Idem, "Was the Aleppo Codex Actually Vocalized by Aharon Ben Asher?", *Tarbiz* 34 [1965], pp. 136–155 (in Hebrew).

David Samuel Loewinger, "The Aleppo Codex or *Diqduqe Hatte'amim*", *Tarbiz* 38 [1969], pp. 186–204 (in Hebrew).

Two Chapters from *Diqduqe HaTe'amim*

Below are two chapters from Dotan's edition. The first, Chapter Five, deals with the pronunciation of the "*shewa* of similarity", and the second (Chapter Six) with the vocalization of the word בֵּן (="son"). The texts here are vocalized (unlike their appearance in the manuscripts).

Chapter Five – *shewa* of similarity

סִימָן שְׁתֵּי אוֹתִיּוֹת, אֲשֶׁר בְּתֵיבָה אַחַת צְבוּתוֹת, זוֹ לְעוּמַּת זוֹ חֲרוּזוֹת.

כָּל הַמִּקְרָא עַל זֶה, מִפִּי כָּל סוֹפֵר וְחוֹזֶה, הַסִּימָן הַטּוֹב זֶה, עוֹד לֹא יִרְזֶה.

אִם גַּעְיָא לְאוֹת רִאשׁוֹן, תִּקְדֹּם בִּנְעִימַת לַחְשׁוֹן, יִפְתַּח פִּיו בְּאוֹת הָרִאשׁוֹן.

כְּגוֹן: יִסְכְּהוּ צַאלִים צֶלְלוֹ (אִיוֹב מ, כב), מְלֵלֵי גָלְלֵי (נחמ' יב, לו), יְלְלַת הָרֵעִים (זכ' יא, ג), אֲשֶׁר לְקָקוּ (מ"א כא, יט), רִבְבוֹת אַלְפֵי (במ' י, לו), בְּרִבְבוֹת נַחֲלֵי שֶׁמֶן (מי' ו, ז).

וְאִם אֵין גַּעְיָא אֶצְלָם, לֹא יִפָּתְחוּ לְעוֹלָם, אֲבָל גּוֹלְלָם, לֹא יִפְצְחוּ בְמֹלָם. כְּמוֹ: רִבְבוֹת אֶפְרַיִם (דב' לג, יז), חִקְקֵי-אוֹן (יש' י, א), הִנְנוּ אָתָנוּ (יר' ג, כב), הִנְנִי אֲנִי (יח' לד, כ וְעוֹד).

וְהַכֹּל לָזֶה דּוֹמֶה, וְטוֹעֶה בָזֶה הוֹמֶה, כְּעוּר וְסוֹמֵא, לַבּוּרִים יְדַמֶּה.

חוּץ מִן ד' פְּסוּקִים, עַל זֶה פּוֹסְקִים, וְעָלָיו חוֹלְקִים.

כִּי גַעְיָה לָהֶם סְמוּכָה, וְעִמָּהֶם מְשׁוּכָה, וּבָהֶם תְּמוּכָה, שְׁמוּרָה וַעֲרוּכָה.

וְהֵם לֹא נִפְתָּחִים, וּבָהּ לֹא נִפְצָחִים:

בְּצַר לָהֶם יְשַׁחֲרֻנְנִי (הו' ה, טו), זֶבַח תּוֹדָה יְכַבְּדָנְנִי (תה' נ, כג), אָז יִקְרָאֻנְנִי... יְשַׁחֲרֻנְנִי וְלֹא יִמְצָאֻנְנִי (מש' א, כח), וּמְשַׁחֲרַי יִמְצָאֻנְנִי (מש' ח, יז).

This rhymed chapter provides a simple rule for pronunciation of the "*shewa* of similarity", i.e. when a *shewa* appears under the first of two identical letters: If it also has a secondary stress mark (*ga'ya*) – it is a sounded *shewa*, and if it has no *ga'ya*, it is silent. There were later grammarians in whose opinion every *shewa* under the first of two identical letters was pronounced, but from this chapter, we can see that that was not the opinion of the Masoretes. Only in certain cases was the *shewa* to be sounded.

The exceptions from the rule are highly extraordinary: They are six words in which the cantillation sign appears on the first of the two similar letters. From the point of view of the Masorete every cantillation sign (and especially a disjunctive one) may be regarded as a stress mark (*ga'ya*), and perhaps all the more so if a secondary stress mark (*ga'ya*), is sufficient to make the *shewa* pronounced, a primary stress mark (a cantillation sign) should clearly do so. For that reason the rule is given, stating that not to be the case, and in the cited words the *shewa* is silent. The six words are:

יְשַׁחֲרֻנְנִי (=״and beg for my favor״, Hos. 5:15)

יְכַבְּדָנְנִי (=״honors me״, Ps. 50:23)

יִקְרָאֻנְנִי... יְשַׁחֲרֻנְנִי וְלֹא יִמְצָאֻנְנִי (=״They shall call me… they shall seek me but not find me״, Prov. 1:28)

יִמְצָאֻנְנִי (=״will find me״, Prov. 8:17)

Chapter Six – בֵן and בֶן

כל בן אשר במקרא סמוך ומוקף
עם אב או עם איש או עם מעשה או עם מעשה אביו
בג' נקודות יהיו:
כמו: בֶן-אברהם (בר' כה, יב ועוד), בֶן-איש (וי' כד, י ועוד), בֶן-אשה אלמנה הוא (מל"א ז, יד),
בֶן-בליעל (שמ"א כה, יז).
חוץ מן ד' במקרא:
ותלד בֶן-ששי ליעקב (בר' ל, יט), וימלט בֶן-אחד (שמ"א כב, כ), ולמפיבשת בֶן-קטן (שמ"ב ט, יב),
בֶן-פרִיץ (יח' יח, י).
וכל בן בטעם גריש – כגון בֶן חכם (מש' י, א) – ולעולם בשתי נקודות.
חוץ מן ז' במקרא בטעם גרש והם בג' נקודות:
ושחט את בֶן הבקר (וי' א, ה), בֶן הישראלית (וי' כד, י), זכריהו בֶן ירבכיהו (יש' ח, ב), בֶן יאיר
בן שמעי (אס' ב, ה), זכריה בֶן משלמיה (דה"א ט, כא), את בת משלם בֶן ברכיה (נחמ' ו, יח),
הלבֶן מאה שנה (בר' יז, יז).

This rule is not rhymed, and it deals with whether the word בן (=״son״) should be vocalized with a *zere* (ε) or a *segol* (e). The Masora says that the vocalization depends on the status of the word: if it comes before a hyphen, it should be vocalized with a *segol*, but if it carries its own cantillation sign – with a *zere*. Both of these generalizations have exceptions. In fact, according to Dotan, the vocalization does not depend on the existence or absence of a hyphen, but on the grammatical status of the word: The separate form is vocalized with a *zere*, and the construct form with a *segol.* However the Masora preferred to describe the vocalization as dependent on the musical status of the word, perhaps because that was clearer to the reader than the grammatical status.

Additional explanations and a more extensive discussion may be found in Dotan's edition, which contains the chapters themselves, a commentary, an analysis and footnotes.

14 The Masora and Biblical Exegesis

Is there exegesis in masoretic notes?

The purpose of the Masora is to preserve the text of Scripture. It does so with great care as we have seen in the chapters of this book. By establishing a uniform text, accurate in spelling, pronunciation and cantillation signs, the Masora creates the basis for the study of Scripture and its interpretation. Clearly, anyone who wishes to study Scripture and interpret it needs the accurate text set forth by the Masoretes. The reader will read this text, the student will study it and the exegete will interpret it.

However the question remains, does the Masora engage in exegesis? Did the Masoretes regard interpreting Scripture as part of their task? Is Biblical exegesis reflected in masoretic notes? We shall try to answer these questions in this chapter.

Masoretic notes that disregard the meaning of a word

A general rule in the Masora is that *it follows the pronunciation of the word*. The Masora combines homonyms even if they are not written identically or have different meanings.

Listing words that are not written identically is a common occurrence in the Masora, e.g.:

מ"ג-א דה"א טו, טז: מַשְׁמִיעִים ג' ב' מל' וחד חס' - ויאמר דויד (שם) וכל ישראל מעלים (שם, כח) ועמהם הימן (שם טז, מב).

[MM (=Masora Magna) of MS A, I Chr. 15:16 – מַשְׁמִיעִים ("making heard") 3 occurrences, twice *plene*, once defective: "David said" (Ibid.), "All Israel brought up" (Ibid. 15:28); "And with them Heman" (Ibid. 16:42).]

The Masora cites three occurrences together, and the various spellings: in the first verse and the last the spelling is *plene* (מַשְׁמִיעִים), but in the second verse defective (מַשְׁמִעִים).

Moreover, the Masora lists together words even when they differ grammatically. Thus, for example, it lists together masculine and feminine forms or singular and plural forms, such as:

מ"ג-א מל"א ב, טז: מֵאִתָּךְ ה' וסימנהון והיה אני (מ"א יח, יב) שאלה (מ"א ב, טז) שאלה (שם, כ) ויאמר הקשית (מל"ב ב, י) שתים (מש' ל, ז).

[=MM **A** I Kings 2:16 – מֵאִתָּךְ (= ""of you") 5 occurrences and their sign is "When I" (I Kings 18:12); "request" (I Kings 2:16); "request" (Ibid., 2:20); "And he said you have asked a difficult thing" (II Kings 2:10); "two things" (Prov. 30:7).]

https://doi.org/10.1515/9783110594560-014

In the words of Adonijah "I have one request to make of you" (I Kings 2:16) the word מֵאִתָּךְ ("of you") is addressed to Bathsheba, and is, of course in the feminine form. Batsheba's words "I have one small request to make of you" (Ibid. 2:20), are addressed to Solomon and the word מֵאִתָּךְ is the masculine form in its pausal form (that appears at the end of a phrase). Nevertheless the Masora lists them together without any distinction, because they are pronounced identically.

מ"ג-א דה"ב לד, יג: עֹשֵׂה מְלָאכָה ד' - והאיש ירבעם (מל"א יא, כח) ועמך לרב (דה"א כב, טו) ועל הסבלים (דה"ב לד, יג) יורדי הים (תה' קז, כג).

[=MM A II Chr. 34:13 – עֹשֵׂה מְלָאכָה (="doing the work") 4 occurrences: "This man Jereboam" (I Kings 11:28); "and with you an abundance" (I Chr. 22:15); "over the porters" (II Chr. 34:13); "others go down to the sea" (Ps. 107:23).]

Regarding Jereboam (I Kings 11:28) it is said "and when Solomon saw that the young man was a capable worker (עֹשֵׂה מְלָאכָה)", in singular form, but in Psalms 107:23–24, "Others go down to the sea in ships, ply their trade (עֹשֵׂי מְלָאכָה) in the mighty waters; they have seen the works of the Lord" the expression appears in plural form. Despite the grammatical difference and the difference in spelling – singular form with the letter *he* and plural form with the letter *yod* – the Masora lists both verses together, since the pronunciation of both forms is identical. The purpose of the note was evidently to distinguish between this expression and another common expression עֹשֵׂה/עֹשֵׂי הַמְּלָאכָה (the same, but with the definite article in the second word).

A. Dotan (*Leshonenu* 54 [1990], p. 162) cited an example of a masoretic note that combined occurrences of one word – i.e. all pronounced identically – with five different meanings grammatically. The Masora cites six occurrences of the word *nissa* in Scripture, two of them written with letter *sameh* and *he* (נסָּה) and the rest with *sin* and *aleph* (נשָׂא). These are the verses included in the note:

והאלהים נִסָּה את אברהם (בר' כב,א)

"And God put Abraham to the test" (Gen 22:1) – pi'el, past tense, third person, root: נס"י.

ויואל ללכת כי לא נִסָּה (שמ"א יז, לט)

"Then he tried to walk, but he was not used to it" (I Sam. 17:39) – *pi'el*, past tense, third person, root: נס"י.

אם נשאת נָשָׂא לנו (שמ"ב יט, מג)

"Has he given us any gifts?" (II Sam. 19:43) – *nif'al*, past tense, third person, root: נש"א.

ועל כל נשא ושפל (יש' ב, יב)

"Against all that is lofty – so that it is brought low" (Is. 2:12) – *nif'al*, present tense, singular.

חירם מלך צר נָשָׂא את שלמה (מל"א ט, יא)

"King Hiram of Tyre had supplied Solomon" (I Kings 9:11) – *pi'el*, past tense, third person.

נָשָׂא לבבנו אל כפים (איכה ג, מא)

"Let us lift up our hearts with/to our hands" (Lam. 3:41) – *qal*, future tense, first person plural.

In this case the Masora points out the difference in spelling, but does not refer to the grammatical difference.

Moreover, it even combines homonyms *that have entirely different meanings.* M. Breuer cited several cogent examples (in his article "Masora and Grammar", *Israel: Linguistic Studies in the Memory of Israel Yeivin*, Jerusalem 2011 [Heb.], pp. 45–47):

מ"ג-א יש' כא, יא: מְלֵיל ב' - ותאמר מי מלל לאברהם (בר' כא, ז) שמר מה מליל (יש' כא, יא).
בתרייה מל'

[=MM **A** Is. 21:11 - מְלֵיל 2 occurrences: "And she said: Who would have said (מלל) to Abraham" (Gen. 21:7); "Watchman, what of the night (מליל)" (Is. 21:11).]

גינצבורג, המסורה, סעיף נ 56: וְנָבִיא ז' – [...] – וְנבא לבב חכמה (תה' צ, יב)

[=Ginsburg, *The Massorah*, Par. נ56: וְנָבִיא ("And a prophet") – 7 occurrences – [...]; "that we may obtain (ונבא) a wise heart" (Ps. 90:12)]

מ"ג-ש1 יר' לג, ו: אהרן בן אשר ומערב' ורפאתים מל', מדנח' מסרי ורפאתם ל' חס' (שם). ידעו
כי רפאתים מל' (הושע יא, ג). ואין בקר ברפתים כת' חס' א' (חב' ג, יז).

[=MM **S1** Jer. 33:6 – Aharon Ben Asher and the western sages: ורפאתים in *plene* form – "and I will heal them (ורפאתים)" (Jer. 33:6). The eastern sages' Masora comment is: ורפאתם in Jer. 33:6 is the only defective occurrence; "they knew not that I healed them (רפאתים)" (Hos. 11:3) – is *plene*; "And no cattle are in the cowsheds (ברפתים)" (Hab. 3:17) – is written without *aleph*.]

Regarding this last example Breuer says: "The ability of the Masora to combine words according to their sound alone – ignoring their meaning – reached its apex here in an astonishing way."

Citing meanings in masoretic notes

Sometimes the Masora operates differently and does not ignore differences of meaning. Some masoretic notes list together homonyms with different meanings and point out the differences. For example:

מ"ג-ל בר' ד, ד: וְהֶבֶל ג' והבל הביא גם הוא (שם) לתהו והבל כחי כליתי (יש' מט, ד) שקר החן
והבל היפי (מש' לא, ל). קדמיה שם אנש.

[=MM **L** Gen. 4:4: וְהֶבֶל 3 occurrences: "And Abel also brought" (Ibid.); "I have spent my strength for empty breath" (Is. 49:4); "Grace is deceptive, beauty is illusory" (Prov. 31:30). The first occurrence is a man's name.]

מ"ג-א שו' ד, טז: וּבָרָק ג' - וברק רדף (שם) ותשר דבורה (שם ה, א) וברק ממררתו יהלך
(איוב כ, כה). בתרייה לשון ברקין.

[=MM **A** Jud. 4:16 – וּבְרָק 3 occurrences: "as Barak pursued" (Ibid.); "Deborah [and Barak] sang" (Jud. 5:1); "the gleaming tip from his gall-bladder" (Job 20:25). The last means lightning]

מ"ג-א יה' יט, כא: חַדָּה ה' - ורמת (שם) וישם פי (יש' מט, ב) ואתה בן אדם (יח' ה, א) ולשונם חרב חדה (תה' נז, ה) ואחריתה (מש' ה, ד). קדמיה שם קריה

[=MM **A** Jos. 19:21 – חַדָּה 5 occurrences – "And Remet" (Ibid.); "He made my mouth" (Is. 49:2); "And you, O mortal" (Ez. 5:1) "whose tongue is a sharp sword (Ps. 57:5); "But in the end" (Prov. 5:4). The first is a name of a town.]

מ"ג-א שמ"א יב, כה: הָרֵעַ ה' ג' בישין ותריין טבין – ואם הרע תרעו (שם) חדלו הרע (יש' א, טז) למדו הרע (יר' יג, כג) וכל הרע לאיש מתן (מש' יט, ו) בכל עת (שם יז, יז) ...

[=MM **A** I Sam. 12:25 – הָרֵעַ 5 occurrences, 3 bad and two good: "For if you persist in your wrongdoing" (Ibid.); "cease to do evil" (Is. 1:16); "who are practiced in doing evil" (Jer. 13:23); "and all are the friends of a dispenser of gifts" (Prov. 19:6); "a friend at all times" (Prov. 17:17)...]

In the first three notes one verse is exceptional in terms of meaning. The first הבל is the name of a man and not an abstract noun; the last וּבְרָק is not a proper noun, but a lightning; the first occurrence of חַדָּה is not an adjective, but the name of a city. In the last note are three verses in which the word הָרֵעַ is an infinitive meaning "to do evil" and two verses in which it means 'the friend'. The Masora called these two forms "bad" and "good" (in Aramaic), distinguishing between the two meanings.

It is difficult to determine when the Masora points out the difference of meaning and when it does not. Sometimes a masoretic note appears in two different manuscripts, one pointing out the difference and one ignoring it. Evidently the Masora did not have an exegetical intention in these notes, since in most cases there is no question regarding the meaning of the word and the definition given in the Masora presents nothing new. The purpose may have been to warn those engaged in Masora and the Scriptural text not to forget to combine proper nouns and verbs or adjectives and the name of a town. It may also have come in order to eliminate the astonishment of readers upon seeing the strange combination of unlike words together, as if to say explicitly: I know that these words have different meanings, but they should anyway be combined because their pronunciation is identical.

Masoretic use of distinction of meaning

Some notes make use of the distinction in meaning in order to simplify and abbreviate the description of the text of Scripture that they are relating. In these notes the Masora limits the discussion to one meaning of the word, ignoring its use with other meanings, or dealing with each meaning of the word separately. For example:

מ"ג-א יה' טו, מב: עָשָׁן ה' שם קריה ...

[=MM **A** Jos. 15:42 – עָשָׁן 5 occurrences as a place name]

מ"ג-א שמ"ב כד, ג: וְיוֹסֵף ג' לשון תוספת ...

[=MM A II Sam. 24:3 – וְיוֹסֵף 3 occurrences meaning addition...]

מ"ג-א יר' נא, נז: שְׁנַת ה' בשינה ...

[=MM A Jer. 51:57 – שְׁנַת 5 occurrences meaning sleep...]

מ"ג-א דה"ב לא, י: לְבִיא ב'... וכל לשון אריה דכות'

[=MM A II Chr. 31:10 – לְבִיא 2 occurrences... and all occurrences meaning "lion".]

The Masora lists here עָשָׁן as a place name and not as a noun, וְיוֹסֵף as a verb and not a proper noun, שְׁנַת meaning sleep and not a construct state form of the word שָׁנָה (=year), לְבִיא meaning "to bring" and not "lion". The purpose of the Masora here is not to interpret the meaning of the words, but on the contrary: the distinction is common knowledge, serving as a basis for the description.

In this kind of notes the Masora sometimes points out grammatical distinctions, such as:

מ"ג-א יח' טז, לט: אוֹתָךְ י"ו מל' לשון נקבה...

[=MM A Ez. 16:39 – אוֹתָךְ 16 *plene* occurrences in feminine form...]

מ"ג-ל יר' יט, י: אוֹתָךְ ט' מל' בלשון זכר...

[=MM **L** Jer. 19:10 – אוֹתָךְ 9 *plene* occurrences in masculine form...]

The Masora preferred to treat the masculine and feminine forms in separate notes, evidently in order to avoid creating a long and cumbersome list of verses.

Exegetical use of distinctions of meaning in the Masora

When the Masora makes use of distinctions of meaning, it assumes that the meaning of the word is understood and well known, thus it can serve as the basis for a note concerning the text of Scripture. However in the rare cases in which the meaning is not totally clear, the situation can be reversed, and conclusions may be drawn from the masoretic note regarding how the word was understood. For example:

The Masora tries to determine the spelling of *lekha*: When should it be written לְךָ and when לְכָה? The former spelling occurs 495 times in Scripture and the latter 33 times. In order to simplify the description the Masora makes use of the meaning, asserting that generally when it is an imperative form from the root "to go" it is written in *plene* form (e.g. לְכָה אִתָּנוּ וְהֵטַבְנוּ לָךְ, "Come with us and we will be generous with you", Num. 10:29), but when it is a pronoun it is written in defective form, לְךָ,

without the letter *he*. However this general rule has a small number of exceptions, and the Masora (MM **D**, Gen. 27:37 and more) cites four verses in which the pronoun is written in *plene* form (e.g. שִׂמְלָה לְכָה קָצִין תִּהְיֶה לָּנוּ, "there is clothing for you, be a chief over us", Is. 3:6) and three verses in which the meaning "to go" is written in defective form (e.g. in the words of Balak, לְךָ נָּא אִתִּי אֶל מָקוֹם אַחֵר, "Come with me to another place", Num. 23:13). It is usually easy to distinguish between the two meanings, i.e. between "going" and a pronoun. However in one verse, Ps. 80:3, it could be interpreted either way. The Masora lists the word among the pronouns written in *plene* form without the letter *he*, and Rashi drew from this his interpretation of the verse[1]:

ולכה לישועתה לנו [="and your help to us"]. This is not the language of going, but לך [="your"]; and such it is in the Masora: ולכה איפוא [="What then can I still do for you?"] concerning Jacob (Gen. 27:37), שִׂמְלָה לְכָה [="when you have no news worth telling", II Sam. 18:22], ולכה אין בשורה מוצאת קָצִין תִּהְיֶה לָּנוּ [Is. 3:6] etc.

For additional study

– Examine the following masoretic note from Masora Magna in the Aleppo Codex on Jer 29:1:

אל יתר ב' - וילך משה וישב (שמ' ד, יח) ואלה דברי הספר (יר' כט, א). ותריין על יתר - כוננו חצם (תה' יא, ב) ומשלם על יתר (תה' לא, כד).

אל יתר 2 occurrences – "Moses went back" (Ex. 4:18), "This is the text of the letter" (Jer. 29:1). And both 2 occurrences of על יתר – "set their arrow" (Ps. 11:2), "and more than requites" (Ps. 31:24).

What is the meaning of יֶתֶר in each of the verses cited here? Is the fact that the Masora ignores the meaning of the word understood or is it strange?

– Study the following list taken from *Okhla weOkhla*, Frensdorff ed., list 92 (Figure 14.1):

---

1 ולכה לישועתה לנו. אין זה לשון הליכה אלא כמו לך וכן הוא במסורת: ולכה איפוא דיעקב (בר' כז, לז) ולכה אין בשורה מוצאת (שמ"ב יח, כב) שמלה לכה קצין תהיה לנו (יש' ג, ו) וגו'.

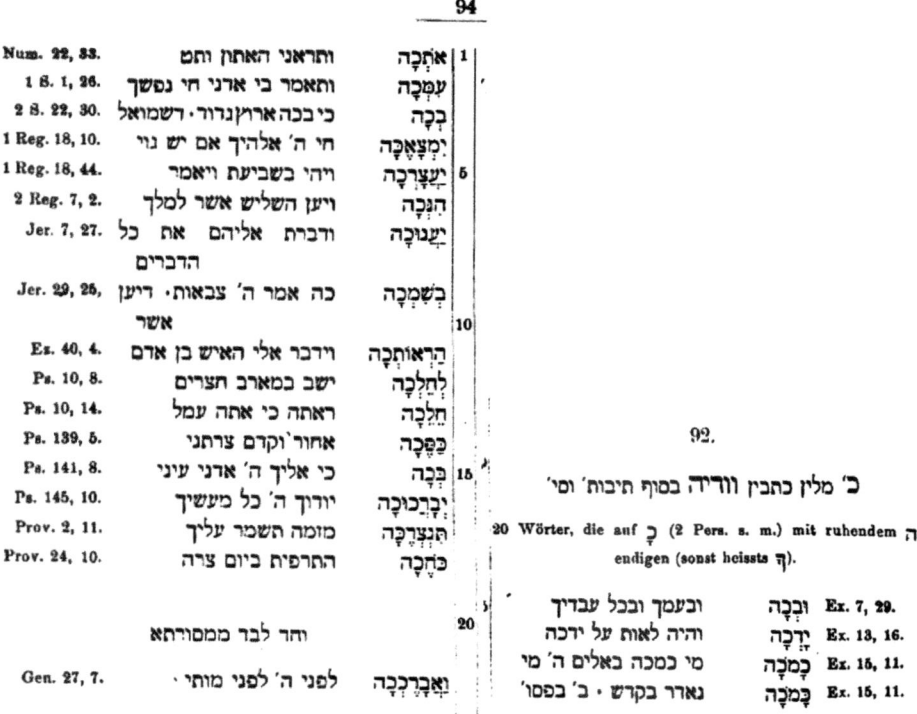

Figure 14.1: List 92 of *Okhla weOkhla*

Now examine Rashi's commentary on Psalms 10:8 below:

"לחלכה" (תה' י, ח), "עליך יעזב חלכה" (שם, יד) - שניהם במסורת מן מלין המשמשין כה
במקום ך כגון ובכה ובעמך (שמ' ז, כט) תבונה תנצרכה (מש' ב, יא) ככל אשר צויתי אתכה
(שמ' כט, לה) הנצבת עמכה (שמ"א א, כו). למדנו ממסורת שחלכה כמו חילך, חיל שלך.

[=לחלכה (="his eyes spy out the hapless", Ps. 10:8), עליך יעזב חלכה (="To you the helpless can entrust
himself", Ps. 10:14) – both in the Masora of the type of words that use *kaf he* instead of final *kaf*, like
ובכה ובעמך (="on you and on your people", Ex. 7:29), תבונה תנצרכה ("discernment will guard you",
Prov. 2:11), ככל אשר צויתי אתכה (="just as I have commanded you", Ex. 29:35), הנצבת עמכה (="who stood
here beside you", I Sam. 1:26). We learn from the Masora that לחלכה is like חילך (="your power").]

Explain what the intention of the Masora was, and how Rashi derived his exegetical
conclusion from it.

- On the verse לוֹ תֹּאמַר צֵא דָּוָה כְּמוֹ תִּזְרֵם [="you will cast them away like a menstruous
  woman¸ 'Out!' you will call to them", (Is. 30:22)], the Masora Parva in the Aleppo
  Codex says: ל' בטינוף (*leita betinnuf*, i.e. Only here the meaning of this word is
  'dirt'; a similar note is found in other manuscripts).

R. Yesh'yahu diTerani's commentary on this verse:

צא תאמר לו - מלשון "ומצואתו לא רחץ" (מש' ל, יב).

Like "[a generation that] yet are not washed from their filthiness" (Prov. 30:12).

(cf. also Radak's commentary on this verse).

Explain the masoretic comment. What makes the purpose of this note remarkable, in light of what has been said above in this chapter?

– Examine Rashi's commentary on Daniel 12:13. Check the two interpretations he had before him, and how he decided between them according to the Masora.

"Two occurrences with two meanings"

One kind of notes that deals with meaning is particularly common, notes that give "two occurrences with two meanings", i.e. words that occur twice in Scripture, each time with a different meaning.[2] Dozens of such notes appear in the Masora Parva in the margins of the manuscripts, and these were collected in long masoretic notes, such as one that appears in the masoretic collection *Okhla weOkhla* (see above, Chapter Four), which includes nearly one hundred pairs of words (list 59 in Ms. P, list 60 in Ms. H). The beginning of the list is presented in Figure 14.2.

In these notes the Masora *does not define* the two meanings, but only points out that the two occurrences have different meanings. Thus the interpretation inherent in these notes is a kind of "silent commentary" that still requires study and exegesis, in order to understand how the Masora interpreted the word under discussion in each of the verses discussed.

In most cases the meaning of the word is clear, and it can be easily perceived that we have before us two different meanings. Here are three examples taken from the list above:

דברי אָגוּר בן יקה =) "The words of Agur son of Jakeh", Prov. 30:1) – the former is a verb meaning to fear (or: piled) and the latter a proper noun.

כבודם בקלון =) "two berries or three on the topmost branch", Is. 17:6); שנים שלשה גרגרים בראש אָמִיר =) "but for fear of the taunts of the foe", Deut. 32:27); לולי כעס אויב אָגוּר the latter a verb meaning change.

אָמִיר =) "I will change their dignity to dishonor", Hos. 4:7) – the former is a noun meaning the top of a tree, the latter a verb meaning change.

---

2 Lists of "2 occurrences with different meanings" were discussed at length in Aron Dotan's book, *The Awakening of Word Lore: From the Masora to the Beginnings of Hebrew Lexicography*, Jerusalem 2005 (Heb.), pp. 77–115. Cf. also A. Dotan, "Homonymous Hapax Doublets in the Masora", *Textus* 14 (1988), pp. 131–145; R. I. (Singer) Zer, *Masora and Exegesis*, unpublished M.A. thesis, Touro College, Jerusalem 1999 (Heb.), pp. 26–34. 54–56; R. I. (Singer) Zer, "Ben Asher and the list of Homonyms לישנין בתרי תרין', *Leshonenu* 66 (2004), pp. 103–111 (Heb.).

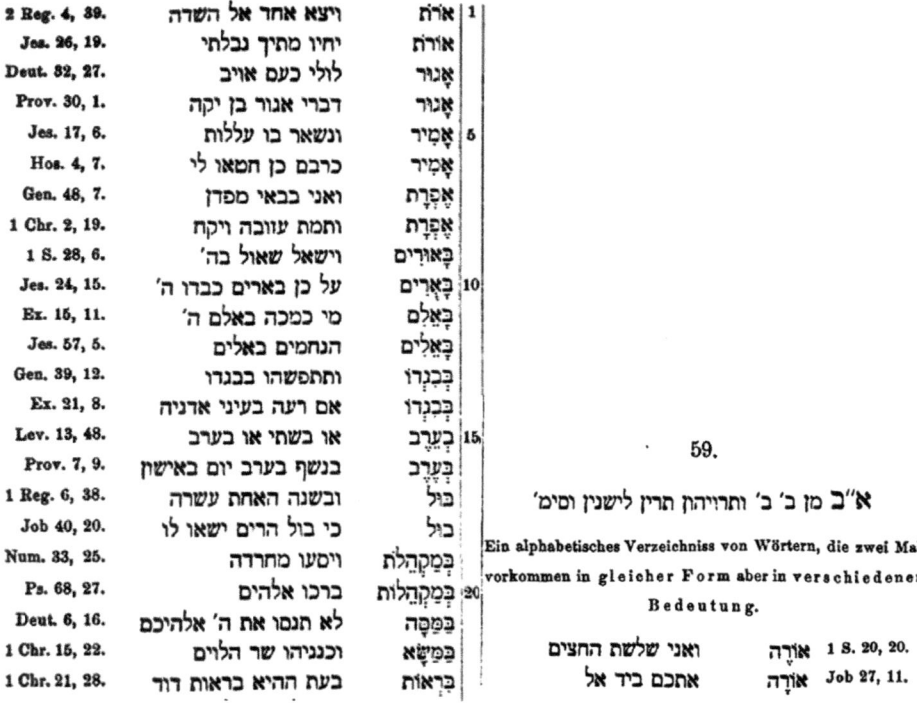

Figure 14.2: A section from a masoretic note on "two occurrences with two meanings", *Okhla weOkhla* Frensdorff ed., p. 62.

ותתפשהו בְּבִגְדוֹ (="she caught hold of him by his garment", Gen. 39:12); לא ימשל למכרה בְּבִגְדוֹ בה (="he shall not have the right to sell her, since he broke faith with her", Ex. 21:8) – the former meaning garment and the latter meaning breaking faith.

However there are cases in which it is difficult to determine whether a word has one meaning or two. Sometimes this depends on interpretation of the verses, and sometimes it depends on whether two close meanings should be considered one word or two.

בִּלֶּדְכֶן את העבריות וראיתן על הָאָבְנָיִם (="when you deliver the Hebrew women, look at the birth-stool", Ex. 1:16); וארד בית היוצר והנהו[3] עֹשֶׂה מלאכה על הָאָבְנָיִם (="So I went down to the house of the potter, and found him working at the wheel", Jer. 18:3) – Are the birthstool and the potter's wheel two different words or are they sufficiently similar to be regarded as one word?

הַתַּנִּין אשר בים (="the Dragon of the sea", Is. 27:1); ואצאה בשער הגיא לילה ואל פני עין הַתַּנִּין (="I went out by he Valley Gate, at night, toward the Jackal's Spring", Neh. 2:13) – Is this Spring in the area of Jerusalem a separate term, or was it called that way because of the same animal mentioned in Isaiah?

---

3 The qere of this word is והנה הוא.

Such masoretic notes have exegetical value, and some of the early Bible commentators tried to find the interpretation reflected in these notes. For example, Rashi says the following regarding the verse יוֹמָם יְצַוֶּה ה' חַסְדּוֹ וּבַלַּיְלָה שִׁירֹה עִמִּי (="By day may the Lord vouchsafe His faithful care, so that at night a song to Him may be with me", Ps. 42:9):

שירה עמי - תהא חנייתו בתוכנו. שירה לשון חניה, כדמתרגמין "ויחן" - 'ושרא' (בר' כו, יז ועוד). זו למדתי מתוך מסורת הגדולה שחבר את זה עם "ויהי שירו חמשה ואלף" (מל"א ה, יב), באלפ"א בית"א של שתי תיבות החלוקים בפתרונן, לימד שאין זה לשון שיר.

[=עמי שירה – may he encamp among us. שירה means encampment, as in the Aramaic translation of ויחן (Gen. 26:17 and elsewhere): ושרא. This I learned from the Masora Magna that combined it with ויהי שירו חמשה ואלף (="and his songs numbered one thousand and five", I Kings 5:12), in the alphabetic list of two words with different meanings. One can conclude that this (the word שירה in our verse) does not mean a song.]

The composition that Rashi refers to as "Masora Magna" is the collection *Okhla weOkhla*. Rashi refers to the list described above, which is an alphabetical list of pairs of words with two different meanings. This list contains a pair of verses in which the word שִׁירֹו appears. In the verse regarding Solomon the meaning is "his songs", thus in the verse under discussion (Ps. 42:9) it must have a different meaning.

Also Rashi's grandson, Rabbenu Tam, used the masoretic list of homonyms drawing exegetical conclusions from it. He referred to the word בְּשָׂרִים in the list, which occurs in the following verses: חַיֵּי בְשָׂרִים לֵב מַרְפֵּא [="a calm disposition gives bodily health", Prov. 14:30] and לֹא נָאוֶה לִכְסִיל תַּעֲנוּג אַף כִּי לְעֶבֶד מְשֹׁל בְּשָׂרִים [="Luxury is not fitting for a dullard, much less that a servant rule over princes", Prov. 19:10]. Menahem ben Saruq cited the second verse under the root בשר in his dictionary *Mahberet*, and Dunash ben Labrat took exception to that, insisting that in the second verse the word is from the root שר (the letter *bet*, being an auxiliary letter).[4] R. Jacob ben Meir (Rabbenu Tam) defended Menahem's assertion regarding the word as taken from the root בשר. However, he himself pointed out that the masoretic note seemed to contradict his interpretation because it asserted that the two verses used the word with different meanings.[5]

According to Rabbenu Tam, the Masora may speak of homonyms also when a word is used both literally and metaphorically. In his opinion that was the case regarding the word חֲרַשְׁתֶּם – in both occurrences it meant plowing: first literally (Jud. 14:18) and later metaphorically: "you have plowed wickedness" (Hos. 10:13). The same applies to בְּשָׂרִים, first to be taken literally (Prov. 14:30) and secondly as a metaphor for people (Prov. 19:10).

---

4 For the remarks by Dunash and Rabbenu Tam, cf. *The Responsa of Dunash ben Labrat*, ed. Filipowski, London and Edinburgh 1855, pp. 10–11.

5 כי שני בשרים הם בכל הקריה. ואע"פ כי המסורה גדולה חברם עם הנפתרים בתרין לישנין, כאשר חבר "חרשתם בעגלתי" (שו' יד, יח) עם "חרשתם רשע" (הושע י, יג) בתרין לישנין, יען "חרשתם בעגלתי" חרישה ממש, ו"חרשתם רשע" דוגמא. כמו כן הפליג "חיי בשרים" הנשמע בשר ממש, ו"משול בשרים" אנשים בית אדוניו ולא בשר ממש.

Radak (R. David Kimhi) also mentions the masoretic note on homonyms in reference to a verse from Ezekiel that deals with the punishment that will come upon the
Ammonites: "I will pour out My indignation upon you, I will blow upon you with the fire
of My wrath: and I will deliver you into the hands of barbarians [וּנְתַתִּיךְ בְּיַד אֲנָשִׁים בֹּעֲרִים],
craftsmen of destruction", (Ez. 21:36). Radak suggests two interpretations of the word
בֹּעֲרִים:

> בוערים - כסילים ונמהרים שיהרגו פתאום, כמו "בינו בוערים בעם" (תה' צד, ח). ויש לפרש
> בוערים מעניין "כאש תבער יער" (תה' פג, טו), רוצה לומר: מכלים ושורפים כאש, וכן אמרה
> המסרה על "בינו בוערים": ב' בתרי לישני.

> בֹּעֲרִים – fools and rash persons who may suddenly kill, as in בינו בוערים בעם (="Take heed, you
> most brutish people", Ps. 94:8). בוערים may also be understood as כאש תבער יער (="As a fire burns
> a forest", Ps. 83:15), i.e. destroying and burning like fire, and consequently the Masora said regar-
> ding בינו בוערים: "two words with different meanings".

First Radak interpreted the word as it was used in Psalms. And then he suggested a
second interpretation, pointing out that it suited the masoretic note (since according
to the first interpretation the two verses do not contain homonyms). The difference in
approach to masoretic notes between Rashi and Rabbenu Tam on the one hand and
Radak on the other is noteworthy. While the former both see themselves as obligated
to the Masora, Radak makes do with pointing out the fact that the Masora subscribes
to the second interpretation. He does not hesitate to give a different interpretation
first, that does not suit the Masora, and that would seem to be the understanding he
preferred.

The intention of the Masoretes in notes on homonyms

Thus we have seen that the masoretic notes on homonyms may be useful for exegesis,
and some commentators exploited this potential, clarifying the exegetical intention of the Masora. Nevertheless, the original intention of the Masoretes demands
explanation. Why did the Masoretes write so many notes saying "two occurrences
with two different meanings"? In order to preserve the accurate text of Scripture it
would have sufficed to write only "two", without relating to the exegetical issue. The
entire masoretic apparatus was created only in order to preserve the accurate text of
Scripture in every detail, which is the main purpose and intention of the Masora. We
have seen above masoretic notes that ignore entirely exegetical differences between
the verses they discussed. So why did the Masora make so much use of these notes
on homonyms?

At first glance one might assert that the Masoretes had another purpose, the
interpretation of Scripture, and this purpose was in addition to their primary goal,
preservation of the text; and maybe that Biblical exegesis here became the main goal

and casted a shadow on preserving the text. In my opinion this is not correct, and it does not explain the multiplicity of notes on homonyms, that hold the main exegetical potential of the Masora apparatus.

In this context we should stress what was already mentioned above: The exegesis inherent in the notes on homonyms is a kind of "silent exegesis", since the masoretic notes do not provide straightforward interpretation of the verse. They provide only a negative statement – that the word in one verse should not be regarded as having the same meaning as in another verse. Consequently the exegetical information provided by these notes is more restricted than that in other notes that state explicitly "a person's name", "a place name", "meaning lightning", "good and bad" and the like.

In my opinion we should look for the background to the development of these notes on homonyms elsewhere – in the context of the Accumulative Masora (see above Chapter Four). Accumulative masoretic notes combine short masoretic notes creating long and "sophisticated" lists. Most of the lists combine unique words using various criteria. However there are many such lists that combine pairs of words. In most cases the two elements in the pair have some contrast between them, such as one that has a *mapiq* in the letter *he* and the other lacking a *mapiq* (*Okhla weOkhla*, Frensdorff, list 44), one that opens with an auxiliary letter and the other not (as in the first list in *Okhla weOkhla*), one that opens with an auxiliary letter vocalized with a *shewa* and the other with a *patah* (lists 45–50), or that have a difference in the letters of the word itself (list 7: the first word contains *dalet* and the second *resh*), in its vowels (lists 5, 55) or stress (list 51). The list of "two occurrences with two different meanings" (no. 59 – see above, Figure 14.1) should be seen in this context. Here too there is a contrast between the two elements in the pair – a difference of meaning.

This list comprised a special challenge for the Masoretes because including additional elements in the list was not a technical matter alone, but required examination, study and interpretation. In the light of the existence of a classic list in the collection *Okhla weOkhla* Masoretes looked for additional items that fit that definition and inscribed them in notes in the Masora Parva and Masora Magna. Evidence of the aspiration of the Masoretes to expand the list may be found in masoretic lists that conclude new pairs of words that were not included in the list of *Okhla weOkhla*; these lists include between 25 and 83 items.

The following is the title of such a list in the Farhi Tanakh from 1383[6]:

שמנים וארבע תיבות מפוארות במקרא בשתי לשונות, מה שלא [נמצא] במסורת גדולה ולא
במסורת קטנה, לא במסורת בני בבל ולא במסורת ארץ ישראל ולא בדברי סופרים, והם נפלאים
ונאים מכסּפים, מפי בן אשר מאֻלפים.

---

6 Cf. Dotan, *The Awakening* (above, note 2), p. 87.

[=84 noble words in Scripture with two meanings, not found in the 'great Masora' (i.e. *Okhla weOkhla*) or in the 'small Masora' (i.e. the Masora Magna and the Masora Parva), nor in the Babylonian Masora or the Masora of Eretz Israel or in the writings of scribes, and they are more wonderful and beautiful than silver, taught by Ben Asher.]

Scholars have debated whether the declaration that Ben Asher himself wrote this list is reliable or whether later writers attributed it to him in order to enhance their own work. At any rate the pride of the author of the list over having brought together so many items that had not been put together before is apparent.

Finally the masoretic notes on homonyms provide a "silent commentary" on many verses in Scripture, and in that way resemble to a degree the cantillation marks (and also certain roots in the dictionary of Menahem Ben Saruq, which are sorted into groups of meaning, without indicating explicitly the meaning of each group). The importance, the intellectual challenge and the special beauty of revealing a hidden interpretation while demonstrating skill and sharpness of intellect, should not be denied. However, a distinction should be made between exploiting the exegetical potential of the Masoretic comments and the question of the intention of the creators of the Masora. The fact that these notes have exegetical ramifications does not mean that the Masoretes meant to provide their readers a commentary on Scripture. Had they wanted to do so, they would have cited the meaning of the word in every verse they cited. Their motivation was evidently to expand this list of "two occurrences with two different meanings" and to find as many items as they could that belonged to that category.

Mention should be made of Aron Dotan's discovery of two lists from the Geniza that constitute a link between masoretic lists of this kind and the lexicological editing of linguistic material.[7] In the first list the emphasis on unique occurrences of linguistic forms is broken down and words with two different meanings are cited even if they are not unique occurrences. Sometimes the word is cited in its elementary form instead of its declined form with auxiliary letters (such as: כפר – וכפרת אתה; in the verse itself the form that appears is בַּכֹּפֶר [="with pitch", Gen 6:14]). In the second list further steps were taken from the Masora to the dictionary: It includes items that provide three or four different meanings, and the list explains each meaning in Arabic.

For additional study

– Examine Rashi's commentary of the word נבליך [="your lutes", Is. 14:11] and the commentary of Radak on מדין [="saddle rugs", Jud. 5:10] and חרשתם [="you plowed", Jud. 14:18]. What is the exegetical conclusion that may be derived from the Masora quoted by the commentators, and what is the interpretation they prefer?

---

7 Cf. Dotan, *Ibid.*, pp. 146–164.

Sevirin notes

Sevirin (סבירין) notes in the Masora warn the reader against erroneous reading. The following is such a note that appears in Masora Magna of **L**[M] on Num. 13:22:

וַיָּבֹא ו' סבירין לשון סגין וקורין לשון יחיד, וסימנהון	
ויעלו בנגב ויבא עד חברון	במ' יג, כב
עדיו יבא ויבשו כל	יש' מה, כד
ויבא אל הגוים אשר	יח' לו, כ
ויבוא אליה כבוא אל אשה זונה	יח' כג, מד
אלי אנשים מזקני (יהודה) [ישראל]	יח' יד, א
וברותי מכם המורדים	יח' כ, לח

[=וַיָּבֹא – 6 occurrences in which you would presume [or err to think that] they are plural, but they are read as singular and they are the following:

"They went up to the Negeb and came into Hebron", Num. 13:22

"to Him shall men come in confusion", Is. 45:24

"But when they came to those nations", Ez. 36:20

"And they would go to her as one goes to a prostitute", Ez. 23:44

"Certain elders of (Judah) [Israel] [came to me]", Ez. 14:1

"I will remove from you those who rebel", Ez. 20:38]

Reading the first verse, "They went up to the Negeb and came into Hebron", one might assume that the verb וַיָּבֹא is plural and should be read וַיָּבֹאוּ, and the Masora warns the reader, reinforcing the correct reading, וַיָּבֹא. The same applies to the rest of the verses, such as "Certain elders of Israel came to me" in which the reader might err and read ויבואו instead of ויבוא.

What is the meaning of the term *Sevirin*? R. Elia Levita ('*Bahur*'; Italy, 1469–1549), suggested two explanations (in his work *Masoret HaMasoret*, Chapter eight):

דע כי סבירין הוא ענין מחשבה כוזבת, כל שאדם חושב ומדמה בלבו שהוא כן ואינו כן... כן יש
מלין הרבה במקרא שסבירין בני אדם שהם כן ואינן כן....

ויש מפרשים סבירין לשון סברה, ופירוש: לפי הסברה היה ראוי להיות כד... אבל לא סבירא לי
כי לפי זה היה להם לכתוב מִסְתַּבְּרִין, ודוק.

[=Know that *sevirin* is a matter of wrong thinking, anyone who thinks and imagines something, but it is not so... so there are many words in Scripture that people think are so, but they are not so.

And some explain *Sevirin* as logical presumption, meaning: according to logic it should be so... but that does not seem to me to be correct because they should have used the term מִסְתַּבְּרִין, and be exact.]

According to the first explanation, people err and think that the word should be read unlike the testimony of the Masora. But according to the second explanation there is an exegetical preference for the rejected reading. In contemporary Hebrew the second explanation seems more likely, but it is difficult to attribute this meaning to the language of the Masora, as Levita pointed out correctly.

We should point out that there are additional masoretic terms that are used to describe this phenomenon. In the Masora of Tiberias we find the term מטעין (=err) and in the Babylonian Masora the parallel term מישתבשין (making a mistake). Both terms refer to people who make mistakes regarding the text of Scripture, and the Masora seeks to avoid these mistakes and point out the correct and accurate reading.

Like the term *Sevirin*, we find the Babylonian term דחזי להון [="that seem to be"], as in the following examples[8]:

יעשה דחזי להון **תעשה** ה' ומיש' (=ומישתבשין)

כבר	שמ' כה, לט
פרכת	שמ' כו, לא
ששת ימים דכי תשא	שמ' לא, טו
והבאת	וי' ב, ח
וכל אשר יפול	וי' יא, לב

[=יעשה that seems to be תעשה – 5 occurrences; and people make mistakes (while reading them):

"A talent [of pure gold]", Ex. 25:39

"[You shall make a] curtain", Ex. 26:31

"Six days" in the portion *Ki Tisa*, Ex. 31:15

"When you present", Lev. 2:8

"And anything on which one them falls", Lev. 11:32]

In the instructions for making the Menorah (in the first verse in this list) we would have expected the verb to be in the imperative form: "And *make it* (תֵּעָשֶׂה) of one talent of pure gold" and not in the third person: "*He will make it* (יֵעָשֶׂה) of a talent of pure gold". In the commandment of the Sabbath (third example) we would expect it to say "On six days work may be done (תֵּעָשֶׂה)" in feminine form because the word מלאכה (work) is feminine, but Scripture uses the masculine form of the verb (יֵעָשֶׂה).

The term דחזי refers to the most logical version, determining that it is the more appropriate reading, i.e. understood and required by the context. Nevertheless, the version of the Masora should be accepted, and one who follows the "appropriate" reading makes a mistake.

Some scholars have maintained that the purpose of these masoretic notes was to propose corrections to the masoretic text or to document variants that differed from it. Some compared the *sevirin* notes to notes regarding *qere* and *ketiv*, and saw in both

---

8 Y. Ofer, *The Babylonian Masora of the Pentateuch, Its Principles and Methods*, Jerusalem 2001 (Heb.), p. 457.

kinds of notes documentation of textual variants in Scripture.[9] However these opinions are not convincing and conflict with the way the Masora works. The purpose of the Masora is not to preserve disagreements, but to decide between different opinions, and the *sevirin* notes serve to reject the assertions of the erring and the mistaken, maintaining the one and only masoretic text. Mentioning other variants was required in order to preserve the masoretic text by taking exception with the non-masoretic variant.

That is what must be said regarding the *purpose* of the Masora. Regarding the logic of the variant readings, in most of the verses in these lists, the proposed reading is more reasonable than that of the Masora itself, since in such places in Scripture where the masoretic text presents a difficulty, there is a fear that readers will err and replace the difficult reading of the masoretic text with the "easier" reading.

Now is the time to formulate the two key questions that should be asked about the comments of *sevirin*:

(1) What is the origin of these versions that are different from those of the Masoretic text?

(2) Is the intent of the Masora to say that from the interpretative aspect, the rejected version is appropriate for the intention of Scripture?

Regarding the question of the source of these alternative readings: Some of them may stem from ancient versions of Scripture that were rejected by the masoretic text. Sometimes this may be substantiated from the text of translations or other testimonies on the text of Scripture. However, in most cases it seems that there was no ancient source for the rejected variant, but the Masorete observed around him readers who erred in reading (without any source) or feared that they would err in certain verses, and he therefore posted a warning sign in the form of *sevirin* note.

In this context something should be said about the development of these notes. Masoretic notes pertaining to the "יבא" that might be read "יבואו" in different manuscripts give conflicting numbers of occurrences. The note in Ms. **L**[M] quoted above lists *six* verses, two of them reading יָבֹא and four of them reading וְיָבֹא and similar notes appear in Mss. **C** and **S**. The masoretic note in Ms. **S1** and in the printed Miqraot Gedolot (Venice 1524–25) counts *eight* verses. A third masoretic note (quoted by Ginsburg, par. ב 119 a) cites 12 verses, and a fourth masoretic note – found in Mss. **B**, **L**[M] – goes even further and cites 14 verses with the word יָבֹאַ alone![10] The more that the Masora expands the circle and adds additional verses, the more this interpretation becomes tenuous, and in some cases it is hard to see how the Masora regarded the plural form as more reasonable than the singular.

---

9 Cf. A. Geiger, *The Bible and its Translations*, Jerusalem 1949 (Hebrew translation), p. 150; C. D. Ginsburg, *Introduction to the Massoretico-Critical Edition of the Hebrew Bible*, with Prolegomenon by Harry M. Orlinsky[2], New York 1966, p. 187. Regarding *ketiv* and *qere* see above Chapter Six.
10 For detailed data – cf. M. Breuer, *The Masorah Magna to the Pentateuch (MS L*[M]*)*, New York 1992 (Heb.), pp. 591–592.

This phenomenon reveals clearly the development of such a masoretic note. Every Masorete tried to add to the list of his predecessor, finding more verses that corresponded to the framework of "יבוא" that might be read "יבואו". There are no objective criteria for that, since the question if the plural form would have been appropriate in this verse – or if one might by mistake read it in plural form – is an exegetical question, and if the Torah has "seventy faces", there are seventy-seven possibilities of misinterpretation and mistaken reading that those who make mistakes might make in reading Scripture! Ordinary masoretic notes concern textual facts, cite such matters as three occurrences of *plene* form or four occurrences of defective form or five cases of *qere-ketiv* of a certain kind. All of these are objective facts that cannot be expanded. However the list of "warning signs" is not fixed and it may be expanded by use of the rich imagination of the individual making the list.

In the light of this, *all* of the *sevirin* notes cannot be seen as stemming from ancient textual variants, nor do all of them suggest variants more reasonable than that of the Masoretic text. The tendency of the Masoretes to expand the lists led them to make many additions over and above the preliminary nucleus of these notes.

The exegetical significance of *sevirin* notes

Let us turn now to the second question we posed above, the question of interpretive significance. We have claimed above that the intention of the Masoretes in *sevirin* notes was not exegetical. However, do they reflect a degree of interpretation? Is it possible to assert that "every note of *sevirin* and 'two meanings' is a note of commentary", as one scholar has claimed?[11]

Indeed some medieval exegetes made use of these notes in their commentaries. Below for example is the commentary of Radak on a problematic verse regarding the daughter of Jephthah (Jud. 11:34):

וַיָּבֹא יִפְתָּח הַמִּצְפָּה אֶל בֵּיתוֹ וְהִנֵּה בִתּוֹ יֹצֵאת לִקְרָאתוֹ בְּתֻפִּים וּבִמְחֹלוֹת
וְרַק הִיא יְחִידָה אֵין לוֹ מִמֶּנּוּ בֵּן אוֹ בַת

[="When Jephthah arrived at his home in Mizpah, there was his daughter coming out to meet him, with timbrel and dance! She was an only child; (literally:) he had *from him* no son or daughter.]

Radak: אין לו ממנו – Jonathan translated ממנה 'from her': no other child from her, i.e. he had no son or daughter from this daughter, who was still unmarried as it says 'she had never known a man' (Jud. 11:39). And likewise the Masorete said: 'six occurrences in which you would think the reading is ממנה, but the reading is ממנו'. And it is also possible to interpret ממנו as it is written, for Jephthah's wife may have had sons from a different man before she married Jephthah, and

11 Y. Shashar, *Ms. JNL 24° 5702 (Sassoon 507) and Its Role in Formation of the Accepted Tiberian Masoretic Text,* Ph.D. dissertation (Heb.), the Hebrew University of Jerusalem 1983, p. 253.

he raised them in his home and they were considered his sons, however from himself he had no other son or daughter except for this daughter.

Radak gives two interpretations: According to the first one the word ממנו refers to Jephthah's daughter, and according to the second to Jephthah himself. Radak reinforces the first interpretation by citing the Aramaic translation of the verse, which translates ממנה [="from her"], and also by citing the *sevirin* note of the Masora.

The underlying assumption behind Radak's view should be elucidated: According to the second interpretation, the word ממנו [="from him"] refers to Jephthah himself and there is no reason to read the verse differently. However, according to the first interpretation, the verse demands the word ממנה, since the reading ממנו creates a grammatical problem. The intention of the Masora is to warn the reader to read the *lectio difficile*, which is correct, and not to solve the problem by altering the text. The assumption here is that meaning of the text is clear and evident. The version given in the *sevirin* note provides the *correct meaning*, however the Masora warns the reader that the *correct reading* is different.

However there may be another possibility: The Masora is concerned with the text of Scripture, and warns against a tempting and likely reading (that suits the first interpretation). The masoretic reading should be accepted, but the question of its interpretation remains open: Perhaps the second one, which does conform to the Masoretic text, should be preferred!

Here is another, better-known example from the story of the scouts (Num. 13:22):

וַיַּעֲלוּ בַנֶּגֶב וַיָּבֹא עַד חֶבְרוֹן

[="They went up into the Negeb and came to Hebron"]

We have seen above a masoretic note citing this verse among "six occurrences in which the word would be thought to be in plural form, but read in the singular". That follows the plain meaning of Scripture according to which the verse refers to the twelve scouts. On the other hand Rashi's well-known interpretation is "וַיָּבֹא עַד חֶבְרוֹן" – Kaleb alone went there and prostrated himself on the tombs of the patriarchs etc." Is it absolutely clear that the Masora understood the verse differently from Rashi? Perhaps not: the Masora warns against reading ויבואו, which would be the obvious reading according to the plain sense of Scripture, insisting that the correct reading is וַיָּבֹא. Beyond that the verse remains open to interpretation: one may adopt the plain sense or prefer Rashi's interpretation.

Of course there are many cases in which the verse may be interpreted in only one way, following the suggestion offered by the *sevirin* note, and there is no other more suitable interpretation for the text established by the Masora. For example, in the description of the people who came before Ezekiel:

וַיָּבוֹא אֵלַי אֲנָשִׁים מִזִּקְנֵי יִשְׂרָאֵל וַיֵּשְׁבוּ לְפָנָי (יח' יד, א)

[="Certain elders of Israel came to me and sat down before me" (Ez. 14:1)]

The subject of the sentence, אֲנָשִׁים [="persons"], is perfectly clear, and the commentators have only to justify the lack of grammatical agreement apparent here. Some simply point out the phenomenon ("a singular form applied to plural" – Menahem Ben Shimon), some find an explanation for an exception of this kind ("hinting to each and every one" or "referring to the group as a whole" – both interpretations were cited by Ibn Kaspi, who rejected the former and accepted the latter), and others provide a literary explanation for the linguistic exception ("all in agreement for evil" – Rashi and similarly Radak).

In summation: The purpose of the Masoretes in these notes, called *sevirin*, was to preserve the text of Scripture and warn against deviation from the masoretic text. Usually the note warns against a variant that seems to be simpler and clearer, and consequently a tempting source for error. Sometimes conclusions may be drawn from a masoretic note on how Scripture should be interpreted, and some of the early commentators did so. However, arguments from the Masora are never decisive since another interpretation may be given to the masoretic version, opposed to that derived from the version rejected by the masoretic note.[12]

For further study

–   ופקדיו אשר צוה ה' את משה [="and each was recorded as the Lord had commanded Moses" (Num. 4:49)] – cf. Rashi as quoted by Ramban on this verse, and Ramban's own interpretation. What are the conclusions drawn by the commentators from the Masora? Did they regard the interpretation of the Masora as binding?
–   Explain the exegetical use made by Radak of *sevirin* notes from the Masora on the following verses: על פני הבאר [="over the mouth of the well" (II Sam. 17:19)], וילקט ממנו [="picked from it" (II Kings 4:39)], ויבוא אליה [="and they would go to her" (Ez. 23:44)].

Scribal correction (תיקון סופרים)

A masoretic list in Ms. Paris of *Okhla weOkhla* carries the title "18 words that Ezra corrected" (List 168; ed. Frensdorff, p. 113). This list presents 18 verses in which it would

---

12 The question of exegesis inherent in a *sevirin* note depends to a degree on the meaning of the term. If it means that the other variant is clearer and more reasonable than that of the Masoretic text, it may also have exegetical significance. However, if it means that some people are of the opinion that it should be read differently, it would not seem to have any exegetical weight since that variant was not accepted. However the matter is not absolute: the Masora does not warn the reader against every variant, but only against those which are likely to be read by mistake.

have been appropriate to write the text in a certain way, but it was regarded as offensive towards heaven, and consequently written differently. Here are two examples from the list:

"ואברהם עודנו עמד לפני ה'" (בר' יח, כב) - הי' צ"ל וה' עודנו עמד לפני אברהם, שהרי כתיב "וירא (ה' אל אברם) [אליו ה']" (שם, א). ותבע מן השכינה שיתעכב לו עד שיגמל חסד למלאכים, ומפני זה כנה הכתוב.

[="While Abraham remained standing before the Lord" (Gen. 18:22) – It should have said "and the Lord remained standing before Abraham", just as it said "The Lord appeared (to Abraham) [to him] (Ibid. v.1). And he demanded the Holy Presence wait until he extended hospitality to the angels, Scripture used euphemistic language.]

"כבודם בקלון אמיר" (הושע ד, ז) - כבודי הצ"ל [=היה צריך לומר] אלא שכנה.

[="I will change their dignity to dishonor" (Hos. 4:7) – It should have said "*my* dignity", but Scripture used euphemistic language.]

A similar note appears in Ms. **C** (Masora Parva on I Sam. 3:13 and other places: "18 words read according to corrections of scribes and sages"), in the printed edition of *Miqraot Gedolot* and additional manuscripts. All of them list 18 occurrences, and most of them use the term תיקון סופרים ["scribal corrections"]. Medieval sages disagree regarding the meaning of the expression (and so do modern scholars): Did the appropriate version ever exist and the scribes changed it, or was the text always as it is – euphemistic – but hinting at the other meaning. Norzi, The author of *Minhat Shai* (on Zech. 2:12) described this problem as follows:

And regarding the meaning of *tiqqun soferim* some write that the members of the Great Assembly made these changes from what was first written. And so it appears from *Midrash Yelamdenu* and thus wrote R. Natan, author of the *Arukh* in the entry כבד regarding *tiqqun soferim*, that in the early books was written בבבת עיני[13] [...], but the commentators do not agree, for how could we believe that the scribes added or detracted [...]. However the correct explanation is that which was written by R. Shlomo ben Adret (Rashba), that the scribes and sages took great care and found regarding each one of these texts that the main intention was not the literary meaning of the words written in the book, but otherwise.

Be that as it may, it is still surprising that the Masora deals with this issue, which has no connection with determining the text of Scripture. There was no doubt regarding the correct writing and the correct reading of these words, and the Masora does not deal with the history of the Biblical text. Scribal correction pertains to interpretation of the text, and the Masora usually does not deal with such subjects!

---

13 The correction here is from בבבת עיני (the pupil of my eye) to בבבת עינו (the pupil of his own eye). The reading in the Masoretic text is the latter.

In fact all of the verses that the masora indicates as *tiqqun soferim* are discussed in midrashim that preceded the masoretic notes: *Mekhilta* and *Sifrei, Gen. Rabba* and *Midrash Tanhuma*. Both expressions, תיקון סופרים and כינה הכתוב appear in midrashim, and in Lieberman's opinion reflect the disagreement about the essence of the phenomenon: The *Mekhilta* and *Sifrei* maintain that Scripture used euphemistic language – Scripture and not the scribes. *Midrash Tanhuma* on the other hand asserted explicitly that the scribes changed the text.

Perhaps it is not by chance that we do not find notes on *tiqqun soferim* in the Masora of the Aleppo Codex or Ms. Leningrad. I believe that the Masoretes of these two manuscripts felt that such notes do not serve the main purpose of the Masora – determining the accurate text of Scripture, and consequently they did not include them (we explained similarly, above in Chapter Four, why these two Masoretes refrained from including notes in the style of "Accumulative Masora").

The main "contribution" of the Masora regarding scribal corrections is in their number, eighteen. This number is not found in the midrashic sources. Once the number was given to this list of verses, it came to resemble typical masoretic lists, that open with a title stating the number of entries followed by the list of verses itself. Cf., for example the lists called "*Qal vahomer* – 5 occurrences in the Torah" and "*Qal vahomer* – 5 occurrences in Prophets and Writings". This matter also stems from midrashim (*Gen. Rabba*, 92:7), and these lists were also included in the collection *Okhla weOkhla*, pars. 182–183, not far from the lists of *tiqqun soferim*. The same applies to masoretic notes in Masora Magna of the Rabbinic Bible (Venice 1524–25) on I Kings 13:2 – "Four were called by their names before they were created: Ishmael, Isaac, Solomon and Josiah (cf. *Pirqei deRabbi Eliezer*, Chapter 31).

For further study

S. Lieberman, "Corrections of the Soferim", *Hellenism in Jewish Palestine: Studies in the literary transmission, beliefs and manners of Palestine in the I century B.C.E.–IV century C.E,* New York 1962, pp. 28–37; M. A. Zipor, *Tradition and Transmission: Studies in Ancient Biblical Translation and Interpretation,* Tel Aviv 2001 (Heb.), pp. 79–165.

Midrashic homilies in the Masora

Occasionally masoretic notes include midrashic homilies that interpret the verses. Generally speaking, most of these homilies serve to explain textual variants between similar verses, either in terms of words, or vocalization and cantillation signs. First a note of comparative Masora appears, followed by a midrashic explanation for the difference, such as the following examples (see Figures 14.3 and 14.4):

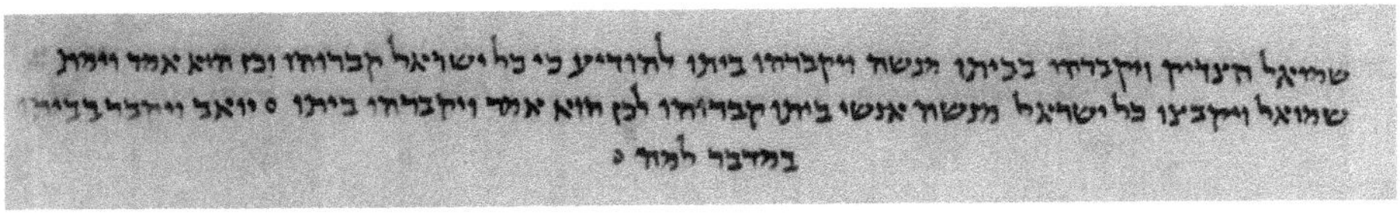

Figure 14.3: A midrashic homily in the Masora of the Aleppo Codex, II Chr. 33:20.

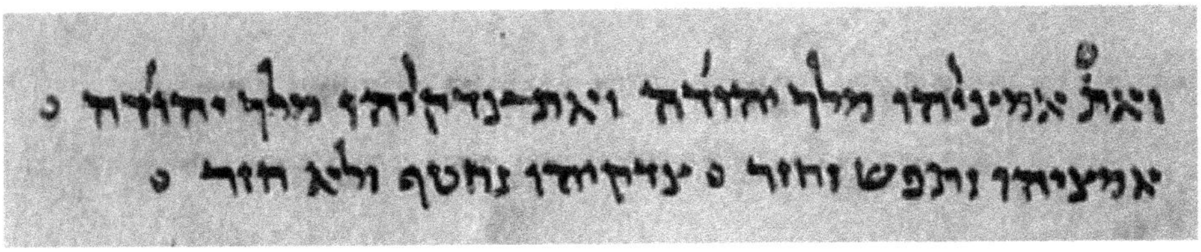

Figure 14.4: A midrashic homily in the Masora of the Aleppo Codex, II Chr. 25:23.

מ"ג-א דה"ב לג, כ: שמואל הצדיק (שמ"א כה, א) ויקברהו בביתו; מנשה (דה"ב לג, כ) ויקברהו
ביתו. להודיע כי כל ישראל קברוהו, וכן הוא אמר "וימת שמואל ויקבצו כל ישראל" (שמ"א
כה, א). מנשה אנשי ביתו קברוהו לכן הוא אמר ויקברהו ביתו. יואב (מל"א ב, לד) ויקבר בביתו
במדבר - למה.

[=MM Ms. **A** II Chr. 33:20 – Samuel the righteous - ויקבְּרהו בביתו "and they buried him in his home"
(I Sam. 25:1); Menashe - ויקבְּרהו ביתו "and the people of his home buried him" (II Chr. 33:20). This
teaches that all of Israel buried him [=Samuel], as it said "Samuel died and all Israel gathered"
(I Sam. 25:1). Menashe – his family buried him and thus it says ויקבְּרהו ביתו. Joab - ויקבר בביתו
במדבר "And he was buried in his home in the wilderness" (I Kings 2:34) – why?]

מ"ג-ל° במ' ז: בכל הקרבנות כתוב "קרבנו" בר מן יום [הראשון שהוא קרבן] נחשון, שהוא
"וקרבנו" (שם, יג). למה הוסיף וו? מלמד שבאותו היום נתחדשו ששה דברים. לכך הוסיף
וקרבנו, ונתקיימה לאיש האלהים.

[=MM Ms. **L**[S] Num. 7: Regarding all the sacrifices it is written קרבנו (="his sacrifice") except for the
first day, the sacrifice of Nahshon, which says וקרבנו (="and his sacrifice", Num. 7:13). Why was
the additional *waw* added? To teach that on that day six new things were introduced. Therefore
they added וקרבנו, and it was fulfilled for the man of God.]

מ"ג-א דה"ב כה, כג: ואת אמצִיהו מלך יהוׄדה (שם) ואת-צדקִיהו מלך יהוׄדה (יר' לד, כא).
אמצִיהו נתפש וחזר צדקיהו נחטף ולא חזר.

[=MM Ms. **A**, II Chr. 25:23 – "King Amaziah of Judah" (ibid.), "King Zedekiah of Judah" (Jer. 34:21).
Amaziah was taken captive and returned. Zedekiah was taken and did not return.]

The latter homily deals with two similar expressions, both in their words and in
their cantillation signs, but with one small difference in the latter. In the verse on
Zedekiah, the word ואת is hyphenated together with the name Zedekiah, but in the

verse on Amaziah the word has a cantillation mark of its own (called *telisha qetanna*). According to the homily this difference hints at the different fates of these two kings. Regarding Amazia it says "King Joash of Israel captured Amaziah son of Joash son of Jehoahaz, king of Judah, in Beth-shemesh" (II Chr. 25:23), but from the continuation it is clear that he returned to his kingdom. Zedekiah, on the other hand was kidnapped (נחטף). The term חטף in the Masora refers to quick reading, and in this case reading a word that is hyphenated without a cantillation sign of its own. This expression is applied here to Zedekiah, who would eventually fall into the hands of the king of Babylonia, be kidnapped and never return to his kingdom.

Conclusion

The exegetical potential of masoretic notes is very rich, and divided into a variety of types. Early exegetes, such as Rashi, Rabbenu Tam and Radak, made use of the Masora as an aid to their exegesis. To examine masoretic notes and derive from them conclusions regarding the meaning of the verses – carefully – is no small challenge.

Nevertheless all of this rich exegetical material, some of which was cited here, does not contradict the basic assumption, that the basic trend of the Masora was not exegesis, but only maintaining the text of Scripture. Occasionally the Masora digresses into interpretation, either for some need of its own, using distinctions of meaning in order to determine the text or warning against the temptation to make mistakes (*sevirin*), or in addition to its work, in order to create a sophisticated masoretic note (on homonyms) or as an additional justification for distinctions in reading (homilies).

For additional reading

R. I. (Singer) Zer, *The Exegetical Element in the Atypical Masora Lists*, Ph.D. dissertation, the Hebrew University of Jerusalem 2007 (Heb.).

15 The Masora and Halakha

Introduction

This chapter concerns the status and authority of the Masora in the course of generations. We shall examine whether the Tiberian version as reflected in the masoretic notes in the manuscripts from Tiberias were considered authoritative, to the point that they had the power to replace other versions of Scripture that were accepted in various Jewish communities. We shall also examine the attitude of halakhic authorities towards masoretic notes in various periods and locales from earliest times until our own.

The text of Scripture reflected in the Talmud vs. the Masoretic text

During the time when rabbinic literature was created – the halakhic and aggadic midrashim as well as the Babylonian Talmud and the Jerusalem Talmud – Torah scrolls and copies of Scripture in the Jewish world differed from each other in textual details, mainly orthography. Centuries later the final Tiberian version of Scripture was defined, and perpetuated in the notes of the Tiberian Masora. Thus it is not surprising that in certain places the Tiberian Masoretic text differs from that which was available to the sages of the Talmud and the midrashim. We do not have manuscripts of Scripture from the Talmudic period, but testimony regarding the text of Scripture they used may be found in verses quoted and in homilies on verses in rabbinic literature, the Talmud and the Midrash.

The differences between the Tiberian Masoretic text and the Scriptural text reflected in the Talmud and Midrash were revealed in later generations. Many of the "Rishonim", the earlier scholars, pointed out the discrepancies in various places in Scripture and tried to resolve them. The issue was particularly severe when a practical halakhic issue was at stake: In such places the question of authority arose in all its severity. The Babylonian Talmud is the authoritative source of Halakha on the basis of which Halakha is decided. Does this authority apply also to the text of Scripture? Can it overrule the authority of the Masora or could the latter be more authoritative in matters of the text of Scripture?

In the following example from Tractate Shabbat (55b) Rashi and the Tosafists differed, taking contradictory positions on the matter at hand. The Talmudic passage discusses the sons of Eli and the nature of their sin:

> R. Samuel son of Nahmani said in the name of R. Jonathon: Whoever maintains that the sons of Eli (Hofni and Pinhas) sinned is merely making an error ... Rav said: Pinhas did not sin... But it is written מעבירים [="you (plural) make [the Lord's people] to transgress", I Sam. 2:24]?! R. Huna son of Rav Joshua said: the word is written מעברים [with only one yod]![1]

---

[1] The defective spelling hints that only one of Eli's sons sinned (even though the verbal form is plural). Or: the word can be read מַעֲבִרָם (he causes them to transgress).

https://doi.org/10.1515/9783110594560-015

Rashi noted the disagreement between the text of Scripture cited by Rav Huna and that of the Masoretic text. Evidently this disturbed him and brought him to say:

> I have difficulty with the name of the sage mentioned here. For I say that it is a big error and the whole paragraph should be deleted from the Talmud. Since in well-checked books the spelling of the word is מעבירים (*plene*), and also the 'great Masora', which lists all the words that a *yod* is read and not written does not list this word, and they are all listed according to number...

Rashi found that in the accurate books of Scripture available to him the text of the word מעבירים was *plene*, and he cited the 'great Masora' (i.e. the collection called *Okhla weOkhla*; see above, Chapter Four) as further evidence. Thus Rashi had difficulty resolving the words of the Talmud with the Masoretic text, and his solution was exceptional and surprising: Rashi deleted the entire sentence from the Talmud! Evidently he did so because of the contradiction he found between the Masoretic text and that cited in the Talmud.

A contrary approach to the problem is found in the words of the Tosafists (*Ibid.*, incipit: מעבירם):

> Our Talmud disagrees with our books, which write מעבירים (should be: מעברים). Similarly we found in the Jerusalem Talmud regarding Samson "And he led Israel for forty years" (Jud 16:31) meaning that the Philistines feared him twenty years after his death as they did during his lifetime. Yet in all of our books it says "twenty years".

The Tosafists had no qualms about admitting simply: "Our Talmud disagrees with our books". Their conclusion is that the accepted text of the books should not be changed even if we find a different version in the Talmud.

In order to reinforce this principle, the Tosafists quote a different source, in which a homily is based on a text of Scripture that differs from that of the Masora. Here the discrepancy is not between *plene* and defective spelling, but an entire word. The Jerusalem Talmud (Sota 1:8, 17b) points out a contradiction between two verses regarding Samson. One says that he judged Israel for forty years, and the other for twenty years.

And the Tosafists remark that in "our books" both verses state "twenty years" (Jud 15:20; 16,31), and if so, there is no basis for the homily in the Jerusalem Talmud.

The principle to be derived from the words of the Tosafists was expressed explicitly by R. Abraham b. R. Isaac of Narbonne, author of *Sefer HaEshkol* (twelfth century):

> And we follow the Masora in accurate books even if it contradicts homilies in the Talmud and Midrash (Laws of the portions read throughout the year, *Sefer HaEshkol*, Ed. B. H. Auerbach, II, p. 62).

To illustrate his point the author provides a list of occurrences in which the variant reflected in rabbinic homilies does not conform to the Masoretic text:

> הפילגשים (="concubines" [plene spelling], Gen. 25:6/Gen. Rabbah par. 61), כלת (="finished" [defective spelling], Num. 7:1/Pesiqta Rabbati par. 5 and parallels: ביומא דעלת כלה לגנתא [="in the day that **a bride** arrives to her canopy"], and likewise מעבירים (I Sam. 2:24, the verse discussed

above), and קרנת (="the horns", Lev. 4:25,30, 34/Sanhedrin 4a and Zebahim 37b), and כדר [לעמר] (=Chedor[laomer], Gen. 14:1/Hullin 65a), nor did we find in our books להכרותו (="to urge him", II Sam. 3:35/Sanhedrin 20a).

Specifically in the most notable example, the one which the Tosafists used to support their method, the author of *Sefer HaEshkol* does not concur:

> And the Talmud speaks regarding this matter not according to the plain sense of Scripture: It is written in one place "He [Samson] led Israel for forty years" and in another place it says: "He led Israel for twenty years". Rabbi Aha said this teaches that the Philistines feared him for twenty years after his death just as they feared him for twenty years during his lifetime.

> They knew that the scripture does not say about Samson "He led... for forty years", but they came to interpret two verses: During his lifetime it says "he led Israel in the time of the Philistines twenty years" (Jud. 15:20) and at the end they repeated upon his death: "they buried him...and he had led Israel for twenty years" (Jud. 16:31), as if he continued leading them for twenty more years and together that is forty years.

That is to say, the reading in the Jerusalem Talmud in the Bible does not differ from the Masoretic text, but the homily explains the repeated reference to the twenty years of Samson's leadership, seeing the two references as consecutive, twenty years in his lifetime and twenty years after his death.

This example is important because it represents one of the three ways by which exegetes and scholars treated the problem of variants that did not conform to the Masoretic Text of the Bible: one way was to recognize the fact that the Scriptural variants in the Talmud differ from the accepted text; a second was to reconcile the homily in such a way that conformed to the Masoretic text, claiming that they do not reflect a different reading of Scripture; the third way was to question the authority of the Masora and prefer the reading reflected in the Talmud.

For additional study

Examine Rashi's commentary on Tractate Shabbat 55b (quoted above), and in the collection *Okhla waOkhla* (ed. Frensdorff, list no. 128). Explain how Rashi used the masoretic list in order to determine the Masoretic text of I Sam. 2:22. Examine the verses cited in the list, and consider how to answer the evidence Rashi gives.

Collecting Scriptural variants reflected in rabbinic writings

Different writers and projects have tried to collect testimony from rabbinic literature (Talmud and Midrash) regarding scriptural variants that do not conform to the Masoretic text. Some of the collections tried to minimize the extent of the phenomenon, reconciling the homilies with the Masoretic text, much as we saw above in a citation from *Sefer HaEshkol*. Other collections simply documented the phenomenon, and they too were aware that not every occurrence testified to the existence of a different version of Scripture.

Among the former mention should be made of the books *Mishpehot Soferim*, *Sefer HaMesillot*, *Sefer Darkhei HaShinnuyim*, as well as the work by Rabbi Reuven Margaliyyot, *HaMiqra weHaMasora*. Among the latter the collection edited by V. Aptowitzer is noteworthy.

Particularly noteworthy in this context is the extensive enterprise of Yedidya Shelomo Norzi in his work *Minhat Shai*. In this massive work, arranged according to the books of the Tanakh, numerous testimonies are quoted from rabbinic literature, commentaries, grammars, Kabbalistic writings and even books of sermons. Norzi was aware that in very many places the text cited differs from the Masoretic text. He determined the reading on the basis of masoretic literature, but nevertheless cited evidence of different readings from a variety of early and late sources.

In order to illustrate that not every homily is testimony to a Scriptural variant, he presented a collection of homilies that differed from the Masoretic text, some of them very different and even strange, saying (*Minhat Shai* on Malakhi 2:15):

> The way of the homily is to expound in many ways even if they conflict with the cantillation signs, and we learn [their words] without questioning them. [...] And not only regarding cantillation signs, but even vocalization and letters. [...] There is no doubt that all the words of our sages of sacred memory were spoken with the greatest wisdom and valued beyond the purest gold.

In other words, the sayings of the sages are deep and contain sublime ideas, but they have no bearing on the text of Scripture, nor do they invalidate the simple meaning of the text.

A wide-ranging effort to collect and analyze textual variants was conducted for the edition of the Tanakh by the Bible Project at the Hebrew University of Jerusalem. The second apparatus in this edition deals with variants from the Judean Desert Scrolls and rabbinic literature; the editors testify that "recording rabbinic literature is a first attempt to overcome the obstacles that stand in the way of anyone wanting to implement this material in a scholarly apparatus". Even though the editors examined the Mishna and Tosefta, both Talmuds and the works of Midrash, they do not regard their work as complete because for every source there are numerous manuscripts, and frequently the reading that differs from the Masoretic text is documented in a single manuscript or only a few manuscripts.

An important distinction was made between the versions documented as variants in citations and those that are derived from the homilies themselves, since the latter do not seem to depend on the work of the scribes who copied the manuscripts. Nevertheless there are many reasons to cast doubt and in the words of the editors: "There are few occurrences in which we feel confident that the homily could not be interpreted differently".

For additional study

R. Akiva Eiger, *Gilyon HaShas*, on Babylonian Talmud, Shabbat 55b (In Hebrew); S. Waldberg, *Sefer Darkhei HaShinnuyim*, Lemberg 1870 (in Hebrew); S. R. Edelmann, *Sefer HaMesillot*, Vilna 1875 (in Hebrew); S. Rosenfeld, *Mishpeḥot Soferim*, Vilna 1883 (in Hebrew); V. Aptowitzer, *Das Schriftwort in der rabbinischen Literatur*, 5 vol., 1906–1915 (photocopy New York 1970); R. Margaliyyot, *HaMiqra weHaMasora*, Jerusalem 1964; Y. Maori, "Rabbinic Midrash as a Witness of Textual Variants of the Hebrew Bible: The History of the Issue and its Practical Application in the Hebrew University Bible Project", *Studies in Bible and Exegesis* III (1993), pp. 267–286 (in Hebrew); E. Tov, *Textual Criticism of the Hebrew Bible*, Minneapolis 2012, pp. 32–34; M. Kahana, "The Biblical Text as reflected in Ms rome 32 of the Sifri", *Meḥqerei Talmud: Talmudic Studies* I, Jerusalem 1990, pp. 1–10 (in Hebrew)

The responsum of R. Shelomo b. Adret (Rashba)

Many discussions have been conducted over the years regarding the textual variants derived from the Talmud. The starting-point for most of these discussions is a responsum by R. Shelomo b. Adret (Rashba, thirteenth-century Spain). This responsum requires detailed treatment because it reflects the characteristic state of the Masoretic text during the Middle Ages. One minor textual error occurred in the transmission of the responsum at a critical point, essentially reversing its meaning. It may not be an exaggeration to say that the Masoretic text was "saved" thanks to the error in Rashba's responsum. The following is the question posed to Rashba: (*Responsa of Rashba attributed to Ramban*, no. 232):

שאלה: אם נפסל ספר תורה בחסרות ויתרות שיהיה כנגד המסורה, שאני אומר אין ספרי המסורה מעולין מספרי התלמוד שאמר פלגשם כתיב, וכן ואשמם כתיב, וכן כלת כתיב. ובספרים שלנו פלגשים ביו"ד ואשימם ביו"ד כלות בו"ו וקרנות בו"ו, הפך מזה שאמרו חכמים. ואין אנו חוששין לספרי התלמוד לתקן הספרים לשנותם, שכך אני מקובל ממך. ואיך נחוש לספרי המסורה חדשים מקרוב באו? ויש לי ראיה לקבלתי זו מפ"ק דקדושין, דאמר דבשעה רב יהודה ורב יוסף לא הוו בקיאי בחסרות ויתרות, כל שכן אנו. ומי שדרש פלגשם ואשמם וכלת, יש לנו לומר שמצאו כן בספריהם. אבל אנו לא נחוש להם, וספרינו נחזיק כמה שהם.

אמנם אני איני תמה על פסוקי דרשות של הגדה כדאמרן. אבל קרנת קרנת חושש אני להם, כיון שבית שמאי ובית הלל מודים להם, ולא נחלקו אלא ביש אם למקרא או יש אם למסורת, ושניהם עושין דין על פי החסר והיתר. ודעתי היה לתקנם, אלא שאני ירא בדבר ואשמר לי עד יבא דברך ויורנו. ובסכות בסכת מצאנוהו בספרינו כמו שאמרו חכמים. הודיענו דעתך בזה.

[=**Question:** If a Torah scroll was declared invalid because of a problem of *plene* and defective orthography that differed from that of the Masora. And I say that the books of the Masora are not better (or: stronger) than books of the Talmud, that said it is written פלגשם, or ואשמם and likewise כלת. But in our scrolls [we find] פלגשים, with a *yod* and אשימם with a *yod*, כלות with a *waw* and קרנות with a *waw*, the opposite of what the sages said. And we do not see the need to correct them on the basis of books of the Talmud, as I have learned from you. So how could we consider correcting them on the basis of books of the Masora that have only recently appeared? And I have evidence for my tradition from the first chapter of Qiddushin that says that in the years of Rav Yehudah and Rav Yosef there were not experts regarding *plene* and defective spelling, and we even more so. And whoever gave a discourse on spellings such as פלגשם and ואשמם and כלת, we should say that they found those spellings in their scrolls. But we should not be concerned about that, and leave our scrolls as they are.

Indeed I am not surprised at verses in homilies of Aggada such as those I have mentioned. But regarding קרנת קרנת, I am concerned, because both Beit Shammai and Beit Hillel agree, and they only disagreed regarding the precedence of the written text or the oral tradition [for the Halakhic conclusions], but both of them determine the Halakha according to defective and *plene* forms. And I would have thought to correct them (=the Torah scrolls), if I were not fearful about it; and I refrain until I receive your word and teaching. And regarding בסכות and בסכת, we find that [the spelling of these words in] our scrolls is like what the sages said. Please inform me about this.]

There are two parts to the question: The first part deals with the authority of the Masora in general. Opposite the Masora are "our scrolls", i.e. the spelling of Scripture as found in Torah scrolls in the provenance of the questioner and the respondent. The questioner asks whether books of the Masora have the authority to change the accepted spelling, and he expresses his own opinion that the decision of the Masora should not overrule local practice. For that reason he provides an inference from minor to major: He had already heard from Rashba that the accepted spelling in scrolls should not be changed on the basis of spelling reflected in the Talmud. And if so, even more so the accepted spelling should not be changed on the basis of books of the Masora, which "have only recently appeared" and whose authority is clearly less than that of the Talmud.

This approach seriously reduces the authority of the Masora in general. Surprisingly enough Rashba agrees and reinforces the assertion:

תשובה: מדעתי שכן האמת, שאין מוסיפין וגורעין בכל מקום ומקום בספרים על פי המסורת ועל פי מדרשי אגדה, לפי שנחלקו במקומות בארצות על פי חכמיהם הבקיאים בחסרות ויתרות, וכמדומה לי אפילו במקרא ומסורת, כמחלוקת בן אשר ובן נפתלי, ובין מערבאי למדינחאי.

[=**Response:** In my opinion that is true: we do not add or detract anywhere in the scrolls on the basis of the Masora or Midrashei Aggada, since they (=the Masoretes) differed in places and countries according to their sages and their expertise in defective and *plene* spellings, and it seems to me even in Scripture and Masora (=cases of *Ketiv* and *Qere*), as in the disagreements of Ben Asher and Ben Naftali and between the western [sages] and the eastern [sages].]

That is to say, the abundance of internal disagreements within the Masora cast doubt on its authority in general. This approach is completely different from that of Rashi, who relied on the Masora and regarded it as a compelling authority for determining not only the text of Scripture, but also its meaning (see below in the list for additional study). Obviously this approach contradicts the explicit declaration of the author of *Sefer HaEshkol* regarding the authority of the Masora.

Rashba's approach reflects a situation in which the status of the Masora is not that strong. The books of the Masora were not that widespread and were not available to scribes. There were verses that the local Torah scrolls did not conform to the masoretic notes as to their spelling, and even when contradictions were discovered, they did not rush to correct the scrolls because the authority of the Masora was not absolute.

In the second part of the question the questioner raises a serious problem with regard to the text of Scripture in the Talmud: In most cases the accepted opinion was that "our scrolls" should not be corrected on the basis of variants in the Talmud, an opinion expressed by the Tosafists, to which Rashba subscribed and which he had taught to his correspondent at an earlier time ("as I have learned from you"). But we accept the authority of the Talmud in matters of Halakha. What should we do when the Talmud bases a halakhic ruling on the text of Scripture? How can we undermine the basis of a Talmudic law, and nevertheless accept the ruling that stems from it?!

Rashba accepted this argument and maintains in his responsum:

ומכל מקום, בכל מה שבא בתלמוד דרך עיקר דין בכקרנת קרנת (סנהדרין ד ע"א ועוד) וכבסכת (סוכה ו ע"ב ועוד) לטוטפת (סנהדרין ד ע"ד ועוד) ובן אין לו ביו"ד דרשינן עיין עליו מדלא כתיב בלא יו"ד כמו 'מאן בלעם', שעליו דנין עיקר ירושה שממשמשת והולכת (יבמות כב ע"ב) - בזה ודאי מתקנין המיעוט.

וכן בכל מקום ומקום, אפילו בחסרות ויתרות, מתקנין המיעוט על פי הרוב, דמקרא מלא דבר הכתוב 'אחרי רבים להטות', ושנינו במסכת סופרים: 'אמר ריש לקיש ג' ספרים נמצאו בעזרה ספר מעון וספר זעטוטי וספר הוא' (סופרים פ"ו ה"ד)...

[=And nevertheless, regarding what appears in the Talmud as the essence of the law such as homilies on קרנת קרנת (Sanhedrin 4a and parallel passages) and such as בסכת (Sukka 6b and more), לטוטפת (Sanhedrin 4b and more) and ובן אין לו with a *yod*, and [because of this *plene* spelling] the Talmud says 'Hold an inquiry concerning him', regarding how the expression מאן בלעם is written without a *yod*, which figures in the discussion of a principle in inheritance law (Yebamot 22b) – **here we certainly correct the minority** [of scrolls].

And likewise in every place, even regarding defective and *plene* spelling, the minority [of scrolls] is corrected on the basis of the majority, as we learn from the scriptural injunction "follow the majority", and as we have learned in tractate Soferim "Resh Laqish said there were three scrolls in the Azara, *Sefer Ma'on*, *Sefer Za'atutei* and *Sefer Hu*" (Soferim 6:4).

In the second paragraph quoted here Rashba refers to an internal difference between "our scrolls", i.e. between Torah scrolls found in his location. In such a case the ruling goes by the majority of the scrolls (and not according to the Masora! – see the beginning of the responsum). However, if that is the case, the first paragraph makes no sense. If the ruling is that the version reflected in the Talmud should be accepted when it has halakhic consequences – that should apply with respect to all the Torah scrolls. What is the meaning of "we correct the minority"? After all, correcting the minority is the norm without relation to the variant in the Talmud or to its halakhic pertinence.

Clearly a scribal error occurred in the transmission of Rashba's ruling. The correct version of the responsum is documented in some of the sources (Meiri, *Qiryat Sefer*, ed. Hershler, Jerusalem 1956, p. 254; Responsa of Tashbez, III, no. 160; Responsa of Radbaz IV, no. 101). It reads that in the case of a halakhic ruling of the Talmud בזה ודאי מתקנין

[="we certainly correct"]! This may have been no more than a scribal error in which the word המיעוט [="minority"] was added because the expression appears in the follo-wing line of the responsum. However, the addition of this word was so significant that it reversed the impact of Rashba's ruling. It may have been an intentional correction and not just a scribal error. Such a hypothesis was suggested by Prof. S.Z. Havlin in his discussion of the issue.[2]

At any rate many later scholars cited this responsum of Rashba, and the approach that was accepted in practice in Jewish communities supported the Masoretic text. Most of the scholars who dealt with the text of Scripture accepted the authority of the Masora and did not regard it as conflicting with "our scrolls". Their attitude was the opposite: The text of the scrolls conformed to the Masora and was determined by it. It is also possible that the "professional tradition" of the scribes was firm and stable, and the scribes were reluctant to diverge from it because of the opinions of halakhic authorities. As far as the difference between the text of the Masora and the text of the Talmud, here the erroneous version of Rashba's responsum was accepted, according to which the Masoretic text should not be replaced on the basis of variants in the Talmud.

This is how Yedidia Norzi, the author of *Minhat Shai* (sixteenth and seventeenth centuries), described the situation in his gloss on Lev. 4:34:

> And I have already informed you that whenever the Talmud or the Midrash disagrees with the Masora regarding defective or *plene* orthography we follow the Masora. Not only in Aggadic homiletical interpretation, like 'פילגשם', 'כלת', 'ואשמם', but also in places where a halakhic rule is drawn, like here (the spelling of the word קרנת) according to the School of Shammai and the School of Hillel. And in addition [I should say that] all Torah scrolls and all scribes give the same spelling, without any dispute. And in the responsum of Ramban no. 232 [=the responsum of Rashba above] he was asked about this [...] and Ramban answered that everywhere, even regar-ding defective and *plene* orthography, the minority of scrolls should be corrected on the basis of the majority, as in the scriptural injunction "follow the majority".

For further study

S. Z. Havlin, "Establishing Correct Manuscript Readings: Quantity or Quality?" (Heb.), *Me'ah She'arim: Studies in Medieval Jewish Spiritual Life in Memory of Isadore Twersky*, Jerusalem 2001, pp. 241–265; J. S. Penkower, "Maimonides and the Aleppo Codex", *Textus* 9 (1981), pp. 40–41, n. 3; S. Z. Leiman, "Masorah and Halakhah: A Study in Conflict", in: M. Cogan et al., *Tehillah le-Moshe, in Honor of Moshe Greenberg*, Winona Lake, Indiana 1997, pp. 304–305, notes 37–38.

---

2 "It is ironic that in the text of this responsum itself a printer's error (perhaps not accidental) occurred in a critical place and misled many" (p. 251). Cf. *Ibid.*, pp. 253–254, note 35.

Masora vs. Halakha today

Recently, in the wake of discoveries and research into ancient manuscripts of the Tiberian Masoretes, and in particular the Aleppo Codex, the question of the authority of the Masora vs. Halakha has come to the fore. This question has many facets, and the decision is not uniform in every case. Nor are the circumstances identical to those of earlier times: In earlier times the issue was the Masoretic text vs. variant readings in the Talmud and Midrash, but today the Masoretic text faces halakhic decisions of ancient halakhic authorities regarding the Masora itself!

The questions that are discussed today relate to *plene* and defective orthography and to open and closed passages. The problems concern the Torah itself and also the Prophets and Writings, and we shall discuss them one at a time.

The orthography of the Torah and that of the Prophets and Writings

We discussed the data from the Masora above in Chapter Three. We observed there that the orthography accepted in Jewish communities is very close to that of the Tiberian manuscripts and their masoretic notes. Nevertheless there are at least eight instances in which the text accepted in Ashkenazi and Sephardi communities differs from the Yemeni one, the Aleppo Codex (documented in the list made by Rabbi Sitthon in Aleppo), and most of the Tiberian manuscripts and their masoretic notes. This fact came to light only recently. Thus the question arises whether this information could influence the accepted tradition of orthography in Sephardi and Ashkenazi communities today. The answer is clearly negative: The ruling on the orthography of the Torah accepted in most communities was that of the Ramah (R. Meir Halevy Abulafia) in his book *Masoret Seyag LaTorah*, written in the early thirteenth century. His ruling was supplemented in a few passages by R. Menahem di Lonzano in his work *Or Torah* from the early seventeenth century. The text that emerges from these rulings was accepted in Sephardi and Ashkenazi communities, the guides for scribes called *Tiqqunei Soferim* were based on it, and hundreds and thousands of Torah scrolls were copied according to it in most Jewish communities. Thus one should not expect it to be rejected and replaced by the Masoretic text discovered in our times. Even Rabbi Breuer himself, who was the first to clarify and reveal these facts, did not fathom the Masoretic text replacing the accepted way of writing Torah scrolls. He only suggested cautiously and hesitantly that "a new community, that had not yet adopted a permanent custom – and that consisted of descendants of different communities – should consider raising their level by selecting a Torah scroll written according to the Yemeni custom" (*The Aleppo Codex and the Accepted Text of the Bible*, Jerusalem 1977, p. 9 [in Hebrew]). However there is some doubt whether anyone has done so.

The situation is entirely different with regards to books of the Prophets and Writings. No significant halakhic ruling was ever made regarding them, mainly because most communities did not copy them on parchment like Torah scrolls. In these books, the orthography should be determined according to the accurate and ancient manuscripts and according to the Masora comments. Rabbi Breuer determined the Masoretic text of Prophets and Writings in his edition of the Tanakh and explained how he did so in the aforementioned book (1977). In recent years there has been a process of adopting this version by scribes who write scrolls of books of the Prophets and Writings and by the editors of guides for scribes.

Open and closed passages and the style of writing songs

In Chapter Five we discussed the subject of open and closed passages as well as the way in which songs should be written. Here we shall review the conclusions from the point of view of relations between the Masora and Halakha.

We observed that the Masora did not achieve total clarity regarding passages. The Tiberian Masora did not deal with the subject at all, and the Babylonian Masora – and the lists of passages, most of which stem from Babylonia – were unable to reach a decision. It was Maimonides who determined the matter of passages and the writing of songs in the Torah, and his ruling was based on the Keter, which later came to be known as the Aleppo Codex. Here we shall address the issue from a different point of view: To what degree did the practical ruling regarding passages and songs in the Torah conform to the Aleppo Codex? The same question will be asked regarding the Prophets and Writings.

As far as the Torah is concerned all of the Jewish communities accepted Maimonides' ruling in principle to rely on the Aleppo Codex. However regarding certain details there was some doubt and in practice they diverged from the Aleppo Codex. In Leviticus, Ch. 7 the communities disagreed regarding Maimonides' intention, and evidently the actual usage in the Aleppo Codex did not conform to either interpretation. In two additional passages (Ex. 34:1, פסל לך ["Carve two tablets"], and Deut. 27:20, ארור שוכב עם אשת אביו ["Cursed be he who lies with his father's wife"]), testimony on the Aleppo Codex indicates that Maimonides' ruling did not conform to the Codex, however, it is possible that there was a small space in the Codex that Maimonides interpreted differently from the other witnesses to the manuscript.[3]

---

3 Cf. Y. Ofer, "M.D. Cassuto's Notes on the Aleppo Codex", **Sefunot - *Studies and Sources on the History of the Jewish Communities in the East***, NS vol. 4 (19), 1989, pp. 325–330, 335, 341 (in Hebrew); Y. Ofer, "The Aleppo Codex and the Bible of R. Shalom Shachna Yelin", in: M. Bar-Asher (ed.), **Rabbi Mordechai Breuer Festschrift** – *Collected Papers in Jewish Studies*, Jerusalem 1992, pp. 305–308 (in Hebrew).

In writing the Song at the Sea and the Song of *Haazinu* and the lines before and after them there are some differences between the Aleppo Codex and contemporary Torah scrolls:

1. Most communities (with the exception of Yemen) ruled that *Haazinu* should be written in seventy lines (as stated in Tractate Soferim) and not in 67 like the Aleppo Codex. Here Maimonides' words were altered, and those who differed from the Aleppo Codex relied on the later version of Maimonides' books.

2. In the same communities the lines after *Haazinu* were written differently from the Aleppo Codex, because these lines in that manuscript are wider. Here there is no different version of Maimonides' ruling, and those who do otherwise base themselves on another custom and rely upon the saying of Maimonides that a different way of writing in these lines does not invalidate the scroll (cf. Maimonides, Laws of the Torah Scroll, 7:10).

3. Even the Yemeni tradition differs from the Aleppo Codex in one detail of the Song of *Haazinu*, and that because Maimonides' ruling was ambiguous: Maimonides says that the word גם comes at the beginning of the 39th line of the song. In the Aleppo Codex the line begins with the words גם בתולה [="and a maiden", Deut. 32:25; Figure 15.1], but in the Yemeni practice with the previous words גם בחור [="both a youth"] (Figure 15.2).

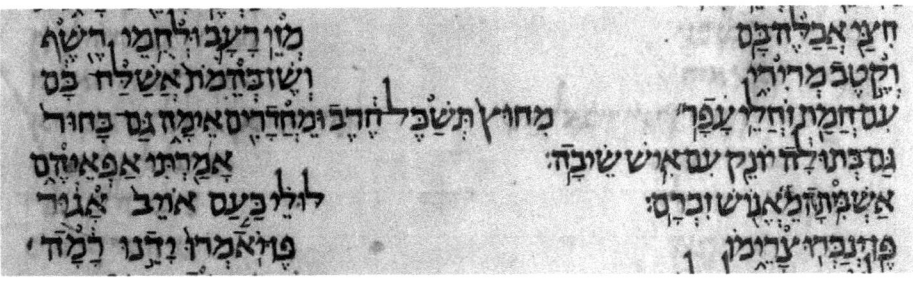

Figure 15.1: Lines from the song of *Haazinu* in the Aleppo Codex.

מזי רעב ולחמי רשף	חצי אכלה בם
ושן בהמת אשלח בם	וקטב מרירי
מחוץ תשכל חרב ומחדרים אימה	עם חמת זחלי עפר
אמרתי אפאיהם	גם בחור גם בתולה יונק עם איש שיבה
לולי כעס אויב אגור	אשביתה מאנוש זכרם
פן יאמרו ידנו רמה	פן ינכרו צרימו

Figure 15.2: Lines from the Song of *Haazinu* in *Tiqqun Soferim* of the Yemeni custom Compare lines 3–4 to Figure 15.1.

4. The last lines of the Song at the Sea are written in a way that differs from their writing in the Aleppo Codex (which is known only from testimony since that part of the Codex is missing). Maimonides did not describe the lines of the Song at the Sea verbally as he did regarding the Song of *Haazinu*, but copied it in its entirety as it should be written. However there are differences in different manuscripts of *Mishne Torah* as to the way these lines are written.

The Song of *Haazinu* is extant in the Aleppo Codex today, and we have reliable testimony regarding the Song at the Sea, but the way in which the two songs is written was already determined in tradition and in the Torah scrolls of different communities, yet no one can imagine changing it.

For further study

M. Goshen-Gottstein, "The Authenticity of the Aleppo Codex", *Textus* 1 (1960), pp. 17–58; J.S. Penkower, *New Evidence for the Pentateuch Text in the Aleppo Codex*, Ramat Gan 1992 (in Hebrew), pp. 32–50.

Passages in the scroll of Esther, passages in the Prophets and in the four scrolls

Maimonides ruled that the Aleppo Codex was authoritative only regarding the Torah, and did not mention anything about the Prophets and Writings. The question remains whether to apply the same instruction to the rest of the Tanakh.

We discussed this question above in Chapter Five, where we pointed out that the regulations regarding the Scroll of Esther differs from those for books of the Prophets or the other four scrolls. With regards to Esther, the Halakha was determined by R. Moses Isserles in the *Shulhan Arukh* that "all its passages are closed", and such is the practice in all Jewish communities today, not only Ashkenazi ones. With regards to the Prophets and the other four scrolls (Song of Songs, Ruth, Lamentations and Ecclesiastes) – the situation is different. Writing these scrolls in the manner of Torah scrolls is practiced mainly in Ashkenazi communities that follow the teachings of the Vilna Gaon, and even though most of the scrolls were written according to a tradition of passages that differed from the Aleppo Codex, the ambition to follow the Codex began in the mid-nineteenth century by expert scribes among the followers of the Vilna Gaon, and received support from the leading rabbis of Jerusalem. After the Aleppo Codex was made accessible and evidence regarding how the scrolls were written in it came to be known, a polemic broke out in 1995 about whether the tradition of the portions in the Aleppo Codex or another tradition should be the basis for writing scrolls (see above, Chapter 5 and Figure 5.5). The polemic has not yet been resolved, but it would seem that writing according to the Aleppo Codex is becoming more predominant.

For further study

D. Yitzhaki, "Open and closed passages in the scroll of Esther" (Heb.), *Zefunot* 4,3 (1992), pp. 100–103; D. Yitzhaki "Customs of Writing the Scroll of Esther" (Heb.), in Y. Buksbaum (ed.), *Qovez HaMo'adim: Hannuka, Purim, Tisha Be'av weTa'aniyot*, Jerusalem 2002, pp. 376–420; Jordan S. Penkower, "An Esther Scroll from the 15th century: determining its type among five traditions (Oriental, Sefardi, Ashkenazi, Italian, Yemenite)", *Textus* 26 (2016), pp. 209–270.

Should the reading of two verses in the Scroll of Esther be repeated due to doubt?

The status of the Scroll of Esther ("the *Megilla*") is different because the Halakha demands that the Book of Esther be read on the holiday of Purim from a scroll written according to the laws of writing Torah scrolls, and consequently, very many Esther scrolls were written over time. This in opposition to other books of the Writings that are not read in public and were only rarely copied on parchment like Torah scrolls, and also to books of the Prophets and the other four scrolls, which only a small minority of communities read from specially-prepared parchment scrolls.

The orthography of the Scroll of Esther was determined in recent generations in Ashkenazi communities by the rulings of R. Shelomo Ganzfried in his book *Qeset HaSofer* (first published in 1834). An examination conducted by Rabbi Mordechai Breuer revealed that in six places the orthography in *Qeset HaSofer* differs from that which emerges from most of the masoretic manuscripts and notes. It will be interesting to see to what degree the instructions of *Qeset HaSofer* spread among other Jewish communities, and whether Rabbi Breuer's assertion will influence the writing of Esther scrolls, rejecting the text established by the author of *Qeset HaSofer*. Evidently only a small number of the Esther scrolls in use today conform in every respect to the Masoretic text.

In two of the places where this difference exists the issue is not only spelling, but reading as well: In Esther 8:11 the disagreement is between ולהרג [="and massacre"] and להרג [="massacre"]; in 9:2 between לפניהם and בפניהם ["them"]. In many communities it has become the practice to read the word, the phrase or the entire verse twice, using both alternative readings, due to doubt. Rabbi Breuer published a special booklet, in which he maintained that in the light of what is known about the Masoretic text there is no justification for this practice, since the Masoretic text is clearly known from ancient manuscripts and masoretic notes: ולהרג (8:11), לפניהם (9:2). Here too, the accepted custom is so widespread and established in Halakhic literature that it would be difficult to overrule it.

For further study

M. Breuer, *The Aleppo Codex and the Accepted Text of the Bible*, Jerusalem 1977, pp. 23–25 (in Hebrew) [See also: *Leshonenu* 58 (1994–1995), p. 293 (in Hebrew)]; idem, *Miqraot sheyesh lahem hekhre'a* (="verses that their current version could be determined"), Alon Shevut 1990 (=*Megadim* 10 [1990], pp. 97–112) (in Hebrew); Y.S. Spiegel, "On doubts and on strict rulings", *Megadim* 11 (1990), pp. 113–115 (in Hebrew); idem, "More on the double reading of verses in the Scroll of Esther", *Megadim* 20 (1993), pp. 97–98 (in Hebrew); J.S. Penkower, "*Minhag* and *Massorah*: On the Recent Ashkenazic Custom of Double Vocalization of זכר עמלק (Deuteronomy 25:19)", *Studies in Bible and Exegesis* IV (1997), pp. 122–126 (in Hebrew).

Index of Manuscripts

Biblical Manuscripts and printed editions

Most important manuscripts

Ms. A, The Aleppo Codex, The Keter This important manuscript is mentioned throughout the book, and therefore the page numbers are not specified here. See especially Chapter 8 (pp. 131–150)

Ms. B, British Library Or. 4445 8, 49, 51, 55, 199, 224–225

Ms. C, Cairo 34 8, 41, 43, 52–53, 57–59, 90, 187, 199–202, 209, 211, 213, 226, 260

Ms. L^M, Cairo 14 21, 157–161, 166, 226, 254, 256

Ms. L, Ms. Leningrad, SP Evr. I B19a 7, 21, 32, 36–43, 47, 55, 70, 77, 80, 82, 92–94, 151, 154, 157–158, 187, 190–193, 199–200, 209–214, 217, 223, 229, 261

Ms. S, Heb. 24^0 5702 (formerly Sassoon 507) 9, 41, 161, 166–169, 199

Ms. S1, formerly Sassoon 1053 8, 30, 41–43, 46–47, 134, 199, 56

Other biblical manuscripts

Ashkar-Gilson 176
British Library Add. 15451 192
Berlin 680 80
Sassoon 368, Farhi Tanakh 252

Manuscripts from Sanct. Petersburg, National library

SP Evr. I B 3, Ms. P 226
SP Evr. II B 9, Ms. L20 162
SP Evr. II B 17 134–135
SP Evr. II B 34 83
SP Evr. II B 115 83
SP Evr. II B 1475 83
SP Evr. II C 1, Ms. Ls 229–231, 262

SP Evr. II C 144 113
SP Evr. II C 156 65
SP Evr. II C 159 81

Biblical Printed Editions (arranged according to year of appearance):

Mikraot Gedolot, Second Rabbinic Bible, D (1524–1525) 10, 31, 38, 41, 44, 93–94, 123, 186, 204–206, 256, 260–261

Kennikot (1776–1780) 179–184

Letteris (1862) 190–193, 206–207

Ginsburg (First ed.: 1894; Second edition: 1926) 93–94, 183–184, 190, 192, 203, 207–208, 211

BH^3 (1937) 38, 93, 187, 193, 217

Koren (1961) 37, 93–94, 190, 192, 203, 211–213, 218

Biblia Hebraica Sttutgartensia, BHS (1968–1976) 38, 93, 187, 193, 217

Dotan (Adi, 1973) 193

Hebrew University Bible Project (1973-) 184, 187, 192–193, 213, 217, 267–268

Mossad Harav Kook, Breuer (1977–1982) 43, 213–216

Mikraot Gedolot Haketer, Cohen (1992-) 33, 45, 63, 109, 148, 150, 181, 187, 192–193, 202, 204, 217–218

Horev, Breuer (1998) 148, 214–216

JPS (1999) 187

Jerusalem Crown, *Keter Yerushalayim* (2000) 37, 44–45, 148, 187, 214–216, 218

Biblia Hebraica Leningradensia, Dotan (2001) 193, 203, 213

Biblia Hebraica Quinta, BHQ (2004-) 38, 93, 187, 193, 217

Non-biblical important Manuscripts

Oxford Hunt. 80 (*Mishne Torah*) 119, 122
Sanct Petersburg NL Evr. II B 1549, MS11 (Babylonian Masora) 154, 164, 165

https://doi.org/10.1515/9783110594560-016

Index of People

*Sages who lived before 1700 are marked with an asterisk.

https://doi.org/10.1515/9783110594560-017

Index of Terms

Abstractions of verbal Nouns 224–225
Accordance (software) 21
Accumulative Masora 17, 49–60, 225–227,
 252, 261
Acrostic 55, 58
Adat Devorim 196
Aleppo Codex Committee of Trustees 11, 137
Ashkenaz 31, 34, 46–47, 66, 72–73, 76, 82, 94,
 114, 120–121, 124, 147–148, 151, 184–185,
 192, 204

Babylonian Masora 32, 64–66, 69, 76, 113–114,
 116, 123, 151–169, 204, 226, 253, 255, 273
Babylonian Masora Terms 155, 160, 255
Babylonian vocalization 151–153
Ben Zvi Institute 11, 131, 133
bgdkpt (Hebrew letters) 4, 233–234

Cairo Geniza 64, 65, 83, 114, 123, 125, 136,
 151–154, 164, 175, 187, 253
Cambridge Geniza Fragments 90, 114, 123, 153
Comparative Masora 156, 261

Dagesh 4, 191, 192, 194, 196, 208, 227,
 233–234
Diqduqe HaTe'amim 134, 195, 227, 234–238

Emet (Job, Proverbs, Psalms) 78, 189, 215
Error Correcting Codes 108–128
Euphemism 98–99, 106

Filling signs 135
Friedberg Geniza Project 187

Ga'aya (pl. Ge'ayot) 15–16, 22, 149, 182,
 189–202, 204, 218, 227, 235, 236

Haftara (pl. Haftarot) 47, 73, 147, 214

Italy 34, 46, 66, 114, 184, 192, 204, 205,
 211, 254

Jerusalem Talmud 5, 76, 79, 151, 204
Judean Desert Scrolls, Dead Sea Scrolls 3, 5,
 34, 35, 61, 102, 138, 163, 170–176, 213,
 217, 267

Ketiv and *qere* 14, 44, 56, 85–107, 196, 204,
 207, 209, 212, 249, 255–257, 269

Mahberet Menahem. See Menahem ben Saruq
 (Index of People)
Mahzor Vitri 3–004, 91
Mapiq 252
Masculine and Feminine 100, 223, 232,
 241–242, 245, 255
Masoret Seyag LaTorah 31, 46, 185, 272
Menahem ben Saruq 221, 226, 229–231,
 250, 253
Mil'el and *milra'* 56, 224
Minhat Shai. *See* Norzi, Shelomo Yedidya (Index
 of People)

Nehardea (in Babylonia) 65, 113, 116, 158–163

Okhla we-Okhla 10, 21, 51–60, 96–98, 112, 163,
 221, 224, 246–253, 259, 261, 265, 266
Open and closed passages 43–45, 46,
 61–84, 111–121, 144–146, 148, 211,
 213–215, 272–276
Or Torah. See di Lonzano, Menahem (Index of
 People)
Or Zaru'a 76
Oxford Geniza Fragments 185

Passages in Esther 275–276
Pausal forms 27, 87, 223, 232, 242
Permanent *qere* 92, 93, 99

Quires 5, 131, 133

Samaritan (Torah version and vocalization) 151,
 170, 172–174, 176–177, 182
Sedarim 13, 197
Sefarad (adj. Sephardi, Sephardic) 31, 34,
 46–47, 66, 72, 76, 82, 120–121, 148, 151,
 184–185, 195, 211, 215, 272, 276
Sefer HaEshkol 265–269
Sefer Hahilufim 131, 196–199
Septuagint 34, 163, 170, 172, 174, 176
Sevirin 254–259, 263
Shrine of the Book (Israel Museum) 131–132,
 138, 148, 170, 176

https://doi.org/10.1515/9783110594560-018